BENJAMIN CONSTANT

BENJAMIN CONSTANT

A biography

Dennis Wood

London and New York

First published 1993
by Routledge
2 Park Square, Milton Park, Abingdon, Oxon, OX14 4RN

Simultaneously published in the USA and Canada
by Routledge Inc.

711 Third Avenue, New York, NY 10017

First published in paperback 2011

Phototypeset in 10/12pt Garamond by
Intype, London

British Library Cataloguing in Publication Data
Wood, Dennis Michael
Benjamin Constant: a biography
I. Title
848.609

Library of Congress Cataloging in Publication Data
Wood, Dennis.
Benjamin Constant : a biography / Dennis Wood.
p. cm.
Includes bibliographical references and index.
1. Constant, Benjamin, 1767–1830—Biography. 2. Novelists,
Swiss—19th century—Biography. 3. Intellectuals—France—
Biography. I. Title.
PQ2211.C24Z95 1993
944.06'092—dc20
[B]

ISBN13: 978-0-415-01937-8 (hbk)
ISBN13: 978-0-415-51315-9 (pbk)

CONTENTS

PLATES

PREFACE

It may be helpful to state from the outset what this book is not. It makes no pretence at being the full and definitive biography which its subject demands: to do justice to such a life, one that was so cosmopolitan, eventful and filled with emotional agitation would require several volumes and many hundreds of pages of text and notes. Such a biography will have to await the complete publication of the works and correspondence of Constant, a project that will run well into the next century. Nor is the present work a study of Constant the novelist, the political theorist, the historian of religion, the autobiographer, the diarist or the letter-writer: many books and articles have already been devoted to these areas by specialists more competent than myself – Stephen Holmes on Constant's political thought, for example, and Pierre Deguise on Constant and religion. Even as a biography the present volume does not set out to deal fully with every aspect of Constant's intellectual activities or with his very many publications as did Kurt Kloocke in his *Benjamin Constant: une biographie intellectuelle* (1984). Its purpose is more modest: to provide the English-speaking reader with a concise and factual account of an important historical and literary figure, an account which includes the findings of the most recent research, some of it my own. To this end I have translated all quotations into English, while also giving the text in the original language where the wording is of particular importance. (When quoting from original documents in French, English or German I have retained their spelling and punctuation.)

My hope, nevertheless, is that both the general reader and the specialist in French literature will find something of interest in the pages that follow. Only two significant attempts at a full biography of Benjamin Constant have been made in English, by Elizabeth W. Schermerhorn (1924) and Sir Harold Nicolson (1949). Both are long out of print but, more important, both predate the many important discoveries made in the past forty years, for example that of the semi-autobiographical *Cécile* first published in 1951 by Alfred Roulin. Sir Harold Nicolson's biography, the most readily available, is a delight to read, elegant, witty and shrewd, but in some areas it is now inaccurate both in its facts and the judgements that depend on those facts. My intention is to tell the full story within a necessarily limited compass, devoting proportionately more space to Constant's early, formative years than has sometimes been the case. It goes without saying that there are gaps in our knowledge which the edition of Constant's complete works and correspondence may yet fill (at the time I am writing only one volume of each has so far gone to press), as well as subsequent volumes of the systematic *Chronologie* of Constant's life and works, of which only the first, covering the years 1767–1805, has so far appeared. It seems useful nevertheless to *faire le point*: to take stock and attempt to summarize the present state of our knowledge about Constant's life. If there is any other claim to originality in this book, besides its giving as many of the ascertainable facts as possible, it is to be found in a tentative reinterpretation of Constant's personality in the light of modern clinical studies of attachment and bereavement by John Bowlby (1907–90) and others – a study which, incidentally, I began long before Bowlby's compelling life of Darwin appeared in 1990. Madame de Charrière once called Constant 'a true chameleon', and changeability – violent swings of mood from energetic elation to the most profound and overwhelming melancholy and fatalistic despair – was a central feature of his character. There is a *mystère Constant* which the first four chapters of the book in particular seek to identify and understand.

Two articles which I wrote for the journal *French Studies* in the early 1980s provided the starting point for Chapter 2 of this book: I recall the kindness and generosity of the then editor, Professor Malcolm Bowie, with deep gratitude. My colleagues on the team editing Constant's complete works and correspondence have offered encouragement and stimulus on many occasions, particularly Simone Balayé, Dr C. P. Courtney, Professor Paul Delbouille, Professor Alison Fairlie and Dr Kurt Kloocke, as well as my friends and colleagues in Birmingham, Dr Ceri Crossley, Dr David Hill, Dr Alex Hughes, the late Professor Derek Lomax, Professor R. E. F. Smith and Dr Marcus Walsh. My Head of Department, Professor Jennifer Birkett, Professor Michael Butler of the School of Modern Languages, and the Dean of the Faculty of Arts, Professor Leon Pompa have also greatly facilitated my work.

I should like to thank the many librarians, archivists and owners of private collections who have helped me over the years in my research, particularly Jacques Rychner, Director of the Bibliothèque publique et universitaire, Neuchâtel; Jean-Daniel Candaux and other members of the staff of the Bibliothèque publique et universitaire, Geneva; the staff of the Bibliothèque cantonale et universitaire, Lausanne; Etienne Hofmann, Christian Viredaz and the staff of the Institut Benjamin Constant, University of Lausanne; Dr Alain Rivier of Vevey and his family for permission to consult the Rivier archives at Le Désert, Lausanne; Professor Claude

Reymond; Annie Angremy of the Département des manuscrits, Bibliothèque nationale, Paris; Dr Matthes, the staff of the Niedersächsisches Staatsarchiv, Wolfenbüttel, and the Von Marenholtz family for access to the Von Marenholtz family papers; Professor Dr Paul Raabe, Director of the Herzog August Bibliothek, Wolfenbüttel and his staff, especially Dr Gillian Bepler; the university libraries of Göttingen and Erlangen, and the Stadtarchiv Erlangen; the Bodleian Library, Oxford, and university libraries of Cambridge and Edinburgh; the Harrowby Mss Trust, Sandon Hall, Stafford; the National Library of Scotland and the Secretary and members of the Speculative Society, Edinburgh; Peter Fox, Librarian of Trinity College, Dublin; and Dr Ben Benedikz, Rare Books Librarian, University of Birmingham.

I am grateful to the Leverhulme Foundation for a Fellowship in 1986 which enabled me to make a number of discoveries in Germany, and to the British Academy, Pro Helvetia Foundation and the University of Birmingham for their generous support of my research through travel grants. At Routledge, Richard Stoneman's forbearance since 1986 has been worthy indeed of the Constant family motto, 'In arduis constans'. My wife Katherine and my sons Orlando and Francis have shown exemplary patience and given unstinting support: this book is dedicated to them.

Birmingham, Whitsun 1992

BRIEF CHRONOLOGY

1767	25 October: Henri-Benjamin Constant de Rebecque born in Lausanne, Switzerland, the son of Juste de Constant de Rebecque, an officer in the service of Holland. 10 November: death of Benjamin's mother Henriette, *née* de Chandieu. Benjamin entrusted to nursemaids.
1772	Juste puts Benjamin in the care of Marianne Magnin, later his second wife. Subsequently the boy is educated by a number of unsatisfactory tutors.
1780	Benjamin spends two months at Oxford with his father.
1782–3	Student at Erlangen University, Germany. Fights duels.
1783–5	Student at Edinburgh University, friendship with John Wilde and James Mackintosh. Begins study of the history of religions. Attends many debates at the Speculative Society. Gambling debts.
1785	Affair with Madame Johannot in Brussels.
1786–7	Friendship with the novelist Isabelle de Charrière whom Constant meets while staying in Paris. Runs away to England and Scotland during the summer of 1787.
1788	After staying with Madame de Charrière near Neuchâtel, Switzerland, Constant takes up a post at the Court of the Duke of Brunswick (1788–94). Unhappy at Court.
1789	Marries Minna von Cramm, a lady-in-waiting at the Court of Brunswick, whom he divorces in 1795. Friendship with Jakob Mauvillon, who dies in 1794.
1793	Friendship with Charlotte, *née* von Hardenberg.
1794	Meets Germaine de Staël in Switzerland, will have a long relationship with her.
1795	Beginning of Constant's political activity in Paris, publishes pamphlets.
1799	24 December: Constant elected to the Tribunate.
1800	Passionate affair with Anna Lindsay (1800–1).

1802	Constant excluded from the Tribunate for his opposition to Bonaparte.
1804	In Weimar with Madame de Staël. Meets Goethe, Schiller and Wieland.
1806	October: begins affair with Charlotte von Hardenberg, and the novel from which *Adolphe* and *Cécile* will eventually emerge.
1807	Torn between Madame de Staël and Charlotte. Falls under influence of a pietistic circle in Lausanne.
1808	5 June: secretly marries Charlotte. Completes *Wallstein* while at Coppet.
1811–14	In Germany with Charlotte; works on book on religion. Writes *Ma Vie* and gives final shape to *Cécile* (probably 1810–11). 12 February: death of Juste de Constant.
1814	Constant briefly supports Bernadotte. Returns to Paris, unrequited passion for Juliette Récamier.
1815	Rallies to Napoleon during 'Hundred Days', followed by semi-exile.
1816	January–July: in London gives readings of *Adolphe*. 7 June: *Adolphe* published in London. Returns to Paris. Political ambitions.
1817	14 July: death of Madame de Staël in Paris.
1819	Constant elected to French parliament as Deputy for the Sarthe. Becomes celebrated liberal opposition orator and campaigner. Leg injury after accident, later walks with crutches. Possible affair with 'Eliane' (1818–19).
1824	Publishes first volume of *De la religion* and third edition of *Adolphe*.
1825–6	Campaigns for Greek independence and against the slave trade in Africa.
1827	Elected Deputy for Strasbourg. Great popularity in Alsace. Spied on by police.
1829	Constant's health declines despite spa treatment.
1830	After July Revolution, Constant is made a member of the Council of State by King Louis-Philippe (August). In November he fails to gain election to the French Academy. Illness, creeping paralysis. 8 December: death of Benjamin Constant. 12 December: state funeral, burial at Père Lachaise cemetery in Paris.
1833	*Du Polythéisme romain* published.
1845	Death of Charlotte Constant.
1895	*Journal intime* published for first time.
1907	*Ma Vie (Le Cahier rouge)* published for first time.
1951	*Cécile* published for first time.

A NOTE ON BENJAMIN CONSTANT'S FAMILY

In view of the complex family background to Constant's life and its importance in, for example, his claim to French nationality and in his relationship with his father, uncle Samuel and cousins, it may be useful to outline the salient facts here. On his father's side Baron Henri-*Benjamin* de Constant de Rebecque, known to his contemporaries and posterity as *Benjamin Constant*, had ancestry that could be traced back as far as the thirteenth century to the Rebecque family of Aire-en-Artois in northern France. He owed his Swiss Protestant identity to the fact that during the Reformation the Protestant Augustin Constant (d. 1593) moved from Aire-en-Artois to settle in Geneva. Benjamin Constant's grandfather on his father's side, Samuel de Constant de Rebecque (1676–1756), was a distinguished army officer in the service of Holland who re-established the family's aristocratic credentials, re-adopted the surname *de Rebecque* and the title of baron. In 1721 he married Rose-Susanne de Saussure (1698–1782), Benjamin's grandmother, a strong-willed woman known as 'la Générale', and they had four sons and a daughter. Of these, three of the sons survived into Benjamin Constant's lifetime: Benjamin's father Louis-Arnold-*Juste* de Constant (1726–1812), who like his father entered the service of Holland as an army officer, and later became estranged from 'la Générale'; and Benjamin's two uncles, David-Louis, known as *Constant d'Hermenches* (1722–85), an officer in the Dutch and later the French army, a friend of Voltaire and correspondent of Belle de Zuylen, later Isabelle de Charrière; and François-Marc-*Samuel* de Constant (1729–1800), author of sentimental novels and of works on economic and ethical matters. Constant's aunt on his father's side, Suzanne-*Angélique*-Alexandrine, Marquise de Gentils-Langalerie (1731–72), who died when he was very young, was the mother of his first cousin Charles, Chevalier de Langalerie (1751–1835), leader of the *Ames intérieures* of Lausanne to whose religious practices Constant was attracted in 1807. For Benjamin the most important relatives of his own generation on his father's side were the children of his uncle Samuel, his cousins *Rosalie*-Marguerite (1758–1834), who remained unmarried and became a close friend and lifelong correspondent; her sister

1

Louise-Philippine, known as *Lisette*, also unmarried (1759–1837); their brother Juste ('le Jeune') (1760–93), an officer in the service of Holland, who died after being wounded at Tourcoing; and *Charles*-Samuel (1762–1835), involved in commerce with China and sometimes known because of this as *Charles le Chinois*, often a severe (and occasionally shrewd) critic of Benjamin and of his father Juste.

Constant's mother, *Henriette*-Pauline de Chandieu (4 September 1742–10 November 1767), traced her ancestry back to one of the leading Protestant figures in the French Reformation, Antoine de La Roche Chandieu from the Dauphiné region, who sought refuge in Geneva in 1564 and later Lausanne, and who acquired citizenship of Geneva. The first wife of Henriette's father, Benjamin de Chandieu-Villars (1710–84), Françoise-Marie-Charlotte, *née* de Montrond (1722–77), gave birth to ten children of whom four daughters survived: Constant's mother Henriette who died shortly after he was born; her sister *Anne*-Marie-Pauline-Andrienne (1744–1814) who became Comtesse de Nassau on marrying Count Lodewijk Theodoor de Nassau La Lecq (1741–95) in 1768, and who lost her only child Louis, aged 24, in 1794 – *Anne de Nassau* was always one of Benjamin's closest and most cherished relatives and he corresponded with her until her death; Henriette's elder sister *Catherine*-Louise-Jacqueline (1741–96) who married Salomon de Charrière de Sévery (1724–93) in 1766; and Henriette's youngest sister Antoinette-*Pauline* (1760–1840) who was to marry Jean-Samuel de Loys (1761–1825) in 1784. None of Constant's eight cousins by these various marriages were as important in his life as his uncle Samuel de Constant's children, but worthy of note are Catherine de Charrière de Sévery's son Wilhelm (1767–1838), with whom there was mutual antipathy, and Pauline de Loys's daughters Antoinette (1785–1861) and Andrienne (1789–1850) – Constant considered marrying one or other of them in January 1806 (see Constant, *Œuvres*, p. 560, journal entry for 2 January 1806).

As will become clear in a later chapter, Benjamin Constant was unaware until some years after the event that his father Juste had at an unknown date married Jeanne-Suzanne-Marie, known as *Marianne Magnin* (1752–1820), a clever village girl from Bettens who was Constant's governess from an early age and whom he intensely disliked. Juste had in fact forcibly taken her away from her parents in 1761 when she was 9 in order to have her educated at his own expense, with the intention of later making her his mistress. Contrary to what might be expected, Marianne became devoted to Juste, who was twenty-six years older than herself. After the death of Henriette de Chandieu, whose loss permanently and profoundly affected him, Juste turned once again to his *protégée*, and there exist both a promise of marriage to Marianne signed by Juste and dated 22 July 1772 and a marriage contract dated Dijon, 11 July 1792. By this second marriage to Marianne Juste had two more children, Charles-Louis, known as

Charles de Rebecque (1784–1864), who pursued a military career and later one in agriculture, and *Louise*-Philippine (1792–1860), who married Claude-Louis-François-Marie Balluet d'Estournelles (1772–1837) in 1817. Although at first resentful of the consequences for his own income of Juste's 'second family', after the death of their father in 1812 and of their mother in 1820 Benjamin Constant increasingly assumed a semi-parental role vis-à-vis his half-brother Charles and his half-sister Louise. He grew especially fond of Louise d'Estournelles, who herself later became a novelist. Constant's wife Charlotte Constant, *née* von Hardenberg, had a son by her first marriage, Wilhelm, later Baron von Marenholtz (1789–1865), but Benjamin Constant had no children of his own by either of his two marriages. There is, however, a strong possibility that he was the father of Germaine de Staël's daughter Albertine (1797–1838), later the wife of Victor, Duc de Broglie (1785–1870). Constant always showed Albertine the greatest affection, but after her marriage in 1816 they became somewhat estranged, largely as the result of her own and her husband's rather puritanical disapproval of Constant's character and past conduct.

INTRODUCTION

The inglorious collapse of the Communist régimes of Eastern Europe between 1989 and 1992, an unexpected and extraordinary turn of events which seemed to mark the beginning of a new era for humanity, drew a less dramatic response from French intellectuals than uninformed observers in Britain or America might have expected. This muted reaction was undoubtedly the result of a major shift in attitudes which had already taken place in France in 1977–8 and at the time was attributed to a group of former Marxists and veterans of 1968 known collectively as *les nouveaux philosophes*, 'the new philosophers', of whom Bernard-Henri Lévy and André Glucksmann were the *chefs de file*. The revolt against Marx in France – prompted by the revelations in Aleksandr Solzhenitsyn's *The Gulag Archipelago* (1973–5) about Soviet labour camps as much as by observation of conditions in the Soviet empire – dislodged the USSR from the pedestal it had hitherto occupied among the French intelligentsia, and in the late 1970s brought about a revival of interest in liberalism and liberal democracy, words which during the preceding radical decade no self-respecting intellectual would have uttered without a sneer. This qualitative change in thinking naturally led to a re-examination of the origins of the liberty which had for too long been taken for granted in the West – the right to disagree with the government in power and to organize peaceful opposition without fear of arbitrary arrest, imprisonment or exile, freedom of conscience and worship, an unmuzzled press, the inviolability of property ownership and so on. Coincidentally the 150th anniversary of Benjamin Constant's death fell in 1980, and the event was marked by a conference, publications and broadcasts[1] in which his struggles as a liberal parliamentarian and humanitarian campaigner were accorded the general public recognition in France and Switzerland which they deserve.

For, as the century of Hitler and Mussolini, Stalin and Pol Pot draws to a close, it is fitting that we should remember the man whom Sir Isaiah Berlin has called 'the most eloquent of all defenders of freedom and privacy'.[2] At the end of his life Constant wrote:

4

For forty years I have defended the same principle: freedom in all things, in religion, philosophy, literature, industry and politics. And by freedom I mean the triumph of the individual both over an authority that would wish to govern by despotic means and over the masses who claim the right to make a minority subservient to a majority.[3]

For too long Constant's reputation as a freedom-fighter – a much abused term but entirely appropriate in his case – was obscured by a sometimes rather forced moral outrage at his sexual promiscuity, inspired initially by the critic Sainte-Beuve and Madame de Staël's descendants, the De Broglie family.[4] His courage and resilience in sticking to his principles through illness and disappointment remain exemplary for the generations that have followed. In the English-speaking world this side of Constant's activity has received a considerable amount of attention lately from political scientists, notably Stephen Holmes and Biancamaria Fontana,[5] but it would be unrealistic to say that it yet matches interest in Constant as the author of *Adolphe* and the lover of Madame de Staël. And yet there is a connection. Constant stated:

Literature is linked to everything else. It cannot be separated from politics, religion or morality. It is the expression of people's opinions on each of those matters. Like everything in nature it is at once both cause and effect. To describe literature as an isolated phenomenon is not to describe it at all.[6]

As recent commentators have increasingly emphasized, in Constant's case that link between literature and the rest of his writings and activity was very strong, and intimately connected with what one might call the problematics of freedom.

Constant was born into several forms of oppression and servitude. These were not the most obvious hardships of poverty or a lowly position in the social hierarchy, but real nonetheless, and he was acutely aware of them early in his life. His ancestors had fled from France to French-speaking Switzerland to escape persecution for their Protestant beliefs, and the memory of that was still very much alive in the family. His Swiss homeland – the canton where he lived as a child that is, the Pays de Vaud – had been under the domination of the German-speaking Bernese since the sixteenth century, with the result that Vaudois aristocrats, like his father Juste de Constant, were excluded from political office in Lausanne and were forced to pursue a military career in the service of another country, in his case Protestant Holland.[7] The death of Benjamin's mother a few days after giving birth to him left him at the mercy of a loving but moody and unpredictable father who – when he was not away in the Netherlands – alternated between indulgence and heavy-handedness, and who later put him in the care of a peasant-girl Marianne Magnin who was probably already Juste's mistress, and subsequently of a rather motley assortment of private tutors. Early stirrings of rebellion by Benjamin against those tutors (one of them, the Englishman Nathaniel May, found him more than a little truculent[8]), perhaps against Marianne, and by implication against Juste were followed by political *engagement* against the Pays de Vaud's oppressive masters the 'Bears' of Berne, as he called them, responsible for Lausanne's genuine, albeit mild servitude, then against the monarchy in France, against Napoleon and against the excesses of the Bourbon Restoration. In what was to become a lifelong political vocation, there was, of course, no readily available continental model for Constant to follow at this time: he naturally looked to Britain and to the great Opposition orators of the House of Commons, a noble ideal he had glimpsed during a happy and formative period at Edinburgh University in 1783–5 and which never left him. By temperament he was in any case an inveterate individualist, far better suited to being an opposition sniper than to holding ministerial office or automatically toeing a party line.

'The least government [is] the best government'[9] was Constant's belief from the mid-1790s onwards, an idea that has become an axiom of modern liberalism of the more economically conservative kind – a development, incidentally, of which he would not necessarily have approved. He detested unfairness, but his primary concern was with unfairness of the most fundamental kind, loss of freedom. His craving for political liberty for his fellow citizens and his desire to preserve the sanctity of their private lives and personal beliefs were matched by his own permanent need for independence from others, from father and from family but also from the women in his life – a factor which blighted his many love affairs. This preoccupation with freedom and this fear of dependence on others – or by others on him – give to Constant's writings an anguish-laden urgency which continues to speak to our own times. The need for personal freedom is dramatized in his best-known work, his novel *Adolphe* (1816), through the characters of Adolphe and Ellénore, where the individual's desire for freedom is set against the power of the wider social group – all the more powerful because the individual has internalized its expectations and shibboleths consciously or unconsciously. Adolphe's apparently straightforward task of freeing himself of a woman he has grown tired of is complicated by society's hostility to Ellénore as a 'kept woman' which makes him protective towards her, and by his own need to be independent and pursue a career worthy of his intellect and talents within that same society. A superficially simple story written in Constant's characteristically limpid, incisive and often memorable French prose thus generates a remarkably complex range of responses and reflections on the part of the narrator and subsequently the reader.[10] The revelations in Constant's diaries similarly concern his painful sense of responsibility towards the women he had loved, his own fluctuating desire to be free from them, but his terror at the idea of causing them suffering.

Political liberty and personal independence: these continue to be the two principal focuses of interest for modern commentators on this exceptional man's life, a man whom some continue to find repellent. It will be evident that the present writer does not find him so. The sheer mass of Constant's letters, diaries and other autobiographical writings as well as accounts of his life by contemporaries give the picture of a man of formidable intelligence as well as intellect, erudite, perceptive, humane and frequently funny at his own expense. Like Montaigne, he invites us to see ourselves mirrored in his contradictions: he could be changeable and filled with self-doubt, then pugnaciously dogmatic – and he was not above opportunism either, particularly under the Directory, as his fiercest twentieth-century critic Henri Guillemin has continually pointed out,[11] although by any reckoning Constant would more than make up later for any *arrivisme* with exhaustingly hard work in the best of causes, a fact Guillemin invariably neglects. Constant was certainly no Machiavelli, and that indeed is his endearing quality: his two best-known attempts to back political winners – Prince Bernadotte, and later Napoleon during the Hundred Days – turned out to be almost laughably bad choices.

We live in an age when lip service is routinely paid to a rather hollow Europeanism and internationalism, but here was a man of cosmopolitan background and upbringing who spoke three languages fluently and read several more, who actually lived as a European and poured virulent invective on narrow nationalism and empire-building, notably condemning French intervention across the Pyrenees to reinstate a conservative Bourbon monarch in Spain, but whose concern for oppressed peoples led him to campaign for Greek independence and against slavery in Senegal. At the same time Constant applauded the fact that small communities, towns and provinces wished to run their own affairs in their own way, to cherish the uniqueness of their own local traditions, history and speech, and to reject attempts at centralization: 'Variety is life', he wrote famously, 'uniformity is death'.[12] After all, defending a region's right to retain its own specific character, its entitlement to be different from others, was absolutely consistent with upholding the individual's right to freedom of thought and expression. For Constant was a Lausannois and a Vaudois and, no doubt as the result of his Swiss origins, a federalist.

Constant's lifespan of 63 years covers an era of sometimes violent political and social change, unparalleled perhaps before our own time. He experienced the *ancien régime*, observed the Revolution from a distance, and lived under the Directory, Consulate, Empire, First Bourbon Restoration, 'Hundred Days', Second Restoration and July Monarchy. He was born in the middle of the Enlightenment, in 1767, the year when Voltaire published *L'Ingénu* and Sterne was about to publish his *Sentimental Journey*. In 1830 when he died Victor Hugo's Romantic drama *Hernani* had already unleashed a furious literary storm in Paris and Tennyson had published his *Poems, Chiefly Lyrical*. It was Hugo who paid tribute to Constant in his diary on 9 December 1830:

> Benjamin Constant, who died yesterday, was one of those rare men who are able to sharpen, hone and polish the ideas of their time, those arms of the people which will break any that an army can throw against them. It is only revolutions that can thrust such men to the fore in society. It takes volcanoes to produce pumice stone.[13]

Yet Constant's ceaseless public activity and political campaigning were often conducted against a private background of acute depression, occasionally of despair. As he noted with a degree of feeling:

> Of all the scourges to which human beings are a prey, the worst is dejection [*le découragement*]. It prevents them from judging their position and seeing what their resources are. This sickness, which afflicts individuals, can also overwhelm organized groups.[14]

The possible reasons for that recurrent dispiritedness in Constant will be the starting point for our consideration of his life and achievements.

1

'THE GRIEF THAT DOES NOT SPEAK': CONSTANT AND HIS FATHER (1767–1783)

Give sorrow words: the grief that does not speak
Whispers the o'er-fraught heart, and bids it break.
(*Macbeth*, IV. iii)

It was a calamitous beginning. Scarcely was Benjamin Constant born, on 25 October 1767, a frail baby who was not expected to live, than the attention and anxieties of his family were directed away from him to his 25-year-old mother, Henriette, *neé* de Chandieu. There may have been complications at the birth; we do not know. What is certain is that Benjamin Constant's mother died on the sixteenth day after his birth, that is on 10 November 1767, no doubt after unimaginable suffering.[1] Benjamin immediately became the focus of a quarrel between his two grandmothers as to who should have charge of him. The argument was won by Henriette's mother, Françoise-Marie-Charlotte, *neé* de Montrond (1722–77), but the tensions which already existed between the Constant and Chandieu families were aggravated: as Constant grew older they were indeed to become chronic.[2] Benjamin was baptized on 11 November at the Calvinist church of Saint-François in Lausanne, and the following day Henriette de Constant was buried in the Saint-François cemetery. Shortly before the funeral, her husband Juste, desperate at the loss of the woman he had married only the previous year, was stricken with a seizure: he was unable to move, he could not get his breath, his pulse apparently stopped, and he was only saved by the intervention of a doctor.[3] A second tragedy was thus narrowly averted. Colonel Juste de Constant lived on to return to Holland and the Swiss regiment of which he was commanding officer there. Meanwhile his son was no doubt left in the care of a nurse or nanny about whom we know nothing, whom Benjamin Constant never mentions and who concerned herself with the mundane task of keeping him alive. From time to time during these early months he would suddenly find himself in the midst of a constellation of grandmothers and aunts who would briefly take him in their arms, and then leave him to return to their daily social round.

Benjamin Constant almost never speaks about the first five years of his life, and it is not difficult to see why. During those years he wanted for nothing material. As an infant prodigy he was doted on and spoiled, his every utterance was applauded, and he soon learned how to captivate an audience of female relatives. Nevertheless his later life seems to tell a different and sadder story about the pattern of his childhood experience. Let us begin with the first catastrophe of his existence, the loss of his mother. There is no way of knowing how such a separation can affect so young a baby, and child psychologists maintain a prudent silence on the subject. All the evidence tends to suggest that the effects of what happened to Constant could have been mitigated, as common sense would suggest, by the establishment of a continuous and loving bond with a substitute for the mother, for example a nurse. Whether this happened in Constant's case we do not know. Constant's father Juste was a highly impulsive and quarrelsome man and, for all we know, may have changed his son's nurses as he would later change his tutors – often. The long-term effects of such treatment have been exhaustively documented in our own century, notably by such clinical specialists as Michael Rutter and the late John Bowlby, and several of their conclusions remind us unmistakably of Benjamin Constant.[4]

But before considering them, there is another crucial factor to consider in respect of Henriette de Constant's death: the reaction to it of her husband. We saw a moment ago the extraordinary effect of grief on Juste de Constant, a seizure which brought him close to death. And we can add to this the knowledge of the couple's happiness during the sixteen months of their marriage (22 July 1766 to 10 November 1767), a fact about which Gustave Rudler was sceptical when he wrote his magisterial 1909 study *La Jeunesse de Benjamin Constant*, but which the correspondence surrounding Henriette's death seems to confirm. Losing her left Juste de Constant in total disarray, the more remarkable for his being in normal circumstances a stern and exceptionally strong-willed personality. He had, for a while, no idea what to do with himself or his son. Then his composure returned, he made arrangements for Benjamin's immediate future and left to rejoin his regiment in Holland. Thereafter Juste returned periodically to Lausanne, and we can easily imagine the bewilderment of his young son whose pattern of life his return disrupted and who would become attached to him on each visit only to undergo another inevitable separation.

Yet perhaps more important even than repeated separation was Juste's attitude towards Benjamin. Portraits of Benjamin Constant from early childhood to middle age reveal a striking facial resemblance to Henriette, whose sandy hair he also inherited.[5] Each sight of his son would renew Juste's sense of loss, a grief it was not in his character to display, but which it would be only too natural for Benjamin to glimpse now and then. The mystery of death, and especially that of one's own mother, is, of course, incomprehensible to a very young child, and it must certainly have troubled one as precocious and intelligent as Benjamin Constant. A look or a cross word from his father, the gossip of a servant, perhaps, would be enough to suggest to him that he had some part in the mystery. Not knowing anything about the physical details of birth, Benjamin felt nonetheless some responsibility for what occurred after his own. Jean-Jacques Rousseau offers us a case for comparison, as we can see in this well-known passage from the *Confessions* (1782):

> I was born weak and sickly. I cost my mother her life, and my birth was the first of my misfortunes. I have never been able to understand how my father had borne her loss, but I do know that he was inconsolable for ever afterwards. He believed he could see her in me, while never being able to forget that I had taken her away from him. He never put his arms around me without my feeling in the force of his embrace a bitter sense of loss: this rendered it still more tender. Whenever he said, 'Jean-Jacques, let's talk about your mother', I would reply, 'So we're going to cry again, are we, father?' I only had to say that for his tears to begin to flow. 'Bring her back to me', he would sob, 'console me for losing her. Fill the empty space in my heart. Would I love you as much as this if you were only my son?' Forty years after losing her he died in the arms of his second wife with the name of the first on his lips, and the memory of her face deep in his heart.[6]

As we would expect of Rousseau, all the complexity of motive and feeling is brought out in this intensely moving passage: Isaac Rousseau's reproaches, his heightened sense of his son's vulnerability, above all the constant reminder of his dead wife in his son's very looks. Painful as it was, this was an essentially healthy reaction towards Jean-Jacques on his father's part. There was no bottling up of grief, and although Rousseau was clearly upset by the situation and powerless to prevent its recurrence, he was left in no doubt about either his father's quite involuntary feelings of blame and resentment or about the abiding reality of his love for him. It is my belief that in this, as perhaps in other ways, Constant was emotionally less fortunate than Rousseau. Such a scene as the one just described in the *Confessions* had no counterpart in Constant's experiences. For reasons which he must have tried long and hard to fathom, Constant only knew a father who was critical, ironic, lacking in warmth, above all who seemed permanently unable to come out into the open with what he had on his mind.

John Bowlby has written eloquently about the possible effects of such a failure of communication:

Without understanding and sympathy there is a danger that the child's thoughts and feelings will become locked away, as though in a secret cupboard, and there will live on to haunt him. Then, whenever some adverse event or threat of it penetrates to that secret cupboard, with or without his realising it, he becomes anxious and distressed and prone to develop symptoms, the reasons for which neither he nor his family may understand.[7]

This lack of directness on Juste de Constant's part was allied to an emotional restraint which must have seemed very much like rejection to a little boy who saw his father so infrequently. A child has no understanding of a person's character and its history beyond what it sees. Benjamin Constant could not know at this age that genetically the Constant family was afflicted with a certain oddity in behaviour, compensated for – if compensation it can be called – by considerable intellectual vigour.[8] All Benjamin could see in his father was an apparent indifference – which he would later rationalize as being timidity – which chilled him to the quick and destroyed all hope of trust or intimacy between them. The obvious conclusion, in a child's mind, was: 'What have I done to displease him?' and there was an immensely disturbing answer ready to hand: that he was responsible for his mother's death. John Bowlby describes such a situation and its consequences:

How prone children are spontaneously to blame themselves for a loss is difficult to know. What, however, is certain is that a child makes a ready scapegoat and it is very easy for a distraught widow or widower to lay the blame on him. In some cases, perhaps, a parent does this but once in a sudden brief outburst; in other cases it may be done in a far more systematic and persistent way. In either case it is likely that the child so blamed will take the matter to heart and thereafter be prone to self-reproach and depression. Such influences seem likely to be responsible for a large majority of cases in which a bereaved child develops a morbid sense of guilt; they have undoubtedly been given far too little weight in traditional theorizing.

Nevertheless, there are certain circumstances surrounding a parent's death which can lead rather easily to a child reaching the conclusion that he is himself to blame, at least in part. Examples are when a child who has been suffering from an infectious illness has infected his parent, and when a child has been in a predicament and his parent, attempting rescue, has lost his life. In such cases only open discussion between the child and his surviving parent, or an appropriate substitute, will enable him to see the event and his share in it in a proper perspective.[9]

'Open discussion': the contrast with Rousseau and his father is instructive.

That passage of the *Confessions* about a bereaved husband's anger, sorrow and resentment must have been alarming and depressing for Constant when he eventually came to read it. There was no such communication with Juste de Constant. There was love of a kind, of course, in Juste, as Constant later knew, but a love which, very early, became ambitiousness on Benjamin's behalf and a desire to rush him into an 'adult' world of intellectual achievement. No tears, no tender feelings, no mothering: Benjamin was under pressure to become a *bel esprit*, an intellectual and a salon wit – and the sooner the better. What damage Juste did to his son by this and other manifestations of a crass disregard for ordinary common sense we shall see later in this book. But we are still at the beginning of the story and that harm was, by the age of 5, already beginning to show itself in Benjamin Constant.

Evidence about Constant's early childhood is extremely scant and fills only a dozen pages out of the seven hundred which make up volume I of the comprehensive *Chronologie de la vie et de l'œuvre de Benjamin Constant*, edited by Dominique Verrey in collaboration with Etienne Hofmann, covering the years 1767–1805.[10] It was not until 1810 or 1811 that Constant himself began setting down his early experiences in a systematic and non-fictional form, though there may have been earlier unrecorded attempts. This precious but unfinished account of the years 1767–87 was given the title *Le Cahier rouge* in 1907 by its first editor after the red cover of the notebook, but Constant's title was *Ma Vie* – *My Life* – as can be seen from the first page. On 2 February 1812 Juste de Constant died, and subsequently Benjamin seems to have revised the text of *Ma Vie*, to what extent is unknown. At all events it was neither completed nor published by him and the narrative ends in November 1787, just before Constant's reunion with his friend Isabelle de Charrière. Where Rousseau's *Confessions* sustain an unbroken flow of events and commentary, stretching back before his birth and reaching the moment when Rousseau sets pen to paper, *Ma Vie* in its early sections is marked by curious gaps and silences. As Constant's account moves away from childhood towards late adolescence the writing leaves behind the initial form of brief entries year by year as in a chronicle and begins to resemble a continuous story. When he began writing, Constant may not have intended so detailed a record, with the dialogue, description and reflection that we see in the later sections of *Ma Vie*, and this might explain the lopsided nature of the whole. One might suppose that after a jerky and uncertain beginning, Constant with practice got into his stride and by the time he reached the mid–1780s was writing with confidence. But is this *really* the case? I suspect not. Nor was it the case, I believe, that Constant considered accounts of childhood experiences to be lacking in interest: Rousseau had shown they could make absorbing reading. I would suggest rather that a return to the details of his childhood would have been a return to an infernal region, to a time of unrelieved emotional suffering for Constant that he could hardly bear to recall. And the evidence of the text seems to bear this out. *Ma Vie* begins thus:

> I was born on 25 October 1767 in Lausanne, Switzerland, the son of Henriette de Chandieu, who was from a formerly French family which had taken refuge in the Pays de Vaud for religious reasons, and Juste Constant de Rebecque, a colonel in a Swiss regiment in the service of Holland. My mother died as a result of giving birth, a week [or eight days] after I was born.
> [1772] The first tutor of whom I have a reasonably clear recollection was a German named Stroelin, who used to beat me, then smother me with his embraces so that I wouldn't complain to my father. I always kept my promise to him not to, but what was going on was found out in spite of my silence, and he was dismissed. He had had the ingenious notion of getting me to invent Greek in order to teach it to me, that is to suggest that the two of us create our own language which only we could understand. I became enormously keen on the idea. First of all we devised an alphabet into which he introduced Greek letters. Then we began a dictionary in which each French word was tranlated by a Greek one. All of this imprinted itself on my mind to a remarkable degree because I believed I was the inventor of it all, and I already knew very many Greek words and was in the process of applying general rules to what I had made up – that is I was learning Greek grammar – when my tutor was thrown out of the house. I was 5 when that happened.[11]

One's first reaction is astonishment when confronted by that second paragraph, an astonishment tinged with pity and a degree of disbelief. But let us go back to the preceding paragraph. Even the editor of the Pléiade edition of Constant's *Œuvres* goes beyond the usual factual annotation and remarks that there is something rather strange afoot in Benjamin Constant's simple statement about his mother and father: 'It is surprising that Constant recalls his mother's Huguenot ancestry without adding that the Constant de Rebecque family was also a French family that took refuge in Lausanne as early as the sixteenth century for religious reasons.'[12] Juste de Constant is deliberately cut out of the glorious heritage of Protestantism with its tenacity in the Faith, an omission too striking not to be at some level intended. What might be interpreted as muted aggression towards his father has to be taken together with the fact that this is almost the only time in all his writings that Constant mentions his mother. In later life the offer of a portrait of her by Constant's half-sister Louise brought a tart reply from him: he refused to accept it as a gift and insisted that it should be treated like other portraits and paid for.[13] It is not hard to visualize the frustration and the confused emotions of a man who cannot remember his own mother – Tolstoy, who lost his mother when he was 23 months old, was a prey to similar feelings.[14] But there was clearly more to Constant's attitude than this.

Undoubtedly the strangest hiatus in *Ma Vie* is the chronological jump between its first and second paragraphs. Is it a case of bad memory, or of nothing worth recounting? Or a deliberate suppression? One's suspicions are increased by that altogether remarkable second paragraph. It comes to the reader out of a total and unexplained void, and the story it contains clearly burned in Constant's memory some forty years later with an incandescence all of its own. Suddenly we see Constant being savagely beaten by his German tutor – possibly one Friedrich Jakob Ströhlin (1743–?), if C. P. Courtney's tentative identification is correct;[15] his sobs are suppressed by his tutor taking him in his arms and caressing him; the tutor fears Constant will denounce him to his father; Constant promises not to betray him, and adheres faithfully to the promise. In the latter part of the paragraph the same evil genius devises a game, one in which his pupil Constant 'invents' the Greek language and generates a Greek grammar. At this point the tutor's ill-treatment of Constant is discovered through no fault of the boy himself, and Ströhlin is dismissed by Constant's father.

It must be said at once that there is something strangely familiar about the story. We find similar elements in Montaigne's account of his own upbringing in the essay 'De l'institution des enfants' ('On educating children'). There we have a comparable inventiveness in pedagogy, attributed to Montaigne's father, who takes on a German tutor to teach his infant son Latin; by the age of 6 Montaigne can speak nothing else; he is taught Greek by his father as a game:

> We tossed our declensions back and forth to each other like those who, by means of certain board games, learn arithmetic and geometry. For amongst other things he had been advised to get me to enjoy learning and having to do work without using any form of constraint, so that I did it of my own volition, and to allow my mind to develop gently and freely without coercion or the imposition of discipline.[16]

Even Ströhlin's beatings are like a scene from the Marquis de Sade's *Justine ou les malheurs de la vertu* (1791) – and Constant almost certainly knew the writings of Sade. We must ask the question, therefore: is Constant's story true? And I believe the answer we must give is: perhaps true, but arranged, arranged in conformity with Constant the writer and self-explorer's wishes and intentions. In *Ma Vie* as in other of his autobiographical works, there is clearly a desire, akin to the psychoanalytic 'talking cure', to liberate himself from past sufferings and nightmares through writing about them, so that he can at last become fully master and maker

15

of his own history, as the title *Ma Vie* indeed suggests. And one hardly needs to be a Lacanian to see that its narrative is a search for himself, for wholeness, an attempt to locate himself in time and space, above all perhaps – and notwithstanding the text's humour – an attempt to come to terms with loss, absence and incompleteness.[17] Now beyond this point our reading must be conjectural if we are to pass through to the deeper significances that may lie beneath the surface meaning. But it must be apparent to every reader of Constant's story about his tutor that the passage is charged with a talismanic value for its author that will forever remain tantalizingly beyond our grasp unless we do take a few judicious risks.

What, at the level of mere common sense and intuition, hides on the underside of this incident? One of the keys to the mystery is the young Constant's unexplained complicity with Ströhlin. The obvious – though not necessarily correct or complete – answer is a need for companionship and physical affection, a need so great that it is even worth enduring the repeated torment of beating to satisfy it. This interpretation has the virtue of being entirely in keeping with the facts of Constant's early childhood and his relationship with his father as far as they can be reconstructed. Sir Harold Nicolson's biography rightly emphasizes the absence of love from Constant's childhood world:

> [It is not] right to underestimate or to ignore the effect upon his character of the tremendous disaster of his mother's death. It removed the discerning watchfulness which might have enabled him to develop gradually, rather than by fits and starts; it gave him in childhood the disconcerting feeling that he did not belong to anybody, absolutely, anywhere; it rendered him ignorant of gentleness; it induced him throughout his life to confuse love with passion; it denied him maternal control, which alone could have curbed his wayward precocity; and above all perhaps it left him completely at the mercy of his capricious father.[18]

According to this theory, therefore, Benjamin Constant would willingly submit to Ströhlin's violence for an indefinite period in order to benefit from physical contact with him and to enjoy his all too brief show of mothering. It is an unbearably poignant explanation: Constant turned to a perhaps paedophile sadist to find the love he was denied everywhere else. The hypothesis is plausible, perhaps more so than the other possibility that it was the sheer intellectual delight of learning Greek that made Constant remain silent about Ströhlin's conduct. True, Constant himself almost suggests that this was the reason, but he stops short of actually saying so and the lack of direct explanation on his part leaves other possibilities open. In any case, according to the alternative explanation of Constant's behaviour, what he himself gives or does not give as the reason for his complicity with Ströhlin may be far from the real reason. I am referring, of course, to the reading a Freudian psychoanalyst might give of the situation. At the beginning of this discussion I pointed to a literary parallel in another French introspective, Montaigne, for what we see in the Ströhlin anecdote. I did so in order to underline the uncertain status of the *Ma Vie* passage as a record of historical fact. Indeed the Freudian fundamentalist would go further.

The peculiar tonality of the Ströhlin incident and the prominent position it is accorded as *liminaire* to the whole of *Ma Vie*, its *valeur fondatrice* – laying an important foundation for what is to come – would suggest it has a fundamental mythical or symbolic power for Constant. In other words it could be viewed as a fantasy. Freud's well-known analysis of his own dream about Irma led him to his classic definition of the function of dream, and by extension daydream: every dream is a wish which is repre-sented as fulfilled.[19] Looked at from a psychoanalytical point of view, the reverse side of the Ströhlin story is rather different from what one might call the 'common-sense' view. It is a fantasy of wish fulfilment. And what, then, might those wishes be in an adult remembering his situation as a child of 5 who had lost his mother at birth and who thereafter had an absent and neglectful father? The conclusion of the Freudian might be that the scene dramatizes first of all Constant's desire to punish himself for his mother's death for which he holds himself responsible; the instru-ment of this self-punishment is a substitute for the father towards whom he feels guilt. (There could also be a reversal of Constant's retaliatory and aggressive feelings towards Juste.) The second element in the scene is the relieving of the guilt, the expiation of the sin, and the restoration of Constant's self-esteem. Freudian theory is reinforced by the text itself where Constant congratulates himself on his heroic fidelity to Ströhlin: he does not denounce him, he keeps his word. The cycle of guilt, self-punishment and expiation goes on as long as Constant wants it to. Para-doxically he is the *master* of the situation and he wishes it to continue: he wilfully keeps his father in ignorance (for reasons that are not adequately explained by the text, of course). When Ströhlin is finally sent packing, it is through the intervention of Constant's 'real' father: it is therefore not Constant's fault. That, or something like it, might be the framework of an orthodox Freudian reading of this complex passage.

Is the passage, then, a record of historical fact or is it a fantasy about Constant's guilt and aggression vis-à-vis his father? 'A little of both' must, I believe, be the prudent answer. The part played by the game of Greek and the secret complicity that surrounds it is more teasingly problematical. The role played by Ströhlin in Constant's acceding to language, to the discovery of a private language which finally turns out to be a valuable public one, is that of the good and kindly disposed pedagogue. The older Constant has every reason to be grateful to him for his Rousseauistic *éducation négative* – allowing him to learn for himself – for introducing him to a means of later spiritual enrichment. But Ströhlin, now absolved of his crimes and viewed in a favourable light, Ströhlin the innocent, is nonetheless punished when he is dismissed by Constant's father. It is strangely like the earlier punishment of Constant, and brings out the ambivalent status of all three characters in the drama: Benjamin, Ströhlin and Juste are all at different moments guilty and innocent, masterful and dependent. Evil comes out of the apparently good, good comes out of apparent evil. It is indeed extraordinary that the Freudian doorway to Constant's psyche should open onto what some of the profoundest critics of his writings have already glimpsed: a world of coexisting antagonisms, of jostling contradictions. In this one passage of Constant's *Ma Vie* we see almost a mythical presentation of his whole life: in it all the now angry, now helpless, now loving paradoxicality of his existence is released and comes at us at high pressure. This opening text is, in a word, an oxymoron, a forcing together of opposites: domination and submission, dependency and independence, guilt and expiation.

There is, of course, one other and vital part of the story we have not yet touched on. This is Constant's passage from being a dumb, suffering infant to the acquisition of a language which he would make peculiarly his own. The entrance into language marks, in the terminology of Jacques Lacan, the entrance into the so-called symbolic order – that is the end of the pre-oedipal phase and the child's acceptance of the 'Nom du Père', the 'Name-of-the-Father' (also, in Lacan's punning way, the 'Non du Père', the paternal 'No' to incestuous desires), where words are organized by the symbolic father and governed by his laws and authority: thus the child enters the social order and accedes to culture through rational discourse, leaving behind childish babble. But for Freudian – Lacanian or otherwise – and non-Freudian alike there is a symbolic value in the Ströhlin episode, in the everyday sense of the word 'symbolic'. In it, a vehicle of culture, of civilization, is handed on to Constant, a means by which he was later to achieve fulfilment: he became a fine Greek scholar and an expert on Greek religion. Constant would also use the Greek alphabet while writing in French for as it were coded self-expression in his private diaries, the *Journaux intimes* of 15 May 1811 to 26 September 1816 – indeed he was perhaps already doing so when he wrote *Ma Vie* if it was composed in 1811.

The foregoing reading rests necessarily on a Freudian hypothesis. But Freudianism itself is an unproven theory, *pace* the Freudians, as Jeffrey Masson, the French novelist Christiane Rochefort and others have lately argued very strongly. What if we do not accept the validity of psychoanalytical interpretations of Constant's childhood? There is a third way of viewing Constant's childhood which steers a middle course between common-sense empiricism and the rigid categories of Freud and his disciples. This is the school of thought best represented by John Bowlby, which is largely based on the results of clinical work with children. It is illuminating to consider in the light of Bowlby's findings not only the Ströhlin passage but also another text from the *Journaux intimes*, an entry dated 20 April 1804:

> While I am speaking about pain, I must set down here a memory which is not from my own experience but which nevertheless two months ago filled me with sombre emotions which well up every time it comes to mind. It is the story of a woman of twenty-three who was hanged in England for fraud. There was nothing remarkable about her personality. She is not reported to have been beautiful, witty, sensitive or distinguished in any way. But in all the details of her sufferings, from the beginning of her trial until her execution, there is such a depth of human misery that one is gripped and chilled by what happened whenever one reflects on it. Caught in the act and brought before the court, she made no attempt to defend herself, but throughout her trial continually fainted. Condemned to death and taken back to prison, she remained, until the day appointed for her execution, motionless, on the same spot in her cell, and ate nothing. When the suffering one undergoes is seen by the public, is the subject of other people's opinions, no matter whose, there is some compensation in that suffering, if only in the fact of braving what others think of one. But in this case it was solitary suffering, treated with disdain by others who were content to walk past and ignore it as if it were a completely natural occurrence. That kind of suffering weighs solely and entirely on the individual victim. Finally, on the day she was to die, the poor woman allowed herself to be taken to the gallows without offering any resistance, without appearing to notice what was happening around her, and the first and last sign of life she gave was to let out a long scream when she felt the tumbril disappearing from under her feet. There is in this account such a picture of human wretchedness – a weak human giving up without a struggle, not even expecting anyone else to show the slightest interest, crushed by the iron hand of an implacable society – that it inspires a particular degree of pity. That pity, while not unmingled with contempt, nonetheless touches the very bottom of one's heart.[21]

The most awesome, the most terrible thing Constant could conceive of in his whole existence was silent, lonely, helpless suffering. For a person like Constant to tell this story must have been like holding his hand in a flame. And yet it is told with the unflinching directness and with the persuasive conviction in its observations we associate with the author of *Adolphe*. It comes from a man who has journeyed to the bottom of himself, and for whom the story of the Englishwoman had the intensity of a vision. There can be little doubt that the Constant who writes thus is identifying himself with the sufferings of Ann Hurle, the woman in question,[22] and that Constant learned to sympathize with her absolute and bewildered defencelessness and her distress 'which people were content to walk past and ignore as if it were a completely natural occurrence', having lived through such experiences himself and probably at an early age. Such memories are indelible. The permanent fear that one will one day be abandoned again received, of course, its most famous and moving expression in Dickens's recollection of the time he was set to work in Warren's Blacking Factory:

> No words can express the secret agony of my soul as I sunk into this companionship; compared these every day associates with those of my happier childhood; and felt my early hopes of growing up to be a learned and distinguished man, crushed in my breast. The deep remembrance of the sense I had of being utterly neglected and hopeless . . . cannot be written. My whole nature was so penetrated with the grief and humiliation of such considerations, that even now, famous and caressed and happy, I often forget in my dreams that I have a dear wife and children; even that I am a man; and wander desolately back to that time of my life.[23]

The appalling fate of Ann Hurle and the treatment of the 5-year-old Benjamin Constant at the hands of his tutor, these two stories told by the older Constant seem to point to a single possibility: that in the years that are of such crucial importance in the development of a personality, in the first five years of one's life and beyond, Constant felt unloved and abandoned. And, as is too often the case, he perhaps never escaped completely from the tyranny of that deprivation. Although the evidence that can be now gathered about those years of Constant's life may be scant and although Constant himself maintains a strict silence on the subject (a silence which is probably itself eloquent), there is an irrefragable logic in the pattern of his later attitudes and responses that brings us back again and again to early unhappiness. Let us recapitulate the essential features of Constant's first years: he lost his mother shortly after his birth; his father, despite remarrying later, was deeply and permanently scarred by Henriette's death, and, as Rosalie de Constant, Benjamin's cousin, records in her *Cahiers verts*, speaking of Juste de Constant: 'Ce malheur a influé sur tout le reste de son temps', 'this misfortune influenced the rest of his life'.[24] She adds: 'His son's upbringing caused him a great deal of tribulation: he [Juste] was clearly affected by the misfortune of having lost his mother'.[25] Even without having such a burden to carry, Juste was already noted for his ironic detachment from those around him, as well as for his vanity and general aloofness; he was also secretive and devious, moody, impulsive, liable to change his attitudes and opinions from one minute to the next, unable to show affection, prone to using sarcasm to indicate his displeasure.

The effect of Henriette's death can only have been to exacerbate all these tendencies in Juste de Constant. He was never able to show his feelings directly and openly, and, where Benjamin was concerned, those feelings must in any case have been complex. Juste's whole career as an army officer had reinforced his distrust – and perhaps fear – of emotion, a condition which Ian Suttie once described in *The Origins of Love and Hate* as 'a taboo on tenderness'.[26] His mourning for his wife can only have been prolonged and rendered more painful by this, and would not have helped him in his relationship with his son, whom moreover he saw only occasionally. Benjamin inherited certain of these characteristics from his father genetically – changeableness and the fretful restlessness or *inquiétude* of the whole Constant family – but appears also to have inherited from elsewhere the ability not only to feel but also to *display* very strong emotions. The little boy's expressions of joy or sorrow can only have been a source of embarrassment to his father who, while encouraging his son's already prodigious intellectual powers, neglected Benjamin's feelings. By the time Benjamin Constant had reached adulthood, he could describe their chronically difficult relationship in the following terms: 'He is silent and I am cool. Each of us in his own way has grown very subdued in his relationship with the other, and while we love each other a great deal, we are often at a loss to know what to say to each other'.[27] We have the confirmation of Constant's friend Sismondi (1773–1842), if any were needed, that the description of Adolphe's father in Constant's novel is an exact portrait of Juste de Constant in his relationship with Benjamin:

> Unfortunately his behaviour where I was concerned was high-minded and generous rather than loving. I was very aware of his right to my gratitude and respect. But we had never taken each other into our confidence. He had an ironic turn of mind which did not suit my own character. At that age all I wanted to do was abandon myself completely to primitive and passionate feelings which transport the individual beyond the common realm of everyday experience, and which inspire only disdain for the people and things around one. I found in my father not a severe critic but an unemotional observer who was given to making caustic remarks, a man who would begin a conversation with a pitying smile on his face and soon after would be impatient to end it as quickly as possible. In all of my first eighteen years I cannot recall ever having had a conversation lasting an hour with him.[28]

Why Juste should have been unable to show the love he felt, why he hid from his feelings behind irony we do not know. A clue would seem to

lie in his having been brought up 'avec beaucoup de sévérité', 'very stric-
tly', by his puritanical officer father, Samuel de Constant (1676–1756),[29]
and had a hardly less formidable and strong-willed mother, 'la Générale'
Rose-Susanne de Constant (1698–1782) with whom he seems to have had
a particularly bad relationship, indeed one which in later years took on
the character of a vendetta on his part. Ian Suttie throws light on the
possible development of both Juste and Benjamin Constant:

> The repression of affection seems ... to be a process likely to be
> cumulative from one generation to another. The mother who was
> herself love-starved and who, in consequence, is intolerant of tender-
> ness, will be impatient of her own children's dependency, regressive-
> ness and claims for love. Her suspicion and anxiety really amount
> to a feeling (rooted in self-distrust), that children are naturally bad
> (St Augustine!) and require to be 'made' good by disapprobation
> and the checking of all indulgence of 'babyishness'. This creates a
> corresponding anxiety in the children about retaining approbation
> and winning more. The child feels too early that love must be
> *deserved* or *earned*, and excessive anxiety may easily reach the point
> of despair ... it may lead to a jealous competitiveness, the quest
> for power, position, 'prestige', possession. Love has now become
> aggressive, anxious, covetous. Unintentionally the mother has
> imparted her own inhibitions (on tender feeling) to her children, has
> substituted the ideal of duty for that of good-fellowship and estab-
> lished a morality of guilt and distrust in place of that of benevolence
> and confidence which I maintain would have developed naturally.[30]

This seems to hit the nail exactly on the head. The poison of *défiance* was
passed on from one generation of the Constants to the next, distrustfulness
both as regards others and oneself. In Juste's case the results were worse
than with any of his brothers. One reason for his putting Benjamin in the
care of Marianne seems to have been because he did not trust his mother;
he feared she would criticize and denigrate him while he was away, and
that he would thereby lose his son's love and respect. Ambition later
drove Juste into a series of ruinous lawsuits, which he should have known
there was a strong likelihood he might lose, in order to restore his honour
after a mutiny. Through Juste's influence, what Ian Suttie calls 'jealous
competitiveness' became – involuntarily – part of Benjamin Constant's
nature, especially during his youth. Finally, anxiety about being loved
came to be both a source of vulnerability and the focus of a cluster of
often contradictory attitudes in the older Benjamin Constant.

It is at this point in our investigation that the work of John Bowlby
with disturbed children has its relevance. What Suttie describes above is
the course of what is, for all its sadness, a fairly common misfortune. But
what if you have lost your mother at birth, if it is your remaining parent

who is treating you like this – on the rare occasions, that is, when you see him? What if, left only with a nurse, you begin to brood on your mother's death, come to the conclusion that it was your own fault, but are unable subsequently to discuss your feelings of guilt with your father, a father who declines to talk to you for any length of time and who recoils from any display of emotion? The likely conclusion must be that such a person will sooner or later, unless the situation improves dramatically, be likely to show symptoms of neurosis. The special circumstances and personality of the sufferer will obviously affect the course of the neurosis, but it could nonetheless persist for a very long time. The problem would be aggravated by ill-treatment at the hands of your tutor, and by the sudden appearance of a substitute mother at the age of 4 replacing whoever had looked after you before (even this, as we shall see, happened to Benjamin Constant as well). We noted earlier in this chapter John Bowlby's comments on a child's susceptibility to blaming itself for its parent's death. Such self-reproach could lead to bouts of depression and the development of a morbid sense of guilt. But there is a still worse possibility: according to Bowlby, young adults who have lost a parent during childhood are more prone than others to consider committing suicide. Reasons for making a suicidal gesture include: (a) a wish to elicit a caregiving response from an attachment-figure who is felt to be neglectful – the well-known 'cry for help'; and (b) a wish to punish an attachment-figure and so coerce him or her into being more attentive.

Reasons for completing a suicide include: (a) a wish to destroy the self in order to assuage an overpowering sense of guilt for having contributed to a death; and (b) a desire for revenge against a dead person for having deserted, which can take the form either of redirecting towards the self murderous wishes aroused by a deserting person, or else of abandoning another in retaliation.[31] Despair of ever finding another loving relationship and a wish for reunion with the dead person are other reasons which, clinical evidence suggests, induce people to go through with the act.

Now in Constant's life chronic anxiety, depressive episodes and examples of his proneness to dejection and melancholia are too numerous to mention and well documented. As for suicide, even if we leave aside his notorious attempt in 1795 to win the love of Madame de Staël by possibly faking a suicide scene, there is at least one account in Constant's writings of suicide contemplated and one of suicide actually attempted. The suicide attempt is the well-known tragicomic scene recounted in *Ma Vie* when Constant swallowed part of a bottle of opium rather than submit to the humiliating confession before a stranger that he had not won the love of Jenny Pourrat.[32] The contemplation of suicide occurred, according to Constant's letter of 31 August 1787 to Isabelle de Charrière, during a boat trip on Lake Windermere:

I have just experienced a kind of storm on Lake Windermere, the largest lake in this whole region, two miles from this village [Patterdale]. I wanted to drown myself, the water was so dark and so deep that the certainty of finding peace so very quickly tempted me greatly. But I was with two sailors who would have pulled me out again, and I don't intend to drown myself – as I poisoned myself – in vain.[33]

Now although both of these incidents are treated with Constant's usual humorous verve, and the second is a parody of the well-known scene of a storm on the Lake of Geneva in Jean-Jacques Rousseau's *Julie ou La Nouvelle Héloïse* (1761), it is nevertheless difficult to escape from the conclusion that there was a measure of seriousness about his suicidal wishes on both occasions. At the end of *Ma Vie*, in connection with a challenge to a duel with François du Plessis-Gouret about which he seemed unconcerned at the time, Constant writes significantly:

I wouldn't claim to be any braver than anyone else, but one of the characteristics which nature has given me is a great contempt for life, and even a secret desire to leave it, so as to avoid anything unpleasant that might yet await me.[34]

There may well have been other moments when Constant thought about killing himself. Bowlby, quoting K. S. Adam, concludes: 'the presence of a consistent, stable nurturant figure of some sort seem[s] to be of great importance in protecting against the development of significant suicidal ideation'.[35] It would, of course, be absurd to suggest that the early loss of a parent and the absence of communication between the surviving parent and child are the only reasons why people might think of committing suicide. Nor are guilt for that loss or aggression redirected against oneself the only explanations of Constant's character and attitudes. But taken with the urge towards suicide his behaviour points significantly in the direction of a chronic condition which can only fairly be called neurosis. Naturally we are dealing not with certainty but with probability here. That probability increases, however, when we list the special qualities and foibles that Gustave Rudler, Georges Poulet and many others – not least Constant himself – have found in his character:

- an obsession with death;
- uncertainty about the future;
- detachment, indifference to all around him;
- a tendency to indecision.

Above all the most *constantien* of qualities is an oscillation between one quality and its opposite: between a desperate desire for freedom, and passive submission to the will of another or fate; between frenzied activity and total inactivity; between tears and laughter; between involvement in the affairs of the world and abnegation; between aggression and pity. And the mind that views all this stands apart from such Pascalian *contrariétés* or contradictions, critical of that of which it is a part. It is, of course, precisely this ability to see a multitude of people within himself that is the very stuff of a great artist, what Keats, speaking of Shakespeare, famously called '*Negative Capability*, that is, when a man is capable of being in uncertainties, mysteries, doubts, without any irritable reaching after fact and reason'.[36] Constant certainly had this rare faculty, though it did not prevent him, in all his creative writing, from searching for 'facts and reasons'. However it is no disparagement to the active creative intelligence of Constant the novelist to see the shaping of that intelligence in the experiences and relationships of his early life. And for a child who appears to have inherited some of the gentleness and sensitivity of his mother the fundamental experience of those early years can only have been one of traumatic rejection. In order to grow up into an adult who feels secure in himself and able to give love, a secure and stable bond of affection is essential during childhood. On this, good sense and clinical observation concur. When unable to form that lasting bond, or when that process of attachment is repeatedly disrupted the long-term consequences are:

- acute distress in the child, a phase of protest and despair which leads eventually to its detachment from people and from the world around it; that is, a defensive withdrawal;
- an inability to form lasting bonds and compulsive self-reliance;
- anxiety associated with separation persisting into adult life, and a tendency to be overdependent and overeager to please.[37]

When the situation a child finds itself in discourages it from expressing its emotions, it is driven in on itself to bear its sorrows alone, and the harm it suffers is likely to be greater. In many respects separation anxiety and the symptoms of what Bowlby calls 'disordered mourning' tend to be similar, and Constant's predicament was such as to produce in him the reactions of both. Although, Bowlby notes, there may be no *intellectual* impairment in a child thus afflicted, other results of separation and bereavement can include:

- ambivalence towards any person who is loved;
- compulsive wandering, perhaps with the urge to recover the lost loved one;
- 'depersonalization' or 'derealization', that is a sense of inner emptiness and the sense that a glass wall separates the sufferer from the world around him or her;

- vulnerability to another loss or the threat of a loss which will produce a feeling of unrelieved hopelessness;
- aggression, truculence, defiance against attachment-figures;
- a manic exuberance and apparent euphoria, a tendency to present oneself in an attractively comic light.[38]

The correspondence between such a pattern of behaviour and the well-known traits of Constant's character which I outlined earlier is unmistakable. No doubt we all behave from time to time in one or two of the ways listed above: the point is that Benjamin Constant behaved in *all* of those ways – and frequently – during adolescence and early manhood. My contention is that this resulted from the emotional deprivations he experienced as a child and which, at some level in his mind, he never forgot. It seems quite implausible that a pattern of response of such complexity could be innate.

I have so far avoided discussing the most interesting and provocative view of Constant's life and work to be published in recent years, that of Han Verhoeff in his *'Adolphe' et Constant: une étude psychocritique* of 1976.[39] I have done so in order to be able to summarize beforehand the biographical facts and character traits to which Verhoeff alludes in his theory. Writing as an admirer and follower of the French Freudian literary critic Charles Mauron but also drawing on the work of Melanie Klein, Verhoeff traces the central theme of *Adolphe*, which he sees as Adolphe's ambivalent attitude to Ellénore, to Constant's loss of his mother shortly after his birth. Verhoeff defines Adolphe's treatment of Ellénore as being characterized by aggressiveness towards her, an aggressiveness which alternates with a self-identification with her sufferings. This pendulum swing between a need to love and be loved, and a desire to hurt the one by whom one is loved is what typifies all of Constant's relationships with women. Verhoeff traces the tendency to what he calls the behaviour of an *abandonnien* or *abandonnique*, using the terminology of the Swiss psychoanalysts Charles Odier and Germaine Guex.[40] Central to Constant's psychology is the feeling of having once been let down by his mother when he was at his most helpless and needing her love. Henriette's death, Verhoeff concludes, was ever after felt by Constant to have been an abandonment of him. It made him behave towards the women he knew in later life with both a resentful desire for retribution and an ineradicable longing to be mothered and cared for by them. The mixture of pity and scorn Constant felt for the sufferings of women were an expression of his permanent *comportement d'abandonnien*, 'abandonian' behaviour. For Verhoeff, even Ellénore's abandonment of her children in *Adolphe* echoes Constant's anger and resentment at the way he felt he had been treated in his earliest days: she becomes a 'bad mother'.

Verhoeff's theory is an attractive one and fits a lot of the evidence. The principal drawback with it, apart from the strangely disappointing analysis of *Adolphe* to which it leads, is, I think, its exclusiveness. Verhoeff leaves aside all other environmental factors, and above all neglects Constant's relationship with his father and with his governess from the age of 5 (and later his stepmother), Marianne Magnin. If Constant came to feel guilty about his mother's death because of his father's continuing grief during his childhood, this would surely have occupied a dominant place in Constant's mind. This is not to underestimate the sense of loss which Constant felt when he compared himself with other children who had mothers, or to minimize the effect on him of paternal absence or changes of nurse, one of which at least occurred when he was 4, and which might also have been viewed by him as an abandonment. It is, rather, to restore a sense of balance to the picture by including Juste de Constant's real *Trauerarbeit* alongside Benjamin's conjectured mourning, and to leave a decent space for actual childhood *experience* of separation. Having said this, one is nevertheless impressed by Verhoeff's arguing of his case and handling of the available evidence, and left with the sense that here at last a critic has said something profoundly true about Constant's relationship with his character Adolphe. One is all the more struck by Verhoeff's hypothesis when re-reading the passage quoted earlier about Ann Hurle, the English-woman hanged for fraud. After describing her repeated faintings at her trial, her refusal of food and her silence right up to the moment of her execution, Constant writes:

> There is in this account such a picture of wretchedness – a weak human being giving up without a struggle, not even expecting anyone else to show the slightest interest, crushed by the iron hand of an implacable society – that it inspires a particular degree of pity. That pity, while not unmingled with contempt, nonetheless touches the very bottom of one's heart.[41]

It is, of course, the phrase 'pour n'être pas sans mélange de mépris', 'while not unmingled with contempt' (or 'scorn'), that is so unexpected and disconcerting, and so out of tone with what has gone before. Verhoeff, who does not mention this passage, examines a similarly disquieting comment on the behaviour of the dying Julie Talma in Constant's *Journaux intimes* (entry for 1 April 1805):

> Dined with Madame Talma. She was so irritable, so hard on her servants that I had to remind myself constantly that it was because of her illness. Oh wretched human nature! The poor woman, who is so republican and democratic in her outlook, put on a show of aristocratic vanity that quite entertained me.[42]

Verhoeff sees in this and similar remarks an element of cruelty and derision, feelings comparable, I think, with the contempt Constant feels at Ann Hurle's silent acquiescence in her fate. Of course there are rational explanations for Constant's comments in both contexts; I suppose one could adduce the hard truthfulness about his own feelings of a psychological realist; a belief that life is a battle which ought to be fought to one's last breath;[43] that people ought, even *in extremis*, to live out their political convictions. And yet it is hard to resist the suspicion that Constant's lifelong preoccupation with the deaths of women he knew and his dwelling at such length on the details of their decline and agony had roots that plunged very deep indeed in his experiences and personality. With that suspicion goes a feeling that the fascination was for Constant morbidly voyeuristic and at the same time sprang from a horrified sympathy amounting almost to identification with the sufferer. We do not have to accept every jot and tittle of the Freudian Law in order to find Verhoeff's explanation of Constant's ambivalent attitude to the dying Julie Talma plausible:

> Aggression here is in the observer's gaze. The eager fascination with which he contemplates the suffering and death of this woman who is older than him also looks like revenge. This time he doesn't want to miss the event, as he did when his mother died. He is there, and behind his genuine grief is also felt an obscure sense of satisfaction.[44]

So far in this chapter we have dwelt at some length on Constant's possible response to the death of his mother and the difficulties in his relationship with his father. Such problems were made worse by Juste's bad choice of tutors for his son, of which Ströhlin was only the first. But Juste had another plan for his son's future which would have equally far-reaching consequences. In 1772 when Benjamin was 4 years old his paternal grandmother, 'la Générale' Constant, asked to be allowed to bring him up. Juste refused and instead put him in the care of a young woman of 20 by the name of Jeanne-Suzanne-Marie Magnin (1752–1820), known as Marianne Magnin. Benjamin was taken away from his grandmother for whom he had real affection, and away from whatever nurse she or Juste had entrusted him to, and sent to live with Marianne, a person he hardly knew, at the house of Pastor Samuel-Benjamin Perey (1726–89) at Cuarnens, on the outskirts of Lausanne. (Later Benjamin lived with her at La Maladière, a property Juste de Constant had acquired in 1764, where he had a large house built in 1771–2, and to which he later gave the name 'Le Désert'.[45]) If we are to believe Constant himself, he did not realize until much later in life the truth about Marianne: that, when she was a peasant girl of 9, Juste de Constant had taken a liking to her and, partly goaded into the deed by an argument with his relatives, had taken her away from her family, virtually kidnapping her; that he had given her a good education – this included the usual accomplishments plus an understanding of the running of a country estate – his plan being that she would eventually take charge of his estates; that subsequently she appears to have become Juste's mistress; and that they later married in secret at some unknown date.[46] The whole extraordinary story, which exemplifies as well as anything the stubborn wilfulness of Juste, had begun in 1761, long before his marriage to Henriette de Chandieu. His nephew, Charles de Constant, describes how it happened in a letter to his sister Rosalie:

> It was pure chance that made my uncle take Marianne, an argument about education with my aunt, Madame de Charrière [de Bavois] who mentioned a very intelligent little girl at Bettens to him; my grandmother never forgave him for what he did. When he married [Henriette de Chandieu], the Chandieu family demanded that [Marianne] be put in an out-of-the-way place so that she would never reappear on the scene. This was done. But when he became a widower so soon afterwards this cancelled the agreement. Life is often more the result of the circumstances we find ourselves in than of our calculations. I always believed Marianne was simply unfortunate and not a guilty party in all of what happened.[47]

Thus, even before his son was born, Juste had prepared the ground for yet another unhappy relationship in Benjamin's life. There is no evidence that Marianne had yet become Juste's mistress before his marriage to Henriette de Chandieu, although it is not impossible. And it is certain that Juste's grief for his wife's death was genuine and long-lasting: like his son in later life, Juste was perfectly capable of loving two women passionately at the same time. However, when Marianne became Constant's full-time guardian in 1772 she was 20 years of age. We know the date of a promise of marriage which Juste signed – 22 July 1772 – and there exists a marriage contract dated Dijon, 11 January 1792: Marianne may possibly have married him secretly in 1792.[48] She bore Juste a son, Charles de Rebecque in 1784 and a daughter, Louise de Rebecque, later Baroness d'Estournelles, in 1792. Now the strangest part of the whole story is that Constant, an exceptionally alert and receptive child, remained in total ignorance of Marianne's real status, an ignorance which outlasted his adolescence and ended only in 1800 when, at the age of 33, his father decided he was old enough to know the truth![49] It is difficult to believe. However, the structure of one's childhood relationships is an immediate 'given' which is sometimes not questioned until much later life, and this seems to have been the case with Benjamin Constant. For many years, therefore, Marianne occupied the role of protector, perhaps of elder sister, and of substitute mother, before becoming, very late in the day, his stepmother. If, in this whole episode which is so reminiscent of Molière's *L'Ecole des femmes* (*School for Wives*), Juste played the role of an implausibly successful Arnolphe to Marianne's Agnès, the older man turning his young ward into his wife, Benjamin also had his part to play, and it was

29

an unenviable one. Taken away from whatever security he had known to a strange house with a 20-year-old village girl he did not know, Benjamin became a pawn in a game he could not possibly understand. For Juste, who nonetheless idolized Benjamin, the boy was a means of defying his mother, 'la Générale', and taking revenge on her, among other things, for her earlier disapproval of his forcible abduction and adoption of Marianne. For Marianne, Benjamin was something like a bond imposed on her by Juste lest she be tempted to free herself from her by now highly compromising relationship with him. What Benjamin himself felt about the arrangement emerges from his later comments. On the one hand he could write to his half-sister Louise in 1819 or 1820 when Marianne was on the point of death:

> Please tell your mother how much I sympathize with her in her illness and how much I hope that she will recover soon. I shall never forget her tender care of me in my childhood. Nothing has ever weakened my affection for her and nothing ever will.[50]

On the other hand in 1792, and nearer the events, when Juste proposed giving Marianne a third of his wealth, Constant objected bitterly to being thus partially disinherited 'in favour of a harpy I don't even know'.[51] In other words Constant's feelings towards Marianne were always ambivalent and tended towards hostility whenever he saw himself replaced by her in the affections of his one surviving parent.

In trying to gauge the effect of the relationship that grew up between Benjamin and Marianne during the two years (1772–4) she looked after him, I would suggest that it is essential once again to consider it primarily in the light of Benjamin's relationship with his father. From a Freudian point of view the situation was relatively simple: Benjamin's oedipal feelings, left unsatisfied by the death of his real mother, would have been redirected towards this young substitute mother. Marianne introduced the missing third term which was added to the father/son dyad, and as a result Constant experienced what Jacques Lacan would consider a corrective, normative oedipalization. This would later have produced precisely the kinds of aggression and tenderness that we see in Constant's references to Marianne, and a sense of being abandoned yet again when Constant learned of – or suspected – the nature of Marianne's relationship with his father. One could add that according to the Freudian principle of *Verneinung* – denial, the absence of a thing implies desire for it. And Marianne Magnin is totally and inexplicably absent from *Ma Vie*. But there were other important factors involved in Constant's feelings about Marianne, of which the most notable was money. Marianne succeeded over the years in diverting a large proportion of Juste de Constant's remaining wealth away from Benjamin and towards herself and her children. If we are to believe Gustave Rudler, Benjamin Constant inherited from his Chandieu ancestors an acute concern about money matters,[52] and his fury at seeing his own birthright constantly dwindling is not hard to imagine. Before Juste died in 1812 Marianne had, understandably, made every effort to safeguard her own children's future, but had considerably worsened his relationship with Benjamin. Benjamin's future prospects were in jeopardy, and the stresses and strains this imposed on him should not be underestimated. But the other factor involved was, no doubt, Constant's abiding fear of losing the love of his father to someone else or to someone else's children. All this, of course, happened long after 1772–4. Whatever the truth or otherwise of the theory of a redirected Oedipus complex, Constant's situation must have felt one of total isolation. As Sir Harold Nicolson vividly puts it, he was a

> lonely little boy of six years old, interned at La Maladière under the guard of a woman whom he already much disliked. A perplexed, vivacious, clever little boy with red hair, whose disconcerting father was absent for months on end among the small garrison towns of the Low Countries.[53]

This gloomy picture is undoubtedly an accurate one.

The young Benjamin Constant found real affection and, when he needed it, a reliable source of sharp and unsparing criticism in his cousin Rosalie de Constant (1758–1834). She was the daughter of Juste's younger brother, Samuel de Constant (1729–1800), a man very different in character from Juste. Gifted with some literary talent as a sentimental novelist, but reserved and lacking in confidence, and somewhat too thin-skinned and sensitive to cope with the misfortunes life heaped upon him, Samuel lost both his dearest brother Germain-*Philippe* (1724–56) and his wife Charlotte, *neé* Pictet (1734–66), through illness. This second death left him with four children to bring up on a very modest income.[54] Already having herself known a tyrannical grandmother, Marguerite Pictet (1734–66), at the age of 8 Rosalie, with her sister Lisette and her brothers Juste and Charles, found herself without a mother. Rosalie was a hunchback, the result of a childhood fall in which she had dislocated her shoulder, and she was short-sighted into the bargain. But this did nothing to sour her good nature.[55] In a family marked by extremes of diffidence and indecisiveness on the one hand and of stiff-necked authoritarianism on the other Rosalie was an exemplar of reasonableness and clear thinking. In her friendship with her cousin Benjamin, who was nine years her junior, she could be relied on for her unsentimental kindness and support as well as for needle-sharp home truths about his character and behaviour. She had a Calvinist's unswerving respect for the truth, however uncomfortable that was at times, but also a modesty about her own worth which added greatly to the force of her observations. In later life Constant would express his appreciation of his 'chère cousine' in the following terms:

31

Seeing you and talking to you is one of the greatest pleasures in my life. If you don't always approve of what I do, you understand what I say, and the latter compensates me a little for the former. I say 'a little' because I would like to do only those things that you approve of. But it's already a rare piece of good fortune to be understood. The intellect alone is not enough to understand someone, the heart has to be involved too, and that is why one is only understood by those one loves and by whom one is loved.[56]

That ability to understand Constant was to prove a very mixed blessing indeed for Rosalie, as it would later be for Isabelle de Charrière. Nevertheless there is no doubt at all that from the first they loved each other as younger brother and older sister. Rosalie was generous in maternal affection, Benjamin was starved of that mothering: he was lively and extrovert, she was shy: they complemented each other perfectly. Moreover by the time Benjamin and Rosalie first knew each other they had both lost their natural mother, as we have seen, a loss which certainly reinforced their attachment to each other. They cannot have seen one another very often – Rosalie lived in Geneva, Benjamin in or near Lausanne – but Rosalie was always a fixed and stable point in Constant's life when so many other relationships were both unsettled and unsettling. From the age of 12 Benjamin saw Rosalie more frequently and they corresponded. That correspondence was interrupted by Constant for four years, from 1782 to 1786, during the time he spent studying in Erlangen and Edinburgh. Although hurt by her cousin's silence, Rosalie resumed their exchange of letters which continued thereafter until Constant's death in 1830.

We shall return later to the relationship between Constant and Rosalie. There does however appear to be something of mystery surrounding the absence of correspondence between them from 1782 to 1786. The collection of letters published in 1955 by Alfred and Suzanne Roulin begins with a letter from Constant dated 19 March 1786, at which time relations between Constant and his uncle's family were strained because of Constant's impossible behaviour: he had succeeded in annoying almost everybody by his vanity and cutting humour. But it is the silence that precedes this letter of March 1786 which is so puzzling, given what we know of Constant's affection for Rosalie. From 1780 to 1782, as Alfred Roulin says:

[Rosalie] was to see her young cousin, the mischievous Benjamin more often, and appreciate still more the liveliness and charm of his precocious intellect. For his part, the solitary boy became more and more attached to this older girl who understood him so well and had so much affection for him. She became the tenderest and most devoted of sisters to him.[57]

32

In 1782 Constant was 14 years of age, Rosalie 23. It is not inconceivable that at such an age Constant felt a kind of calf-love for his cousin of which he was ashamed, but which experience of the world and relationships with other women helped him to overcome. This is, at least, one of the possible inferences to be drawn from the *Lettres de d'Arsillé fils*, the unfinished autobiographical novel which Constant was later to write in collaboration with Isabelle de Charrière. But there is no evidence of this elsewhere, and it remains pure speculation.

There can be no doubt about the young Constant's quickness of mind or his ability to amuse and charm: no doubt either about his being a conceited little monster with a violent temper. At the age of 6 or 7, while directing a playlet with his cousins Wilhelm and Angletine de Charrière de Sévery and demonstrating to them all the tones of voice that were needed, he had shocked Angletine by hitting her for the inadequacy of her acting. As Angletine's mother wrote in a letter: 'One has to applaud Benjamin continually, otherwise he's not happy. It's less he himself than his father who hopes for applause.'[58]

Constant showed early talent as a witty, sophisticated, allusive writer of letters, as shown by those that have survived to his father, to his cousin Wilhelm de Charrière de Sévery, and above all to his paternal grandmother, 'la Générale', from whom he had unwillingly found himself separated since his father's decision to put him in the care of Marianne in 1772. As C. P. Courtney has rightly observed: 'Benjamin's childhood letters to his grandmother, which are desperate cries for affection, take on an extra dimension if they are read against the deplorable family background.'[59] For the anger and hostility that 'la Générale' felt about Juste's behaviour had even extended to Benjamin, even though grandmother and grandson still loved each other very much. Nonetheless Benjamin's letters are a delight, and the boy clearly felt confident enough even to allow himself what seems to be a degree of sexual innuendo when writing to his 'chere et excellentissime Grandmere' on 19 November 1779. He told her that when playing the harpsichord – he was a talented keyboard player – his largos and adagios always finished up as prestissimos, and his minuets ended in some frisking about: 'an incurable affliction, and impervious to reason', he added tongue in cheek.[60]

Constant cannot long have remained ignorant about sexual matters. Leaving aside his professed unawareness of Marianne's role in his father's life, we have his account in *Ma Vie* of what followed the two years he spent under Marianne's tutelage. When he was 7, in 1774, his father, anxious to obtain the maximum profit from Benjamin's intellectual precocity, took him to Brussels and began supervising his education himself. But Juste was no teacher. As he said in a letter to Marianne a year or so before: 'I have too much of a temper and not enough patience to bring up a child properly.'[61] He therefore entrusted Benjamin in 1775 to a surgeon in his own regiment, a Monsieur de La Grange, who was an atheist and libertine, a vain and stupid man who began by trying to seduce the daughter of Benjamin's music teacher, Ferdinand-Philippe-Joseph Staes (1748–1809) and ended by moving into a brothel in order to be nearer to his pleasures, taking Benjamin with him.[62] At this point, during the summer of 1776, Juste learned of de La Grange's depravity and took his son away.[63] This early awakening of Benjamin's sexual curiosity was soon followed by several months of intensive reading, chiefly of erotic novels and atheistic works. During this period he lived with his music teacher, played truant from lessons with his other tutors and waited for his father to make more permanent arrangements for his education. Juste, displaying an unrivalled capacity for having the wool pulled over his eyes, chose as tutor for his son a Monsieur Gobert, a Frenchman and former lawyer who had been forced to leave France for one shady reason or another, and was now proposing to set up a tutorial establishment in Brussels with a mistress he pretended was his housekeeper.[64] As a result Benjamin spent his days as unpaid copyist of a manuscript work composed by Gobert. By the time a furious Juste de Constant took him away from Gobert, however, Benjamin had had the last laugh: his handwriting was so bad and he had made so many mistakes that he had got no further than the preface.[65]

In late 1778 and early 1779 Juste tried once again to educate Benjamin himself at his La Chablière property outside Lausanne (at this period Juste owned four properties around Lausanne – La Chablière, Le Désert, Beau-Soleil and La Vallombreuse). Although he was extremely intelligent and widely read, Juste again appears to have found the task irksome, and this time chose an ex-monk, Monsieur Duplessis, to take over from him.[66] Duplessis had many good qualities: he was learned, witty and kind, but he inspired only contempt in Juste because he was not strict enough with Benjamin. Nonetheless under Duplessis's guidance Benjamin made some progress as they both followed Juste around Europe, from Switzerland to Brussels and then on into Holland. After little more than a year Juste's patience was exhausted and he dismissed Duplessis who, according to *Ma Vie*, later went mad after an unhappy infatuation and shot himself. Thus in 1780 ended the first phase of Benjamin Constant's formal education.[67]

The impact of such a succession of experiences on the young Constant is summarized in *Ma Vie*. After recounting the Gobert episode Constant states that he was 'convinced for the third time that those whose job it was to educate me and put me on the right path were themselves very ignorant and immoral men'.[68] On each occasion the father who had proved so poor a judge of character in the first place was later forced to rescue his son from the consequences of his folly. But in the cases of Duplessis and Benjamin's next tutor, the Englishman Nathaniel May, a curious complicity formed between father and son. Juste encouraged Benjamin to look down on the man he was employing to teach him. The problem seems to have been that Juste could never be content to leave his son without an image constantly before him of what he should become. That image was, of course, largely one of himself, Juste de Constant, superior, ironic, a man to command men, an enemy of 'mediocrity'. Benjamin, for the reasons outlined earlier, was throughout his boyhood perpetually anxious to please and placate a father he loved but of whom he was often more than a little afraid. He tried to accept his father as a model for himself, and also absorbed Juste's high expectations of future intellectual glory for him. This anxious dependence, alternating with outbreaks of rebelliousness – a pattern which was to repeat itself so often in his later life – was firmly established by the time Benjamin had reached early adolescence. His father was not disappointed in his literary hopes for Benjamin: from a very early age the boy poured forth poems, translations and astonishingly witty and mature letters addressed to his relatives. In 1779 when he composed his first piece of any real significance, *Les Chevaliers. Roman héroïque par H . . . B . . . C . . . De R . . .* [*The Knights. An Heroic Romance by H . . . B . . . C . . . De R . . .*], he wrote on the back of the fly-leaf an 'Epître à Monsieur Juste Constant', 'Epistle to Monsieur Juste Constant':

> Dear Father, I have been told that fathers find their sons' writings excellent even though they are often only a collection of literary reminiscences that have been thrown together without art. To prove such a rumour is false, I am honoured to present you with this work. I am sure that even though I composed it you will not find that it is any good and you will not even have the patience to read it.[69]

The romance, which is indeed reminiscent of the *Chanson de Roland*, Ariosto and other sources, is unfinished, and the dedication may not have been as disingenuous as it appears. Benjamin may indeed have feared that it might not come up to his father's high standards and have been unable to continue. In the event such fears were groundless. Juste obviously found the romance's vein of self-mockery to his liking and had it lavishly bound.

According to *Ma Vie*, so convinced was Juste de Constant of his son's abilities and promise that the following year he took him to Oxford where he intended him to matriculate at the exceptionally early age of 13. The truth of the matter, however, seems to be that Juste's relationship with his mother, 'la Générale', had now reached a nadir: harsh words had been exchanged over Benjamin's upbringing and Juste wished to put himself and his son beyond her reach for a while. He wrote a very revealing letter to his brother Samuel from Oxford on 10 July 1780, first published by

35

C. P. Courtney in 1985, which says as much about Juste himself as it does about his mother and Benjamin:

> I have been here for about three weeks. Quite apart from other reasons I have, I thought it was the best I could do to complete his study of languages. There are no distractions here: we see only people who are hard at work and whose diligence is always rewarded. Up to now I have had reason to be pleased that I chose to come here, however expensive it may have been. I think my son will make progress and that he will soon understand English. He works a great deal and with relish. I assure you, my dear Brother, that you judge the boy too favourably. He no longer shows any signs of having retained the promise he once had that he would distinguish himself academically. His boisterousness was taking over from his intellect and, as he was allowed a great deal of freedom, he sometimes came out with strange things which people took to be marks of genius. But as his boisterousness diminishes, so do his apparent gifts, and all that is now left is a great love of study. You will see him and judge him similarly. It is true that my mother has written some very harsh things, and that my fear of being contradicted by her and of the many problems she might cause me encouraged me to come to England – something I had long had the intention of doing – in order to be free and undisturbed: those are the things I need in order to be able to continue to supervise my son's studies. Besides, my mother is extremely embittered where I am concerned, and she will take anyone who happens to be present into her confidence on the matter: I am afraid my son might be one of that number, and would lose the trust I want him to have in me. The best thing I could do for her sake and mine was to go away until she had got over her grievance about me, so that I could enjoy the freedom I feel I need. It's not too much to ask at 55 years of age to be allowed to oversee my own son's education. I regret very much not being with my mother and not looking after her as I have for so long, but she has grown tired of my marks of attachment and respect, and in order to justify her present conduct she finds fault in me and accuses me of having secret plans and projects which exist only in her imagination. It hurts me a lot, but after having done everything I could to dispel the fears she says she has, the only thing left for me has been to give up and leave, doing rightly or wrongly the thing which I had intended to do. I wrote to tell my mother that I was going to England, but she refused to open the letter.[70]

Juste had a friend who in 1780 was a Fellow and Senior Dean of Arts at Magdalen College, Nathaniel Bridges (1750–1834),[71] and he perhaps hoped that, possibly with Bridges's help, Benjamin would find a tutor who would help him to pick up the English language quickly. Benjamin was never to matriculate at Oxford: even if Juste had secretly hoped that his son might begin studying at the University at this early stage, it would very soon have become clear to him that, despite his uncommon mental powers, Benjamin could not compete with students who were two or more years older than him, and of course still less in a language, English, which he was only beginning to acquire. Father and son spent only late June to August 1780 in Oxford, during which time Benjamin took English lessons: they then returned to Holland, reaching The Hague in early September. However they were now accompanied by a young Englishman who had been recommended to Juste, perhaps by Bridges, as a teacher of good character, Nathaniel May (1761–1830), and who was at this time a student at Lincoln College, Oxford.[72] According to *Ma Vie* Juste had learnt his lesson as regards tutors, and employed Nathaniel May under a much looser arrangement than that adopted with his predecessors. May was to teach Benjamin Greek and English, it seems. He remained with the Constant family for almost a year.

Thanks to the researches of C. P. Courtney who in 1966 edited Nathaniel May's letters to his sister Jane written while working for Juste de Constant, we have an accurate idea of his character against which to measure the dismissive account which Constant was to write thirty years later in *Ma Vie*:

> Hardly had Monsieur May joined us on our our journey and my father already found him laughable and insufferable. He confided in me his impression of him, with the result that I considered my new companion worthy only of mockery and perpetual derision. . . . Monsieur May spent a year and a half accompanying us in Switzerland and Holland. . . . My father, who wanted only to be rid of him, seized the first opportunity that presented itself and sent him back to England.[73]

Nathaniel May's letters tell a strangely different story. He speaks repeatedly and in glowing terms of Juste's politeness and efforts to make everything agreeable for him, and appears quite unaware that, if we are to believe *Ma Vie*, his host found him absurd. There is, perhaps, a solution to this apparent contradiction in the character of Nathaniel May which emerges from his correspondence with his sister. A devout Anglican with Evangelical leanings (he was later to become more closely associated with the Evangelical movement of which Nathaniel Bridges was a leading Oxford representative), the 20-year-old May must have appeared exasperatingly innocent, pedantic and humourless to the mercilessly ironic and sophisticated Juste, who furthermore never made any secret of his scepticism in matters of religion. In all probability May never realized when Juste was being tongue in cheek, and his French was certainly too poor to enable him to catch any ironic nuances or inflections. As a result he appears to have sailed happily through the year he spent with Juste and Benjamin, enjoying the sights of Europe and having plenty of leisure for his own studies, entirely unaware of the mirth he continually inspired in all around him. From May's reports to his mother and sister it is also evident that Benjamin profited considerably from his tuition (May's letters are of course in English): '[Constant] labours very hard and has made great improvement. He is far advanced in the Greek, understands the English very well and speaks it very fluently'.[74] But there were also indications of Benjamin's increasing unruliness, behaviour that only Juste could deal with: 'Young Constants passions are sometimes very strong[;] it is only the presence and authority of his Father that can govern him. If he will not conduct himself well with me I shall not stay with him long'.[75] Some months later things were going rather better:

> The Young Gentleman has given me little reason to complain for some time[;] he has a great friendship for me but nobody ever has or ever will be able to preserve any influence over him but his Father, who keeps him in very great awe. I was never required to be answerable for his conduct and was only required to assist him in his studies.[76]

At some point soon after 23 May 1781 Nathaniel May left Juste's service, apparently by mutual agreement. Indeed the account given of May in *Ma Vie*, after such a rogues' gallery of bad tutors, was perhaps distorted for aesthetic effect, since, long after it was written and thirty-five years after the events it described, Constant sought out Nathaniel May, who was by then vicar of Leigh in Kent, and entrusted to his temporary safe-keeping his most precious possession, the manuscript of his book on polytheism on which he had been working more than half his life.[77] Faintly ridiculous he may have been, but May's integrity had clearly remained fixed in Constant's memory.

Just before Nathaniel May returned to Oxford and while he was still helping Benjamin with his work (they were staying in the garrison town of Geertruidenberg), Benjamin fell in love, it seems, for the first time. The object of his affection was the daughter of the commanding officer David Grenier (1721–90), a friend of his father's. Too shy to tell her of his feelings for her, interrupted when she began questioning him about his love, Benjamin was soon obliged to leave Geertruidenberg to follow his father back to Switzerland.[78] During that autumn of 1781 Benjamin took lessons from a local pastor, Philippe Sirice, known as Le Doyen Bridel (1757–1845), later noted for his work on Swiss folklore and patois. Once again the arrangement was unsuccessful. Bridel, according to *Ma Vie*, was a self-important pedant who assumed an air of familiarity inappropriate to his dealings with the son of a Vaudois aristocrat and which Juste soon found unacceptable. Bridel was dismissed.[79]

All Juste's efforts to secure for his son the degree of personal attention that only a private tutor could give had now failed. Perhaps only May had achieved anything with Benjamin, but his obtuseness made him in the long term unsuitable in Juste's eyes. Having avoided all educational institutions for so many years he was at last forced to send Benjamin away from home. On 6 February 1782 Benjamin Constant matriculated at the University of Erlangen.[80] The choice of this German university was the result of Juste's chance meeting with the Protestant Margrave of Ansbach-Bayreuth, Christian Friedrich Carl *Alexander* (1736–1806), an amiable and cultured eccentric whose court was essentially French in outlook. It was a happier choice than all the others had been. Benjamin, now nearly 14 years old and emancipated from the close supervision of Juste or his tutors, divided his time between his studies at the University – of which Margrave Alexander was *Rector Magnificentissimus* and a great benefactor – and attendance at Court.

Little is known of the precise nature of his reading or other activities within the University. From his earlier and later studies we can assume the Greek and history dominated his interests, and that his knowledge of German and of German literature originated during the year and a half he spent at Erlangen. It was a fine university, cosmopolitan and open to new ideas, with many distinguished scholars among its teachers.[81] The following year, probably in April 1783, Constant wrote to his cousin, Wilhelm de Sévery, who was his own age and a student at the Military Academy of Colmar, describing his life at Erlangen:

The detail of my occupations can be briefly summarized. I work for about eight hours a day. I go horse-riding every afternoon, and every evening I go to pay my respects to the Margravine. Sometimes I play cards and I have supper there. She is kinder to me than I deserve, she treats me with great cordiality. She allows me to visit her Court every evening, a distinction she has granted only to me, and she has obtained for me a post as Gentleman of the Bedchamber to the Margrave. I cannot express all my gratitude to her. All that I lack here is a friend, but I shall not, I think, find one to my liking here.[82]

In fact apart from attending lectures, which were mostly given in Latin, it would seem, and of which a great variety were available in his fields of interest – Latin and Greek language and literature, ancient and modern history, theology – as well as possibly attending private tutorial sessions, Constant appears to have been a rather solitary student, devoting all his energies to studying on his own. In the middle of his stay news reached him of the death of his grandmother, 'la Générale' Rose-Susanne de

Constant, which occurred on 14 October 1782. Although his reaction is not recorded, it can only have been one of profound grief: one of his earliest objects of love and attachment had been taken away from him, and the loss may have had a deleterious effect on Constant's subsequent behaviour in Erlangen.

For company he had members of the Court, and he appears to have been temporarily adopted by 'Madame la Margrave', the Margravine who no doubt felt sorry for him in his lonely exile. This Margravine was either Friederike Caroline of Saxe-Coburg, the sickly wife of the Margrave who had for long years neglected her in favour of his various mistresses, or the Dowager Margravine, Sophie Caroline Marie of Brunswick-Wolfenbüttel (1737–1817), sister of the Duke of Brunswick and widow of the previous Margrave. Gustave Rudler opts for the second of these on the grounds that the notoriously unhappy Friederike Caroline would have been unlikely to cheer anyone up.[83] From the letter quoted above, which Rudler appears not to have seen when he wrote *La Jeunesse de Benjamin Constant*, it might look as if it were indeed she who befriended Constant, but since Constant refers to 'la vieille margrave' in *Ma Vie* we must conclude with Rudler that Constant is most likely to have been the *protégé* of Sophie Caroline of Brunswick-Wolfenbüttel. At Court Constant made his first and fateful acquaintaince with the pleasures of the gaming table. He also fought at least two duels,[84] either with other young men at Margrave Alexander's Court or with fellow-students at the University. This was not exactly what his father had had in mind when he sent him to Erlangen, as a letter from Juste to his friend Sir Robert Murray Keith dated 18 April 1783 reveals:

> [Benjamin] is in Erlangen at the moment where I took him so that he can acquire that gravitas and bombast which characterizes Messieurs the German professors, highly respectable gentlemen every one, but whose ability to hit hard is the single best corrective to an excess of liveliness in a student.[85]

Ma Vie tells a very different story from what Juste would have wished. On the one hand Benjamin undoubtedly studied seriously for long periods while at Erlangen. But on the other he felt free at last to indulge in 'mille extravagances', many acts of folly, and to draw attention to himself he took, ostensibly as a mistress, a girl of doubtful reputation. He did not like her, nor did the girl allow their relationship to become a physical one, yet he kept up the elaborate and expensive pretence of keeping her as his mistress – and this in spite of the Margravine's disapproval. In fact the more the Margravine, his erstwhile friend, revealed her hostility to the girl, whose mother had in the past offended her, the more attached to his 'mistress' Constant became. He went further and, encouraged by the Margravine's old enemy, the girl's mother, indulged to the full his talent for savage mockery at the expense of his protector. The Margravine was justifiably outraged by Constant's behaviour and saw to it that his father was informed. Juste immediately ordered his son to leave Erlangen and to join him in Brussels. Soon afterwards Juste took Benjamin with him to Edinburgh so that he could begin his studies once more, in a different and, he hoped, more suitable environment. It was to prove a fateful and – for once – farsightedly wise decision on Juste's part.

Writing some fifty years nearer to Benjamin Constant's lifetime than Gustave Rudler, and drawing on the personal memories of Constant's contemporaries, Edouard Laboulaye records in 1861 that Constant never knew the love of a mother and was unable to find that warmth in his relationship with Juste. On the subject of his father's second marriage and family, Laboulaye implies that Benjamin felt excluded and distanced as a result of it, and that his unsatisfactory relationship with the irascible and overbearing Colonel, in which there was always an element of fear, influenced the whole course of his life.[86] There can be no doubt that the young Benjamin Constant's troubled relationship with his father did indeed set the framework for the rest of his life and affected in some way all of his subsequent activities, attitudes and friendships. The experience of rejection which I have suggested he felt in his earliest years came not only from the loss of his mother (a fact on which he must have brooded as soon as he became aware of it), but also from the severing or disruption of so many of his ties with the living: with his paternal grandmother and with his nurse at the age of 5, and with his father, so often leaving him to rejoin his regiment on the other side of Europe. Fear of rejection leads to fear of love itself, and there can be little wonder at the ambivalence of Constant when offered love in later life. To this can be added the anguish which is always associated with partings in his work: separation was what had permanently threatened his childhood existence, beginning with that first brutal and inexplicable separation from his mother about which he had been told, and constantly repeated with a thousand more or less painful variations. Parting carried with it an undefined menace – that of being possibly final.

Fear of rejection, fear of separation: there was enough there to make for a childhood of more than average misery. But to have Juste de Constant as a father, with his aggressiveness, his propensity for cutting sarcasm and his limitless desire for his son's literary glory, this surely was misfortune on a grand scale. And yet somewhere and somehow Benjamin did find a little love, the proof being that in the end he was able to love and cherish at least his second wife Charlotte and to accept her rather maternal love in return. He was also capable of great and lasting loyalty to his friends. But the residue of these early, dark, often lonely years was also there, poisoning his hopes and ambitions and infecting his relationships. He was anxious, depressive and throughout his life overwhelmingly obsessed with the idea of death, perhaps secretly guilty and self-reproachful for having survived his mother. His friend Jean-Jacques Coulmann observed that the ever-present thought of death blighted Constant's whole existence, affected all his relationships and made him seem offensively indifferent to people.[87] Certainly Constant's sense of futility amounting perhaps to a questioning of his right to be alive at all could well have come from an early bond with a substitute mother having been severed. In the view of Ian Suttie a person's relationship with his or her mother is a socializing one and one which gives us a sense of ourselves and of our worth. With Constant such serene self-acceptance came late if it came at all, and his persistent tendency, especially in his youth, to self-destructive behaviour could well have originated in an early experience of rejection. Insecure, sometimes unable to see himself as loved or lovable, unable to identify entirely with an aggressive and domineering father, it would not have been surprising if Constant had been drawn to a number of forms of sexual deviation. A feeling of guilt and inferiority perhaps produced the sado-masochistic scene which opens *Ma Vie*, either in reality at the age of 5 or as a fantasy in the mind of the 44-year-old writer. It could also have produced a bisexual identification which may not only have led him to attach great value to friendship with older men, probably with an element of hero-worship or intellectual competitiveness involved, but also, and most important, to that profound but never permanent identification with feminine passivity and suffering that would characterize his greatest writing, and would culminate in *Adolphe*.

2

'THE CHARMS OF FRIENDSHIP'
(1783–1785)

My father only remained in Scotland for three weeks. After he left, I began studying with great enthusiasm, and then began the most agreeable year of my life. Among the young students of Edinburgh it was the accepted thing to work. They had set up several literary and philosophical societies: I attended the meetings of some of them, and I made a name for myself there as a writer and orator, even though I was working in a language that was not my own.

(*Ma Vie*, entry under 1783–4[1])

When, in November 1783, Benjamin Constant enrolled at Edinburgh University as a member of Professor Andrew Dalzel's advanced Greek class, the 'classis provectiorum', another student, formidably precocious like Constant, was registering as a member of the beginners' class, the 'classis tyronum'. The University Matriculation list gives his name as 'Gualterus Scott'.[2] This curious fact is worth recording not in an attempt to rewrite the history of Franco-British literary relations, but merely to illustrate the lack of research on Constant's period as an Edinburgh undergraduate until recent years. Too many commentators were content with Gustave Rudler's statements on the question – detailed and largely accurate as they admittedly are[3] – and with those of Constant himself in *Ma Vie*. The loss of all of Constant's correspondence with his Edinburgh friends compounded the mischief and led critics to suppose that there was nothing more to be said on the matter. And yet no one to my knowledge ever remarked on the fact that Constant and Sir Walter Scott were students at Edinburgh at the same time, albeit in somewhat different circumstances, Scott being 12 years of age and living at his parents' house near the University and Constant, now 16, lodging with the Professor of Medicine, Andrew Duncan,[4] and living the altogether more independent life of a student in a foreign city. They may even have had acquaintances in common: among other members of Dalzel's 'classis provectiorum' with Scott in December 1784 were Charles Ross, James Johnstone and James Wauchope, all future members of the Speculative Society, but Wauchope in particular a member of a family well known to Constant.[5] One of the greatest ironies and missed opportunities of literary history, no doubt, is the fact that after Constant left Edinburgh, Walter Scott became a member of the Speculative Society and the Secretary of that distinguished debating club:[6] his minutes of its proceedings are deposited in the Society's archives and his death mask still stands on a table in its debating hall. Benjamin Constant and Sir Walter Scott lived parallel lives, certainly worthy of the attention of a modern Plutarch. Insufficient attention, then, has been paid to the people Constant could have met or did meet in Edinburgh, Scott being among those Constant *may* have met, though there is no evidence that he ever did. There are still large areas of Constant's Edinburgh experiences that remain obscure and unmapped, but there are too some significant remains in the form of letters and documents that, surprisingly, have been overlooked by literary archaeologists, and which enable us to form a clearer idea of Constant's activities, to identify those people he *did* know well, and even to understand their significance in his life.

According to *Ma Vie* Constant arrived in Edinburgh with his father on 8 July 1783 where they were welcomed by old friends of Juste de Constant.[7] It had been in Juste's mind for some months that his son would profit from studying at a Scottish university, and on 18 April 1783 he had written to an old friend, Sir Robert Murray Keith, British Ambassador in Vienna:

> I am sending my son to Scotland to finish his studies there. . . . He is only 15 and his one passion is literature. Being in the company of the learned men of your country can only reinforce his preference. If he can get to know some of them, he will be able to acquire what he still lacks.[8]

But Juste de Constant had other reasons for sending Benjamin to Edinburgh, as he confessed more candidly in a further letter to Keith dated 2 June 1783. He was worried about a son 'born with all the talents imaginable, but also with the most violent emotions which cannot be tamed' and continued:

> I had hoped that his liking for study – which I worked hard to instil in him – would act as the most effective brake on him. He is making progress, but his tastes are widening and it is to be feared that he may give in to them entirely. My sole concern now is to move him on to a new place as soon as I see that the acquaintances he is making are dangerous ones [*dès que je m'aperçois que ses liaisons deviennent dangereuses*]. I gain time that way, but also I do not succeed in rooting out the evil. At the moment he is in Erlangen where he has behaved quite well. However I must take him away from there now. As he has a particular liking for your literature, I

thought a period in Edinburgh would be useful for him. He is good at Latin and Greek, and it is only in your country that he will find true scholars. The letters of recommendation you have sent me will enable him to meet men for whom he already has great esteem. Perhaps studying under them will produce the result I desire, that is that he will spend more time with the dead than with the living.[9]

Others had doubts about Juste's plans, including General Robert Douglas who wrote to Keith:

The young man is, they say, a prodigy, but people add that the father spoils him by proving too much his good qualities, & that he will destroy the boy's intellectuals with learning him too much. I have a great opinion of Constant, but here, I almost join with the voice of the multitude, & am much afraid that, with all the pains, prodigious expence, & the often changing of his son's education, the young man will never turn out the scavant and home de lettres w[ch] his very sensible, but too fond father has laid down for a rule, & positive maxim that his son shall be.[10]

After a stay of three weeks in Edinburgh with his son, Juste de Constant left him under the protection of the historian William Robertson (1721-93), Principal of the University, who appears to have taken a personal interest in Benjamin's progress.[11] We may assume that during the months of late summer and autumn 1783 Constant familiarized himself with the city, and probably met other students in his lodgings at the house of Professor Andrew Duncan. His host, Andrew Duncan the elder (1744-1828) was 'both generous and hospitable to his pupils' and a man of 'very social instincts' and 'evenly balanced temperament',[12] and one can speculate that it was through him that Constant met one of his drinking companions, the doctor Richard Kentish.[13] By November 1783 Constant was certainly acquainted with – and probably the friend of – at least two outstanding Edinburgh students, Charles Hope[14] and John Wilde. It was through their sponsorship that Constant became a member of the Speculative Society, a remarkable institution which deserves a few words of description. 'The Spec', as it is still affectionately known to its members, was founded by six Edinburgh students in 1764 as a debating society, and built its own hall in which to hold its meetings. When, in the early nineteenth century, its hall had to be demolished, it was given rooms in the new University buildings, and there it still holds its meetings weekly between October and March. Although its premises are no longer those that Constant would have known, it remains essentially the same Society with the same purpose. Nowadays, however, the Speculative Society's members tend to be mainly young advocates, whereas in Constant's day they were undergraduates. In the atmosphere of enthusiastic intellectual inquiry of late-eighteenth-century Edinburgh, student societies – medical, scientific, theological and literary – proliferated: the Speculative Society has outlived almost all of them, and has been as exceptional in the calibre of its members – Constant, Sir Walter Scott, Robert Louis Stevenson among many others – as in its longevity.[15]

The Speculative Society's Minute Book records that at the first meeting of the 1783–4 session held on Tuesday 11 November 1783, with Charles Hope in the chair, there were received: 'Petitions from Baron Constant, attested & presented by M[r.] Hope & Mr. Wylde, and Allen Dalzel, attested & presented by Mr. Wylde & Mr. Js. Clerk praying to be admitted members.'[16] According to the usual practice a ballot of members was held the following week and we read in the Minutes for the meeting of Tuesday 18 November 1783 that 'The Society agree[d] to admit Mr. Dalzel & Baron Constant Members, & the latter was received accordingly'.[17] From that date the Society was to be one of the main focuses of Constant's life in Edinburgh. As students did not live in the University but in lodgings, and as many could ill afford to heat their rooms in the winter months, student societies were an obvious solution both to the unconvivial isolation and the cold.[18] While it is doubtful whether Constant ever experienced such privations, his life became likewise centred on at least two societies and the friendships that he made there. At the same time that autumn of 1783 he was beginning his University courses in Greek and History, and by the end of the year his name was on the Matriculation Roll of the University among the 'Discipuli D. And. Dalzel, Ling. Graecae Professoris' in the 'classis provectiorum' and among the 'Discipuli D. Alex: Tytler Fraser, Historiae Civil: Profess.' As one would expect, fellow students were often fellow members of societies: in Constant's History group, for example, there was a Russian, Dimitri Poltoratski, who joined the Speculative Society shortly after him.[19]

These, then, are the salient facts about Constant's first months in Scotland. By themselves, however, they tell us few of the things we would most like to know about his highly formative period in Edinburgh. Fortunately there are other and more valuable sources of information which, taken together with the chronological framework we have established, enable us to enter into Constant's world in an altogether more vivid way. The first of these, and by far the best known, are the *Memoirs of the Life of Sir James Mackintosh*, edited from Mackintosh's manuscript by his son and published in 1835. In *Ma Vie* Constant singles out James Mackintosh, 'at present a high court judge in Bombay',[20] as one of his closest friends at this time: Mackintosh for his part describes 'Baron Constant de Rebecque' as 'a Swiss of singular manners and powerful talents, and who made a transient appearance in the tempestuous atmosphere of the French Revolution',[21] and who was a fellow member of the Speculative Society.

It is Mackintosh who is able to tell us vividly what it felt like to be a student at Edinburgh in the 1780s:

> I am not ignorant of what Edinburgh then was. I may truly say, that it is not easy to conceive a university where industry was more general, where reading was more fashionable, where indolence and ignorance were more disreputable. Every mind was in a state of fermentation. The direction of mental activity will not indeed be universally approved. It certainly was very much, though not exclusively, pointed towards metaphysical inquiries. Accurate and applicable knowledge were deserted for speculations not susceptible of certainty, nor of any immediate reference to the purposes of life. Strength was exhausted in vain leaps, to catch what is too high for our reach. Youth, the season of humble diligence, was often wasted in vast and fruitless projects. Speculators could not remain humble submissive learners. Those who will learn, must for a time trust their teachers, and believe in their superiority. But they who too early think for themselves, must sometimes think themselves wiser than their master, from whom they can no longer gain anything valuable. Docility is thus often extinguished, when education is scarcely begun. It is vain to deny the reality of these inconveniences, and of other most serious dangers to the individual and to the community, from a speculative tendency (above all) too early impressed on the minds of youth.[22]

'Metaphysical inquiries', 'vast and fruitless projects', 'think themselves wiser than their master': as we shall see presently, these phrases are singularly appropriate for Constant's impossibly vast project of writing a history of polytheism (i.e. the belief in many gods) conceived in 1785 soon after he left Scotland, and which may well have been inspired by a reaction *against* the lectures of Professor Alexander Fraser Tytler, as we shall also see later. What Mackintosh calls, in another context, 'the pleasures of revolt' and 'independence of established authority'[23] were the very hallmarks of student life in Edinburgh whether manifested in 'Bacchanalian orgies'[24] or in the calmer pursuit of 'Oratory, History & Composition'.[25] It was to the encouragement of this latter *trivium* that the Speculative Society was dedicated, and it provided a channel of expression for that radical Whiggishness which characterized not only many of its members but also the intellectual atmosphere of the city.

It is regrettable that the practice of taking detailed notes of what was said at the Society's debates was not yet in force during Constant's period in Edinburgh, nor was it permissible to record in the Minutes on which side an individual member voted. The only clear indication of a member's voting intentions comes from his being named in the Minutes as a teller for the Ayes or the Noes. Nonetheless the *Minute Book* gives us a valuable insight into the political and moral preoccupations of Constant and his associates; in it we see a very wide range of political, historical, philosophical and ethical subjects dealt with. Entries take the form of a list of members present, preceded by the President's (i.e. chairman's) name; petitions from men wishing to be admitted as members; the results of ballots on the applications for membership received the previous week; the title and author of a 'Discourse' or essay read to the Society; the 'Question for this Evening's debate'; the names of the member who opened the debate and those who spoke to the motion; the tellers for the Ayes and Noes; the voting figures and whether the motion was passed in the affirmative or negative. What we can glean from the *Minute Book* is meagre but significant: that the young Constant had regicidal and perhaps proto-feminist leanings, for on 6 January 1784 he voted retrospectively for the execution of Charles I, and on 21 December 1784 in favour of giving women a 'learned education'.[26]

Among Constant's close friends at the Speculative Society, James Mackintosh – afterwards the Right Honourable Sir James Mackintosh (1765–1832) – was, like several other Edinburgh acquaintances, a student of medicine when he was admitted to the Speculative Society on 21 December 1784. Mackintosh had been drawn to Edinburgh by its reputation as having the finest teachers of 'physic' and science in Europe. Medicine was not his first love, however, and he would have preferred to be a bookseller ('conceiving that no paradise could surpass the life spent among books')[27] or a lawyer, but was persuaded otherwise by financial considerations. Later, however, he was to pursue a career closer to his desires: in 1795 he was called to the English Bar, and in 1803 appointed Recorder of Bombay and given a knighthood. Towards the end of his life he was to become a Member of Parliament and Privy Councillor.[28] All commentators on Mackintosh's life agree on the breadth of his reading, the retentiveness of his memory and the clarity of his understanding in fields which interested him, politics, legislation, history, philosophy – fields which were, of course, also beginning to occupy Constant's mind. But his character at this period was very different from Constant's. He was, despite his claim to have been 'speculative, lazy, and factious',[29] a rock of moral integrity, kindness and practical sense set in the midst of the turbulent and sometimes murky seas of metaphysics and political philosophy on which his fellow students were driven hither and thither. He was a polymath who immediately assumed an easy authority over his contemporaries by the strength of his personality and by his mental powers. That this model of discipline and intellectual effort made a lasting impression on Constant and, no doubt, encouraged him to persevere in fields remote from the writing of fiction is clear from a letter Constant wrote to Mackintosh twenty years later. Assuring him that his opinion is still 'of so great value' to him, Constant continues:

I have often boasted of your friendship, when your literary and political eminence were my only mode of communicating with you, unknown to yourself, and when I had but very faint hopes of your remembering me. You may, therefore, well believe that the renewal of that friendship has been one of the greatest pleasures I have ever experienced.

> Your old and ever
> Devoted and attached friend,
> B. CONSTANT.[30]

This does not have the ring of a well-turned but hollow compliment. To a young man of 16, Mackintosh, this *integer vitae scelerisque purus*, two years his senior and with all the virtues, can only have reinforced Constant's dissatisfaction with his own character and uncertainties and with the lack of purpose of his own disordered life until then. Mackintosh became a friend, but a distant one no doubt, and remained an ideal model. This impression may have been emphasized by the very brevity of their time together, four months (from December 1784 to April 1785), and by Constant's enforced departure in highly unbecoming circumstances. They had a common interest in the history of religion (which was to develop during Mackintosh's stay in India), and Mackintosh's *Memoirs* record one conversation between them, which took place on 15 February 1785:

> My first essay [in the Speculative Society] was on the religion of Ossian. I maintained, that a belief in the separate existence of heroes must always have prevailed for some time before hero-worship; that the greatest men must be long dead, believed to exist in another region, and considered as objects of reverence before they are raised to the rank of deities; that Ossian wrote at this stage in the progress of superstition; and that if Christianity had not been so soon introduced, his Trenmor and Fingal might have grown into the Saturn and Jupiter of the Caledonians. Constant complimented me for the ingenuity of the hypothesis, but said, that he believed Macpherson to have been afraid of inventing a religion for his Ossian.[31]

The controversy about the authenticity of James Macpherson's *Works of Ossian* (1765) continued to divide the literary world, and this exchange reveals, as one might expect, Constant's total scepticism on the subject. It is a measure of how his Edinburgh education was increasing his capacity to ask questions and to doubt that earlier, on 2 December 1783 when he had been present at a Speculative Society debate on the question 'Are the poems of Ossian authentick?', it had been decided that the poems were authentic *without a division*.[32] Constant's remark may also betray his anticlericalism (Macpherson did not dare to venture into an area which might involve him in a religious dispute). Alternatively it may simply point to

Constant's own growing awareness of how complex the history of religions was, a result of his recent studies: on 23 November 1784 he chose as the subject of his Speculative Society 'Discourse' 'the Influence of the Pagan Mythology on manners and character'.[33] The Discourse, like all others from that period, was unfortunately not preserved.

By an odd coincidence mention of the Ossian controversy leads us automatically to think of Malcolm Laing (1762–1818), 'one of the best of [the historian] Robertson's successors' as Constant calls him in *Ma Vie*.[34] In an appendix to his *History of Scotland from the Union of the Crowns to the Union of the Kingdom* (1802), Laing was to maintain that Macpherson's Ossian poems were of modern origin, and that Macpherson had based them on virtually nothing of truly archaic provenance. This iconoclasm was entirely in the character of Laing, one of the finest Scottish historians and, in Mackintosh's words, 'The scourge of impostors and terror of quacks'.[35] Laing, an ardent liberal and future friend of Charles James Fox, was called to the Scottish Bar in 1785, but although 'most acute and ingenious' he was handicapped by 'an inconceivable rapidity of utterance', according to Mackintosh.[36] Another contemporary, Thomas Macknight is more inclined to be charitable: '[his] eloquence flowed from his mouth with *cataractic* force & velocity'.[37] Mackintosh and the *Edinburgh Review* both regretted Laing's tendency to strain after a brevity which sometimes obscured his meaning.[38] But Laing's impassioned liberalism and his hostility in debate to the power of the aristocracy were completely in tune with Constant's views at this time.

There was, however, at least one member of the Speculative Society still more passionately radical than Laing, and willing in later life to risk even the hangman's rope for his beliefs. This man was Thomas Addis Emmet (1764–1827) who, during Constant's time in Edinburgh, was studying medicine, and who, after visiting medical schools on the Continent between 1785 and 1788, returned to his native Ireland. On the advice of Mackintosh he gave up medicine for the law, was called to the Irish Bar in 1790, and became legal adviser to the United Irishmen. He was the elder brother of the more famous Robert Emmet (1778–1803) who was to be executed for leading the abortive uprising of July 1803.[39] Thomas Macknight says the following on the subject in a memoir:

Thomas Addis Emmet – brother of Emmet who was conspicuous in the Irish rebellion 1798 and suffered in the cause – was perhaps the most splendid orator I ever listened to. In a few sentences after he began, on a favourite topic, political or even moral, we were hurried in imagination into the region of the Stars – with an endless variety of brilliant similes – it resembled a Sky-rocket darting among the clouds & throwing out an infinity of dazzling points; and whatever we thought of the *argument*, we could not help being astonished &

captivated with the fluency & beauty of the *illustration*. I never heard Grattan or Flood – but I question, if either of them could have surpassed Emmet. What became of him I have not learned. He went, I think, to America, and for aught I know, may be still alive there.[40]

'What became' of Dr Emmet is, of course, part of Irish history: he was lucky to escape with his life for his part in the 1798 uprising; was imprisoned in Scotland at Fort George until 1802; tried to enlist Napoleon's support for the 1803 conspiracy for which his brother was hanged; then emigrated to New York and ended his days as one of America's most distinguished lawyers.[41] He was already six years in his grave when Macknight wrote down his memories of him. It is strange and perhaps instructive that Constant does not mention Emmet, who played such a leading role in the Speculative Society between 1783 and 1785. Mackintosh perhaps gives a clue about this silence: 'Emmett did not reason, but he was an eloquent declaimer, with the taste which may be called Irish, and which Grattan had then rendered so popular at Dublin.'[42]

'Emmett did not reason': to a disciple of Helvétius who was as steeped in French Enlightenment thought as Benjamin Constant, the *clinquant*, the flashiness of Emmet's furious oratory would appear strange and outlandish, and the violence of his espousal of the cause of the United Irish Society disturbing. By 1810–11 when he came to write *Ma Vie*, Constant had very firm views about usurpation and the use of military force. One can imagine that a man like Thomas Addis Emmet, for him as for the Speculative Society, lay beyond the pale, in the full sense of that phrase: indeed the Speculative Society, for all the radicalism of some of its members, had long since expelled Emmet from its number for disloyalty to the British Crown.

Mackintosh, Laing, Emmet: these were the most prominent members of the Speculative Society in the period which concerns us. But there was one other member who, on Constant's own admission, was the most important of all because of the deep friendship which grew between him and Constant: John Wilde.

Of all those young men the one who seemed the most promising was the son of a tobacco merchant named John Wilde. He had an authority over all of the rest which was almost absolute, even though most of them came from better families or were well off by comparison. He was immensely learned, tireless in his enthusiasm for his studies, brilliant in conversation, and of excellent character. After having reached the rank of Professor through sheer merit and having published a book which had begun to make a favourable reputation for him, he went completely mad and now, if he is not dead, is chained up in a cell and sleeping on straw. Oh wretched human race, is this what we and our hopes are destined to come to?[43]

Such a series of superlatives in this passage from *Ma Vie* indicates the extent of Constant's admiration and attachment. There was something special about John Wilde, and all the sources we have about his life concur on this. We do not know when he was born. A letter in the Speculative Society's archives from Robert Paterson to Robert Balfour who, at the time the letter was written, 7 February 1843, was preparing the excellent 1845 *History of the Speculative Society of Edinburgh*, reports on a fruitless search of Edinburgh baptismal records:

> The register of Baptisms in my possession does not go farther back than January 1766. And the only individual of the name Wyld that I find is the following and I rather think it is not the person you refer to – Alexander son of John Wild and Elizabeth Wilson was born the 21st and Baptized the 28th of September 1768.[44]

It is possible, of course, that this refers to the birth of a brother of John Wilde – whose name was spelt consistently 'Wilde' by himself but variously by others. It does at least seem certain that John Wilde was born in Edinburgh and that his father, a merchant of the same name, dealt in tobacco and had premises on the High Street, Edinburgh – not an unlucrative trade in the eighteenth century, but not to be compared with an income from land and estates. Indeed Wilde appears to have been poor in 1787. John Wilde's name first appears in Edinburgh University's Matriculation records under 11 December 1777 when he enrolled in Andrew Dalzel's advanced Greek class. Now at this period students registered and began to work towards a degree at anything between the ages of 14 and 20 (Walter Scott's beginning at 12 was exceptional), and on this reckoning John Wilde was probably born some time between 1757 and 1763. As a resident of Edinburgh like Walter Scott, he is more likely to have started university studies early rather than late, say at 14 or 15, which would give a *circa* of 1762/3 for his birth. He would therefore have been several years older than Benjamin Constant. Having begun in 1777 with Andrew Dalzel, Wilde continued in 1778–9 studying 'Literae Humaniores' – Latin – under John Hill, Logic and Metaphysics under John Bruce and Mathematics under Dugald Stewart, as well as attending Dalzel's Greek classes. In 1779–80 he studied Moral Philosophy with Adam Ferguson, Mathematics with Dugald Stewart and Greek with Dalzel. The last entry in the University Matriculation records states that he attended Robert Dick's Civil Law lectures in 1782–3. These lectures were also attended by other present and future members of the Speculative Society, to which Wilde had been admitted on 28 November 1780. Between 1783 and 1788 John Wilde presided over its meetings many times, and was made an honorary member on 5 February 1793.[45] When Benjamin Constant made his petition to be admitted to the Speculative Society on 11 November

1783 he was, as we have seen, sponsored by John Wilde and Charles Hope.

What kind of man was Wilde that he should draw forth from Constant expressions of such warmth and sadness in *Ma Vie* twenty-seven or twenty-eight years after they first met, and some twenty-three to twenty-four since he had last seen him? Mackintosh, referring to Wilde's later insanity, remarks that he 'has now, alas! survived his own fertile and richly endowed mind' and adds that as an orator he 'had no precision and no elegance; he copied too much the faults of Mr. Burke's manner'. But this failing in John Wilde was clearly compensated in Mackintosh's eyes by the fact that, 'He was . . . full of imagination and knowledge, a most amusing speaker and delightful companion, and one of the most generous men'.[46] In a remarkable passage in a memoir on the Speculative Society by the Reverend Thomas Macknight we are able to glimpse Wilde 'as in life', probably around May 1784:

> When I returned to Edin^r. after some years residence in England, I found John Wylde and James Mackintosh (then studying for the degree of M.D.) the *shining* personages of the Society. Wylde possessed an astonishing range of *miscellaneous* information. But at *25*, he had no more *vigour* of mind, than at *18*; and he could understand or relish no philosophy, but Lord Monboddo's *Antient Metaphysics*, on which his mind perpetually brooded. Mackintosh was the most acute Metaphysician, I ever knew; but his voice had a degree of coarseness, or want of *tone*, which excluded him from the class of *Orerotundo* speakers. Edwards on Free Will he considered as the standard of Metaphysical writing: and Park's Preface to Bellendinus, then newly published, was the object of his highest admiration. His power of memory was perhaps never excelled, as conjoined with such strength of Intellect – whatever he read he could instantly recollect, and bring to bear on his argument.
>
> It was in conversation that Mackintosh's talents appeared to greatest advantage. Many a delightful *symposium* I enjoyed with only him and Wylde (whom he called the greatest genius he ever knew) – after the meeting of the Society was over. We sat for hours listening to his recitations & remarks. I have heard him repeat 20 pages of the Life of Savage by Dr Johnson, from memory. But that elegant piece of writing, created in Wylde an admiration of the wayward Poet, which proved of the utmost detriment to Wylde himself. It was the means of betraying him into that careless dissipated style of life, which doubtless accelerated the effect of that tendency to aberration of mind, which at so early a period of his existence removed him from the business & Society of the world.[47]

The Reverend Macknight, feeling, no doubt, that he has gone a little too far in indiscretion, then apologizes: 'In these last observations I have perhaps been too particular' – too particular, that is, for a general *History* of the Society for which they are intended. We cannot but be grateful to him, however, for such refreshing candour. It illustrates once again how the memory of John Wilde has the capacity to evoke powerful feelings. More important, however, is the light these remarks throw on areas of Wilde's personality that have hitherto been obscure. Thanks to Macknight we know that John Wilde was something of a bohemian, unconventional and undoubtedly living in literary poverty when Constant knew him. The note of censoriousness at Wilde's way of life is struck again in a letter addressed to Benjamin Constant on 12 September 1824 by one Frederic Macfarlan. Recalling their mutual associates in the Edinburgh of the 1780s Macfarlan mentions 'Dr Thos Macknight, long one of the ministers of Edinr, & even then 40 years since one of the first scholars of that City so justly renowned for fine scholars'. Then Macfarlan comes, as it were, to Hecuba:

> John Wylde, long professor of Civil Law, who gave his lectures all in elegant Latin: yet, (so feeble is man, even in his best state!) long before last Century ended, lost the use of reason in great measure. How truly wise is it to be *sober* minded, even in the very whirlwind & tempest of applause![48]

Independently of each other, Macfarlan's smug satisfaction at a noble mind o'erthrown by too much acclaim, and Macknight's more heartfelt regrets point to a similar conclusion: John Wilde's eventual madness had a moral origin in his way of life. But it could hardly have been a way of life uncongenial to a man like Constant, a young man who despised the safe and the orthodox. Freedom was what Constant valued most, and Wilde's unfettered existence untrammelled by convention and his diet of ideas and works of the imagination must have appeared invincibly attractive. This was, of course, the career Constant must already have chosen for himself, that of a man of letters, and he must have begun to live it, at least in anticipation, at this time. Whether the 'careless dissipated style of life' of Wilde was directly responsible for Constant's return to the gaming table is open to doubt: Wilde's active participation in the Speculative Society's meetings – he spoke in almost every debate – may on the contrary have encouraged Constant's own regular attendance and put off that evil day. What Wilde did offer Constant was the friendship of a generous and clear-sighted man who did not spare him positive criticism where it was needed. We can see this in a recently published portrait of Constant in John Wilde's hand:

Character of H. B. Constant

By nation a Swiss, by inclination an Englishman, formed to acquire new talents and improve those he already possesses, while, at the same time, he neglects the first, and perverts the second. Feeling the charms of friendship, and yet reasoning against his feelings, a slave to the passion of love, yet varying perpetually in its objects, constant in versatility, in inconsistency consistent. An affectation of singularity forms a conspicuous feature of his character; and this, tho at present attended with disadvantages, may in time prove beneficial, since, if he continue in these sentiments, he must in the end be a Christian. An Atheist professed, he maintains at the same time the cause of Paganism, and while he spurns Jehovah cringes before Jupiter, while he execrates the bigotry and laughs at the follies of superstitious Christians, yet makes the vices of adulterous Deities the subject of his panegyric and prostitutes his genius to support the ridiculous mummeries of its Priests. In politics warm, zealous, keen, invariable, he resembles an Englishman of the purest times; and here, indeed, alone, we find an exception to his general character. He seems, indeed, to have drawn freedom with his first breath, and sucked the principles of liberty with the milk of his Childhood. But it is impossible, in any respect but this, to pursue him thro the endless mazes of his character. He outdoes even Proteus himself. Now he is one thing, now another; your friend, your foe; your advocate, your accuser; he supports you to day, pulls you down to morrow; composes now a panegyric, now writes a satyr; and yet what is strangest of all, to use a simile resembling one in Helvetius, the basis of his character is still the same, for like the sea in a storm, when the surface is agitated by the most dreadfull tempest, and the billows run mountains high, the bottom is still found undisturbed and peaceable.[49]

Whether this exceptionally interesting portrait of Benjamin Constant was composed, as C. P. Courtney suggests,[50] towards the end of 1784 or later, we can assume that it summarizes the knowledge gained by John Wilde between 1783 and 1785. And that knowledge is of a man who is never the same two days running, who is in perpetual contradiction with himself, and yet in whom there is a still centre that is unchanging and that cannot be reached or touched by all the agitation on the periphery.[51] It is odd that Wilde, who is so acute about Constant's desperate desire to be different (which so often amounted to attention-seeking and exhibitionism), makes no connection between Constant's love of freedom in general and his anxiety about being free as an individual. Perhaps he was too near to Constant to be able to focus on this aspect of their relationship. 'Feeling the charms of friendship, yet reasoning against his feelings': this arresting phrase, taken together with 'your friend, your foe . . . he supports you to day, pulls you down to morrow' suggests that Wilde was offering a closer friendship than Constant was able or willing to commit himself to. 'Yet reasoning against his feelings': what lies behind this? That Constant felt the need of a more intimate bond with Wilde, perhaps, but drew back from it? Certainly literary history offers examples of male friendships that were close and yet, according to those involved, were not homosexual: the obvious examples that spring to mind are Montaigne and Etienne de la Boétie and, more recently, D. H. Lawrence and John Middleton Murry. However, an eminent *constantien* has suggested[52] that Constant may have had homosexual relationships, which is an inference presumably drawn from the enigmatic interlinear addendum in *Ma Vie* under 1785–6 'Amours grecs de Berne', 'Greek love in Berne'.[53] This is therefore, perhaps, an appropriate moment to pause and consider the problem.

The case of Constant's later friendship with Isabelle de Charrière seems to offer something of a parallel with his friendship with John Wilde in that there is absolutely no written evidence – letters or diary entries – to show that their relationship was ever a sexual one. We are therefore thrown back on probabilities, and on the personalities of those involved. There are, as is well known, two extreme positions it is possible to adopt on the question of friendships between people of the same gender, male in this case: that all have a sexual basis, or that none do. Both schools of thought seem, in the late-twentieth century, somewhat crude and unlikely to account for the totality of human behaviour in all its complexity. This is not, of course, to say that there cannot be friendships that are entirely sexual or entirely non-sexual in origin. But if we adopt, for the sake of argument, a position somewhere between the two and examine the Constant–Wilde friendship, what does the evidence suggest? We know that the older Wilde was set apart and above his other Edinburgh friends in Constant's esteem – Wilde's nickname, on account of his enormous erudition, was 'Doctor John'; that Constant's admiration lasted many years, and in 1810 or 1811, when he was writing *Ma Vie*, it still smacked of hero worship; that until mid-adolescence Constant had, to our knowledge, no close male friend outside his family. (As we have seen, he lamented the fact that this was precisely what had been missing from his life in Erlangen.) We know that Wilde – probably several years older than Constant – was, in 1783–5, well on the way to living like a 'wayward Poet' with a 'dissipated style of life'. He lived as a Classical scholar, amid the examples of the male friendships of Antiquity. Most important, he regrets, in his pen-portrait, that Constant will not allow his feelings the upper hand in a friendship – undoubtedly their own – and keeps them in check. What are we then to conclude on the basis of probabilities? If there was a homoerotic element in the friendship – as some have seen in the cases of Montaigne and Lawrence, of course – the same law operated in this relationship as in Constant's relationships with women: a fluctuation between extremes of submission and aggression ('your advocate, your accuser'), between dependence and the panic of claustrophobia – above all an imperative need not to be tied. Is the vision in *Ma Vie* of Wilde's total degradation, chained up in a dungeon on a bed of straw, an expression of a hidden aggression towards him as strong as Constant's continuing affection? For there is in fact no evidence of Wilde's having sunk so low and there may be an element of exaggeration in Constant's supposition. The authoritative *History of the Speculative Society*, published only five years after Wilde's death, merely says: 'Confirmed derangement of mind caused him to spend the last thirty years of his life in retirement.'[54] Whom are we to believe? Was Constant perhaps misinformed, or are we? If he was wrongly informed, the idea of strength confined in a dungeon remained a powerful and disturbing one in his imagination, and recurs in one of the the most striking images of *Adolphe*: 'I thought I was hearing the powerful arms of an athlete being admired, an athlete who lay weighed down in chains at the bottom of a dungeon.'[55] Perhaps Constant needed an image of Wilde plunging down the edge of a precipice he himself could have fallen from. Or perhaps there was still a subconscious envy of Wilde's powers which must for long have excited great intellectual competitiveness in Constant.

We are able, then, to glean an adequate and convincing picture of Constant's friend from the material now available. There is still more that can be deduced from the *Minute Book* of the Speculative Society, however, on Wilde's political views. And they were certainly at odds with those of Constant in several areas, which would account in some measure for the violent swings in Constant's behaviour towards him. Wilde tended towards political conservatism, a cautiousness befitting the son of a merchant, while Baron Constant could indulge in the luxury of radicalism. Wilde voted against Irish parliamentary reform and Irish independence, against the limitation of the peerage, and would not have favoured the execution of Charles I. In general he appears to have been on the conservative side of liberalism, and Constant on the reformist, but his portrait of Constant generously pays tribute to the ardour with which his friend held to his convictions.

There was in Edinburgh another forum for male intellectual emulation where Wilde and Constant could compete with one another. This was the Dialectic Literary Society, about which we learn a little from Frederic Macfarlan's letter of 1824 from which I quoted earlier. Wilde and Constant were both members, along with several other friends from the Speculative Society. Histories of Edinburgh make no mention of a society of precisely that name. The foundation of the 'Dialectic Society' is normally given as 1787, and that of the 'Literary Society' (of which Sir Walter Scott was a member in 1789–90) is likewise believed to have been after 1785 when Constant left the city.[56] However the information given on this period in Macfarlan's letter is convincing, and there is little cause to doubt the accuracy of his statements. In all probability the two societies had their common origin in the 'Dialectic Literary Society' which was clearly in existence during and perhaps before the period 1783–5. In Macfarlan's letter we at last see Constant himself making an impression as a public speaker, even making allowances for a degree of flattery and Macfarlan's eagerness to be remembered by a now famous man:

> Brooklyn by New York, Respected Friend, Benjamin Constant, After forty years, it will be difficult, I fear, to recall to thy recollection the name Frederic Macfarlan. We were then members of the Dialectic Literary Society, in the University of Edinburgh. We were indeed but little, together, except while in the Society. *There* however we really met. For though there were many bright geniuses, & most of them fine scholars, among the first in Edin^r for our time of life; & though all were more or less professedly friends of Liberty; yet none equalled in proper views of liberty, the following 3; Malcom Laing, since, an active Lawyer, & writer of the History of Mary, Queen of Scots. Benjamin Constant, who then, though but young & only lately come to our country was not behind any of us, not only in the love of real liberty, but in the facility of displaying this, in all his speeches; & that too in a Language not Vernacular. This gave me, & I trust to all, no small hopes of his future activity in the field of Eloquence, for Genuine Liberty & the fact has abundantly proved this, in the many & arduous struggles, in which he has encountered every kind of opposition to the real rights of Man, Frederic Macfarlan was the third. Who indeed had this advantage of his fellow students & members of society, in having been, before that, in America, where he was much inflamed with a Love for liberty; which flame still burns.[57]

The Reverend Thomas Macknight, in his memoir on the Speculative Society is more measured in his appraisal of Constant's powers as an orator at this time:

> Baron Constant – whom I remember well. His appearances in the Society did him great credit, altho' perhaps we could hardly have anticipated his occupying so highly distinguished a place as he afterwards did, in the Legislative Council & Government of France. He was much esteemed in the speculative; and his loss seems to have been more regretted in France, than that of any other Legislator.[58]

There was always something strange and disconcerting about Constant which made his later success surprising, and, of course, made him warm to *un original* like his friend Wilde. As Madame de Staël reports after a conversation with Sir James Mackintosh in 1814: 'Mackintosh says you passed for the most extraordinary person in Edinburgh and indeed I think you are in every sense'.[59] For all his oddity – of which some part was, no doubt, a deliberate pose – good reports of Constant's progress were getting back to his father in Holland. In June 1784 Juste de Constant could write to Jean-Baptiste Suard, the *publiciste* or literary journalist: 'People have written to me to say that he deserves my confidence in him and that he is studying with great application and some success'.[60] It was Juste de Constant's plan that Benjamin should be uprooted yet again in October 1784 and sent to Paris where he would live at Suard's house. However this would not allow his son to be introduced to all that was brightest and best in London literary circles: Benjamin would not therefore be arriving in Paris till December![61] In the event Benjamin appears to have hung on in Edinburgh as long as possible, enjoying every minute. Indeed his departure after Easter 1785, when excessive gambling meant that he could put his creditors off no longer, resulted in his having almost completed a second academic year of lectures and society debates.[62]

The picture that emerges of Constant's life outside the lecture halls of Edinburgh is a reasonably clear if incomplete one. In *Ma Vie* he confesses to having got drunk a few times with Richard Kentish,[63] and probably did so with others. But we do not know anything about Constant's being, as Wilde says, 'a slave to the passion of love, yet varying perpetually in its objects'.[64] We do not know whether he kept a mistress, visited a brothel, or was entirely chaste in his affections, although the last would be surprising. There is an allusion in one of Isabelle de Charrière's letters to Constant's 'amie d'Ecosse', 'Scottish woman friend'.[65] Nonetheless the memory of Edinburgh that remained in Constant's mind was one of his own ascetic determination to work hard and achieve academic distinction, whatever extra-curricular excesses there may have been along the way. The first page of *Adolphe* summarizes it thus:

> By dint of stubborn dedication to hard work, in the midst of a very dissolute way of life, I had obtained a measure of success which had set me apart from my fellow students, and had given my father expectations concerning my future prospects that were probably greatly exaggerated.[66]

Of Constant's reading during the period we have no record. Strangely he did not once borrow a book from the University Library, although almost all his fellow students did.[67] On the other hand he donated a copy of Descartes's *Meditations* in Latin to the Speculative Society library, inscribed on the fly leaf in his own hand 'To the Speculative Society from B. Constant'.[68] We must assume that he was able to buy or borrow from friends all the books he needed. Wilde, meanwhile, when he was not immersed in those parts of James Burnett's *Antient Metaphysics* (1779–99) that had so far appeared, was reading Pindar's *Odes* 'Graece et Latine' at the end of August 1783 and in September and October of that year the Italian Davila's seventeenth-century *History of the Civil Wars of France*, an enormously popular account of the religious wars in which Constant's Huguenot ancestors may have taken part.[69]

It is worth considering, for a moment, John Wilde's own curious intellectual obsession with man's primitive origins, given the closeness of his friendship with Constant. The titles of two of the essays Wilde read to the Speculative Society before Constant's arrival in Edinburgh, 'The Savage State' and the 'Origin and Rise of Figurative Language',[70] indicate not, as one might expect, a Rousseauistic bent, but rather the early influence of James Burnett, Lord Monboddo's anthropological disquisitions. Burnett believed – and he was mocked for it – that man could be descended from monkeys. In *The Origin and Progress of Language* (1773–92) he went as far as suggesting that man belonged to the same species as the orang-outang. However man had gradually risen above his fellow animals, and his mind which had originally been subjected to his material body had, little by little, freed itself from matter and was capable of acting independently of his body. The development of human language resulted purely from the development of human society. From John Wilde's comments on Constant's paganism in the *Character of H. B. Constant* it would appear that Wilde was still, at least vestigially, a Christian at heart. Such views as Burnett's about man's descending from the apes must indeed have caused Wilde to 'brood perpetually' on his book. The anxiety Darwin's *Origin of Species* caused to orthodox believers several decades later is well documented. But for Burnett man's real triumph is in the mind's long, upward struggle to free itself from subjection to the body and to matter. The cultivation of our capacity for thought and the pursuit of knowledge are proper to man. And that at least was Wilde's consolation during his endless hours of study. Did the fear that Burnett might be right about our brutish origins contribute to the eventual unbalancing of his mind? Was the effort involved in intellectual self-perfection too much for him? Both hypotheses are plausible.[71] Constant gives no hint in *Ma Vie* or elsewhere that there was any sign of Wilde's impending lapse into madness in 1783–5. If Wilde had moments of black despair or dementia, they are unrecorded: he went on to crown a brilliant academic career by becoming joint Professor of Civil Law with Robert Dick in 1792, and sole occupant of the Chair in 1796. It was not until 1799–1800 that John Wilde had become so much indisposed as to be clearly unfit for lecturing.[72] An arrangement was then arrived at whereby Wilde continued to receive his salary for the Chair, but the work was done by a joint Professor, Alexander Irving.

While his friend was perhaps about to begin his struggle against a private nightmare, Constant in 1783–5 found himself in the altogether more serene atmosphere of the lecture hall. In the 1780s a student's work at Edinburgh University was, in some respects, closer to that of a schoolboy today. Constant's teachers Andrew Dalzel and Alexander Fraser Tytler would perhaps require the occasional essay from him, but there were no written examinations and the stress was on the question-and-answer method. To graduate – which few people ever did – a student was required to spend four sessions working in the University and to study Latin, Greek, Rhetoric and Belles Lettres, Logic and Philosophy.[73] Constant was among the large number of non-graduands: he studied Greek and History in 1783–4, and in the following session failed to register for any subject, probably because of his uncertainty about being recalled by his father and sent to Paris. C. P. Courtney has shown that, although there is no written record, Constant also appears to have studied Physics, Chemistry and Mathematics while in Edinburgh, though with little pleasure, since the only things he loved were 'metaphysics and languages'.[74]

Gustave Rudler states that he was unable to find either a list of lectures given by Constant's Edinburgh teachers or a record of Constant's borrowings from the University Library.[75] As we have seen, Constant did not borrow books from the Library, which solves Rudler's second problem; as for his first, we are exceptionally fortunate in that both Dalzel and Tytler published details of their teaching. In 1780 Dalzel's *Syllabus of Lectures on Poetry* appeared, and in 1821 his *Substance of Lectures on the Ancient Greeks and on the Revival of Greek Learning in Europe* gave an account of Dalzel's teaching which undoubtedly did not differ greatly from that which Constant had known. Tytler for his part published a *Plan and Outlines of a Course of Lectures on Universal History, Ancient and Modern delivered in the University of Edinburgh* (1782), and it was Tytler's course that seems to have made the greatest impression on Constant. Dalzel was, according to Lord Cockburn, 'an exciter of boys' minds': 'He could never make us actively laborious. But when we sat passive and listened to him, he inspired us with a vague but sincere ambition of literature, and with delicious dreams of virtue and poetry'.[76] Whether Constant found Alexander Tytler's lectures entirely to his taste is uncertain. Tytler's outline of the course is largely in note form, so that in some places we do not know the exact nature of his argument. What is overwhelmingly clear, however, is the Whiggishness of his stress on man's gradual progress, but at the same time a pronounced Christian bias, particularly in his treatment of ancient religions. This could not have been to Contant's liking at this time. Some extracts from the lecture summaries will illustrate this:

Of the Egyptians
.... Extraordinary superstitions. – Their morality very reprehensible. – General idea of their character. . . .

History of Greece
.... Origin of the religion of the Greeks. – They received a new system of Theology from their Eastern invaders, which they blended

with their own. – Hence the partial coincidence of the Grecian with the Egyptian and Phenician Mythology. – Error of Mythologists in attempting to trace all the fables of antiquity, and the various systems of Pagan Theology, up to one common source. Reflections on the study of Mythology. – The uncertainty and unprofitableness of such researches. – The ancient Greeks characterised by a spirit of supersitition . . . [77]

Narrow in one sense, Tytler's lectures were nonetheless extraordinarily wide-ranging in every other way: he gave his students a history of the Western World (Egypt, Greece, Rome, then the Middle Ages to the seventeenth century), tracing the rise and fall of civilizations, the origin of laws, the nature of the first governments, and the growth of the English constitution. Tytler did not neglect the importance of religion, philosophy or the arts and sciences. One section of his course may well have had a determining influence on Constant:

Institutions respecting religious worship. – Origin of Idolatry and Polytheism. – Metamorphoses of the Gods. – Apotheosis of heroes. – Institution of the priesthood, and its connection with the regal dignity.[78]

Were Tytler's lectures the spark that began a long slow-burning passion, 'le seul interet de ma vie', 'the only interest in my life', as Constant would call it,[79] that culminated in his books *De la religion* (*Concerning Religion*) and *Du polythéisme romain* (*Concerning Roman Polytheism*)? For all his dismissiveness about mythological researches – no doubt an additional spur to an intellectually rebellious young man – Tytler urged on his students, 'The necessity of prosecuting the study of History according to a regular plan. . . . Fruitlessness of the desultory perusal of detached histories'.[80] According to *Ma Vie* the idea of writing a history of polytheism came to Constant while in Brussels in the late summer and autumn of 1785, that is only a few months after leaving Edinburgh,[81] but it may have been conceived earlier still. Did he remember Tytler and apply to his work on religions that sustained attention Tytler recommended? Constant's book was destined to become a refuge from the many political and emotional conflicts in which he would find himself. And persevering with it as he did was perhaps some tangible link with a lost scholarly Eden where he had first formed the idea of being more than an *étourdi*, an aimless young scatterbrain, and had glimpsed what it would be like to be a great and learned man.

3

ISABELLE DE CHARRIERE
(1785–1787)

I said something to Hochet yesterday which I think is very true. He was talking to me about my former reputation for saying hurtful things about others. I explained to him that at the time I was living with a group of close friends and they had all encouraged me to mock the rest of polite society. I was 18 and thought it very agreeable to achieve success through my witticisms. Besides, all I was doing was to record and express what all of them were saying about each other. I was expressing friendship, but they took it to be hatred.

(Journaux intimes, 28 February 1805[1])

Why Constant loved gambling has never been satisfactorily explained.[2] It was the fashionable thing for a young man of his class to do, certainly, other members of his family also gambled; he was fairly well off, at least as a young man, and could usually afford to do it. But gambling also meant humiliation when he lost all the money he had with him – as he sometimes did – and there was no necessity at all for him to undergo that. He was no impoverished Dostoevsky, trying by one last desperate throw of the dice or turn of the roulette wheel to win enough to feed a family or buy time with his creditors. There was no apparent need for Constant to gamble. Yet, just below the surface and ready to erupt at any opportunity, there was a craving in him, the source of which probably had subterranean links with Constant's attempts at – or contemplation of – suicide. The indescribable exhilaration of entering the *tripot*, the gambling den came, perhaps, from the satisfaction of a deep wish to let go of himself, to put himself in danger, to trust entirely to chance. This is not, of course, the only possible hypothesis that can be advanced, but it comes close to Constant's own view on the matter expressed in *De l'esprit de conquête et de l'usurpation* in 1814:

It has often been said that gamblers are the most immoral of men. This is because they risk each day everything they possess. For them there is no guaranteed future. They live and pursue their activities in the empire of chance.[3]

For the reasons outlined in Chapter 1, Constant's life was dominated by anxiety and uncertainty about the present and the future. Gambling was perhaps both an opportunity to act out such anxious expectation (which of course also included an element of pleasure, albeit somewhat masochistic), and an opportunity to obtain his revenge on destiny. In the ebb and flow of winning and losing, Constant experienced a sense of freedom and power over his own fortunes that had been denied him as a child and continued to elude him in his subservience to his father as an adolescent. The game of cards was, then, a real as well as a symbolic way of playing with his life, and also a form of therapy, since through it he could express his (usually ambivalent) feelings towards his predicament.

According to the Freudian commentator Han Verhoeff, to win while gambling was for Constant the equivalent of winning the love he had always needed but seldom received.[4] Verhoeff's theory appears plausible if we accept that it was the euphoria of occasional success that brought Constant back again and again to the gaming table. There is, however, a further possibility which I would like to propose and one which brings together elements from each of these hypotheses. This is that Constant gambled for the pleasure of gambling: that winning was only a secondary motivation; that Constant played because he needed to live in a state of perpetual crisis, because he enjoyed taking great risks with his life. Verhoeff's suggestion that to win at cards was for Constant like a winning of love can then be taken a stage further. For obtaining a woman's love was never, in Constant's life, the end of the game. The gambler in him could never withdraw from play entirely and was immediately driven on by the anticipated thrill of the next game, forgetful of his winnings from the previous one.

Whether or not such a view is accepted, there was a restless urgency in Constant's activities during his late adolescence suggesting something of the gambler's headlong rush from one risk to the next. It produced in him a feeling of discontinuity in relationships and events which he is certain to have relished as well as deplored. The habit of gambling never let go of him, and right into middle age, when he had become a respected member of the French Assembly, he would take the opportunity of a late-night sitting of the House to slip out to a nearby gaming-house. It was a habit he probably first acquired at Erlangen in 1782–3, and one which abruptly terminated 'the most agreeable year of [his] life' in Edinburgh. In *Ma Vie* Constant describes what happened:

> I lived for about eighteen months in Edinburgh, enjoying myself a great deal, keeping fairly busy and having only good things said about me. But ill-fortune decreed that a little Italian who was giving me music lessons should introduce me to a faro bank run by his brother. I gambled, lost, accumulated debts left and right, and my

whole stay in Edinburgh was ruined. The date my father had set for me to leave came round and I left, promising my creditors I would repay them, but leaving them very displeased with me and having made a very bad impression. I returned via London where I spent three weeks quite fruitlessly, and I arrived in Paris during May 1785.[5]

There are various candidates for the honour of having thus brought Constant's happiest experiences to an end. Perhaps the most likely are the Puppo brothers, Giuseppe and Stephano: Giuseppe is known to have taught singing and his brother languages (French, Italian, Spanish and Portuguese) in Edinburgh in the late 1770s, though no evidence has survived about any other source of income they may have had.[6] The game which proved to be Constant's downfall, faro, was the downfall of many in the eighteenth and nineteenth centuries. In its early form it was simple enough, and involved the player placing a bet on the one card he was dealt: if the dealer, counting through the rest of the cards in the pack, then turned up a card of the same rank first on a pile to his right the player won the amount he had bet. The excitement this generated in adepts of the game is perhaps difficult for us to conceive, but it was considerable enough for faro to be banned by name in some parts of Europe. What seems to have completely enthralled so many gamblers was the tension between staying on in the game or withdrawing – certainly the kind of problem likely to appeal to Constant. Evidently Constant made some bad decisions in Edinburgh or, as is not improbable, the dealer was crooked. It meant he had to leave cherished and admired friends to whom he was perhaps in debt with little hope of seeing them again or perhaps even of being able to repay them.

In late May 1785, if we are to trust the chronology of *Ma Vie*, Constant arrived in Paris where Juste had arranged for him to live under the protection of the Suard family. Unhappily his room was not ready for him, so he had to stay at a hotel. There he fell in with a rich and dissolute young Englishman and soon ran up a fresh set of debts.[7] When at length he was able to move into his room at the house of the literary man Jean-Baptiste Suard (1734–1817), he made a further undesirable acquaintance, that of a Pastor Baumier, recommended to his father by the Protestant chaplain to the Dutch Ambassador, though fortunately, as Constant notes in *Ma Vie*, he was 'humourless, boring and very insolent' and therefore Constant soon tired of him. Baumier lent him money, accompanied him to Parisian brothels and later wrote to Juste de Constant to denounce Benjamin's behaviour.[8]

By August 1785, when Juste took his son from Paris to Brussels, it must have seemed to Benjamin that he was once again adrift, and that the friendship and high-minded intellectual enthusiasm of Edinburgh could not be found again. Paradise was permanently lost, and he was once more a prey to his own fast-developing vices. It was in Brussels, however, that Constant met a woman of whom the later recollection produced in him a genuine pang of regret and a feeling of gratitude that lasted into his middle age. At her invitation they became lovers; for nine years she had been the wife of a Genevan, Joseph-Jean Johannot (1748–1829). Marie-Charlotte Johannot, *née* Aguiton, asked for so little in return, if we are to accept *Ma Vie*'s version of events: she was tender, suffered much from being married to an unfaithful husband, and until she died, says Constant, he was never able to hear anyone say her name without his being deeply moved.[9] Her death is one of the many women's deaths which Constant chronicles, and both its sad circumstances (she took poison because of Monsieur Johannot's treatment of her[10]) and the quality of her love for Constant produce a moment of pathos in *Ma Vie* where, evidently overcome by his memory of her, Constant allows his style to falter as he repeats how long ago it now is, and how little his feelings have changed towards her though she is now dead. The sympathy, the distant pity, and perhaps also the twinge of guilt are, as we saw in an earlier chapter, profoundly characteristic of Constant.

But on this occasion we are privileged in being able to see the other side of the relationship, through three extant letters in Madame Johannot's hand and addressed to her lover Constant shortly before Juste took him away from Brussels in November 1785. And they broadly confirm Constant's picture of the relationship, while adding a note of remorse for her infidelity to her husband which is absent from *Ma Vie*'s version of events. The first letter chronologically deserves to be quoted in full:

> What are you asking of me? Haven't you sufficient proofs of my weakness already without adding another to them, the imprudence of which I might live to regret? No, my dear friend. Even if I had no doubts at all about your discretion, all other considerations would still forbid me from enjoying the pleasure of being with you. It is high time I listened to the voice of reason: it tells me that, far from reinforcing those feelings that are already too powerful in my heart, I ought to be rooting them out. Therefore this will be the last occasion I shall allow myself to speak to you about them. I beg of you, respect my peace of mind enough not to disturb it further. Follow your own destiny, and forget me. The effort will cost you little: make it in order to please society – society which will erase the memory of a woman who had no other merit than to have recognized yours; a woman who, whatever your feelings may be towards her, will always be thinking about you wherever you may be and filled with most earnest hopes for your happiness.
>
> I shall not see you at all today, I shall stay at home. Perhaps you are leaving tomorrow: the very thought of your going prevents me

from writing any more or else I would lose my composure completely. All I ask of you is that you never tell me when you're leaving.[11]

The second letter, in which Madame Johannot refuses to see Constant for the last time before he leaves Brussels lest she lose her self-control, ends with the sentence: 'Farewell. Be happy. If you should ever think about me, forget my moment of weakness.'[12]

The remarkable literary qualities of these letters put us irresistibly in mind of Ellénore's posthumous words to Adolphe:

> What are you asking of me? That I leave you? Can't you see that I haven't the strength to? . . . Is there somewhere I can hide so that I can live near to you but not be a burden on your life? . . . It doesn't become you to be so lacking in feeling. You are kind. Your actions are those of a noble and devoted friend.[13]

And certainly Constant, who kept the letters until the end of his life, must have known each line almost by heart. Two years later, when Constant saw Madame Johannot again in Paris, he was once more captivated by her and when he learned that she had subsequently left the city he experienced 'emotions that were quite extraordinary in their overwhelming power and sadness. It was a kind of premonition, one which her terrible fate was to justify only too well'.[14] That last comment by Constant brings us back yet again to the permanent association in his mind between women, parting and death. But the case of Madame Johannot illustrates the development of a by now equally strong psychological and emotional pattern. It is perhaps going a little too far to describe Constant's affair with her as 'the only absolutely calm relationship which Constant ever experienced',[15] as Sir Harold Nicolson did, but a letter from Constant to Isabelle de Charrière of 4 March 1788 shows the depth of his gratitude to his 'Belle Genevoise, de Brusselles', his beautiful Genevan woman from Brussels, for one thing at least: 'That woman loved me, truly loved me, loved me passionately, and she was the only woman I've known who didn't make me pay for her favours with a great deal of suffering. I no longer love her, but I shall be grateful to her for ever.'[16]

Madame Johannot made no attempt to rope him in tightly to her, quite the reverse. Being some eight or ten years older than him, she was mature and far-sighted enough to realize that their affair must end sooner rather than later, and wished him future happiness and success after his departure from Brussels. Her three letters, 'tristes et tendres',[17] sad and tender, as they are and as Constant describes them in *Ma Vie*, stress the importance of a clean break between Constant and herself. For his good and for her own, they must go their own ways and their relationship must end. According to *Ma Vie*, Madame Johannot took the initiative of nipping in the bud the young Constant's attempt to carry on their correspondence after he had left Brussels: she did not reply to his first letter. She left with him an indelible and bitter-sweet memory, most of all because she had been so exceptionally unpossessive and undemanding. Almost uniquely in his life she was a woman who respected – perhaps more even than he yet did himself – his need to be free and under no obligations towards her. It was she too who, knowing of Juste's intention of taking his son away from Brussels at the end of 1785, forestalled that irresoluteness which would later bedevil all Constant's relationships with women. Her suffering did not make her vulnerably passive: she did what was necessary to prevent that suffering from lasting indefinitely into the future.

From an intellectual point of view Constant's stay in Brussels was a significant one. As we have seen in the previous chapter, it was there that the idea of writing a history of polytheism first took shape in his mind. According to Philippe Secretan (1756–1826), a Swiss tutor whom Juste de Constant had recommended to the Duke of Ursel for the Duke's son, and who acted as a mentor to Benjamin Constant in Brussels from August to November 1785, Benjamin spent much of his time plunged in abstruse metaphysics, again a continuation of his interests and those of his Edinburgh friends earlier in the year. Secretan insisted on taking him out into society, to the theatre and to meet members of the Genevan colony in Brussels, as he records in his *Souvenirs*:

> He had agreeable talents and uncommon erudition, as well as considerable wit. Apart from that, I had the impression that his ideas were in a state of great disorder. I tried to rescue him from the depths of metaphysics and transcendental philosophy into which he enjoyed plunging, and which did not do his health any good.[18]

At the same time Constant was in the grip of a renewed enthusiasm for Helvétius whom he had also read and admired while still at Edinburgh, as is perhaps suggested in John Wilde's *Character of H. B. Constant*. He went as far as lending Madame Johannot a copy of *De l'esprit* (*Concerning the mind*), who sent it back saying: 'I am returning the book about the mind; my own has been too preoccupied to read it.'[19] It is likely that the *philosophe* coterie that met at Jean-Baptiste Suard's Paris house had once again reinforced the dogmatically materialist and atheistic cast of mind in Constant from which in the long run only his later exhaustive study of ancient religions – and no doubt also greater experience of life – would release him. By a strange irony it was, according to *Ma Vie*, a statement by Helvétius in *De l'esprit* to the effect that pagan religion was preferable to Christianity that led by a long and roundabout route not only to his writings on religion which were to become the only interest and consolation in his life, as he was frequently to remark in his letters and diaries,[20] but ultimately to his claim to 'be a member of the Christian church'.[21]

Forty-five years of work began in 1785, a small first step towards which was Constant's translation of a chapter of *The History of Ancient Greece* by John Gillies, brother of Adam Gillies of the Speculative Society. Whether or not the idea was suggested to him by Adam Gillies, with whom he could have been in correspondence at this time as he certainly was with John Wilde, we do not know: all trace of any letters has been lost. But on his return to Switzerland in 1786 Constant set to work on John Gillies's book as soon as he could obtain a copy. His primary intention was to please his father who was by now no doubt hoping for something tangible from the 19-year-old son he had spent so much money educating. In the event Constant translated only Chapter II of the *History*,[22] for he soon discovered that the French King's Librarian, Carra, was in the process of translating the whole book. Thus Constant's own translation became a kind of sampler, a way of gauging the public's reaction to his style and competence as a translator from English. He had also by now conceived a far greater project, as he states in his Preface, that of translating Gibbon's *Decline and Fall of the Roman Empire*. As such a task would have taken a number of years of his life, it is hard not to share Rudler's relief that Constant subsequently abandoned the plan: 'he had better things to do with his talent than wasting it on such an unworthy chore.'[23] In any case such grandiose designs were not, perhaps, entirely Constant's own: in a letter to Isabelle de Charrière of 20 March 1788 he would describe his book as 'a translation I did in a hurry to please my father, which I never revised and which he was absolutely determined to whisk away from me and have printed'.[24] The obvious inference to be drawn from this is that although the subject interested Constant a great deal ('the religion, government, arts, customs and character of the Greeks'), his heart was not entirely in translating someone else's ideas: by now he had plenty of his own, and not all of Gillies's were congenial to him. The *Essai sur les mœurs des tems héroïques de la Grèce, tiré de l'Histoire grecque de M. Gillies*, with its treatment of Greek religion as false and superstitious, contained opinions very close to the orthodox Christian view expounded in Tytler's Edinburgh lectures, and which it must have been unpalatable for the ardently pro-pagan disciple of Helvétius and D'Holbach that Constant now proclaimed himself to be to bring before a wider audience.

Behind this renewal of intellectual activity there was, however, a complex and painful family drama. Constant's homecoming in 1786 after his *Lehrjahre* was far from being an easy one for any of the parties concerned. To begin with, Constant had a horror of his native city of Lausanne which at times bordered on the pathological. On 9 July 1793 he would write to his friend Isabelle de Charrière:

I am completely convinced that Lausanne is uninhabitable for me.

All the lakes, mountains and beauties of Nature at her most radiant could not erase my painful memories, could not rid the city of my irritating relatives nor compensate for the idle tedium of Lausanne life.

(Charrière, Œuvres, IV, p. 118)

And on 23 August 1793: 'Lausanne . . . always fills me with profound melancholy, and has the effect of making me see everything as being black' (p. 157). Since the annexation of the Pays de Vaud by Berne in 1536 Lausanne had lost all autonomy in government. One major insurrection had been crushed and its leader Davel executed in 1723. The consequence for an aristocratic family like Constant's was that, as subjects of Berne, they were permanently debarred from holding political office, this being reserved exclusively for the ruling *Bourgeois* of Berne.[25] Lausanne and the Vaud canton were ruled firmly by a group of patricians in Berne, the Council of Two Hundred, whose representative in Lausanne was the Bailli. Thus the Constants, the Chandieus and families like them harboured political ambitions at their peril, and were left with the army or the church as the only choice of career. And since that church was not the rich Catholic church of France with its bishoprics and sinecures but the church of Calvin, what was on offer was nothing more than the ascetic and scholarly life of a Calvinist pastor. A career in the army meant in fact a life in permanent exile as an officer in the service of a foreign regiment. Benjamin Constant had at least two Calvinist pastors among his ancestors, and his father was, of course, a colonel in a Swiss regiment in the service of Holland. Yet it was not the uninspiring choice of career open to a Vaudois aristocrat which the young Baron Constant resented most. The most irksome thought to him was that he and his fellow countrymen had no say in their own government, and were entirely dependent on the Bernese. For Constant Berne was a tyranny, and all Vaudois were condemned to live under alien rule until their political oppressor could be shaken off. This was the belief in which he had been brought up by Juste, and his father's later experiences of injustice at the hands of 'Leurs Excellences de Berne', 'their Excellencies of Berne', merely confirmed it as a fact. Lausanne was therefore a city in the hands of an occupying power, although the evidence of that occupation was discreetly out of sight. In Constant's mind Lausanne became a symbol of subjection, and worse still its citizens seemed almost to have lost their taste for freedom when in the late eighteenth century their city had become a centre of elegant cosmopolitan *désœuvrement*, idleness and pleasure. If the Lausannois were content to live in a state of complete political docility, Constant certainly was not, and this, as well of course as his need to act on a wider political stage, was a reason for his later change of allegiance to France and his eventual adoption of French nationality.

But the obvious reason is not always necessarily the real reason for a person's feelings and actions, and Constant's reasons were undoubtedly more complex than this. The *démocrate*, the radical republican in him would, as a young man, have found the city's provincial conservatism and rigid hierarchy of social castes a stumbling block to all political progress, and personally stifling into the bargain. Yet even this would hardly account for Constant's animosity against Lausanne. The answer must probably be sought elsewhere, in memories of family life and relationships during childhood and adolescence that the city conjured up in him. As we have seen, Lausanne and the surrounding area had been associated with emotional suffering and above all of helpless dependence – on his relatives, on his nurse, on Marianne, on his father. Lausanne to Constant meant emotional bullying of one kind or another, and at 19 he was now too big to be bullied. Indeed it was a sign of the strength of his defence mechanisms against a renewal of childhood anxieties and miseries that he was able to display a quite exceptional degree of insubordination not only towards his immediate relatives but indeed towards all and sundry in Lausanne, and that far from reacting in a depressive way to the city's political impotence vis-à-vis Berne, he was filled with indignation and harangued his fellow Lausannois on the need for political change.[26]

But there was little rejoicing among members of Constant's family. In their eyes the time he had spent away from Lausanne had ruined his character. They found him on his return from his four apprenticeship years to be insufferably conceited. What they saw before them now was a vain and ambitious young man, ready to humiliate friend and enemy alike with his ironic wit and superior cosmopolitan education. Worse still there was about him the taint of political sedition, a dangerous and unwanted luxury in Lausanne. Besides which each member of his family had a personal reason to resent the change that had come about in his character. Rosalie could not forget that he had not written to her for four years while he was in Erlangen, Edinburgh, Paris and Brussels. And her father shortly would have reason to regret nurturing such a viper in his bosom. Samuel, hypersensitive and unsure of himself at the best of times, had nonetheless taken Benjamin into his confidence and affection, and on his nephew's return to Switzerland asked him to write a *mémoire* on discipline in the Roman army. It would be a constructive way of exhibiting his newly acquired Classical learning – this was no doubt the intention in Samuel de Constant's mind. As with the other project of 1786, Gillies's *History*, Benjamin seems to have been determined to expend as little energy as possible on it, although it is not without significance that the better of the two pieces of work was done for his father. After completing his short piece (fifteen pages of quarto manuscript), in which he merely listed a number of remarkable punishments handed out to members of the Roman army, Benjamin sent it to Samuel in Geneva. When his uncle pointed out justifiably that this was not at all the general and rather philosophical study he had asked for, Benjamin sent him the following reply on 2 May 1786. From its tone it is easy to see why he had now become so unpopular with the rest of the Constant clan:

> Many thanks for the far too generous way in which you have judged the few ideas I assembled in haste on the subject you spoke to me about. If in your first letter you had said that you wanted observations on discipline amongst the Romans and on their concept of honour – which is very different from what you were kind enough actually to propose that I should write – I would have taken more care to tackle the problem you set. But because of what you said in your letter, I limited myself to a number of extraordinary punishments. I had no intention of writing a book or a lengthy essay. All I intended to do was to show you my zeal, at the risk of revealing at the same time my inability to answer your questions. Rather than sending my collection of gossipy anecdotes to the newspapers or keeping it on the shelf of your library, burn it, dear Uncle, and keep me in your affection – which is much better than simply reading what I've written. I send my love to my aunt, to cousins Rosalie and Lisette, and to my dear cousin Charles. I still hope to see you soon, and I hope my enthusiasm will make up for my lack of learning. There is no need, dear Uncle, to remind me to show affection: I would, it is true, have had some difficulty in slipping it into my scribblings about the Romans, but I am happy to show it you when I think of all your kindness towards me.[27]

Samuel de Constant had no difficulty in seeing through the assurances of loyal affection to the disingenuousness and Voltairean sarcasm underneath, and he was very hurt. It was a characteristic misunderstanding. Constant found it hard to resist irony in all its forms – not least, of course, irony at his own expense. As this irony was so frequently mixed in with quite genuine expressions of emotion, it was often difficult to judge which was the real Benjamin Constant. In many cases the answer was, of course, that *both* were the real Constant, each being a result of his alert intelligence standing, as it were, outside and apart from himself and representing to his correspondent or interlocutor the many-sidedness of his response to a situation.[28] Such was no doubt the case in the letter quoted above, but what so angered Samuel de Constant and caused a rift between him and his nephew which was to last some twelve years was the breezy flippancy of the recommendation to burn the essay, and most of all the fatuous remark about his inability to exhibit his feelings for his uncle in an essay on the Roman army. A man as permanently insecure in his relationships with others as Samuel could not fail to take this amiss: he was precisely the wrong man to joke with about affection. Besides which Benjamin's casual and supercilious treatment of Samuel's suggestion that he put his scholarship to good use was insulting to a man of 57, coming as it did from a youth of 19. Gustave Rudler summarizes the results of Benjamin's tactlessness:

> Benjamin responded by believing – or at least claiming to believe – that his uncle was indifferent to him and asking for his affection. Samuel's annoyance was taken up by Benjamin's cousins Rosalie and Lisette. Benjamin met their doubts about him with amusing and sometimes mordant, barbed witticisms about the affection they said they felt for him.[29]

Rudler's own comment is:

> There was in reality sincere affection on both sides between these people who only wished to be close to one another, and it is sad to see them looking for each other, testing each other out, suspecting each other's good faith, provoking each other, and finally falling out. The squabble was to last for more than twelve years.[30]

In Rudler's view the sudden cooling off of relations with Benjamin's uncle and cousins drove the young man in on himself and made him unduly sensitive thereafter to anyone's questioning of the sincerity of his feelings. This may well be so, but it must also be said that the *demi-brouille*, the strains in their relationships had also been provoked by a series of pin-pricks from Samuel and his family which Benjamin had experienced the previous January during a stay with them in Geneva[31]. As in the affair of the *mémoire*, Samuel appears to have reminded Benjamin once too often of the gratitude that he ought to feel towards his uncle for all his kindness. Protesting that he really was grateful, Benjamin had written to Rosalie reminding her how lonely and isolated he would be if she too now turned against him as her father appeared to be doing:

> Don't follow his example. Think of us marooned here at Le Désert, unable to leave because of the snow, rain and cold. Remember me in particular: my stomach, chest and eyes are very bad, and you promised me you would make me forget my ailments. Please consider how cruel it is to take away a poor wretch's last consolation. Obliged to renounce all the vanities of this world, the only resource I have left is your friendship.[32]

Even if we ignore the playfully melodramatic exaggeration of those sentences – an example of Constant's adding a representational ingredient to the expression of feelings he nonetheless *truly* felt and thereby risking being thought insincere – it is nonetheless clear that some time before the feud with his uncle (this letter was written on 19 March 1786, the rift dated from early May 1786) relations were somewhat strained between them and Constant himself believed he had cause to feel aggrieved. Rosalie, while sympathizing with her father's position, continued to correspond with her cousin, but was annoyed when it became obvious that he was not going to keep his promise to return to stay with them in Geneva. By now Constant for his part was tired of – and exasperated by – the wider family's demands on him. It was hard enough to have a father like Juste: any further harassment was emotionally exhausting. In a letter to his friend Isabelle de Charrière of 4 March 1788 he would speak of his family as 'uncles, cousins, the whole angry tribe of them',[33] and later still, looking back on this period of his life he would tell her that he had been 'tortured by people who wanted to extract affection from me as one might squeeze juice out of a lemon'.[34] The episode of the *mémoire* drove a deep wedge between Benjamin and Samuel. At the same time it cannot but have contributed in the long term to Constant's permanent sense of revulsion at emotional blackmail.

There was, however, another reason for Constant's reluctance to leave Lausanne for Geneva, and one which Rosalie and her father must certainly have been aware of. Benjamin was in the process of making a fool of himself with a married woman almost twice his age, Mrs. Harriet Trevor (1751–1829), wife of the British Ambassador to the Court of Sardinia who spent most of his time in residence in Turin. At this point in *Ma Vie* Constant really gets into his stride for the first time and provides a delightfully amusing picture of the whole farcical enterprise. Not surprisingly, it was the heavy gambling which took place at Mrs Trevor's house a mile outside Lausanne that had attracted Constant in the first instance. Then, seeing his hostess, a flirtatious Englishwoman of 35 whose beauty was now fading, perpetually surrounded by half-a-dozen young English admirers – Lausanne was of course at this period virtually an obligatory stopping-point on the Grand Tour – Constant decided to tell her that he loved her and to ask for her love in return. Mrs Trevor replied to his letter offering him 'friendship', not 'love'. Whereupon he caused an extraordinary scene at her house, rolling on the floor and beating his head against the wall, refusing to let Mrs Trevor go near him, threatening to kill himself because all she would offer him was *de l'amitié*. And for three or four months he stuck to his role as star-crossed lover, coming to believe in the part he was acting, 'growing more and more in love every day because every day I came up against a difficulty I myself had created'.[35]

Unusually timid for a young man of his sexual experience, Constant continued to argue about the terminology of the relationship and contented himself with a chaste kiss on her lips. In the meantime Mrs Trevor looked on at this extraordinary performance and little by little assumed a part in the drama herself, weeping when he wept, moved by the great passion she was apparently inspiring in this strange young man. Carried away by it himself, Constant became jealous of a young Englishman who had not the slightest interest in his paramour. Constant challenged the hapless man to a duel when he assured Constant he did not even like Mrs Trevor. The pistols were loaded and ready when the Englishman threatened to explain to their seconds the absurdity of Constant's grievance, and Constant was thereupon forced to abandon his 'brillante entreprise'. He invited Mrs Trevor to Le Désert for dinner, his father being away from Lausanne, and thereby incurred the wrath of Marianne. Perhaps it was because of this last piece of folly which now threatened to bring the family name into disrepute that Juste informed his son that he must prepare to accompany him to Paris. Benjamin left Lausanne in despair on 16 November 1786. With him in the coach were Juste and Benjamin's cousin Charles (1762–1835), son of Samuel de Constant, known as Charles 'le Chinois' because he had already been to China and was now planning a career in commerce. We are indebted to him for a vivid, almost cinematic account of the journey and of Benjamin's state of mind in a letter to his sisters Rosalie and Lisette composed two days later:

> We set out on Thursday morning, my dear Sisters, in a good coach, having taken precautions against the cold. The three of us have entirely different characters, it would seem. It is difficult to describe my uncle. As for Benjamin, still obsessed with his great misfortune, he never talks about anything else. His father argues against his son's philosophical system and moral principles, and from time to time I join in their conversation, but I have to admit I've discovered that I'm just a fool: I can't understand any of my travelling companions' profound arguments. I think about you and what I've left behind, I make plans, I think about life in Paris. I tell Benjamin he's getting on my nerves when he tells me that all human beings are unhappy, that human nature conspires to make us so; I cite examples to the contrary, he says they're an illusion, and I finish up singing a little song to him. Then he tells me quite brutally that my mind is narrow and limited. I feel anger welling up in me, but I content myself with pointing out that I have my pride as well, however misplaced it may be, and that it is very wrong of him to wound it over nothing.[36]

In these few words we have as complete a picture as we could wish for of Benjamin Constant at 19. We see too how different he and his father were from Samuel's side of the family. The unfortunate Charles, five years older than Benjamin but with no head for philosophical speculation, found himself thrust out into the ring every day for a fortnight with two intellectual prize-fighters and unable to escape. Charles's later letters are equally fascinating, as the following remarks will illustrate:

> The company I find myself in is not to my taste. My uncle interferes and disagrees over everything, is interested only in his son whose

response is a tear in his eye and a ready epigram ... my uncle has mocked other people and thwarted their wishes the whole time, Benjamin has been in a state of despair, and I've been bored, albeit rather more cheerfully than my companions. My cousin keeps repeating these four lines of verse:

> You who are poisoning my life
> Do not increase my pain.
> My fate is an unenviable one:
> Why take even my misery away from me?

He addresses them to his father. . . . My uncle, despite the pleasure he takes in contradicting other people, doesn't like to be contradicted himself.[37]

When they arrived in Paris, Juste insisted that his son be addressed as 'Monsieur le baron de Constant', kept him short of money and did all he could to introduce him into literary circles. Charles considered this last venture to be foredoomed: 'I would be willing to bet that Benjamin will never be famous',[38] he observed, but in another letter, of 4 December 1786, he more than made up for his wrong prediction with a paragraph of remarkable insight:

I must talk to you about my uncle: 1) he gets on my nerves; 2) he bores me; 3) I don't like him. All that is perhaps my fault. But his character – suspicious, restless, arrogant, tiresome and given to mockery – is very uncongenial to me. I can well understand Benjamin's despair: it is a direct result of all of this, and I think I can detect that he doesn't love his father; that his father's wish to get in the way of everything he does – without exception – and his disagreeing with everything Benjamin says is making him unhappy. The young man has strong emotions and a passionate love of liberty; he finds his situation a cruel one. Is Benjamin right or wrong? You can judge for yourselves. He's more likely to do something stupid than if he were left alone.[39]

Constant's love for Mrs Trevor soon evaporated now that Paris offered him a thousand different distractions. Their correspondence petered out, and when he saw her again three months later he felt absolutely nothing for her. She on the other hand was astonished at his coolness, and no doubt a little shocked. As usual in *Ma Vie* Constant adds the inevitable unhappy postscript; Harriet Trevor returned to England and by 1811 had become 'virtually insane as a result of repeated attacks of hysteria'.[40] The whole episode of Constant and Mrs Trevor's unconsummated passion is a mysterious and intriguing one in itself, quite apart from the obvious parallels with Adolphe's relationship with Ellénore on which so many critics have commented – the declaration of love to her by letter, love resulting from an obstacle to be overcome, and so on. It is perhaps worth asking what it was that kept Constant from taking advantage of this by all accounts rather scatter-brained woman who was unhappy with her husband and whom Constant must have known was only waiting for him to make the first move. Why, indeed, did he set out to make her love him in the first place? There seems to be something behind this curious *passion cérébrale* that Constant does not explain, and which cannot, I think, be accounted for simply by his desire to be loved, his desire to be the centre of attention (like Molière's Alceste with his Célimène in *Le Misanthrope*), or even the appetite for sexual conquest.

What may perhaps provide a clue to Constant's reasons for behaving in a manner which was extraordinary even by his standards is an interlinear addendum to *Ma Vie* which precedes the entry about Mrs Trevor, and which was referred to in Chapter 2. By the side of the sentence 'If idleness has disadvantages, it has advantages as well', which is itself followed by a preamble leading to a description of Mrs Trevor – 'A new love came along to distract me' – we read in the original manuscript of *Ma Vie*: 'voyage à Berne et à Zurich. connoissance avec Gibbon. Knecht. Amours grecs de Berne', that is, 'Journey to Berne and Zurich. Acquaintance with Gibbon. Knecht. Greek love in Berne.'[41] It is not, perhaps, surprising that scholars should have shied away from pursuing this particular line of research, but it is to be regretted. We know absolutely nothing of Constant's reasons for visiting Berne or Zurich, but it was odd that he should stay in Berne, a city whose government he held in abhorrence, and stranger still that the great Edward Gibbon (1737–94) should also be there, as it seems he was. Gibbon had settled in Lausanne in 1783, he was a friend of Constant's uncle, Salomon de Charrière de Sévery, and appears to have become a friend of Mrs Trevor some time after July 1786:[42] he and Constant had every opportunity of meeting in Lausanne. And yet they seem to have met in Berne, of all places, probably before August 1786, at about which date Constant made his declaration of love to Mrs Trevor. It does not seem that they became close friends, indeed the following year when Gibbon took a greater interest in Constant's considerably less gifted but more modest cousin, Wilhelm de Charrière de Sévery, Constant could not conceal his jealousy and showed it in spiteful comments on Wilhelm's command of English.[43] It may well be that Gibbon found Benjamin to be a rather tiresome coxcomb, forever polishing up an epigram in order to impress: indeed Gibbon had already taken a strong dislike to his father Juste when he had met him on 26 September 1763, and had noted in his *Journal*:

> I spent the afternoon at Madame Grand de St Laurent's at her invitation and there I played cards with Catherine Crousaz and Constant de Rebecque. If I had to bring together the sort of person I really like with the kind for whom I have only aversion and

contempt, I could not have chosen better. That man brings together bad qualities that are diametrically opposed to each other: coarseness and affectation, stupidity and maliciousness, prodigality and avarice. He is in fact a *Monstrum nulla virtute redemptum* [a monster unredeemed by any virtue].[44]

Gibbon's extreme antipathy to the father may well have prejudiced him against the son.

It is easy, then, to imagine Constant's frustration, given his growing taste for historical scholarship. The great man was within a year of completing his *Decline and Fall*, and Constant, as his Preface to his translation of Gillies shows, was in awe of Gibbon's achievement to the extent that he contemplated translating some or all of the six volumes. Nevertheless the 50-year-old Gibbon kept his young admirer at a distance. Whether the failure of their 'connoissance' to develop further had anything to do with what Constant mentions next in *Ma Vie* it is impossible to say. For Constant became the friend of Johann Rudolf Knecht (1762–1820), the son of a rich *Bourgeois* or burgess of Berne, and was in correspondence with him for at least two years thereafter, though there is now no trace of their letters.[45] Knecht, five years older than Constant, was a homosexual, and it is not impossible that the 'Amours grecs' is a reference to the relationship between them; Constant may, on the other hand, simply have meant to write in later at this point in *Ma Vie* an account of Knecht's relationships with others. It is not entirely implausible, however, that precisely at this time in his life, at the age of 18 or 19, Constant should have formed a homosexual attachment, perhaps with the older Knecht himself. In the spring and summer of 1786 Constant's family appeared to have turned against him, and his feelings towards his father were moving towards the crisis of the following year when he was to run away to England. As we have seen from Charles de Constant's letters of November and December 1786, Juste was relentlessly difficult at this period of his life: 'caustique et impérieux',[46] high-handed and with a caustic wit, he was perpetually in disagreement with those around him, a fact which had already forced him to take eighteen months leave from his regiment (May 1785-March 1787). Never at peace with himself, Juste turned his restless critical mind on his son, and when they were together he simply would not leave him alone, but kept up a relentless barrage of cavilling and argument.

Benjamin, who had already internalized the literary ambitions his father had sought for so long to instil in him, must also have developed very early a strong sense of inferiority vis-à-vis this impossibly overbearing old man, and a feeling of guilt whenever – and it seemed to be all the time – he failed to satisfy his many and frequently contradictory demands on him. It would hardly be surprising therefore if Benjamin had no immediate model with whom to identify in order to discover his own masculinity;

if, fearful and timid in his father's presence, he found himself attracted to another man with whom he could identify and who gave him that affection which Juste was seldom able to show to his son (although he certainly felt it); if that man, finally, were such as to evoke admiration as well as affection in Benjamin. In the previous chapter I suggested that John Wilde could have been such a man. Knecht may have been another, though once again there is no actual proof of this. What we do know for certain is that in his letters Constant seems to have poured out his troubles to Knecht,[47] and when his friend was found guilty of pederasty by a Bernese court in 1789, was sentenced in his absence to life imprisonment and had all his property confiscated, Constant wrote the following to Isabelle de Charrière on 4 August 1789:

> I have had a source of real sorrow these past few days, and one which has confirmed my dislike of life: it's this. Do you recall a young man named Knecht whose letters I read to you on your sofa, in your anteroom at the end of 1787 and the beginning of 1788, and which you enjoyed listening to? Well that same Knecht who had a busy career and a comfortable fortune to look forward to, who was learned, witty, full of vigour and good sense, went and got himself involved in that wretched Socratic business in Berne. I was on the point of writing to him when I learned that he was stigmatized, banished and his property liable to confiscation. Gone are all the plans and prospects, the conjectures and the joy inspired by contemplating the future of a friend.[48]

It is clear from this that Constant placed a high value on Knecht's friendship; more than that we cannot be sure about, though no doubt in any relationship there can be scope for a variety of feelings to coexist and for their relative strengths to change over a period of time. If we turn to Constant's 'ridicule amour'[49] for Mrs Trevor, the hypothesis of a recent homoerotic relationship in Berne might go some way to explaining Constant's uncertainty with her, his 'timidité excessive', his excessive shyness, and also perhaps the rather willed and artificial nature of the whole enterprise, the element of play-acting in which, as we have seen, Constant later came to believe. But whatever the reason for his pursuit of her, Mrs Trevor was soon forgotten once Constant reached Paris.

Gambling had by now become a permanent and ruinous part of Constant's behaviour wherever he found himself, and in the French capital he lost no time in divesting himself of most of his money at cards at the house of one Madame de Bourbonne, whom historians have not identified. Not daring to tell his father how much he was in debt, he wrote to the widow of a well-known playwright, Bernard-Joseph Saurin (1706–81) to ask her for a loan. When he arrived the next day to learn her reply, the 63-year-old Madame Saurin (1734–98) had not yet received his letter. She thereupon mistook his embarrassment and hesitancy for a declaration of love. When she realized her error, she handed him the money without a word, and Constant left. *Ma Vie* thus begins again its amusing, self-mocking and sometimes cruel narrative of the *mille folies* committed by Constant's younger self[50] in Paris. But this stay in Paris was to be different. It would, quite literally, change Constant's life. He was, perhaps, in any case beginning to tire of the repetitiveness of his picaresque existence and wanting to wake up to a different self. *Joueur et moqueur*, a gambler and a wit, he would remain, and he would always need to satisfy that side of his character, but in that winter of 1786–7 Constant stood in need of other things as well. He now knew he had no real home and perhaps not even a country that he could call his own: Lausanne meant for him more than ever the antagonism or ostracism of his family; the only real friends he had were six hundred miles away in Edinburgh, and both the circumstances of his leaving Scotland and the cost of the journey back made it unlikely that he would ever see them again. Life with his father meant having to defend his opinions every inch of the way when they were together, and when they were apart Juste's toleration of his misbehaviour as long as it did not cost him money. Unfortunately, as we have seen, it did, and thus Benjamin Constant now found himself virtually friendless, and with his pessimism about the future growing stronger and stronger – as well it might. At this critical moment in his existence he met Isabelle de Charrière.

Whether their friendship, which was soon to develop into a special kind of love, began suddenly or overtook them gradually is uncertain. They may have met at the house of Jean-Baptiste Suard, where Constant's father had once again arranged for his son to be seen and heard, and for his pungent epigrams and pronouncements to be appreciated by Suard's eminent friends, the Abbé Morellet (1727–1819) of the *Encyclopédie*, the philosopher Condorcet (1743–94), General Lafayette (1757–1834), the politician Garat (1749–1833) and others.[51] Juste had then returned to his regiment, much to Benjamin's relief, leaving his son free to air the most outrageous views about those around him. Perhaps to his surprise, he found his behaviour was generally tolerated. Of all the Parisian salons of the day Madame Suard's was one of the most good-humoured. It was either there or at another salon such as that of Madame Saurin, from whom he had borrowed money, that Benjamin, with his cousin Charles with whom he was now temporarily reconciled, first met Madame de Charrière.[52] From Charles's letter to his father of 6 March 1787 we know that by that date he and his cousin were already well acquainted with her.[53] The friendship between Benjamin and Isabelle de Charrière soon became too exclusive for Charles not to feel superfluous. A practical man of business, Charles's own reasons for being in Paris were purely financial: he was looking for a new commercial venture. In the feverish financial atmosphere of Paris that winter he may also have been one of the many from Geneva who were hoping to make a more dramatic improvement in their fortunes. In any case Charles de Constant was hardly the kind of man to appeal to Isabelle de Charrière. To understand why, and the reasons for such an immediate and instinctive sympathy between herself and Benjamin Constant, we must look in some detail at her background and character, and the state she found her life to be in when she met Constant in March 1787.

Isabelle Agneta Elisabeth van Tuyll van Serooskerken was born in the moated medieval castle of Zuylen, at what is now Oud-Zuilen, a village near Utrecht, on 20 October 1740, the daughter of a Dutch baron, Diederik Jacob van Tuyll van Serooskerken and his wife Helena.[54] She was the eldest of seven children, and from an early age she displayed, like Constant, considerable intellectual powers. She received private tuition at the castle, from childhood she spoke and wrote French with the greatest facility and she was thoroughly familiar with the works of the best French authors. Her impulsive and rebellious nature made her critical of the humdrum world of the Dutch provincial aristocracy which was epitomized in the personality of her father, a thoroughly respectable man but dour and stern. In later years Isabelle – or Belle de Zuylen, as she was for long known to literary historians – inevitably came into conflict with the rigid system of beliefs and attitudes of his formidable figure. An unusual and highly intelligent spirit, from early in her life she felt imprisoned in such deadening surroundings.

As the six volumes of her brilliant and extensive *Correspondance* reveal,[55] Isabelle was still essentially the same when she met Benjamin Constant. She resembled him in character to a degree that must have astonished them both. In an early written self-portrait, the *Portrait de Zélide*,[56] it is possible to glimpse already the compulsive talker and arguer, the woman of penetrating intelligence, the reckless, unconventional and self-willed daughter. What we cannot see, but what the several non-verbal portraits of her show, notably the pastel by Maurice-Quentin de La Tour of 1766, is her beauty.[57] Benjamin Constant's uncle, Juste's brother, David-Louis Constant d'Hermenches (1722–85), to whom, characteristically, Isabelle had introduced herself in 1760 at a ball in The Hague, had been so taken by her looks and quick-wittedness that for the next fifteen years he had carried on a passionate correspondence with her.[58] James Boswell who met her in 1762 had thought of marrying her, but had eventually cried off, more than a little intimidated by her disconcertingly powerful mind to which nothing, he feared, would be sacred.[59]

There is a remark by the Princess Halm-Eberstein in *Daniel Deronda* that sums up Isabelle's plight quite admirably: 'You may try – but you can never imagine what it is to have a man's force of genius in you, and yet to suffer the slavery of being a girl.'[60] That cry from the heart from George Eliot would have been applauded by Belle de Zuylen, who, a hundred years earlier, had wrestled with similar problems, and indeed had an extraordinarily similar temperament and attitude to life. Isabelle, as her written self-portrait suggests, found it impossible to assume the passive role expected of a woman by her family and by society. Her character was too strong. Like the pitiless author of 'Silly Novels by Lady Novelists', Isabelle could not bring herself to suffer fools of either sex gladly. But she was similarly passionate and vulnerable, and certainly experienced a degree of ostracism from those who found her too outspoken, and perhaps too honest and clear-sighted, both in her novels and in her life. 'Friendship never had a temple more holy or more worthy of it than Zélide', she had written in her self-portrait. This was indeed to be true throughout her life, and her happiest attachments were to be the – in all probability – sexually unconsummated one with Benjamin Constant, and a series of close friendships with younger women, of a warmth and intimacy akin to that of a mother–daughter relationship (Isabelle was unable to have children), occasionally something more. She has left us a lively satirical tale about the absurdity of pride of ancestry, Le Noble, conte moral, with the deliberately provocative epigraph from La Fontaine 'On ne suit pas toujours ses Aïeux, ni son Pere', 'One does not always follow one's ancestors or one's father', and which the Van Tuyll family immediately tried to have withdrawn from circulation when it appeared in 1763 in the Journal étranger of Amsterdam.[61] Whatever one's views on the autonomous nature of art, it would take a degree of perversity not to recognize in Le Noble (along with all the other things undoubtedly there – the impatience of a progressive mind with social prejudice and so on) a very strong autobiographical element.

It is likely that her long and, for some of the time, clandestine epistolary flirtation with one of Europe's most celebrated womanizers, Baron Constant d'Hermenches, was undertaken in part at least to bolster her sense of her femininity. The affection and flattery of Benjamin Constant's uncle had perhaps been an antidote to an uncertainty about herself as a desirable woman. But also the exchange of intimate letters was a safe and unthreatening form of relationship, and above all a non-sexual one. Within it she could tease and cajole her admirer as much as she liked, knowing that in any case d'Hermenches was a married man and that the likelihood of their relationship ever being physically consummated was remote: they seldom saw each other, and certainly not alone. It is significant that the kind of husband she wanted at this time was a likeable, witty and considerate companion who liked music, not a passionate lover. Indeed the man Isabelle was eventually to marry had most of these qualities, though crucially not all of them.

Before getting that far, she saw, throughout her twenties, potential husband after potential husband either turned away by her father, or, like James Boswell, backing away when they realized that Isabelle was unlikely to make a submissive and obedient wife. All the time she continued to write to Constant d'Hermenches, who was intellectually and emotionally a far more attractive proposition than any of them, though quite out of reach and in any case unlikely to change his promiscuous ways. His letters to her from Corsica show that as a letter writer d'Hermenches was her equal. He was there as a regimental adjutant in the French Army engaged in suppressing Pascal Paoli's uprising, and his account of the 1768–9 campaign, with its Voltairean rapidity of pace and feeling for the ironic and absurd – so like that of d'Hermenches's nephew – was addressed to a woman who had once contemplated translating into French Boswell's strongly pro-Paoli *An Account of Corsica*. This gives a added zest to his observations, as he makes a deliberate point of confronting Isabelle's idealistic theorizing with the shock of his own experience.

D'Hermenches was a relatively enlightened Swiss Protestant aristocrat and friend of Voltaire – almost the only man in Isabelle's life who could hold a candle to her either in strength of mind or power of expression: the other was, of course, to be d'Hermenches's nephew Benjamin. And if we ignore the Lovelace in him, d'Hermenches's letters reveal to us a man of good sense who had Isabelle's best interests at heart. When at the age of 30 and still unmarried she began considering the family tutor, the Swiss nobleman Charles-Emmanuel de Charrière de Penthaz (1735–1808), as a possible husband, d'Hermenches became alarmed. Pointing to the fact that Charrière was so poor that he had to work for his living, he reminded her that she would be much worse off living on her dowry with him in Switzerland than remaining at Zuylen as a spinster.[62] Whatever his reasons for writing so forcefully to dissuade her from marrying Charles-Emmanuel de Charrière (and he could well have known more about his countryman than he was willing to disclose), d'Hermenches's letter was a tactical blunder. Isabelle was already half in love with Charrière. To emphasize only the importance of material advantage was just the kind of statement to reinforce her determination to make any sacrifice for love, and to consider arguments she or her family may have formulated to the contrary as base and unworthy. She was furious with d'Hermenches, and it was two months before she could bring herself to send him a short reply. In it she told him she preferred to ignore his kind of reasoning, and instead to live in hope.[63] By 11 January 1771 a marriage contract had been drawn up between her and Charrière and, despite some last-minute nervousness and hesitation on Isabelle's part, the wedding eventually took place at the village church of Zuylen on 17 February 1771.

'Joyless indeed, but safe' would seem to sum up Isabelle de Charrière's new situation. There is no doubt that her reasons for finally consenting to the marriage were complex and perhaps involved a degree of self-deception. Isabelle's position at Zuylen Castle since her mother's death had been an acutely uncomfortable one: she had encouraged her mother to be inoculated with the cow-pox which eventually killed her, and Isabelle's father had been utterly inconsolable. Monsieur de Charrière had been tutor to her brothers, and she had turned to him more and more. He was very different from her, a shy stammerer but very well read and generally thought of as dependable and a model of unquestionable rectitude. He offered the prospect of a marriage built on shared literary and musical interests, and a well-ordered life untroubled by any excess of passion. Isabelle's state of mind as she approached her thirtieth birthday was such as to welcome so modest a proposal. It is clear from her letters that by then almost any reasonable offer of marriage would not be refused, so pressing was her need to escape from the gloom of Zuylen.

During her honeymoon Isabelle de Charrière wrote to her brother Ditie: 'Do you want to know what our only arguments are about? I often find Monsieur de Charrière too *ordentlyk*, too *overleggende*, and he often finds me to be quite the opposite.'[64] '*Ordentlijk*', that is proper, correct in one's behaviour, and '*overleggende*', serious-minded, given to lengthy deliberation about every course of action. In other words Charles-Emmanuel de Charrière was as maddeningly unexcitable, staid and composed, and as imperturbably dispassionate in his judgements as had been her father Diederik van Tuyll. The only difference was that Isabelle had now thrown away her only chance to escape from servitude to that kind of man. It is hard to imagine a more dreadful realization. Small wonder that on her honeymoon she began to suffer from the first of those vague but recurrent illnesses that would dog her for the rest of her life. Despite her protestations about her feelings for Charrière, there is every possibility that Isabelle's illness was psychogenic, and perhaps as well were many of her 'migraines' of later years. Under these unfavourable auspices her marriage began. She left Holland, never to return, and after spending two months in Paris arrived at Monsieur de Charrière's home, the old manor of Le Pontet at Colombier, near Neuchâtel, on 30 September 1771.

In *Ma Vie*, where Madame de Charrière plays a role of central importance, Constant gives his own version of the circumstances of her marriage and the events of the years which followed:

When she was past 30, and after many passions, of which some had been rather unhappy ones, she had married against her family's wishes the tutor to her brothers, an intelligent man, high-minded and sensitive, but the most phlegmatic and unexcitable man one could ever imagine. During the early years of their marriage she had tried everything to get him to react as emotionally as she did to things, and her torment at only succeeding occasionally had rapidly destroyed the happiness she had looked forward to in what was in many ways a union of two incompatible people. A much younger man than her, not particularly intelligent but good-looking, had inspired a great passion in her. I never got to learn all the details of this passion, but what she did tell me and what I learnt from others was enough to make me realize that her life had been greatly disturbed by it and that she had been deeply unhappy. Her husband's displeasure had upset her peace of mind, and finally when the young man in question had left her for another woman whom he married, she had spent some time in the depths of despair. That despair was put to good account and her literary reputation profited from it, for it inspired the most delightful of her works, *Caliste*, which is part of a novel published under the title *Lettres écrites de Lausanne* [*Letters written from Lausanne*].[65]

I have quoted Constant's statement at length because, since *Ma Vie* first became accessible to scholars, it has been taken as the definitive explanation of Isabelle de Charrière's unhappiness. Philippe Godet, Madame de Charrière's biographer, suggested that she had fallen in love with one Louis de Saussure (1747–1826),[66] and the most recent account of her life and edition of *Ma Vie* by C. P. Courtney put forward a new hypothesis which fits Constant's story better, that the unidentified man was Charles Dapples (1758–1842),[67] second cousin of Charles-Emmanuel de Charrière. Certainly this may have been so – Dapples's age, the date of his marriage and Isabelle's later reactions at the very mention of his name are significant. The truth, however, may have been more complex than this. Although *Ma Vie*, composed in around 1810–11, is often remarkably accurate, it does on occasion seem to twist events and relationships for reasons which remain puzzling: Constant's account of Nathaniel May, his English tutor, is one illustration of this. And it is possible that the passage I have just quoted is not the whole story, indeed it may even have been a deliberate reshuffling of the cards to tell a story less embarrassing to the surviving relatives of Charles-Emmanuel de Charrière, who had died in 1808.

Whatever Monsieur de Charrière was like when Isabelle left with him for Switzerland, it seems that by the 1780s and after ten years of marriage he had begun to look elsewhere for emotional and perhaps sexual satisfaction. A crisis occurred in Geneva, probably at the beginning of 1784, while the couple were staying in the suite of rooms they rented in the city. In his account of this, Philippe Godet – and all other commentators after him – have followed Constant's version of events and seen Isabelle de Charrière as the guilty party.[68] One of the reasons for this has been the disappearance of all of Isabelle de Charrière's letters to her husband written from her self-imposed exile at Chexbres, a village in the hills above the Lake of Geneva, especially those of her second stay from May to September 1784. We only have her husband's half of the correspondence, with its many references to Isabelle's indisposition and unhappiness and his wish for her to return to Colombier: these have been construed as confirmation of Constant's story. They could however be read in a quite different light. An alternative hypothesis can be proposed, one which accords much better with the characters of Isabelle and her husband as they emerge from the recently published complete *Correspondance* of Isabelle.

What really happened *could* have been this. At the beginning of 1781, during Monsieur and Madame de Charrière's fifth stay in Geneva, Charles-Emmanuel fell in love and perhaps even had an affair with Madame Alix de Saussure-Mercier (1765–1828), wife of the Louis de Saussure mentioned by Godet. Isabelle de Charrière suffered greatly and was physically ill, but her husband persisted in his infatuation during their sixth stay in Geneva, January–May 1784, after which she went alone to Chexbres and remained there till September, attempting to come to terms with her situation. She made it clear that she would never return to Geneva, and in October–November 1784 Monsieur de Charrière supervised the sale of the furnishings of their set of rooms there. There was a recurrence of the crisis, for reasons about which we are ignorant, in July 1785, when Isabelle de Charrière left Colombier with no particular destination in mind, then fell seriously ill at Payerne, on the other side of Lake Neuchâtel, and convalesced there until September. When she was fully recovered she left Colombier the following January, again alone, and began an eighteen-month stay in Paris. It is possible that she went there to seek out the man who had warned her against marrying Charrière in the first place, Constant d'Hermenches, to whom she had stopped writing in 1775. If so, she must have been very much distressed to learn that he had died twelve months before at his Paris house, on 26 February 1785. Her consolation was to be meeting, quite by chance, D'Hermenches's nephew Benjamin in early 1787.[69]

Certain remarks in Charles-Emmanuel de Charrière's letters to his English friend Dudley Ryder, First Earl of Harrowby (1762–1847) – letters out of reach of Monsieur de Charrière's family and kept in the Ryder family archives at Sandon Hall, Stafford – about his deep feelings for Madame Alix de Saussure-Mercier and long friendship with her reveal a side of him which until the late twentieth century had remained well hidden.[70] A careful reading of Isabelle de Charrière's correspondence concerning her promiscuous servant Henriette Monachon (1766–?) is also instructive. Henriette gave birth to two illegitimate children, the first a boy Prosper, by an unknown father, in 1792, the second by a known father, a boy Jean-Louis Racine, born in 1796. Isabelle de Charrière defended her wayward servant against all critics until in 1800 her attitude appears to have changed virtually overnight, and she could hardly wait to be rid of her. Could it be that she had discovered a relationship between Henriette and Monsieur de Charrière? There is, too, a popular tradition in Colombier, the reliability of which it is notoriously difficult to evaluate, of course, which maintains that Monsieur de Charrière has a descendant living in the town to this day: as he had none by Isabelle de Charrière, this could only have been the result of an illegitimate union.

From speculation and hearsay we can turn to the certainty of what is known about Isabelle de Charrière's character. She believed strongly, if not in the sanctity of marriage vows, then in their inviolability, and she was firmly opposed to divorce, as she told Constant d'Hermenches in a letter of 12 January 1772, adding: 'Is it worth being happy at other people's expense in this short life? And *is* one really happy when it is at the expense of others?'[71] Indeed one feature above all others dominates Isabelle de Charrière's writings: moral seriousness. Her novels generally have at their centre a moral choice of which the consequences are then explored. Yet the inherent implausibility of Benjamin Constant's statement seems never to have been challenged, even though elsewhere in the *Ma Vie* passage about her there is at least one other distortion of the truth: in her youth Isabelle de Charrière certainly did not have 'many passions', several of which were 'unhappy'; apart from suitors whom she hardly knew there was only Constant d'Hermenches, who never became her lover. Benjamin Constant the novelist seems to have taken over here, and indeed *Ma Vie* does occasionally stray inexplicably from meticulous veracity and gives a thoroughly retouched version of events.[72]

In mitigation of his guilt – if indeed he ever was guilty of infidelity – Monsieur de Charrière would no doubt plead that condign punishment had been subsequently visited upon his head. Isabelle was not a happy wife and spread her unhappiness about her, as the Protestant pastor of Colombier, Henri-David Chaillet (1751–1823), noted in his *Journal* in 1783: 'In one of her outbursts she maintained that virtue did nobody any good, made nobody happy, neither the people tormenting themselves to have it nor those around them.'[73] Pastor Chaillet keenly sympathized with her plight, and ends a remarkable description of her by praising her fearless honesty, despite a barbed aside about her not knowing what virtue was – a remark stemming perhaps from intellectual envy or religious animus. Chaillet could ill-afford to feel superior to anyone: he was hauled before an ecclesiastical court at about this time for a relationship he was having with a woman parishioner, and his sanctimoniousness and hypocrisy had long since become repellent to Isabelle de Charrière.[74] But this complex and highly articulate man has left an image of Isabelle that is rich in significance. Was the tirade against virtue which Chaillet mentions delivered for her husband's benefit, a reminder that her fidelity had done her no good in his eyes? She also attacked prosaic friendships in Chaillet's presence: was it a way of humiliating the neat, precise, unspontaneous, predictable Charrière, and a signal that she too might one day go looking for someone else?[75]

These were desperate years indeed for Isabelle de Charrière during which she must have felt crushed by a malevolent destiny. Her youth was long since gone; she had made what to many seemed an absurd choice of husband; she had devoted more than thirteen years of her life to Charrière, and perhaps now had discovered that she had 'wasted her sweetness on the desert air'. She had no source of income but Charrière, and no home but Colombier, a little Swiss backwater near Neuchâtel which, for Charrière's sake, she had made the focus of her life. Her anguish demanded a release, and after a decade of inactivity she turned again to literature. By the time she met Benjamin Constant in 1787 she had attained notoriety throughout Switzerland with three short novels, *Lettres neuchâteloises* (1784), *Lettres de Mistriss Henley* (1784) and *Lettres écrites de Lausanne* (1785). The first was seen as a satire of Neuchâtel society and, worse, as a deliberate affront to decency because of its portrayal of an unmarried and pregnant seamstress; the second was a bitter and provocative story of a woman driven to despair by temperamental incompatibility with her quietly reasonable husband; the third was a tender study of a widowed mother struggling to find a husband for her daughter among Lausanne society, a man who would both love her and not be deterred by her slender dowry. As Constant remarks, 1787 would secure Isabelle de Charrière's literary reputation with the publication of *Caliste*, a continuation of *Lettres écrites de Lausanne*. She was already in negotiations with the Paris publisher Prault, to whom she had been introduced by Jean-Baptiste Suard, when her friendship with Constant began. From what we have seen of her life until then, and of Constant's, here at least *Ma Vie* cannot be accused of distortion or exaggeration:

> Her intelligence captivated me. We spent days and nights talking to each other. She was very severe in her judgements on all those she saw around her. I was by nature very given to mockery. We suited each other perfectly.[76]

4

ESCAPE
(1787–1788)

The chemists of old called those airy spirits or gases which they had not yet discovered the art of collecting or fixing *spiritus silvestres*, wild spirits, and they did not deign to concern themselves with them. These gases or wild spirits have become the most important part of modern chemistry. In the same way fools and rulers call independent spirits that they don't know how to deal with 'wayward' when in fact they are the most important part of the human race.

(Journaux intimes, 9 August 1804[1])

Benjamin Constant still had one monumentally splendid act of folly to commit. It would mark the beginning of the long slow process of emancipation from his father and the rest of the Constant family. This was his 'escapade d'Angleterre' of June to September 1787. Until then, a word from Juste had always been sufficient to bring his son to heel. Indeed, as we have seen, the whole pattern of Benjamin's life had been imposed on him by others – father, Marianne, tutors or, on occasion, the 'enragée boutique', that is his irate family. The resistance he had offered to their wishes had been minor and short-lived, and his eventual acquiescence inevitable. If, in 1787, Constant tended to view the future with a jaundiced eye, it was precisely because his own individual future was already taken care of by others. However, his friendship with Isabelle de Charrière began a change in him. For she altered Constant's view of himself and thereby affected his behviour in a lasting way. She did so first by her sheer intellectual distinction: her conversation, her ideas, her example as a novelist were a challenge and an encouragement to him to fulfil his own potential as a writer. Second, and perhaps more important, Isabelle de Charrière allowed Constant to be free, a luxury which he had seldom experienced in his life. When he was with her, he could do or say almost what he liked. He could discover himself, and Isabelle created a space for that self-exploration by her love, her tolerance, her understanding, perhaps above all by her sense of humour. The chemistry was exactly right between them – and so was the timing. The affection which now quickly grew between them gave fresh purpose to both their lives.

It is a relief among so many biographical notices that emphasize an allegedly pernicious influence exercised over Constant by Isabelle de Charrière to come across one at least that is more clear-sighted. It is Edouard Laboulaye (1811–83) who, in his long 1861 article, rightly stresses the positive and sustaining nature of her affection. Noting that in the letters they subsequently exchanged there was 'the tone of genuine friendship', he adds that as they were both enemies of 'platitudes', Isabelle naturally encouraged in the future author of *Adolphe* 'that boldness of thought, . . . that need to go deeply into matters which explains the lucidity of his thinking and the clarity of his language'.[2] In *Ma Vie* it is the 'boldness of thought' that Constant chooses to bring out:

> Madame de Charrière had such an original and animated way of looking at life, such contempt for received ideas, such vigour in her thinking, and such a powerful and disdainful superiority over ordinary mortals that, disdainful and out of the ordinary as I also was at 20, I found a hitherto undreamt-of pleasure in talking to her. I unhesitatingly abandoned myself to the delight of conversation with her.[3]

It was in this state of mind that Constant at the same time was entering upon a relationship (and possibly a sexual liaison) with Jeanne-Jacqueline-Henriette Pourrat (1770–1835), known as 'Jenny', the rich 17-year-old daughter of Augustine-Magdeleine Pourrat (c. 1740–1818), hostess of a Parisian literary salon. His primary intention was to marry her and thereby pay off the debts his gambling mania had caused him to amass. The only other choice open to him was to leave Paris and face his father. Understandably he preferred to try his luck with Jenny Pourrat, and wrote to her mother asking for Jenny's hand in marriage. She promptly sent back a polite refusal, explaining that her daughter was already promised to someone else. But Constant had reason to believe that there was still a chance that he might succeed, since Madame Pourrat frequently left him and her daughter together *en tête à tête*. Inexplicably he set about beginning their relationship 'in the most absurd manner imaginable'. At no point could he bring himself to overcome his shyness sufficiently to be able to speak to her of his 'feelings', but instead he wrote to Jenny offering to elope with her, as if she were being forced to marry another man against her wishes – which was not the case. And Constant kept up his strange one-sided correspondence despite Jenny's refusal, never mentioning his letters when they were together. He persisted out of sheer obstinacy: 'I had begun going down that path and nothing was going to make me leave it.'[4]

Meanwhile Constant had taken Jenny's mother further into his confidence, so that Madame Pourrat's lover, Louis-Claude Bigot de Sainte-Croix (1744–1803), had become violently jealous of Constant's friendship with his mistress – who was in her fifties. One day, in order to reassure Sainte-Croix, Madame Pourrat arranged for her lover to meet Constant at her house, and in front of him asked Constant to state that it was Jenny, not herself, who was the object of his yearning. Constant misunderstood completely what the situation required of him, and took her question as an unparalleled affront to his pride: he was expected to admit to a complete stranger that he had failed to arouse the slightest interest in either mother or daughter (which was, of course, the case, at least where Madame Pourrat was concerned). On an impulse he took from his pocket a phial of opium, began saying that he was going to kill himself 'and by dint of saying it I almost succeeded in believing it, even though I hadn't the slightest wish to go through with it'.[5] Partly through self-induced hysteria, partly in the ill-judged hope that such a display would win Jenny's heart, he put the phial to his lips and swallowed some of the liquid. Characteristically, he was also partly serious in his intention to seek a way out of his difficulties: 'given my dilemma I was completely indifferent to the outcome'. Yet equally typical was his suddenly becoming bored with the solemnity of the whole proceedings, a parallel perhaps with his tendency in later life to punctuate moments of great pathos in his readings of *Adolphe* with a *fou rire*.[6] And it was his submitting to receiving medication that destroyed the effect of his grand suicidal gesture. The next day Madame Pourrat wrote to tell him that his plans to elope with Jenny no longer made him acceptable in her house, and she called in Monsieur de Charrière as honest broker in the matter. He interviewed Jenny and reported back to Constant that she had no love for him and was quite happy to marry the man it was intended that she should marry all along, all of which came as no surprise to the erstwhile suicide who had already recovered from the incident. As with Mrs Trevor the major factor in the episode had been 'l'irritation de l'obstacle', chafing against an insurmountable obstacle. But just as decisive had been 'the fear of being obliged to rejoin my father [which] had made me persevere in a desperate venture',[7] and it was either reports of a fresh outbreak of gambling fever in Benjamin or news of the fiasco at Madame Pourrat's that led his father to send a Lieutenant Sigismond Benay from his regiment to bring the prodigal back before his presence in Holland. Were it not for a chance delay in their departure, and for the effect Isabelle de Charrière's friendship was already having on him, there is little doubt that Constant would have gone back to 's-Hertogenbosch with Lieutenant Benay. There, once Juste had got over his anger, he would have left Benjamin to his own devices, with little money and no friends: such, as we have seen, was the usual extent of Juste de Constant's paternal solicitude – scalding sarcasm, followed by condescension or indifference. It was neglect of an unendurable kind, and

Benjamin now no longer found the strength in himself to endure it. He gave Benay the slip, and with only a clean shirt and 31 *louis* in his pocket, he made for the English Channel by coach. Within a day he was in Calais, within two he had caught the Dover packet, and on 26 June 1787 he was on the road to London.[8]

Open defiance of one's parents is hardly unusual behaviour in a 19-year-old, but in a young man as father-dominated as Benjamin Constant it signalled a sharp change of direction. It was to coincide also, significantly, with his first serious attempt at novel-writing. Up to now the only serious pieces he had composed had been *Les Chevaliers*, written to please Juste, and the hack work he had undertaken on Roman military discipline for his uncle Samuel. The translation of Gillies's *History* had likewise been written as an earnest of better academic things to come, and was also a form of placatory offering to Juste. Now, in more than one sense of the phrase, Constant was striking out on his own. When in *Ma Vie* he attributes the fundamental change in him which led to his English escapade to long conversations with Isabelle de Charrière, we must take him seriously. What, then, was the content of those intense discussions, and what ideas and attitudes is Isabelle de Charrière likely to have revealed in them?

Partial answers to the first question are to be glimpsed in *Ma Vie*. The second question demands a brief examination of Isabelle de Charrière's novels and other writings. Our solutions to these problems will lead us later towards answering perhaps the most intriguing and important question of all: what was Isabelle de Charrière's role in Constant's development as a novelist? As far as the first enquiry is concerned, it emerges clearly from *Ma Vie* that Isabelle de Charrière – not surprisingly given the state of her life and of her marriage – was wont to rail against dependence on others, a theme likely to elicit warm agreement from a Constant hitherto so abjectly dependent on a capricious father. No doubt this is what Constant is referring to when he says, 'My head had been turned . . . by all the sophistry I had repeated and heard repeated about independence'.[9] But enforced dependence was merely a sub-section of Isabelle's principal indictment of society – that people seldom take the trouble to think, but fall back on platitudes; that they unquestioningly accept stale ideas and outworn conventions through a mental indolence which was anathema to Isabelle de Charrière's own energetic temperament. She had always taken the line that no one was going to tell her what to think, and she had paid the usual penalty in terms of isolation and social ostracism.

As the epigraph to the 1795 German translation of her novel *Trois femmes* Isabelle de Charrière chose *Cogitans dubito*, a phrase with obvious Cartesian echoes which we could perhaps gloss as 'When I reflect, I doubt', or, more loosely but perhaps closer to the spirit of it, 'The more I think about things, the more sceptical I become'. And indeed she did.

Isabelle de Charrière's conversations with Constant in the spring of 1787 were an incitement to him to think for himself, to take nothing on trust. Even in the midst of his most strenuous efforts to win the hand of Jenny Pourrat in marriage, Constant tells us,

> the person who . . . was really on my mind and in my heart was Madame de Charrière. In the midst of all my romance-filled letters, my invitations to elope, my threats of suicide and my theatrical attempt at poisoning myself, I spent hours and hours, whole nights talking to Madame de Charrière, and in the course of those conversations I forgot my worries about my father and my debts, Mademoiselle Pourrat and the rest of the world. I am convinced that without those conversations my behaviour would have been less foolish. All of her opinions rested on contempt for custom and convention. We outdid each other in making fun of the people we saw; we became intoxicated with our humour and our scorn for the rest of the human race, and as a result of all of this I acted as I spoke, sometimes laughing like an idiot at something I had done in all sincerity and in despair half an hour before. The collapse of all my plans concerning Mademoiselle Pourrat brought me even closer to Madame de Charrière. She was the only woman with whom I could converse freely because she was the only one who didn't bore me with advice or remonstrations about my conduct.[10]

Like many people, Constant grew rather more conservative with the years, and perhaps this, as well as an obscure resentment against the woman who had done so much for him, makes for the disapproving tone that breaks through intermittently in passages like the one quoted above from *Ma Vie*.

We are not obliged to share all the valuations which the writer of 1810–11 felt moved to put on the experiences of the young man he had been in 1787, especially when we possess his letters and other evidence from that earlier period which show him in a different and undoubtedly truer light. And from these and from all we have seen so far it is perfectly obvious that talking to Isabelle de Charrière gave the 19-year-old Constant a unique, positive and longed-for sense of liberation. To begin with, they were so alike that, if they had believed in such a notion, they might have called their meeting providential. They were as mercurial and as restless as each other; and both of them believed they had never been loved enough. Part at least of the 'deeper and much closer relationship' which *Ma Vie* says soon developed between them[11] was a reinforcing of their individual sense of identity. The spiritual estrangement from which each had been suffering was at an end. There was now at least one other person who spoke the same language, who laughed at the same things, and who in very recent years had been through similar turmoil and heartache. It is hardly surprising that Isabelle found little to criticize in Benjamin: he was far too like herself. As Edouard Laboulaye says, she gave Constant the stable affection which allowed him to feel what it might have been like to have a mother – indeed she was almost the same age as Henriette de Chandieu would have been if she had lived. And to Isabelle de Charrière, a childless woman, he was a son, a *polisson*, a wild scamp certainly, but brilliant, destined perhaps for great success in the world, and entirely devoted to her. At this crucial moment in Constant's early manhood Isabelle was in a position to open his eyes to his father's obtuseness towards him – she had had plenty of experience of similar treatment herself – and, perhaps unwittingly, she appears to have prepared the way for his defiance of the paternal edict when it eventually came. On the day he was due to leave for Holland with Lieutenant Benay, Constant says,

> My mind continued to be in a state of great ferment, to which my conversations with Madame de Charrière contributed in no small measure. She certainly could not have foreseen the effect she would have on me, but by talking to me constantly about the stupidity of the human race, the absurdity of received ideas, and by sharing my admiration for everything that was original, extraordinary or bizarre she ended up by inspiring in me a craving to live like her in a way which was out of the ordinary. As yet I had not made any plans, but with some vague idea in my mind I borrowed about 30 *louis* from Monsieur de Charrière.[12]

Isabelle de Charrière could not fail to recognize signs of greatness in Constant which his letters from England would shortly confirm. While there was still time, she continued to urge him to keep his mind free of prejudices and tried by all means possible to encourage his natural aptitude for dispassionate, sceptical investigation. This was not a form of indoctrination, as Constant seems later to have believed: she simply understood better than anybody else what he was like, and merely fostered a tendency that was already apparent in him. It was obvious to her from the start that he had the same unsettling gift of clear-sightedness as herself, and that he must use it. *Ma Vie* gives here an incomplete and therefore misleading picture of Isabelle de Charrière's character and attitudes: we see the scepticism clearly enough; what we are not shown is the moral reasoning that always went hand in hand with that scepticism. Isabelle de Charrière chafed against doctrinaire attitudes and placed such a high value on intellectual independence because she was always intimately aware of the mind's multifariousness and changeability. All the venom which she directed against prejudice and received ideas was distilled out of bitter knowledge that a sensitive and receptive mind may discern vital nuances in a person's character or behaviour, nuances which could make all the difference when it came to judging that person's actions; but she realized too that those fine discriminations are rarely noticed by the bulk of humanity who are too stubborn or too lazy to abandon their crude shibboleths and stereotypes. It was no mere wish to be different from others, to shine or to appear superior that made her adopt a sceptical position. Isabelle de Charrière reasoned invariably in moral terms, and her wish for Constant would have been that he should maintain an open mind because that would help him in the long run to be a better man. To view her as an idle *persifleuse*, mocking merely for the sake of mocking and encouraging the same vice in a younger man, would be as unjust as to accuse George Eliot's novels of encouraging moral indifference. Isabelle de Charrière was aware that minds like hers and Constant's belonged to the same intellectual family as Montaigne: they were predisposed by the colliding oppositions within them and by their own fluidity of mood and thought to see complexity and mutability in all things and all people. If there was one belief above all that Isabelle de Charrière shared with Montaigne (and indeed Flaubert), it was that 'l'affirmation et l'opiniastreté sont signes exprès de bestise', stating things categorically and sticking stubbornly to one's opinions are a sure sign of stupidity.[13] She saw the dangers inherent in such unshakeable certainty, and made sure that Constant saw them too.

A closed dogmatic mind was always odious to Madame de Charrière, not only in the writing of fiction but in religious and political matters. It would not be difficult to illustrate from her *Correspondance* her equal hostility to monarchist and Jacobin, religious fanatic and doctrinaire atheist. Such people were no longer alive to the complex and changing reality around them: more dangerous still, in their firm conviction that they *knew*, that they had access to absolute and infallible truth, there was an arrogance and a pride that flew in the face of a fact which the sceptical Isabelle de Charrière was only too aware of: that we all make mistakes. In her youth Isabelle de Charrière had, for a while, sought dependable certainty in mathematics. And yet it is clear that she remained permanently fascinated by irresolute people like William, the central figure of her novel *Caliste*, an important precursor of Adolphe, fascinated too by indecision and by problems where the grounds for a decision one way or another are most finely balanced. These themes are the basis not only of *Lettres écrites de Lausanne* but also of *Trois femmes* and its manuscript continuation. Questions of choice – often delayed choice – and responsibility for that choice could not but interest this sceptic whose *alter ego* was trenchantly decisive and at times rather too resolute for some of her friends.

Such, then, was the woman who had now set Benjamin Constant's mind in a ferment. She appears thinly disguised in *Cécile* as 'Mme de Chenevière' of whom Constant says: 'Her wide-ranging, bold and original intellect completely captivated me at a time in my life when intellect was much more necessary to me than it is now.'[14] 'Bizarre' is the adjective that attaches itself to her in his memory: it occurs in *Ma Vie*, in *Cécile* and in *Adolphe*.[15] In May 1790 Constant was to tell Isabelle that she would always be 'the dearest and strangest of my memories'.[16] But it was a 'differentness', an oddity with which he was completely at home and in which he discovered himself. We must dismiss once and for all, then, the notion which Constant put about in his later life that at the age of 19 he was a tender plant and that the powerful rays of Isabelle de Charrière's intellect had in some way shrivelled or deformed him. On the contrary, she had been just what he had wanted at that age and, more important, just what he had needed. He was a sophisticated, rather hard-bitten young man who needed a friend who could take all of that in her stride, matching him in worldly wisdom, but who could also, by her tactful trust and affection, offer him a way out of the impasse in which he found himself. As we shall see, the young Constant's letters amply confirm that Isabelle was a tonic to him. If she also helped him to stop being an obedient votary of his father, it would surely in the circumstances be a severe judge who would not add a *tant mieux* – so much the better.

We left Constant, earlier in this chapter, on the high road to London, more than a little amazed at what he had had the courage to do, his mind filled by Isabelle de Charrière with infinite possibilities for what he might yet do and become. His first letter to her, written in haste at Dover as he awaited the stagecoach, is a masterpiece, and begins with the kind of literary allusiveness with which subsequent letters would be crammed:

> There is in the world, without the world being aware of it, a serious German writer who has observed very wisely apropos of a piece of guttering which a soldier was melting down to make musket-balls, that the worker who put the guttering up in the first place never suspected that it would one day kill one of his descendants. Thus it was, Madame – for that is how one ought to begin in order to give one's sentences the right philosophical ponderousness – thus it was, I say, that when I took tea with you every day last week and talked reason I never suspected that for all my reason I was about to do something enormously foolish; that boredom would arouse love in me and I would lose my head, and instead of leaving for 's-Hertogenbosch I would leave for England with hardly any money and with absolutely no idea where I was making for. And yet that is what happened in the strangest of ways.[17]

And so on. The most unmistakeable feature of Constant's letters from England is, of course, their literariness. We begin here with a reference to Goethe's play *Götz von Berlichingen* (1773), followed by a sentence that is quite deliberately reminiscent of Voltaire's *Candide* (1759) playing on the unforeseeableness of Constant's present incongruous situation. It is quite obvious that he relishes at last having just the right audience for fireworks like these. What is more significant still, however, in his brilliant letters from England – their verbal extravagance, the striking of a variety of poses worthy of Rameau's nephew as reimagined by Diderot – is Constant's enjoyment of writing. In what has survived of his correspondence with his family there was little scope for this – his letter to his uncle Samuel quoted in the previous chapter is a fairly representative sample – and we are singularly unfortunate in no longer possessing his letters either to John Wilde or to Johann Rudolf Knecht which might have given us a more appropriate yardstick. But even so it is doubtful whether they could in any way match these letters to Isabelle de Charrière. Their essential difference from his letters to his family is Constant's exhilaration in addressing a writer – he goes out of his way to refer to an incident in her novel *Caliste*, which had recently appeared and was, it seems, highly thought of generally. For a young man brought up to harbour literary ambitions as high as his, this was no doubt a delightful irritant that would not let him rest. And as we shall see presently, it was during his stay in England that Constant set to work on a first novel of his own.

Constant's first letter from Dover is dominated by the idea of freedom. He chose England as a refuge because it was the freest country he knew and, despite his having only 15 guineas in his pocket and very few clothes, he was well pleased with the choice, laughing at himself in the mirror but nevertheless determined to continue in his defiance of his father. He wrote to Juste setting before him the two options for his future which he would find acceptable: marrying a suitable partner, or emigrating to America, taking with him part of his inheritance from his mother. He then cheerfully boarded the coach for London. Once there, he conceived the project of making a tour of England and Scotland, and, in order to carry it through, was not above some deception. He knew the name and address of his father's Anglo-Swiss bankers, Messrs Ripley, Rivier & Co. of 6 Laurence Pountney Lane, off Cannon Street in the City of London, and he paid Philippe Rivier (1747–1816) a couple of visits there. The following is Rivier's account of those visits in a letter to Juste de Constant of Friday 20 July 1787:

> Sir
>
> I received on the 17th the two letters with which you honoured me on the 10th and 14th inst. and I already had the pleasure of seeing your son before receiving them. His visit and his request for £50 sterling to go to Scotland took me by surprise as they were not accompanied by any word from you. But seeing that he was in financial difficulty, I gave him on the 5th inst. £25 sterling on your behalf. Then your two above-mentioned letters arrived and explained the situation. On his second visit he promised to leave the day after tomorrow for Holland as you had asked him to, and this persuaded me to give him a further advance of £15 when he signed the enclosed

receipt for £40. I should be grateful if you would credit my bank Ripley & Rivier for these two sums. With this money I thought he would have more than enough to pay what he owed and for a number of small purchases he says he has made, but now he claims that he only has £7. 13s left and needs another ten *louis* in order to be able to rejoin you. Failing that he will have to await another reply from you. Since I can see that he would like nothing better, I have decided to give him those ten *louis*. When I or one of the employees of our bank see him in the post-chaise on Sunday morning, the day fixed for his departure (something which I promise you can count on and about which I shall inform you by the very next post), rest assured that I will have done everything in my power to exhort your son to be more aware of your kindness towards him and of your love. I hope that he will come to appreciate them and that his behaviour will be more satisfactory in the future. I am sorry that our being out in the country and the great amount of work I am involved in at the moment have not allowed me to receive him in my home as often as I would have wished.[18]

It is highly unlikely that Benjamin ever had the slightest intention of catching the boat to Holland on Sunday 22 July 1787. In fact by then, having secured the money he needed from Rivier, he was 40 miles to the north of London, on the Cambridgeshire–Suffolk border and heading, by a very circuitous route, for Edinburgh.

Constant's stay in London had been a curious affair. He went to the theatre from time to time it seems, lived reasonably well, and made a tentative approach to John Adams (1739–1826), the United States Ambassador and future President about the possibility of emigrating to America. But he was lonely, and bought various pets – a monkey and two dogs – for company (Constant was always inordinately fond of animals). And when the initial excitement of his *fugue* had worn off, he became fearful of his father's anger. He sought out a young English aristocrat, probably Henry Lascelles (1767–1841), known as 'Beau Lascelles', whom he had met in Lausanne but who did not remember him and refused to lend him money to help him on his tour of the island. He also met quite by chance John Mackay (1761–1841), one of his companions at the Speculative Society, who was working in London and due shortly to leave for India. They talked together of John Wilde, to whom Constant thereupon wrote, and from whom he received such a warm reply that he decided to go and stay with him in Edinburgh. Then, also by chance it would seem, he met Dr Richard Kentish (1761–1848), another Edinburgh acquaintance, not a member of the Speculative Society but a former drinking companion, who now had a successful practice in London and a house in Gower Street. An ambitious and rather turbulent Yorkshireman, Kentish was on the point of leaving for Brighton with his wife where he intended to pay court to members of fashionable society who were there for the season. He invited Constant to accompany them. Constant declined, but two days later thought better of it and joined Kentish and his wife in Brighton, expecting 'all sorts of pleasures'. But Kentish had misled him: he knew hardly anyone and spent most of his time at a hospital or earning fees by looking after sick patients. After a week of boredom, Constant returned to London, and a few days later, after deceiving his father's banker, set off on his journey north.

Writing to Isabelle de Charrière from 'Chesterford', that is Great Chesterford near Cambridge, on 22 July 1787 Constant makes a very significant revelation: 'I'm working on a novel which I shall show you. I've written and corrected fifty octavo pages of it. I shall dedicate it to you if I publish it.'[19] Clearly a novel of such length must have been begun before Constant set out on his journey, in all probability in London or Brighton. And he was obviously toying with the idea of publishing it, no doubt after Madame de Charrière had first cast a critical eye over it. As he travelled he continued to work on the book. And those solitary travels on horseback took him through Newmarket, King's Lynn and Wisbech to Wadenhoe in Northamptonshire, where he hoped to borrow money from his father's old friend, the Reverend Nathaniel Bridges (1750–1834), the deeply pious Evangelical rector of Wadenhoe; then away to the north again, having found Bridges was away, via Stamford, Kettering, Leicester, Derby, Buxton, Chorley, Kendal and Carlisle, to arrive in Edinburgh at 6 o'clock on a Sunday evening, 12 August 1787, with only 9 or 10 shillings left in his pocket; back again, after a fortnight of carousing with his old student friends and with 10 guineas borrowed from John Wilde, via Carlisle and the Lake District, Lancaster, Bolton and Market Harborough, to Wadenhoe, where he enlisted the help of the Reverend Bridges but was also obliged to attend lengthy prayer meetings in the rectory during which Bridges in his fervour often beat his head on the floorboards; and finally back to Richard Kentish's house in Gower Street, London. All the time he continued to send Isabelle de Charrière letters filled with literary allusions, parodies and manic clowning. And all the while, it seems, he was thinking about his novel. For on his return journey from Scotland he told her, in a letter dated 'Westmoreland/Patterdale, 29th August 1787':

I've given up the idea of writing a formal novel. I'm too talkative by nature. All those characters who wanted to speak in my place made me impatient. I like speaking for myself, especially when you are the one who's listening. Instead of the novel there will be letters entitled: *Lettres Ecrites de Patterdale a Paris dans lété de 1787 adressées a Mᵉ de C. de Z.* [*Letters written from Patterdale to Paris in the summer of 1787 addressed to Madame de C. de Z.*, i.e. Charrière

99

de Zuylen], that doesn't hold me to anything. There will be a plot of sorts which I shall take up or drop depending how I feel, but I ask you and Monsieur de Charrière (who I hope has not forgotten his foolish friend) to keep absolutely quiet about it. I want to see what people will say or not say about it because I expect to be punished with obscurity rather than honoured by the critics. I've only written two letters so far . . . I write without any great attention to the conventional rules of style or expression, I don't work at any set times, I simply write it down as it comes into my head.[20]

What conclusions can we draw from these remarks? First, that in all probability Constant's novel began as either a third-person narrative or as a series of fictional letters written by a number of correspondents. Second, that Constant found himself unable or unwilling to continue with a novel written in such a form because he felt the need to express his own thoughts and ideas through a first-person narrative. Third, that his preferred form for a novel would be very like his real letters to Isabelle de Charrière, because not only does he wish to speak on his own behalf, he also needs to have present in his mind the idea of a listener as attentive and intelligent as she is. As in his letter from 'Chesterford' quoted earlier, Constant was determined to see his novel in print. Furthermore, in the section of his letter which follows that quoted above, he mockingly alludes to the kind of language used by Jenny Pourrat's mother, turgid phrases like 'do not ask for my *indulgence* when you already have my *friendship*',[21] and indicates that his own style will be simple and natural.

Constant's extraordinary summer idyll in rural England and Scotland ended with his brief stay with the kindly, pious, Low-Church rector Nathaniel Bridges (whom his father had known for many years) at Wadenhoe near Oundle, in Northamptonshire. Bridges was also Rector of Orlingbury, in the vicinity of which was Great Harrowden Hall where lived Lady Charlotte Watson-Wentworth, sister of Charles, Marquess of Rockingham. Bridges took Constant to meet her, and the young man was in awe of this ageing aristocrat so closely connected with a Whig administration that had been idolized by himself and his friends in Edinburgh.[22] But now at length reality was closing in once again on Constant – one might indeed say that the anaesthetic was wearing off and the pain beginning to return. For the fact was that summer was ending and he could no longer put off returning to Holland to face a verbal lashing from his father. As he rode south-east in the direction of Kimbolton, the Great North Road and London on the morning of 11 September 1787, he doubtless wondered if he would ever again taste the exhilarating sense of liberty his English escapade had brought him. Both *Ma Vie* and his letters to Isabelle de Charrière emphasize that one central experience: being alone and free at last. Britain was to remain for him not merely a model of political freedom, but a remembered haven of personal happiness.

On money borrowed from Nathaniel Bridges Constant reached the capital where, according to *Ma Vie*, he appears to have received letters from his father expressing despair at his behaviour, and informing him that his bankers Ripley, Rivier & Co. in the City had been forbidden to give him any more money.[23] When this indeed proved to be the case, he made once again for his erstwhile Edinburgh drinking companion, the ambitious Yorkshire doctor Richard Kentish, whom he had left in Brighton two months previously. At his Gower Street house Kentish received him somewhat coolly, as wary of Constant's capacity for deception as Juste's bankers now were. Constant's request for money was met with an offer of 10 guineas in return for a bill of exchange. It was the kind of humiliation Constant was unlikely to forgive, especially since he had so recently been feted in Scotland by John Wilde and James Mackintosh. After riding to Dover he sent Kentish the dog that had accompanied him on his journey around Britain with a note saying that since Kentish treated his friends like dogs he hoped that he would treat the dog like a friend.[24]

In Calais Constant pawned a watch and rode night and day via Bruges and Antwerp, where he borrowed more money from an innkeeper, towards 's-Hertogenbosch, more widely known at this period as Bois-le-Duc, the Dutch town where his father was stationed. All the time dread of his father's scolding was increasing in him. But the account of his arrival which Constant gives in *Ma Vie* bears eloquent testimony to the extreme oddity of Juste:

I was in a state of the most terrible anguish, and for a while I did not have the strength to ask to be taken to my father's lodgings. Nevertheless I was obliged to take my courage in both hands and go there. As I walked behind the guide I had been given, I trembled both at the thought of the just reproaches that could be made against me, and at the idea of finding my father hurt and perhaps ill because he had been so deeply wounded by me. His most recent letters had upset me greatly. He had written to say that he was ill because of the pain I had caused him, and that if I stayed away any longer, I would have his death on my conscience. I entered his room. He was playing whist with three other officers from his regiment. 'Ah, there you are', he said, 'how did you get here?'

I told him I had travelled halfway on horseback and halfway by coach, day and night. He continued playing cards. I expected an explosion of anger from him when we were alone. The others left us. 'You must be tired', he said, 'go and sleep'. He came with me to my bedroom. As I walked in front of him, he noticed that my coat was torn. 'That's what I always feared would come of this escapade', he said.

He embraced me, said goodnight and I went to bed. I was dumb-founded by the reception he had given me, which was neither what I had feared nor hoped for. While fearing I would be treated with the severity I felt I deserved, I felt the real need – at the risk of being told off – of an open and frank discussion with my father. My affection for him had increased because of the pain I had caused him. I needed to ask his forgiveness and to talk about my future with him. I was longing to regain his confidence, and to have confidence in him. I hoped – and partly feared – that the next day we would speak to each other more openly.

But his manner was unchanged the next day, and despite my efforts to bring the conversation round to the matter, and despite some embarrassed expressions of regret on my part, he did not respond and during those two days I spent at 's-Hertogenbosch no discussion took place between us. I feel now that I should have broken the ice. My father's silence hurt me just as much as mine probably hurt him. He attributed it to culpable thoughtlessness after such inexcusable behaviour on my part; and what I took to be indifference on his was perhaps resentment which he was making an effort to hide from me. But on this occasion as on many others in my life I was held back by a timidity that I have never been able to overcome, and the words I wanted to say were never spoken once I saw no encouragement to go on.[25]

The experience at 's-Hertogenbosch was clearly so fundamental for Constant that we find an echo of it in the opening pages of *Adolphe* where Adolphe and his father are held back by 'la timidité' from open, frank communication with each other.[26] This shyness and his father's distant ironic attitude have far-reaching and ultimately tragic consequences for Adolphe whose already solitary nature is reinforced.

At the end of September 1787 Constant left Holland for Berne, carrying with him memories of his unsatisfactory encounter and discontent with what we might nowadays call an unresolved relationship. Events in Holland, in the form of a mutiny in his father's regiment, were shortly to give him an opportunity to prove his loyalty to Juste, just as those events themselves prove to the objective outside eye what a difficult man Benjamin Constant had to put up with. The circumstances that led to his father's court martial and subsequent unjust treatment were in a sense rehearsed during Constant's journey to Switzerland when he spent hours in argument with his travelling companion, a Bernese aristocrat, took the opportunity to denounce the iniquity of Bernese dominion over his native Pays de Vaud and threatened to liberate it at the earliest opportunity.

These were close to the views of Juste who was very shortly to feel the full weight of Bernese power bearing down on him in the aftermath of the mutiny.

Once in Switzerland Constant lost no time in making straight for Neuchâtel and Isabelle de Charrière's house nearby at Colombier. During his brief stay there the two friends resumed the intoxicating conversations and arguments which had been interrupted by Constant's English *fugue*, and proceeded once again to knock intellectual sparks off each other in a way that neither had experienced before in their lives. The last thing Constant wished to do in such a frame of mind was return to Lausanne, a dismal and subdued city in his eyes whose political servitude to Berne he keenly resented. But return he did, after a couple of days at Colombier, bringing with him a degree of insufferable conceitedness that was soon to irk his relatives. His aunt Catherine de Charrière de Sévery whose son Wilhelm and Benjamin were at daggers drawn at the best of times wrote of Constant:

> The protection that Monsieur Gibbon [Edward Gibbon the historian] gives [to Wilhelm] fills [Benjamin] with the deepest resentment; all his sparkling wit looked merely pallid; the poor boy only has his wit, together with the most appalling conceit which causes him nothing but misery.[27]

But on this occasion Constant's time in Lausanne was to be limited. Juste had been making plans for him ever since they had been in Paris the previous winter, plans which seem at one point even to have included the rather unlikely choice of a military career for Constant,[28] but this time they seemed to offer that degree of independence that Constant now knew to be the essential component in any future arrangement for his well-being. Juste had in mind a post at the Court of the Duke of Brunswick, whom he knew through military service in Holland. The Duke, Karl Wilhelm Ferdinand (1735–1806), was widely known as an intelligent, enlightened ruler of his small north-German state and as an ardent francophile. Rather in the manner of Frederick the Great, the Duke was especially welcoming to writers and philosophers who passed through his territory, men such as Goethe and Mirabeau, as he later was to *émigrés* fleeing revolutionary France to whom he gave employment at his Court.[29] Juste obtained the largely ceremonial post of *Kammerjunker* or Gentleman of the Bedchamber for his son during the autumn of 1787, an appointment which was confirmed on 8 March 1788 (and indeed was later followed by promotion to the rank of *Legationsrat* or Councillor on 27 December 1788). Benjamin was to prepare to leave for Brunswick during December 1787. It was a prospect which, on the face of it, offered everything the young man could want: intelligent company, a large measure of freedom and leisure, the protection of the Duke, financial security and the minimum amount of work.

For a man as complex as Constant, however, it could all go wrong, and indeed the seeds of potential disaster were already germinating. During October or November 1787 Catherine de Charrière de Sévery wrote to her son Wilhelm:

> Yesterday Monsieur de Sévery was at Bellevue [his country house north-east of Lausanne] where Benjamin was haranguing the people with vanity, self-importance and overweening presumption, inter-rupting everyone, condemning the magistrature of Lausanne, criti-cizing and issuing plans for a new government; in a word he is like his father, the difference between them being that unlike him he is not polite and is infinitely less likeable. The Hubers like him [the family of the painter Jean Huber] because they are taken in by his manner.[30]

Constant's response to political repression was as fierce as to any infringe-ment of his own personal freedom, and it had already made him a *démo-crate*, an opponent of monarchs and churchmen. It would make him a natural supporter of the French Revolution when it came. He was about to leave for the Court of Duke Karl Wilhelm Ferdinand, the man who was soon to lead the armies of the European alliance against revolutionary France.

Before joining Constant on his epic winter coach journey along the muddy rutted roads of eighteenth-century Germany, we must not neglect other indications of difficult times ahead for him. The most serious occurred on 29 October 1787 in Amsterdam: the first battalion of Juste's Swiss garrison mutinied. Despite his fellow officers' deserting him, he managed to quell the mutiny, but became involved in a long series of military court cases which would ruin him financially and preoccupy his son for several years.[31] The next is the tragicomic affair of Constant's duel with François du Plessis-Gouret (1755–1833), a lieutenant in a Swiss regiment: on the way to pay a final visit to Madame de Charrière on 18 November 1787 before leaving for Brunswick he got into an argument over his dog with a landowner near Ependes. Constant's hot temper, family pride, and a taste for duelling which was already in evidence at Erlangen, turned the disagreement into an affair of honour. Over the next few days the duel was postponed, and Constant wrote a comic poem on the Du Plessis family and the duel *manqué*. He stayed in Neuchâtel, where he was treated for a venereal infection by Dr Joseph Deleschaut, visited Isabelle de Charrière at Colombier, and the duel finally took place on 8 January 1788, with Monsieur de Charrière as Constant's second: he was wounded in the nipple, Du Plessis in the knee, and the matter was honourably concluded.[32] During the two months that he underwent treat-ment for what was probably gonorrhoea (c. 10 December 1787–10 Febru-ary 1788) he was happy to be away from his family and in all probability wrote the unfinished epistolary novel *Lettres de d'Arsillé fils* in collaboration with Isabelle de Charrière which seems to be a veiled self-portrait depicting the difficulties his personality had caused with his uncle Samuel and his cousins. There is circumstantial evidence, indeed, to suggest that this novel may have been a reworking of the *Lettres Ecrites de Patterdale* of the previous summer: it was not to be published until 1981.[33] Meanwhile Constant learned that his family suspected that he was having an affair with Isabelle de Charrière – something he was, of course, currently incapable of. Annoyed and all the more determined not to change his plans, he stayed on, gambling away some of his money in Neuchâtel and resuming his work on ancient Greek religion. As Madame de Charrière would recall in later years:

> On the other side of the same table [Constant] was writing – on tarot cards which he intended to string together – a work on the spirit and influence of religion, of all known religions. He never read any of it to me, reluctant like myself to expose himself to criticism and mockery.[34]

Finally, after returning to Lausanne he set off for the north of Germany on 17 February 1788, with his father privately expressing his fears to his brother Samuel:

> It is certain that if my son wishes to ensure a comfortable future for himself, he can do so, but I am not without my fears on that subject, and I am afraid of seeing him come back poorer than he leaves. He thinks he is a rich man whose wealth is inexhaustible, but he needs to know and understand how short of money I really am.[35]

A taste for ruinous gambling and risky sexual adventures, intellectual arrogance, political radicalism, a fiery temper – these, then, were some of the benefits soon to be bestowed on Duke Karl Wilhelm Ferdinand's Court in the person of the young Constant. It is perhaps no accident that the uncompleted picaresque narrative of the delightfully witty and self-mocking *Ma Vie* ends at about this point in Constant's career, with the duel with du Plessis. He must have perceived the end of 1787 as a natural fault line running through his life when he later came to compose his autobiographical narrative in around 1810–11, a line that separated the remediable mock-serious disasters of childhood and adolescence from the real and irreparable ones of adult years. And looking back he laid aside his pen, having in all probability no heart to leave behind that world of sunlight and shadows for the deep wintry gloom that was to follow.

5

THE BRUNSWICK YEARS
(1788–1794)

Constant wrote to Isabelle de Charrière from Basle on 20 or 21 February 1788:

> I only have time to say a few words to you because I am not spending the night here as I had thought. The roads are terrible, the wind is cold and I am miserable, more so today than yesterday. It is difficult and painful to leave you for a day, and each day adds to the suffering of the preceding days. I had got so used to the company of your writing, of your piano (although it annoyed me sometimes) and of everything that surrounds you, I had got so used to spending my evenings with you, having supper with the kind Mademoiselle Louise [Monsieur de Charrière's sister], that I miss all of these quiet and cheerful things, and all the delights of bad weather, an uncomfortable post-chaise and dreadful roads cannot console me for having left you. Both my physical and moral well-being owe you a great deal. I have an awful cold, simply from being shut up in a post-chaise: imagine how much I would have been suffering if, as my relatives – alarmed at the threat to my chastity, and more concerned about my continence than my life – had wished, I had left in the middle of my treatment [for venereal disease]. So I certainly owe you my health and probably my life. I owe you more than that, since life is so miserable most of the time, whatever the Reverend Chaillet [pastor of Colombier] says, and you made it sweet, you consoled me for the misery of being alive, of being in company, and of being in the company of Marin, Guenille & Co. [Marianne Magnin and her friends]. I am calculating in my post-chaise how much I am in your debt, because it is a great pleasure to owe you so much and in so many ways. As long as you live, as long as I live, and wherever I am, I shall always say, 'At least there is a Colombier somewhere in the world'.[1]

The journey did not get better: an axle on his coach broke at Rastatt, south-west of Karlsruhe, and while it was being repaired he continued to reflect bitterly in his next letter to Isabelle:

I had spent three months alone [in Neuchâtel] without seeing bad temper, avarice or that friendship which ought rather to be called hatred taking it in turns to torment me. But now, weak in body and spirit, a slave to my father, my relatives, to rulers, to God knows who, I am on my way to find a master, enemies, people who will be jealous of me and what is worse people who will bore me, all this when I am 250 leagues from home.[2]

Writing from Darmstadt on 25 February he compared his present lot with life in England the previous summer, and revealed the real reason for going to Brunswick:

How my feelings, my hopes and my surroundings have changed! By dint of seeing men free and happy I thought that I could become like them: a carefree and solitary summer had given me back some of my strength. I was no longer worn out by other people's moodiness or my own. . . . If in my weakened state I had left in the middle of the winter, I would have died 20 leagues from Colombier. I waited until I could undertake a long journey without risk to my health, a journey I accepted to make solely out of obedience and to which, if I had been the heartless son I am accused of being, I would have objected since I am now 20 years old. I wanted my father to have at least the shadow of a son whom he could still love.[3]

Constant was going against the grain of his own character to carry out his father's wishes, trying once again to wring from Juste some sign of affection and to live up to his father's sometimes exaggerated expectations of him – a recurring theme in their relationship, and one which finds its echo on the first page of *Adolphe*. However, the young man's health was not good: his eyes, already weak and myopic, gave him a lot of trouble, and he mentions sore throats, stomach upsets, fevers and rashes in his letters to Isabelle. As a man of the world he knew what to expect from what he calls 'la vérole', 'the pox', and from treatment for it, which was commonly with mercury and had unpleasant side effects. The thought must have contributed to Constant's increasingly downcast turn of mind.

Constant reached Brunswick (Braunschweig) via Göttingen on 2 March 1788. He found himself in a walled and moated north-German city, still somewhat medieval in atmosphere with an imposing Gothic *Rathaus*. One of the favourite occupations of its inhabitants was walking along the ramparts of the city. There were no less than three Courts in Brunswick, those of the Dowager Duchess, of the Duke her son and of the Duchess her daughter-in-law. It was the last two circles in which Constant was principally to move. The Dowager Duchess Philippine Charlotte of Prussia was punctilious on matters of form and etiquette, and the atmosphere at her Court was stiff and formal. Everyone spoke French more or less well, with an accent that Constant was soon to mock. The Duke, Karl Wilhelm Ferdinand, was known as a fine military leader and a conscientious ruler who, with his able Finance Minister Jean-Baptiste Féronce de Rotencreutz (1723–99), had restored the fortunes of the Duchy after his own father's wasteful incumbency. As Gustave Rudler perceptively remarks:

> Once again Juste de Constant had aimed high on his son's behalf; he was able to – and no doubt did – congratulate himself on having found him a position with a ruler of such high renown. His choice was that of a good father, but one who understood very little about his own son.[4]

The Duke was a serious and cultivated man with many talents, but the ability to communicate easily with those who surrounded him was not among them. His speech was laboured because of his painstaking choice of words, and he rated the lowliest soldier as of more use than his courtiers. Although he no doubt regarded Constant as being among those who were of neither use nor ornament at his Court, he was consistently kind towards him and Juste, despite Constant's increasing political radicalism. Similarly his Minister Féronce, widely read and possessed of an acid wit, took the young man under his wing, while quietly despairing at Constant's inability to organize his life better. The Duchess was of an entirely different species, being English and by nature informal, a lover of anecdotes who was outspoken in her views and the terror of her ladies-in-waiting, whose amorous intrigues she would delight in making public. If the Duke was to act somewhat out of character in helping one of his least dynamic and most reluctant courtiers, *Kammerjunker* Constant, the Duchess his wife was likewise to do so in her later hostility to Constant and her loyal defence of her lady-in-waiting Minna von Cramm. But it was among these ladies-in-waiting that Constant found a friend, an elderly woman whom he mentions occasionally but never names, who made life at times tolerable at Court for him.

Constant's reaction at finding himself in such a milieu was predictable: amused disbelief at first, then boredom and then the most savage mockery he could muster by way of consolation. In fact the strongest evidence we have about this period of his life, apart from *Cécile*, is his correspondence with Isabelle de Charrière where he feels no need to pretend about anything. Shortly after his arrival he describes his life to her:

> I have the prettiest apartment imaginable. I have a room in which

to receive those who come to pay homage to His Highness's Gentleman of the Bedchamber [*Kammerjunker*], I have a small bedroom decorated in the German style, where it is too dark to see (but that is fortunate sometimes), I have a very handsome study, and a harpsichord, a bad one but which I play continually.... I have a bureau (I am so used to titles that at first I wrote 'baron') where I have made an arrangement that pleases me enormously. In some of the drawers I have put all the various Parts and Introductions to my great and magnificent Works. In one of the two others I have put all of your letters and notes to me, and all those from my friend in Scotland [John Wilde]. Also stored away there – and I apologize for this – are three short letters from the beautiful Genevan woman who lived in Brussels [Madame Johannot]. I hesitated for a long while but I finally gave in. That woman really loved me, loved me passionately, and she is the only woman who didn't make me pay for her favours by endless suffering. I no longer love her but I shall always be grateful to her. So where should I put her letters? Surely not in the other drawer, alongside uncles, cousins and the rest of the angry mob [*l'enragée boutique*]. So she had to go into my Heaven, since I couldn't send her to Hell, and there was no Purgatory.

(Letter of 2–7 March 1788[5])

Constant describes a typical day in his early months in Brunswick. He does so in English, a language for which he and Isabelle had a particular affection:

Except with two or three people with whom I may talk and joke upon the weather or some such thing, I never talk to anybody. Visits I make none. I walk a great deal, read the history of Germany, read Greek, play much upon the harpsichord, ride half the day, try new horses . . . do never touch a card, nor a girl, am often low spirited.

(Letter to Isabelle de Charrière of 25–8 April 1788[6])

The Duke's Court was better than many, according to contemporary commentators, being generally friendly and cultivated. There were frequent concerts and the Duke had his own troupe of actors; there were masked balls during the winter, and a club, the Große Klub zu Braunschweig, of which the Duke was the president, devoted to intellectual pursuits, with its own spacious rooms and library. Court ceremonial was elaborate, and Constant's role was to receive guests at receptions and dinners dressed in uniform with a sword at his side. He knew from the outset that he could never fit in. There could be little scope for Constant's characteristic verve and *bizarrerie* to express themselves openly among the formal rituals of Court. And the German nobility he met struck him as stiff, unimaginative and frequently vain. For their part they can have felt little in common with this tall, stooping young man with sandy hair, freckles, spectacles and a lisp whose characteristic mode of conversation was rapier-sharp stabs of irony or paradox, usually at the expense of others. Like so much else about the Duke's Court that is echoed in the first chapter of *Adolphe*, Constant's talent for rubbing fellow courtiers up the wrong way is graphically summarized:

> I was welcomed at Court with that curiosity inspired by any outsider who comes and disturbs a monotonous pattern of existence and a life based on respect for established social convention. For several months I noticed nothing that really held my attention. I was grateful for the consideration which I was shown, but at times my shyness prevented me from making the most of it, and at other times the wearying nature of all the pointless agitation I saw around me made me prefer being alone to the bland diversions I was invited to take part in. Although I had no feelings of hatred towards anyone, few people aroused any interest in me at all. But people are hurt by indifference, and attribute it to malevolence or conceit, not wishing to believe that it is entirely natural to be bored by their company. Sometimes I tried to conceal my boredom, but when I took refuge in total silence, this was attributed to my disdain for others. At other times, tired of saying nothing, I took the liberty of making witty observations and, letting myself get carried away by my sense of humour, I went much too far. In one day I revealed all the absurdities I had observed during a whole month. Those who listened to my sudden and involuntary revelations did not thank me for what I said. . . . Because of this I acquired a reputation for facetiousness, mockery, cruelty. The sharpness of my tongue was seen as proof that my heart was full of hatred, and my witticisms were taken as attacks on everything that was worthy of respect. . . . Thus there was a vague sense of unease about my character among the small group of people around me. They could not give a precise example of any serious misdeed on my part; they could not even deny that some of my actions appeared to stem from generosity or loyalty. But they said I was a man 'without morals', a 'thoroughly unreliable' individual, two descriptions which had the advantage of allowing them to insinuate things which they in fact knew nothing about, and to lead others to make assumptions based only on that ignorance.[7]

Isolated, worried about his health and the way his father's court case was developing in Holland, sinking into ever deeper depression, Constant was thrown an unexpected lifeline by fate in the person of Jakob Mauvillon (1743–94), whom he probably met at the Große Klub zu Braunschweig of which they were both members (Constant joined on 7 April 1788).[8] Mauvillon is one of those writers who have a tenuous existence on the margins of literary history, and he is remembered if at all for having collaborated with Count Mirabeau in the writing of a study of the Prussian monarchy under Frederick the Great which appeared in seven volumes in London in 1788. It was only one of a considerable number of works which Mauvillon had published in the previous twenty years and more, works ranging widely from literary criticism and the defence of German language and culture to a study of the role of gunpowder in modern warfare. Mauvillon's father was French and he himself was bilingual in French and German. His army background had made him an expert on military strategy, which he taught at the Collegium Carolinum in Brunswick, but he also translated into German works on political economy by French writers, was a convinced Physiocrat – a believer in economic *laissez-faire*, a *démocrate* with strongly anti-monarchist views and a freemason, which in a German context at this period went with a staunchly libertarian outlook. So Mauvillon had a similar catholicity of interests to John Wilde or James Mackintosh in Edinburgh, men whom it is clear the young Constant regarded as models to be emulated. But what was this extraordinary polymath like as a man?

It is tragic that not one single letter has survived from the correspondence of men who were in such close accord in their enthusiasms and political allegiances. What we have are a number of testimonies from Constant to the importance of Mauvillon's influence on his development. When Mauvillon died in 1794 Constant wrote to his aunt Madame de Nassau:

> I have lost someone in Brunswick whose death changes absolutely my feelings about living there. This man of letters possessed all the qualities that suited me. He was a man who, during five years of boredom and depression, consoled, supported and encouraged me, a man without whom, in a word, I would have died or become as stupid as those around me. A friend of liberty and enlightenment, this man's high moral stance on ethics, politics and religion corresponded exactly with my own in every detail. . . . Who can give me back that intimacy, that complete conformity on matters of principle, that immediate mutual understanding over our ideas, which coincided, reinforcing and complementing one another? I always left my friend's house feeling more knowledgeable, more lively and more active than when I went in. If I have retained any love for literature, for truth, or for the research which is my only consolation, then it is to him that I owe it. He is dead, and so many dolts are alive! And that mind which was so brilliant and so powerful, that heart which was courageous and free, and that capacity for sustained hard work and patient reasoning, all of that is gone! . . . It is the first time death has robbed me of someone who was really dear to me.

(Letter of 31 January 1794[9])

On 17 March 1805 Constant was to note in his *Journaux intimes* that

111

eleven years later he had still not got over Mauvillon's death,[10] and when he wrote to Mauvillon's eldest son on 18 January 1817 he told him: 'I will never forget my close friendship with your father, whose memory is linked to my earliest literary and philosophical thoughts'.[11] The first meeting of Constant and Mauvillon doubtless took place at the Große Klub, though Mauvillon had a low opinion of the place: he had written to a friend in 1785,

> what you will find unbelievable is that this club which has more than 150 members, included all the intelligent and learned men in Brunswick, offers gambling as the only amusement. The only people who meet there are usually those who want to gamble. Fortunately I quite like gambling, so that's some consolation for me.[12]

As well as their taste for gambling, both men discovered that they had in common a dislike for Brunswick, which Mauvillon found more ugly than Kassel, for example, calling it 'a large ugly town on a completely flat plain', and although its Court was welcoming to foreigners, the aristocracy he found 'extremely arrogant'.[13] What they cannot have failed to notice immediately was each other's forthright manner and plain-speaking. Mauvillon was a firebrand, detested for his liberal views by some at Court, and in a sense already as marginalized as Constant was soon to find himself to be. There were unsuspected links between them: Constant had sat next to Mauvillon's friend Mirabeau at a dinner in Paris the year before,[14] and in 1791 Mauvillon was to write admiringly about John Gillies as being 'one of the greatest experts on Greek antiquity'[15] – Constant had translated and published a short section of Gillies's *History of Ancient Greece* in 1787, and it is likely that Mauvillon already shared Constant's admiration for Gillies and a fascination for his subject. As with John Wilde, and as with Isabelle de Charrière, a deep understanding quickly grew between them, though because of the tantalizingly fragmentary nature of the extant evidence it is difficult to fill in much detail about their friendship. We can surmise that, given the twenty-four years difference in their ages, Mauvillon was an ideal father-figure for Constant, just as Isabelle de Charrière had been a form of surrogate mother. What recent research seems to have established with some certainty is that Constant's political radicalism was reinforced by Mauvillon, and that Constant's growing interest in the history of religion was also encouraged by him. In March 1788 Constant wrote to Isabelle de Charrière:

> What I am writing will be a history of the gradual growth of Greek civilisation . . . and a comparison of the customs and beliefs of the Greeks with those of the Celts, the Germans, the Scots, the Scandinavians etc. . . . I will send you half folio sheets in small handwriting

of my Greeks as they stand at the moment; when I've got a little further I shall ask you for sterner criticism of them.[16]

This study of Greek polytheism was to grow through many transformations and through several decades into Constant's books on Roman polytheism and on religious belief in general published during the 1820s and posthumously.

One commentator, Marcus Fontius, has observed that Constant and Mauvillon must have made a strange pair, rather like Don Quixote and Sancho Panza, the one tall and full of nervous excitement and agitation, the other short, fat and possessed of a calm, unshakeable self-assurance. Mauvillon was undoubtedly a steadying influence on Constant, and cheered him up when his spirits were low. Constant was shortly to be in need of all the consolation he could find. In Holland his father was sliding into an ever deeper morass of legal difficulties which Constant attributed to the malevolence of 'the Bears, our despots', the Bernese aristocracy whom both father and son hated for their oppression of the people of the Pays de Vaud. Juste's regiment, the *Régiment de May* (so called after Friedrich May, its colonel proprietor), was controlled from Berne and dominated by German-Swiss officers who had a grudge against him. In an affair that would soon bring together the complexity of Jarndyce *versus* Jarndyce and the menace of a Kafka story – and which has been ably summarized recently by C. P. Courtney[17] – Juste now found himself accused of misconduct on the evidence of condemned mutineers, his career and entire fortune threatened. A conspiracy on the part of his junior officers led to his being accused of having been responsible for the Amsterdam mutiny in the first place; they now refused to serve under Juste any longer. Juste requested that the *Conseil de Guerre national suisse et grison*, a high-level military court be convened so that he could clear his name. It met in Amsterdam between June and August 1788, and from the names of its judges and its first actions Juste rightly concluded that it was likely to make rulings against him and in favour of his junior officers. In fact the devastating outcome was that *thirteen* sentences were passed not against the officers but against Juste, including six months suspension and the requirement that he pay the legal costs. Juste was ever a fighter – one of the more admirable qualities which he passed on to his son – and knew that he had right on his side. But he was crushed by the weight of injustice and he fled from Amsterdam in panic in mid-August. For a while the Constant family feared he might have taken his own life, but he turned up a month later in Lausanne, perhaps having suffered some form of breakdown. Appearances were not in Juste's favour: his flight seemed an admission of guilt, and he could in any case now be charged with desertion. It was at this point that all the resources of the family were mobilized: Samuel and Benjamin wrote to the Prince of Orange on 19 September

1788 on Juste's behalf,[18] and during that autumn Benjamin asked the Duke of Brunswick to intervene with the Prince of Orange. (The Duke was sympathetic and urged Juste to come and settle in Brunswick.) [19] Benjamin wrote a memoir of the whole affair, but privately hoped that a settlement could be reached. Juste, whose argumentative nature made him a natural litigant, had other ideas and was determined to appeal. When Juste's petition was presented in September 1789, his son was in The Hague to support him.

By that time Constant had a wife and had already been married for four months. During his first lonely and unhappy months in Brunswick he had met a lady-in-waiting to the Duchess, Wilhelmine Luise Johanne von Cramm (1758–1823), known as 'Minna'. The daughter of a former minister at the ducal Court, Carl Gottfried Rudolph von Cramm (d. 1766), Minna came from a good family and was considered the favourite of the Duke's wife. If there is any historical truth in the partly fictional *Cécile's* account of the relationship, Constant married Minna 'out of weakness',[20] and, having done so, loved her out of kindness rather than through feeling any real attraction towards her. What is certainly true, as *Cécile* also states, is that they were completely incompatible in character. On 23 June 1794, surveying the ruins of his son's marriage, Juste wrote to him:

> Always remember who arranged your marriage, remember Deluc [i.e. the Duke] adopted you as one of his children, that he wrote to me in order to remove any obstacles there might be and that if he had not intervened, it is possible that you would not be in the situation in which you find yourself now. It is therefore up to him to remedy all the unhappiness caused by a marriage he wished for and which he arranged.[21]

Constant appears to have entered into marriage almost like a somnambulist. His uncle Samuel wrote to his daughters on 14 October 1788, months before the ceremony took place:

> [Benjamin] does not care about the marriage in question. He is not in love. But the Duke and Duchess wish to see the marriage take place, so he looks on it as a guarantee that his future, his finances and his setting up home will be taken care of.[22]

One of the more curious traits in Constant's character, perhaps linked to early insecurity, was to see marriage, virtually any marriage, as a solution to his problems, as with Jenny Pourrat or later with Amélie Fabri. This one offered not only financial security but also a respectable position in Brunswick society, both with the backing of the Duke and Duchess. Any realistic assessment of whether it would make either partner happy seems to have been almost immaterial.

1 The High Street, Edinburgh in about 1780, by David Allan (1744–96) (National Galleries of Scotland, Department of Prints and Drawings)

2 Benjamin Constant aged about 20, miniature on ivory, artist unknown
(photographic collection, Bibliothèque publique et universitaire, Neuchâtel)

3 Sir James Mackintosh, engraving from Mackintosh's *Memoirs* (1836) after a portrait by Sir Thomas Lawrence (1769–1830)

4 Isabelle de Charrière in 1777, portrait in oils by the Danish artist Jens Juel (1745–1802) (photographic collection, Bibliothèque publique et universitaire, Neuchâtel)

5 Benjamin Constant as a young man, anonymous drawing (photographic collection, Bibliothèque publique et universitaire, Neuchâtel)

6 'Benjamin Constant en 1792', after a silhouette by Marianne Moula (1760–1826) (photographic collection, Bibliothèque publique et universitaire, Neuchâtel)

7 and 8 Ludwig Ferdinand Huber (1764–1804) and his wife Therese Forster-Huber, *née* Heyne (1764–1829), miniatures, artist unknown (photographic collection, Bibliothèque publique et universitaire, Neuchâtel)

10 Benjamin Constant in his thirties, miniature by Firmin Massot (private collection)

9 Germaine de Staël, miniature made by Firmin Massot probably in the spring of 1812 (private collection)

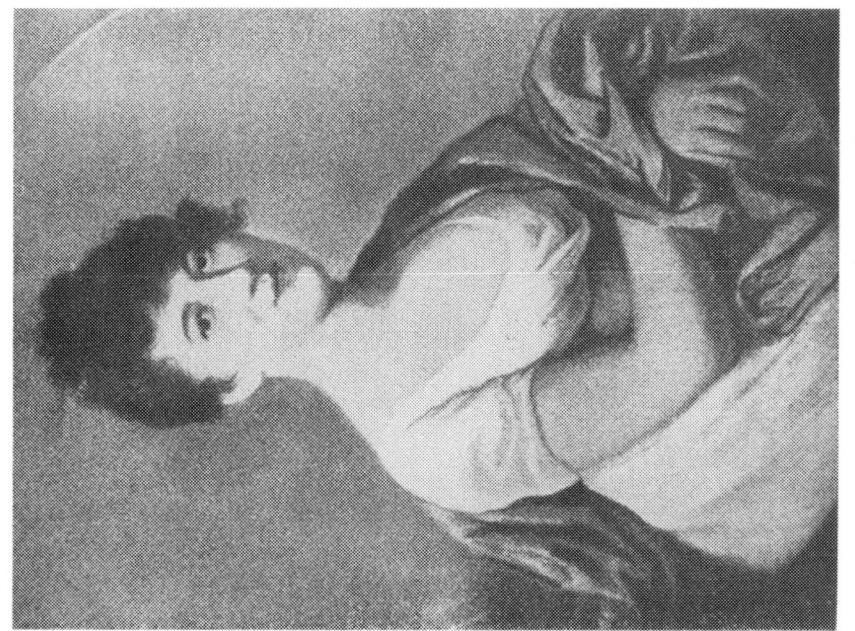

12 Charlotte von Hardenberg (portrait reproduced by courtesy of Constable & Company Ltd)

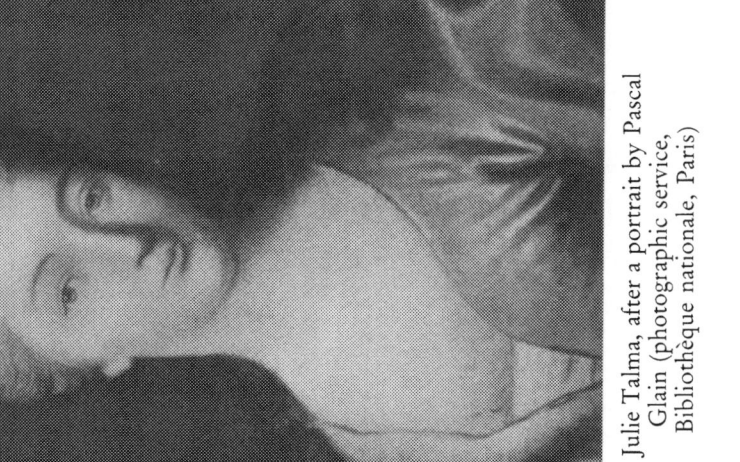

11 Julie Talma, after a portrait by Pascal Glain (photographic service, Bibliothèque nationale, Paris)

13 View of Göttingen in 1791, after a drawing by Heinrich Wilhelm Grape (Städtisches Museum, Göttingen)

14 Portrait in oils of Benjamin Constant dating from 1815 or later, artist unknown (Musée Carnavalet, Paris). Cliché photothèque des musées de la Ville de Paris, © by SPADEM 1992.

15 Engraved portrait of Benjamin Constant from *Discours de M. Benjamin Constant à la Chambre des Députés* (volume II, 1828)

16 Portrait in oils of Benjamin Constant, probably in 1830, signed 'Hercule de Roche' (Musée Carnavalet, Paris). Cliché photothèque des musées de la Ville de Paris, © by SPADEM 1992.

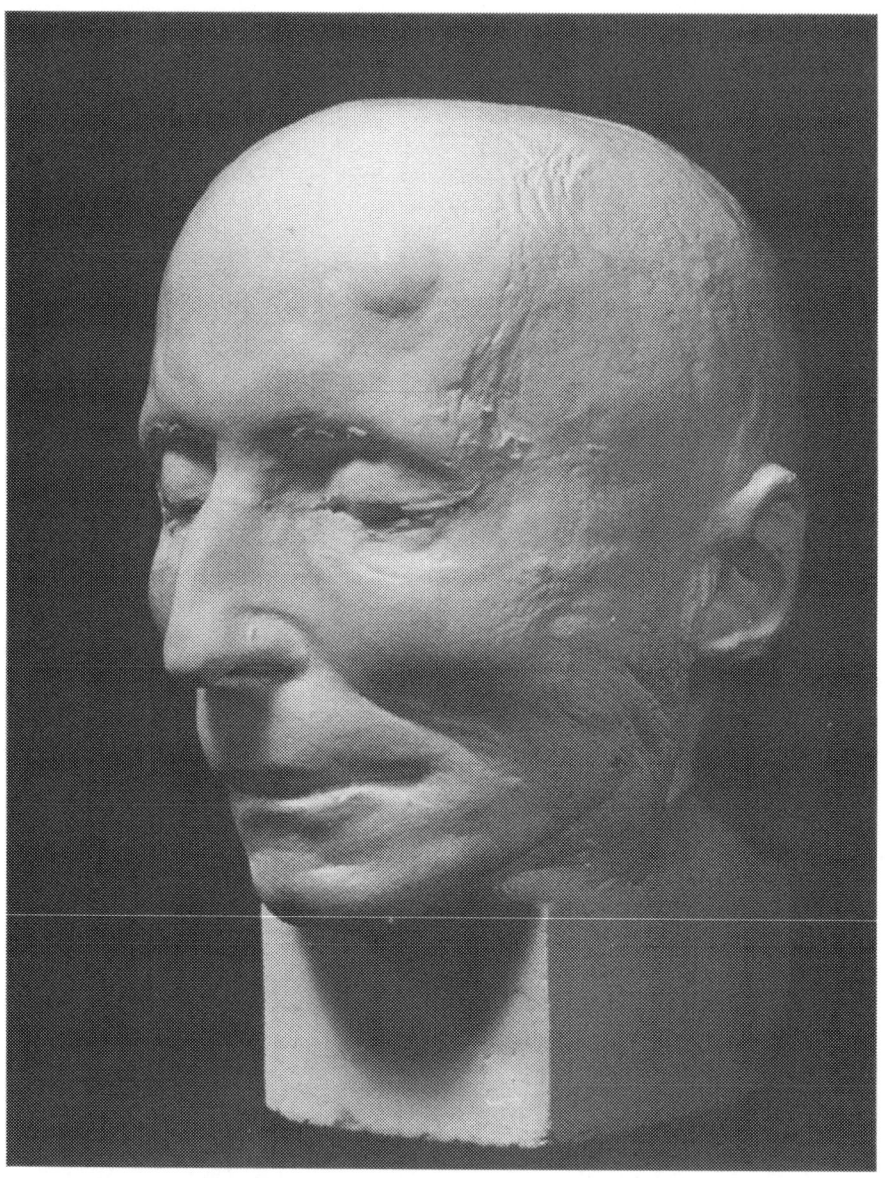

17, 18 and 19 Three views of the death mask of Benjamin Constant made by the
sculptor Gois and recently rediscovered by Kurt Kloocke in the anthropological
collection of the Musée de l'Homme, Paris

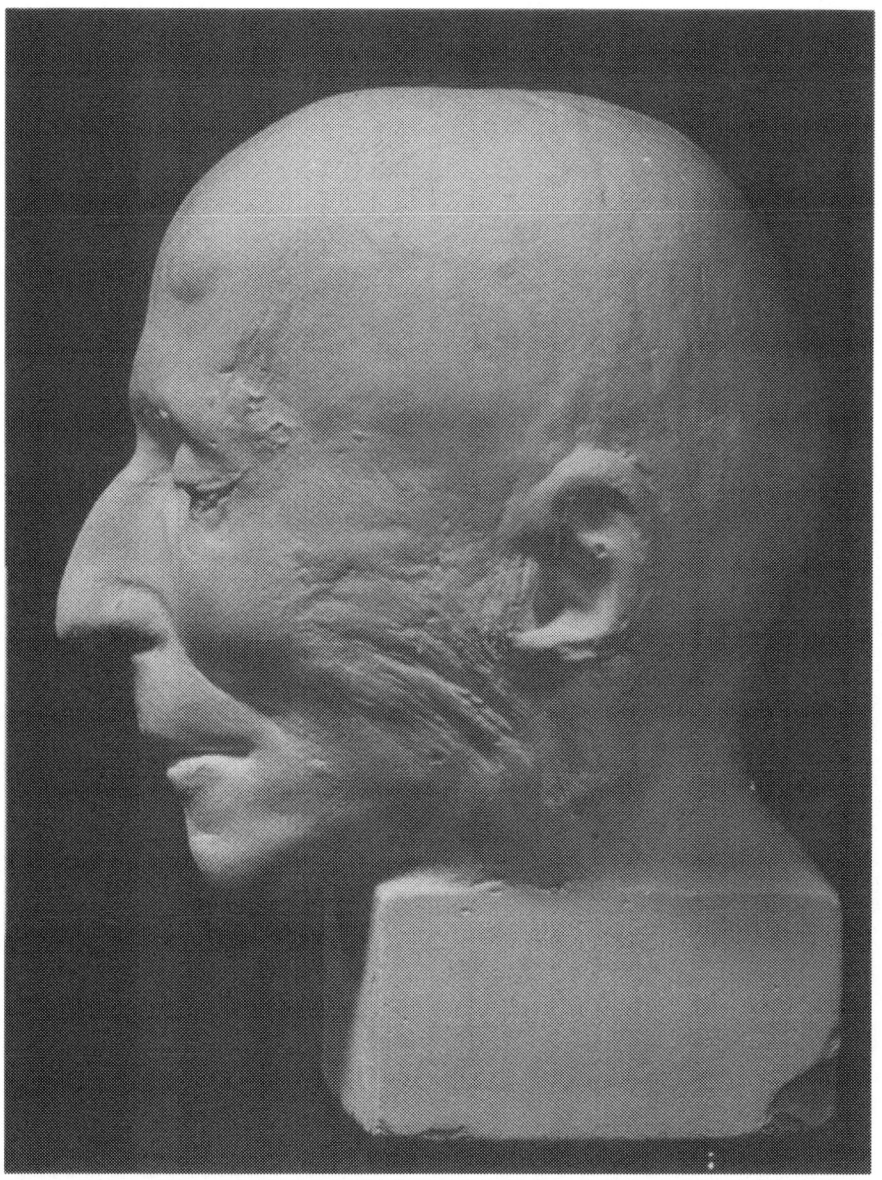

18

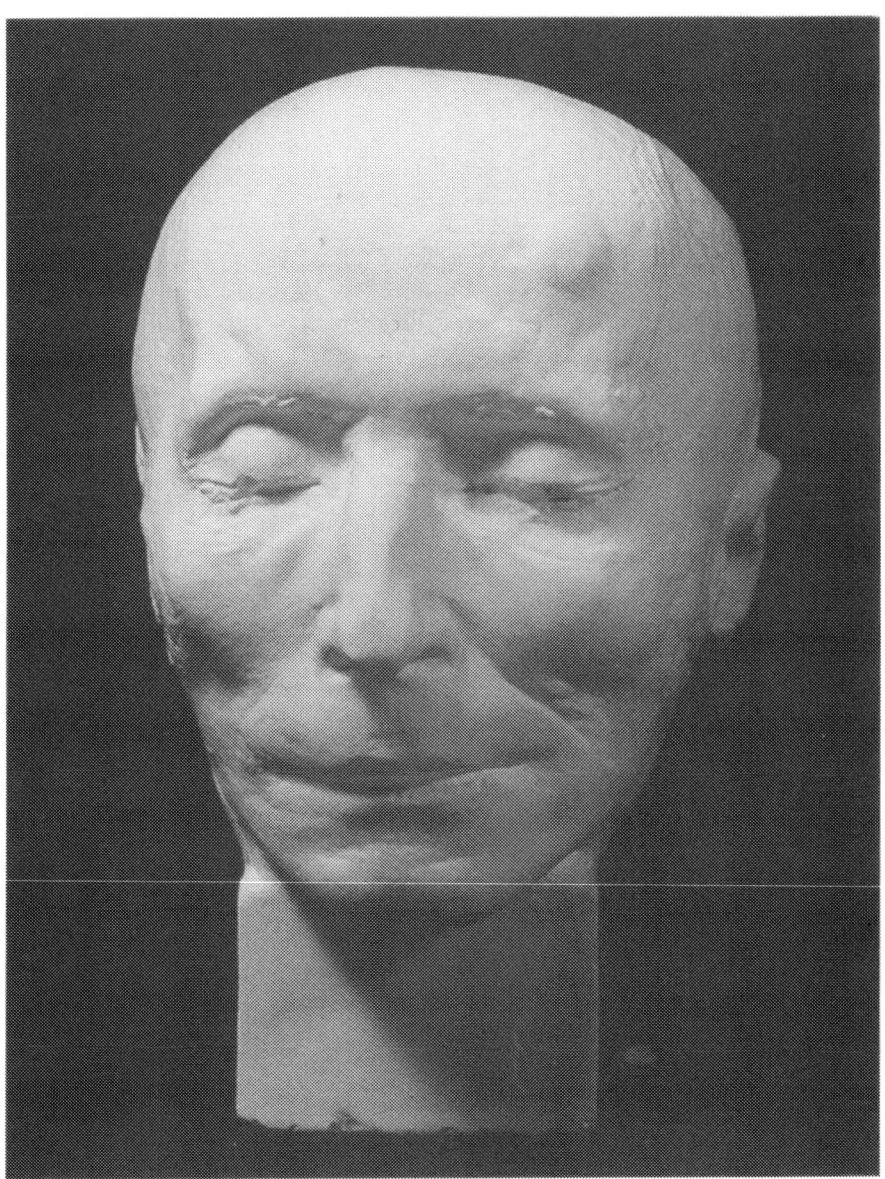

Minna must soon have realized her mistake, seeing Constant's brooding concentration, his increasing passion for solitary study in preparing his work on religion and his unimpaired ability to lash out verbally when provoked – and often, at this period, when not. Constant likewise came to rue the day he met her – according to one account he saw her weeping, asked what was the matter and took pity on her when she said no one loved her.[23] Minna was nine years older than him, was not beautiful – her face was pock-marked, her eyes were red and she was very thin[24] – and belonged to a Court, that of the Duke's wife, which one contemporary commentator said was peopled with 'vermin'.[25] From her early teens she had been at Court, its gossip and intrigue were her whole life; she shared none of Constant's intellectual interests, and had a naturally domineering manner. Almost the only thing she appears to have had in common with her husband was a love of animals, of which she was to keep a very considerable number in their home. Constant was to write bitterly in his *Journaux intimes* on 18 July 1804:

> I ... married her without much thought, she had no money, she was ugly and was two [in fact nine] years older than me. I was caught in the net like a fool. If I had been 30 instead of 21, I would have been able to order her about because she was as weak and timid as she was violent and capricious in her emotions. But I was told what to do by her and those around her from the very beginning. How I suffered![26]

The marriage did not even commence under the best auspices. When the couple's relationship had first begun in September 1788, Constant's father had not yet reappeared in Lausanne, having fled Amsterdam and the military court which condemned him. The shadow of events in Holland lay across their engagement and their first two years as man and wife. In September 1788 Constant left for a brief stay in Holland to sort out his father's financial affairs, which were in a bad way, and to organize his defence. News of the forthcoming marriage became officially public in Brunswick on 12 October 1788, but all of the following winter, as wedding preparations were being made, Constant's one thought was the fate of his father, even to the neglect of his official duties at Court: he wrote to his uncle Samuel on 10 February 1789, 'I no longer live other than through my father and for my father',[27] and to his aunt Anne de Nassau on 30 March 1789:

> I have caused him so much sorrow, I have been so unjust, so biased against him! The only consolation I find in such recollections is that now I am putting things right, and wish to see him spend a happy and tranquil old age as a result of my efforts.[28]

Constant's income and position at court were improved by the Duke who appointed him *Legationsrat* on 27 December 1788,[29] with the prospect of his being responsible for the whole of that part of the Duke's correspondence which was in French.[30] Nevertheless his earnings were still modest and barely sufficient to cover the expense of setting up home in Brunswick. (Despite repeated vows to abstain, he frequently found the attractions of the gaming-table too much for him.) Constant and Minna were married on 8 May 1789, and as a wedding present Juste gave his son 6,600 *livres* and the inheritance due to him from his mother's estate. It also appears that the Duke gave the couple a house and probably a sum of money.[31]

But Constant's thoughts were elsewhere: throughout the winter and spring he had worked ceaselessly, producing in collaboration with his father a stream of factual and polemical documents, the most important of which have been published – some for the first time – in C. P. Courtney's 1990 anthology, *The Affair of Colonel Juste de Constant and Related Documents (1787–1796)*. Constant's summaries of the injustices perpetrated against Juste show his mastery of Ciceronian invective, particularly in the long *Mémoire pour Juste Constant de Rebecque*, as well as his ability to sketch character and motive in just a few words: as C. P. Courtney suggests it is a very early attempt at 'the fictionalization of experience' (p. lii). There was only a brief respite from these preoccupations for Constant and Minna during their stay in Lausanne in July–August 1789. Constant took the opportunity to visit Isabelle de Charrière, but was generally in poor health and depressed. Matters were not improved by his learning that his friend J. R. Knecht, whom he had known in Berne some years before, in circumstances he alludes to enigmatically in *Ma Vie* by a reference to 'Greek love',[32] had been found guilty of pederasty and banished from Bernese territory: another victim of the 'Bears' of Berne.

With the prospect of a return to the legal battlefields of Holland in the autumn of 1789, an increasing note of acrimony entered his correspondence with Isabelle de Charrière. Isabelle knew full well the kind of man Juste was – difficult, quarrelsome and far from being an ideal father to Benjamin – and probably felt that he was not entirely without some blame for the disasters that continued to befall him. She made the mistake of intimating as much to Benjamin on occasion. His reaction was predictable and ferocious. His loyalty to the all-too-human Juste – a man whom Simone Balayé has wittily observed was 'ni juste ni constant',[33] neither fair nor unchanging in his behaviour – is touching for some and irritating for others: Madame de Charrière fell into the latter category, though she learnt to keep her counsel on the matter. She had the feelings of any clear-sighted, well-meaning observer who is frustrated and powerless to intervene in a relationship which has patently never matured, is unhealthily incomplete and unbalanced, and does neither party much good. Constant's gestures alternated between rebellion and submission, and now it was time for the latter, with unsparing efforts to prove himself worthy of Juste's love and esteem. Isabelle had seen the young man she loved and admired living his life under a dark cloud of unresolved emotions about his father and family, and had tried to liberate him, to allow him to become himself. She was to pay a high price for doing so.

Unwittingly – and unjustly on the evidence of their surviving correspondence – she became the focus of deep resentment on Constant's part. From the autumn of 1789 her advice, her jokes, her opinions became unwelcome to him, in a manner not unlike what psychiatrists would call 'negative transference', the process in the course of analysis whereby feelings deriving from an earlier phase of a patient's life are displaced and relocated in the person of the analyst, so that the analyst 'becomes' that figure from earlier life. Like the ideal analyst Isabelle took a very great interest in Constant, tried to be non-possessive about him and, in their long conversations and letters, encouraged him to talk about himself and understand himself. However, one can ask whether by a curious process of displacement, she did not come to signify someone else, whether she did not cease to be the benign friend and, as if now seen through a distorting lens, became the bad mother, the mother he had lost – or who had lost *him* – so many years before. Or indeed whether the suppressed resentments Constant felt vis-à-vis his father were not now channelled against Isabelle. Such speculation is hardly fanciful given that Constant was now entering a period of severe nervous depression during which long submerged feelings can surface in extreme, exaggerated and aggressive forms. The recurring theme in Constant's letters to Isabelle now becomes his accusation that she is full of 'défiance' towards him, that is, that she is distrustful of him, no longer open with him, as if she is forever holding something back from him.[34] A vicious circle is quickly created, familiar to those who have encountered someone going through a severe depression: the aggression coming from Constant, in this case, prevents Isabelle from expressing herself freely, for fear of antagonizing him further. To which Constant's reaction is to see this as proof that Isabelle is indeed holding back, expressing herself in imperiously laconic terms. Isabelle sees that she cannot win, the letters grow shorter and finally the correspondence dries up completely.

Minna returned to Brunswick and from September 1789 to May 1790 – the period when he stopped writing to Isabelle almost completely – Constant laboured intensively on his father's behalf, alone in Holland. His hard work won people's admiration, but, perhaps more important to Constant, it won his father's approval. Juste wrote to his brother Samuel on 2 October 1789: 'I am extremely pleased with my son. He appears to be behaving with much wisdom and prudence. People tell me he is well liked. However things turn out, his journey [to Holland] will do him no harm.'[35] In the meantime, in a fury at Isabelle whom he accused of listening to ill-informed gossip circulating about his father in Switzerland, Constant told her to burn his letters – as he had burnt hers before leaving Switzerland, he added cruelly (letter of 14 September 1789).[36] With the exception of a letter at the New Year, it was not until 11 May 1790 that Constant resumed his correspondence with Isabelle. Working on his father's behalf – and, as it was to turn out, fairly fruitlessly – he had been kept too busy to reflect on the state of his own life. Now he appeared anxious to be on good terms with Isabelle again, but on his return to Brunswick he seemed if anything to be sinking deeper into depression. On 4 June 1790 he told Isabelle, in terms that suggest he had been reading Pascal:

> I feel more than ever the nothingness of all things; how everything seems so promising and nothing lasts; how what we are capable of seems worthy of something better than where we are all destined to finish up; and how that huge discrepancy [*disproportion*] cannot but make us unhappy. In my next letter we shall laugh at the indignation of stathouders and rulers at the French Revolution, which they claim is the result of the innate sinfulness of mankind.[37]

In the same letter he added that while in The Hague he had met Ignazio Thaon di Revel (1760–1835), Minister to the King of Sardinia, a Piedmontese whose view of the universe struck a deep chord in him while in his present state of mind:

> He claims that God, that is the Being Who made us and everything around us, died before He could finish his work, that He had the finest and most grandiose plans imaginable, and His means to achieving them were enormous – indeed some of these means were already in the process of falling into place, just as one puts up scaffolding before erecting a building – but in the middle of His work He died, so that everything that is in the universe at present was created to achieve an end that no longer exists, and we in particular feel destined for something of which we can have no conception. We are like watches without dials, in which the cogs and wheels, which are endowed with intelligence, turn until they are worn out without knowing why, telling themselves constantly, 'Since I'm turning, I must be intended for some final purpose'. This notion strikes me as the wittiest and profoundest piece of madness I've heard, and far preferable to the Christian, Muslim or philosophical madnesses of the first, sixth and eighteenth centuries of our era.[38]

The events of the fateful year of 1789 had passed without making much impact on Constant, other than to give him some measure of satisfaction, and the reference above is among the earliest to an event whose repercussions were to dominate his later political career. Instead he now he occupied himself with writing an account of the failed uprising in Brabant against the Austrians, which in the event was to remain unfinished and unpublished, and planned a Refutation of Burke's *Reflections on the*

Revolution in France, a text famously hostile to what was happening in Paris. That Refutation was never written, but now in his correspondence began the disobliging spectacle of a series of Refutations of Isabelle de Charrière in which Baron Constant accused his fellow aristocrat of being lukewarm in her attitude to the French Revolution, in a manner unpleasantly close to that of a twentieth-century armchair revolutionary chiding a comrade for incorrect thinking (he continued nevertheless to owe Monsieur de Charrière money he had been glad to borrow many months previously in order to survive heavy gambling debts):

> You do not appear to me to be a republican [*démocrate*] at all. Like you I think that all we are really seeing is 'double-dealing and frenzied passions unleashed'. But I prefer the kind of double-dealing and frenzied passions that topple fortresses and get rid of titles and other stupidities of the kind, which put on an equal footing all forms of religious day-dreaming to those which would safeguard and preserve those miserable freaks begotten of the barbarous ignorance of the Jews crossed with the mindless ferocity of the Vandals. The human race is born stupid and led by rogues, that is the norm: but if I have to choose between one lot of rogues and another, I'll vote for the likes of Mirabeau and Barnave, rather than of Sartine or Breteuil.
>
> (Letter of 10 December 1790[39])

Isabelle's position is clear: she welcomed the prospect of reform in France, and indeed many of her writings had been directed towards such an end. However she deplored violence and at all times championed the rights of the individual as against the group, whether that individual happened to be an aristocrat or a commoner. She was afraid that many innocent individuals might suffer in a violent and uncontrolled social upheaval. She was, of course, right in her fears, and later Constant became the forceful advocate of a similar position, while characteristically seldom admitting he had ever been wrong. At this stage, however, he subscribed to the school of thought which would in a later era maintain that one cannot make an omelette without breaking eggs.

To be fair to Constant it has to be stressed that he was going through one of the most severely testing times of his life. His political radicalism, encouraged by the stoical and unbending Mauvillon, was winning him enemies at Court; his father's problems continued to deepen; his finances were shaky and his health had barely improved. Only Constant's marriage seemed still to be holding together, although his long absences from Brunswick would eventually undermine that as well. Small wonder that he wrote to Isabelle at the end of 1790: 'I understand neither the purpose nor the designer nor the painter nor the figures in this magic lantern in which I have the honour to feature' (24 December 1790[40]) and a month later:

119

I am not, shall never be, cannot be happy. . . . Unable to believe in the mysterious and unproven promises of a religion which is in many respects absurd, and seeing no grounds to believe in the hopes of a philosophy which consists merely in words, all I can see here on earth is a great deal of unavoidable suffering . . ., very little pleasure . . ., and at the end of it, sooner or later, nothingness.

(Letter of 21 January 1791[41])

Kurt Kloocke, in his *Benjamin Constant: une biographie intellectuelle*, argues a case for seeing a parallel between Constant's pessimism in Brunswick and the intellectual nihilism of nineteenth-century Germany, but to speak with confidence, as Kloocke does, about a 'crisis of nihilism' seems somewhat excessive as well as anachronistic.[42] References to 'le néant', nothingness, in his letters are symptomatic of serious depression, for which Constant had more than adequate justification, rather than constituting anything like the adoption of a coherent philosophical system. Indeed that depression, like occasional suicidal tendencies, might, as I have argued earlier, have had far deeper roots in Constant's infancy and childhood.

Worse was to come for Constant. On 16 July 1791 the *Conseil de Guerre national suisse* pronounced a final and irrevocable verdict against Juste who in consequence lost his position in the *Régiment de May* and had to pay ruinous legal costs. Juste was forced to sell all his property in the Pays de Vaud, and took up residence across the border in France, at Brevans, near Dole. He also sought the French nationality to which he was now entitled, taking advantage of a new law which allowed those whose ancestors had been driven into exile because of their religious beliefs to return to France: Juste's distant forbears had been Huguenot refugees. Constant immediately appealed to the Prince of Orange on Juste's behalf against the court's verdict, and spent the period from September to December 1791 seeing to the sale of his father's property in Lausanne. Yet another absence from Minna: she had declined to accompany him to Switzerland and on his return to Germany, after a journey on which he had passed through the lines of the opposing armies of revolutionary France and a counter-revolutionary alliance led by the Duke of Brunswick, Constant found a wife who seemed to have definitively changed in her feelings towards him. It is as well that he did not also know that his father was at the same time drawing up a contract of marriage with Marianne Magnin (the document exists, dated Dijon, 11 January 1792[43]); he was not to learn of their legal relationship until some years later, nor that Marianne was about to bear Juste a daughter, Louise – Constant's half-sister – the following June.[44]

Minna's coolness was directed towards a man who, despite at last being back with his wife, seemed exclusively obsessed with obtaining justice for his father. In about June 1792 it appears that she spent some time in the country away from Constant,[45] while he seems to have had his mind fully occupied elsewhere, with political developments in Paris. By September 1792, however, it had finally dawned on him that things had gone irretrievably awry between himself and Minna. On 17 September 1792 he felt moved to send the following balance sheet of his life to Isabelle de Charrière:

> I felt at 18, at 20, at 24 and I now feel again at 25 that I must, for other people's benefit as well as my own, live alone. . . . Literature and solitude, that is my real element. It remains to be seen if I shall be able to find these in a France that is in turmoil or in an obscure retreat somewhere.
>
> My financial position will soon be settled: my wife will be richer than me and I shall leave Marianne [i.e. Marianne Magnin], who already has much of my money, a little more of what remains. All I ask is to have enough to live on, to depend on no one, to be tied to no one. . . . As for my life here, it's unbearable and becomes more so every day. I waste ten hours of the day at a Court where I'm hated because they know I'm a republican [*démocrate*], because I've pointed out everybody's absurdity, which has convinced them I am *a man without principles*. I dare say I'm to blame: blasé about everything, bored with everything, bitter, self-obsessed, with the kind of sensitivity that only causes me misery, changeable to such an extent that I simply look foolish, subject to bouts of melancholia which interrupt all my plans for the future and make me behave, while they last, as if I had given up on everything; and tormented into the bargain by outside circumstances, by a father who is both loving and full of anxiety (and who is at the beck and call of a Marianne who writes me haughty letters), by a wife who is in love with a young scatterbrain – platonically, she says – and who claims still to have some affection for me . . . , how do you expect me to be a success, to be liked by anyone, to carry on living?[46]

And there it was, out in the open: Minna loved someone else, a young Russian prince, a member of the celebrated Golitsyn family – usually known in English as Galitzin – in all probability Dmitri Vladimirovich Golitsyn (1771–1844), a soldier with the counter-revolutionary forces who also appears to have had a penchant for duelling.[47] Meanwhile Juste, to whom Constant had by now sacrificed the best part of three years of his life and possibly his marriage, requested that his son give up over a third of his inheritance to Marianne Magnin:[48] it marked the beginning of many years of sometimes public financial wrangling between them during which Constant may finally have come to see Juste in a more objective light. He would eventually cease to be the periodically submissive and dominated son of recent times and reach a greater degree of maturity in this troubled area of his affective life. While still of course unaware of Marianne's new status as Juste's wife, he could see that he was being replaced in his father's affections by a woman whom he repeatedly calls a harpy or a shrew, and he told Isabelle on 1 January 1793 that he was waiting for a final answer to the reasonable offer of money he had made to Juste:

> If this reply is as I suspect it will be, if it takes the form of an order, accompanied by bitter reproaches, to make further sacrifices in favour of a harpy I'm not even related to [*harpie inconnue*], I shall make them. But then . . . I shall let this harpy replace me alongside my father. I shall pass over to her the task of ensuring his happiness which he does not want me to perform, and I shall think only about my own well-being.[49]

Constant now saw there was no future in his marriage, and during November 1792 found consolation in a sexual relationship with an actress named Caroline about whom he was later to express himself in uncharacteristically lyrical terms to Isabelle de Charrière:[50] she gave him the kind of intense and heady emotional experience that he had not known in years, comparable perhaps with what he had found with Madame Johannot or would later rediscover with Anna Lindsay. Whether Constant's infidelity preceded that of Minna with Prince Golitsyn is unclear, although he expressed no guilt to Isabelle de Charrière about the liaison. What seems certain is that Minna and her friends were making life as difficult as possible for Constant even in his own home. In a vivid manuscript account of the collapse of his marriage known as the *Narré*, and written in the space of a couple of hours on 25 March 1793 with the aim of offering an objective record of what had happened, he stated:

> Thus my life was spent, in scene after scene [with Minna], not knowing how to end her relationship [with Golitsyn] which I had been foolish enough not to nip in the bud, a stranger in my own home, misjudged by those around me, always too weak to cause a public stir, telling myself it was too late and trying to keep my mind off my painful situation. It was precisely that reluctance to dwell on my predicament that came to be misrepresented by others as culpable tolerance and treachery towards my wife.[51]

Constant had lately learnt much about the art of forensic self-defence from the many documents he had written for and with his father, and it is not without significance that the three works of fiction or fictionalized autobiography for which he is best known today, *Adolphe*, *Cécile* and *Ma Vie* (*Le Cahier rouge*), involve in varying degrees self-justification and the indictment of others. The *Narré* – which is careful to mention nothing about Constant's own dalliance with the actress Caroline – offers a gripping picture of the intrigue and perfidy at the Court of Brunswick of which he emerges as the feckless but generally innocent victim. From certain parallels of detail and verbal similarities it appears likely that the *Narré* served as a springboard when Constant later came to write *Cécile*, which gives a fictionalized account of the same events in its first section or *époque*.

Constant was reaching a watershed: his father was all but ruined and living in relatively straitened circumstances under the thumb of the detested Marianne; his own marital problems forced him to envisage living alone and away from Brunswick, where in any case his position had become acutely uncomfortable, a would-be Jacobin in the service of the military leader of the counter-revolutionary armies; in France the Revolution had degenerated into the bloodbath of Robespierre's Terror, which Constant nevertheless felt compelled to defend in his letters to an Isabelle de Charrière whom he now judged to be a reactionary. Only Jakob Mauvillon, stolid and steadfast, offered any solace, and we gain a rare glimpse of Mauvillon's feelings in an unpublished and undated letter he sent to the librarian of the famous Herzog August Bibliothek in nearby Wolfenbüttel, Ernst Theodor Langer (1743–1820), in the period December 1792–January 1793. Langer had made the mistake, it would seem, of expressing views about France that were hostile to the Revolution, to which Mauvillon retorted:

> I share your wishes for a cessation to the barbarity, as long as you think like me that the real barbarians are those who put obstacles in the way of press freedom, and hinder research in theology, philosophy and politics; in short, those who issue decrees about censorship, edicts about religion and who forbid people to read or to think.[52]

In his typically forthright way Mauvillon expresses a radical libertarianism that centres on freedom of the press and of expression, one of the linchpins of Constant's own later political doctrine: clearly Constant's views were being shaped through the stimulus of discussions with his friend.

To the consolations of philosophy with Mauvillon during these last months in Brunswick was now added a new friendship, and one which would ultimately prove to be the greatest consolation of his life. On 11 January 1793, according to *Cécile*, Constant met Charlotte von Marenholtz, the wife of Baron Wilhelm Christian Albrecht von Marenholtz (1752–1808)[53]. The daughter of Hans Ernst von Hardenberg and Eleonore *née* von Wangenheim, she had been christened Georgine Charlotte Auguste (in later life she signed herself Charlotte Georgine Auguste, Countess von Hardenberg) and belonged to a Hanoverian family with very strong links with the English royal house – indeed she had been born in London on 29 March 1769. In 1788 Charlotte had married Baron von Marenholtz, a man sixteen and a half years older than her, and had borne him a son, Wilhelm Ernst August Christian, in January 1789. Like Constant she spoke French, German and English, was well read in the corresponding literatures, and yet despite her cosmopolitan background Charlotte was German to her fingertips.[54] Sir Harold Nicolson speaks in his biography of Constant of 'the general atmosphere of pink ribbons and *Schwärmerei*' that surrounded her.[55] Nevertheless Constant was charmed by their first meeting to the extent of writing the same evening to declare his love to her.

Was he serious? Only partly so, seems to be the likely answer: he was acting out a role in all probability, and waiting to see what would happen, as with Mrs Trevor or Jenny Pourrat, or like Adolphe with Ellénore: a cruel amusement but also a risky one, since he might end up 'feeling the emotions he at first only feigned', again like Adolphe. For Charlotte was not to be underestimated. She did not have the intellect of an Isabelle de Charrière, and if her speech was anything like her written style, judging by the surviving letters to Constant, it can have held few of the sophisticated pleasures of listening to Belle, whose crisp ironic wit and verbal inventiveness matched Constant's own: indeed Constant was to mock Charlotte's style mercilessly in his letters to Colombier. Charlotte could be exceedingly slow on the uptake, naive and easily gulled, as a particularly heartless practical joke which Constant played on her was soon to show.[56] Her tastes were pre-Romantic and tended towards the sentimental. But Charlotte also had considerable personal warmth; she was capable of heroic unselfishness and quiet determination; she had staying power, remaining calm, patient and resilient in adversity – qualities that were to be tested to the limit in the later years of her relationship with Constant.

Constant's letters to Charlotte from this period have been lost or destroyed. Perhaps it is as well for him, since they would doubtless have presented a fairly shocking contrast with what he was writing to Isabelle de Charrière at the same time about the woman he nicknamed 'Le Grand Cachet' on account of the enormous seal on Charlotte's letters. A number of mostly undated letters in French from Charlotte to Constant have survived from the first half of 1793: these love letters are written in an often exclamatory, sometimes rather tedious reach-me-down style, full of protestations and reproaches, cloyingly sentimental too with occasional adolescent simpering and clumsy coquetry. Constant later recognized what literary critics tend to overlook: that a written style that looks stale and affected may nevertheless be the expression of genuine feelings:

> What will you gain, Sir, by destroying the illusion which gives charm to my life? If I am unhappy, will you be any the happier? Am I loved? Why do you fill me with fear? If I am forced to doubt this man, I shall never trust another. No, I am sure of his heart. With such grace it could never prove false to me![57]

The Charlotte who could write these lines – and worse – to Constant in 1793 meant what she said: Constant might snigger, but her sincerity could not be doubted. It may be that he had never met anybody quite like her before. She had a German seriousness and simplicity which, as time went by, seemed to offer a way out of the very French maze of irony and facetiousness he chafed against being trapped in. One might go as far as saying that Constant's attraction to Charlotte offers a valuable insight into his contradictory nature. The real Constant was *both* the man who was drawn to the gentle and uncomplicated Charlotte *and* the disabused salon wit whose paradoxes and asperity proclaimed his unwillingness ever to take anything or anyone at face value. This was the problem that dogged him all his life: how to achieve happiness and success when the opposing poles of his character pulled him violently and unceasingly towards irreconcilable positions. For he already knew there were several potential Benjamin Constants within him: Constant the historical scholar, happy to work for days on end alone in a German library; Constant the sociable gambler and rake; Constant the naturally gifted letter-writer whose talent for amused self-observation might eventually be channelled into autobiography and fiction. Other as yet unsuspected selves would come to light in the future, not least those of the political theorist and the parliamentarian.

For the moment it was the calm and the *douceur* of Charlotte which Constant needed most urgently after the battering he had taken lately from Minna and her allies. Charlotte's marriage to Baron von Marenholtz, who was considerably older than her, had brought neither partner much happiness: Constant's semi-autobiographical *Cécile* suggests that it had only been arranged in the first place because Charlotte's scheming sister, Amalie Magdalene Charlotte von Staffhorst, wished to facilitate the pursuit of her long-standing affair with the Baron by having him marry into the family, although there is no historical evidence of such a liaison. At first the Baron was content to let his wife see Constant every day. Rather like Adolphe and Ellénore, the couple would discuss literature and politics, read Isabelle de Charrière's *Caliste* or the news in *Le Moniteur*, but by the middle of February 1793 the Baron became jealous and Constant and Charlotte were able to see each other only at the theatre or when out walking. Contrary to Sir Harold Nicolson's assumption, it seems that, unusually for Constant, the friendship did not at this stage become a sexual liaison, if we are to believe a later letter to Isabelle de Charrière in which he refers to his 'chaste *amours*' with Charlotte.[58]

The contentment Constant found in this undemanding relationship threw into relief his misery with his wife. According to the *Narré*, events came to a head with Minna at the end of March: she was now being encouraged in her infidelity with Prince Golitsyn by the Countess Anna Ernestine von der Schulenberg. After angry scenes with Constant, Minna

agreed to an eventual separation on 20 March 1793 so that she would not
be dishonoured and would be able to continue her 'petty existence in a
small town', as Constant would later write,[59] while he would regain his
freedom. On about 23 March, according to the *Narré*, Constant discovered
a letter from Golitsyn to Minna referring to the possibility of her becoming
pregnant by him – in *Cécile* the letter is found torn up in an old piano
Constant's father had given him.[60] He now knew for certain that he had
been lied to. On 24 March he went to confront her with the evidence,
and the day after composed the *Narré*. Henceforth there was a *de facto*
separation which soon became common knowledge at Court. Many
blamed Constant for his laxness in allowing Minna's affair with the young
Russian to develop, and the Duchess stood by her lady-in-waiting: once
again it became clear that in Brunswick Constant was almost without
friends – almost, because the Duke and his Minister of Finance Jean-
Baptiste Féronce de Rotencreutz did not abandon him, although they
could see he could have conducted matters very much better. Féronce
could nevertheless not resist asking Ernst Theodor Langer, librarian in
Wolfenbüttel, in a letter dated 12 April 1793: 'Has the story of poor
Constant reached you yet? We have another cuckold and one more whore
in our capital.'[61]

The final blow was to come. Charlotte's father believed that there was
a risk of scandal from his daughter's friendship with a man whose marriage
to Minna was ending so publicly and in such bitter mutual recrimination.
He insisted that for the time being at least Charlotte stop meeting Constant. On 31 March 1793 Constant wrote to Isabelle to tell her that both
women were now lost to him:

> All my ties are now broken, both those that brought me misery and
> those which consoled me. All of them! What a strange weakness in
> me: for a year I have been longing for this moment, I couldn't wait
> to be completely independent, but now it's come I'm shuddering,
> I'm horror-stricken by my solitude, I'm terrified of having no one
> to care for, just as I once complained so much at being attached to
> someone. . . . After I have spent another two or three months at
> Court just to show I have not been dismissed, I shall leave here. . . .
> Please rent quite a large apartment in Colombier for me, where I
> can have a bedroom, a study and library for my books which I shall
> send for and which . . . may comprise 1,500 volumes.[62]

As so often at times of crisis in his life, Constant was planning to return
to a solitary and scholarly existence. But it was not yet to be. Charlotte
was determined not to relinquish all hope of a future together which she
had envisaged after her own separation from Baron von Marenholtz, and
she maintained contact with Constant during April and May 1793. Constant met Charlotte's father in April, and began to worry that she would

have him married again in no time. He left for Driburg, a small spa town not far from Kassel. In fact Charlotte's father was opposed to the idea of her remarrying for some years yet, as Charlotte told Constant during a brief meeting which she arranged with him in Kassel on around 11 May 1793. She intended to visit him again a fortnight later in Driburg, but by then Constant had returned to Lausanne. Their correspondence continued sporadically through 1793, with Charlotte reiterating how much she loved him and voicing her hopes that at some point in the future they could be together again. Constant soon came to consider that he had had a very lucky escape.

The relationship with Charlotte had become burdensome. For the time being Constant preferred to be free, though he still had considerable affection for 'my Charlotte', as he described her to Isabelle: her naivety often irritated him, but he had felt settled and secure enough with her to begin 'a history of his life' at her home in Brunswick early in 1793, possibly an early draft of *Ma Vie*, as his cousin Victor was to report to Rosalie on 29 October 1809.[63] Constant's flagging feelings for her had been galvanized back into life by Charlotte's father's veto, but not sufficiently for him to make any irrevocable move to reclaim her. Nevertheless, he was to recall eleven years later in his *Journaux intimes*:

> I passed through Schmalkalden on my journey from Göttingen to Switzerland, very much in love with Madame de Marenholtz, now Madame Du Tertre. I had fallen in love with her again in the strangest way. I was extremely tired of her when she wanted to marry me, but as soon as she started to tell me that at her father's request she wanted to postpone our wedding, I felt myself once more in the grip of an overpowering passion. Was it wounded pride? I don't honestly think so. But the person who is escaping from you necessarily looks quite different from the person who is pursuing you. You would have something very wrong with your mind if you saw them in the same light.[64]

Yet by the autumn of 1793 he could tell Isabelle categorically that he no longer loved Charlotte (letter of 8 October 1793).[65]

It was a time for taking stock, and Constant told Isabelle de Charrière on 17 May 1793:

> Everything around me lies in darkness, but I must tell you so that you don't feel too sorry for me that the horizon is slowly brightening and I await the most glorious dawn I've yet seen. But I can't bring myself to tell you about a future that is as yet uncertain, to describe desirable things which as yet I only possess in my imagination, or ills which may well not befall me. You may be sure that one way or another I shall have nothing to reproach myself for; that a long

and miserable experience has convinced me that only doing good results in one's well-being, and that to stray from that path produces pain; that I am struggling with all my strength against that indifference for both vice and virtue which resulted from my strange upbringing and even stranger life, and which has caused me so much sorrow. Since it runs against the grain of my character, I shall easily overcome it. I am tired of being self-centred, of mocking my real feelings, of persuading myself that I no longer love goodness or hate evil. And in fact my affecting to be worldly wise, deep, machiavellian or listless has not made me any the happier. Devil take my pride at being world-weary – I am now going to open my heart to new feelings of every kind, I want to feel trust, belief, enthusiasm once again, I want my premature old age which has turned everything around me a uniform grey to give way to a rediscovered youth which will put the beauty back into my life and make me happy once again.[66]

How the 'dawn' and 'rediscovered youth' Constant describes here in uncharacteristically lyrical vein were to come about he cannot have known. But he was right in his intuition that he was intended for better and greater things than he had so far been capable of. His exhausted contempt for Court life had exaggerated his tendency to mordant cynicism; his recent misery with Minna made him wary of any firm commitments; his growing passion for political debate needed an outlet. He found temporary relief at Colombier where he spent three weeks in July 1793 in an apartment which Isabelle had found for him. Their friendship blossomed once again and their political differences seemed less acute now that they were in daily discussion. In August Constant found a publisher for her *Lettres trouvées dans des porte-feuilles d'émigrés* in Lausanne. This epistolary novel about young men and women separated by the revolutionary wars and by opposing political allegiances was a typically honest and fair response by Isabelle de Charrière to the sufferings of individuals caught up in the current turmoil. Constant found nothing to object to in it: quite the reverse, since he corrected the proofs and appears to have collaborated in writing a manuscript continuation.[67]

During the several visits to Colombier which Constant made that summer to escape from the vexations of his relatives and from the tedium of Lausanne he met several of Isabelle's new circle of acquaintances, including *Pierre*-Louis de Malarmey de Roussillon (1770–1802), a likeable young French aristocrat and *émigré* whom Isabelle had befriended, and Ludwig Ferdinand Huber (1764–1804) and his future wife Therese Forster (1764–1829), daughter of the Göttingen professor Christian Gottlob Heyne (1729–1812). Therese Forster's first husband, Georg Forster (1764–94), from whom she was separated, had been one of the revolutionary leaders in Mainz, and she was shortly to acquire a modest reputation herself in Germany as a novelist; Huber was a prolific writer and journalist who would translate several of Isabelle de Charrière's works into German.[68] The couple lived in exile at Bôle near Colombier, and their sympathy with the revolutionary cause immediately put them in Constant's good books. When Isabelle had the temerity to mention Huber's sympathies to Constant, she received a sharp reminder that, notwithstanding the Terror currently raging in Paris, he was still backing the Revolution:

> And what if Monsieur Huber were a Jacobin, what would be the harm in that? Do you believe in the power of propaganda too, then? And what propaganda is he spreading in Colombier? I'm really cross to see you filled with such groundless fears. In Germany we were treated to denunciations, warnings and unmaskings of that kind. The only genuine thing about them was the malevolence of their perpetrators and the stupidity of those who believed them.
>
> (Letter of 30 August 1793[69])

For good measure he went on to deplore the tide of French *émigrés* now flooding into Switzerland. Constant defended Huber as if he were another Mauvillon, and was shortly to begin writing once again in November 1793 on a political theme, composing an imaginary *Dialogue* between Louis XVI and the revolutionary leaders Brissot and Marat, although the work was never finished. (He had recently taken up the threads of his work on religion as well.) Meanwhile he continued to be dogged by his father's legal debacle, and on 13 August 1793 began a lawsuit against a certain Henri Vrindt, Clerk of the Court working for the *Conseil de Guerre* who had been allocated expenses against Juste:[70] the affair, of an extraordinary and nightmarish complexity, was to drag on into 1795.

Constant the enemy of superstition and despotism found refuge once again from his troubles in the company of Isabelle, the friend he nonetheless continued to suspect of being a reactionary. He stayed in Colombier for four months, with some absences, from 2 December 1793 to 5 April 1794. He had at least had the good grace to say to her on 11 November 1793, in a reluctant acknowledgement of political reality: 'The horrors taking place in France distress and stun me. . . . How can I be expected to write when heads are rolling?'[71] On 31 January he was further shocked to learn of the sudden death of Jakob Mauvillon, his indispensable friend and guide, the man who alone had made life tolerable in Brunswick. Constant's immediate reaction was to plan a *Vie de Mauvillon*, a biography which he hoped Mauvillon's widow Marie Louise (1750–1825) would assist him to write by providing information. Grief made him ill for a month, and on 29 March he wrote to his aunt, Anne de Nassau: 'Since my friend died in Brunswick, all that sustains me is thoughts about death, and I consider life to be a kind of lingering death, only shorter or longer depending on the individual.'[72] Meanwhile his separation from Minna was confirmed on 17 February 1794, and the following month Isabelle, no doubt suspecting that he now risked losing his compass bearings, suggested that he write an autobiographical novel: 'You can describe yourself more or less as you are and you can say what you have seen and experienced' (letter of March 1794[73]). As usual Isabelle's advice was sound: at this stage Constant ignored it and did not take up the therapy, although in the long run writing autobiography and fiction based on his experiences would become therapeutic acts of central importance in his life.

Just before Constant left for Brunswick to settle his affairs there in preparation for leaving the Duke's service, he saw Isabelle de Charrière one last time. He was moderating his pro-Jacobin position somewhat as the Terror now reached its height. They discussed recent history, and Isabelle was compelled to see the beginnings of a new political maturity in her friend, as she confessed in her letter to him of 8–11 April 1794:

> These recent days and particularly that evening [3 April] I was struck by your honest, truthful and impartial good sense. You didn't neglect any information that could be obtained about those people you are in the habit of judging on the basis of passion and prejudice. I have accused you sometimes of not revising views you have held for a long time: but this is not the case, for in fact you re-examine and re-evaluate men and things with asonishing patience. The trial of the supporters of Brissot, that of the King, the conduct of R[obespierre] on 10 August [1792], the tenor, spirit and intention of his speeches to the Convention and the Jacobins since that period – you know about all of these things and you spare no one. I found your moral sense to be as strict as your reason is enlightened.[74]

On his journey across Germany he passed scenes of devastation caused by the war between revolutionary France and the counter-revolutionary coalition which reinforced his longing for peace. His affection for Germany was reinforced when he spent a few days in Göttingen during the second half of April 1794 and visited the renowned University Library. In his search for some new political arrangement for when the guillotinings and anarchy had finally subsided in France there was something to be learned from Germany, as he revealed to Isabelle on 20 April:

> I spend my time going to see professors, who are more interesting than I had thought. They question me as much as they can about the situation in France, and are cross or pleased by what I tell them depending on whether they are aristocrats or republicans [*démocrates*]. But I do notice that the aristocracy here is considerably more tempered by education, and the republicans are more moderate

because of the power of self-interest. I have only met one fanatic who wanted France annihilated.[75]

The day before he had written to his aunt Anne de Nassau in praise of the Duke of Brunswick:

My Duke has confirmed the unlimited freedom of the press on his territory. He has put his University on the surest footing. He is remarkable for possessing all the moderation, the wisdom, and the liberal and humane principles that can be expected of anyone. It is a source of pleasure to be in such a man's service.[76]

And for once Constant meant what he said. For despite the Duke's being military leader of the alliance against France, he remained a model ruler, and in *Adolphe* there is a clear echo of him in the enlightened ruler of the fictional German state who resides in the city of 'D***'. Germany was also the place where, as Constant knew, some of the most advanced research in Europe was being undertaken in his own chosen field, the history of religion, and indeed he found to his dismay that a book he had bought – probably Johann Heinrich Voss's *Mythologische Briefe* – had already arrived independently at conclusions that were the fruit of ten years of his own private investigations dating back to his Edinburgh days. It was a jolt that only strengthened his resolve to study more extensively and deeply.[77]

Perhaps the memory of Mauvillon drove Constant harder, for during this last long stay in Brunswick (25 April–8 August 1794) he had frequent conversation with Madame Mauvillon to help him in writing his late friend's biography. He worked many hours a day on his study of religion, using the library of the Große Klub of which he was still a member, and wrote to Langer, librarian at Wolfenbüttel, with the intention of visiting the Herzog August Bibliothek.[78] By 23 May he was able to inform Isabelle: 'I am working hard on my *magnum opus*, and it's coming along well. There are thirty-seven chapters written of which I'm not displeased, but it's hellishly difficult. The Life of M[auvillon] will come afterwards.'[79] By 21 July it was 600 to 700 pages long, he revealed to Isabelle, 'and that's just the first part. I intend to finish it in the next year, and publish it in order to test whether my readership likes it, which consists of a few philosophers scattered here and there, friends of tolerance and liberty. What happiness! What a constant quiet source of enjoyment! What a delight it is to study!'[80]

He was now *persona non grata* to most of the Court, with the exception of the Duke and Féronce, and kept well out of the way, deliberately leading a hermit-like existence while preparations were made for his divorce proceedings. In his diary entry for 17 July 1804 he remembered the contrast, misjudged and despised by many people 'and yet perfectly happy in the midst of all that. My means of finding happiness were quite simple: I was alone and I was working.'[81]

Nevertheless he was unable to avoid seeing Minna and Charlotte's husband. Curiously Charlotte had taken under her wing Caroline, the actress with whom Constant had had a passionate affair shortly before he had met her, and who had fallen on hard times: she was to take great interest in the other women in Constant's life in later years – a mark of both her devotion to him and her extraordinary tolerance. Nevertheless she twice refused to see Constant himself,[82] although she never stopped loving him and appears to have sent him a number of undated letters during this period. Later, on 11 May, she invited him to meet her, but this time it was Constant who refused, fearing that she might commit some *extravagance* such as insisting that they elope there and then (letter to Isabelle de Charrière of 12 May 1794).[83] Shortly afterwards she wrote to tell him that she was on the point of obtaining a divorce from Wilhelm von Marenholtz, who was to take Caroline von Bothmer as his third wife that August. Charlotte then left for Hamburg:

> She has written me an eight-page letter of self-justification . . . in which she informs me that she is renouncing me for ever, but she ends up by telling me how we can get back together again. I have replied that when I saw at the beginning of the letter that she was finishing with me I didn't try to read any further for fear of feeling more acutely what a treasure I was losing.
>
> (Letter to Isabelle of 7 June 1794[84])

And with this piece of calculated cruelty Constant brought to an end a relationship which he would be grateful to renew many years later: even so they continued to correspond that summer. On 5 September he wrote to Isabelle: 'Charlotte is free, her husband has remarried. But I am also free not to marry her!'[85]

Constant's divorce proceedings opened during the second week in June. In the meantime his correspondence with Isabelle de Charrière was becoming increasingly acrimonious. He refused to condemn Robespierre outright, preferring to wait and see what turn events would take, and adopting the line familiar from twentieth-century history that one had to be either for or against the Revolution: 'To occupy the middle ground is to take up a worthless position; at this juncture it is more worthless than ever. That is my profession of faith' (letter of 7 June 1794).[86] Isabelle was outraged by such intransigence when people were suffering on such a scale in France. In fact the argument between the two friends is curiously reminiscent of a famous later quarrel between Sartre and Camus about whether or not Stalin's gulags really existed, with Isabelle playing the humane and realistic Camus to Constant's doctrinaire Sartre. Despite a subsequent reconciliation, Constant and Isabelle were becoming estranged, a fact which clearly caused Isabelle considerably more pain than Constant, who was growing daily more adamantine in his beliefs. He began a correspondence with Huber on the subject of Robespierre's recent decree on religion: Huber was of the same political faith.

Constant left Brunswick on 8 August 1794, and on his return to Switzerland passed the counter-revolutionary army of the Prince de Condé. He was in good spirits during a two-day stay with Isabelle de Charrière (23–5 August), who was pleased to find his politics more moderate than the previous March (letter to Constant of 29 August 1794).[87] But too many hurtful words had been spoken for things ever to be quite the same between them again. Yet it was characteristic of Constant to hold on to the relationship: he had a horror of making any final break, an aspect of his nature which probably went back to his childhood, but which often caused prolonged suffering both to others and himself. Marie Louise Mauvillon, widow of his close friend, was aware of this aspect of his personality:

> Come back [to Brunswick], she writes, come back with all your weaknesses, your failings, with your indecision, your vacillation and your oddity. If you lost a part of that, I would no longer know you, I would no longer have the same confidence in you, or the same pleasure . . .
> (quoted in Constant's letter to Isabelle de Charrière of 5 September 1794)[88]

It would take the equivalent of an earthquake in Constant's life for a relationship like his friendship with Isabelle to alter decisively. But just such an earthquake was about to occur.

6

GERMAINE DE STAEL
(1794–1800)

Constant was kicking his heels in Lausanne, attending to his father's financial affairs, being lectured to by his relatives (as usual), associating with visiting English people whom he always found amusing, writing to Madame de Charrière to defend his belief that repressive measures were a necessary evil in France on the road to a republic where liberty would reign and repression would no longer be needed (he had started dating his letters using the revolutionary calendar – 26 Fructidor, etc. – probably to annoy her). He was also feeling guilty about Charlotte:

> Your last letter but one gave me great qualms of conscience about Charlotte. I feel that I have got into a position with that woman which makes my conduct look false in my own eyes. While I make fun of her with you, I send her from time to time, out of decency, letters filled with affectionate and grandiloquent nonsense, and if anyone compared my letters *to* her with my letters *about* her, I would rightly be considered an evil and treacherous lunatic. Either I must have nothing further to do with her, or stop making fun of her to you or anyone else. And, since I don't want to break off relations with her, I must adopt the latter course. So can I ask you – and I think I have a right to ask it of you – to burn what I've written about her? Thanks to what I say about myself I am already run down enough by people without needing to be criticized still more.

(Letter of 12 September 1794[1])

(Fortunately for posterity Isabelle did no such thing, and Constant, comical and perfidious, attractive and at times repellent, still stands before us in all his complexity in those letters.) It was against this backdrop of his old life, with so many of its threads still hanging loose, that a new life was about to begin for Constant.

Isabelle had lately recommended that Constant go and see 'the author of *Zulma*', that is the novelist and essayist Madame de Staël who lived at Coppet, between Lausanne and Geneva, adding waspishly, 'She is a curiosity not to be missed' (letter of 10 September 1794).[2] Madame de Charrière found her a garrulous busybody, a pretentious name-dropper, whose written style she considered ridiculously overblown, at times to the point of meaninglessness. But seldom in literary history can a depreciatory aside have so backfired against its user. On 18 September Constant met Germaine de Staël at the home of the Cazenove d'Arlens at Montchoisi. Germaine wrote to her current lover, the Swedish Count Adolf von Ribbing, or Adolphe de Ribbing: 'This evening I came across a man of great wit here . . ., not very handsome but extraordinarily amusing.'[3] They got on so well that Constant offered Madame de Staël his entire library of English books in the event of his death and signed a declaration to that effect.[4]

Born Anne-Louise-Germaine Necker in 1766, the daughter of Louis XVI's Director-General of Finances, the Genevan banker Jacques Necker (1732–1804), and Suzanne Curchod (1737–94) (who had been prevented from marrying Edward Gibbon by the intervention of the historian's father, which occurrence had prompted Gibbon *fils*'s famous comment, 'I sighed as a lover; I obeyed as a son'), Germaine had known the world of Parisian literary salons from her earliest years.[5] Like Constant, with whom she shared a similar Swiss Protestant background, she had shown signs of remarkable intellectual precocity. Later her extrovert, energetic and ardent nature, the inexhaustible delight she took in reading and conversation and her many sexual liaisons were to bring her fame and some notoriety. In January 1786 she had married Baron Eric Magnus Staël von Holstein (1749–1802), Swedish Ambassador to France, and her salon in the Swedish Embassy in the Rue du Bac had thereafter become a centre of moderate liberal thought. During the Revolution she had begun to spend time at her father's château at Coppet on the shores of the Lake of Geneva, where she was to live for long periods in later years, and in 1793 had stayed with a colony of distinguished French aristocratic *émigrés* at Juniper Hall in Surrey.[6] When Constant met her in 1794 Madame de Staël was already quite well known as a literary figure, having published controversial essays on Rousseau and on French politics as well as *Zulma*, a short novel which had appeared in April 1794. Germaine de Staël had traits in common with both Constant and Isabelle de Charrière: she was highly intellectual, witty, unconventional, capable of overwhelming enthusiasms, and had been an early victim of anglomania. She felt next to no affection for her cold and spendthrift husband and had taken Count Louis de Narbonne as her lover only two years after her marriage. Narbonne was to be followed by many others, of whom Ribbing was only the latest.

Perhaps sensing that Constant, having experienced such intoxicating company, might now slip away from her completely, Isabelle de Charrière wrote to him on 13 September 1794 trying to patch up their friendship, while not disguising how much the tone of his letters had hurt her. She went too far herself, however, and her tone became embittered. She tried again, this time with a fable in verse in the style of La Fontaine, *Le Lion et le Singe* [*The Lion and the Monkey*] about their relationship.[7] In the meantime Constant was already writing to tell Isabelle how impressed he was by Germaine de Staël as a conversationalist, and accusing Isabelle of being despotic, of wishing to control his freedom to think what he liked, of smothering him with her advice.[8] Isabelle had let herself be driven by Constant's exasperating treatment of her into overstepping the mark and behaving like a mother (a role which of course befitted her years), and a possessive mother at that. Isabelle's tragedy was that, at her age and in the isolated backwater of Colombier where she lived, she had come to need this brilliant young man and his letters much more than he needed her. Constant, despite his air of fragility, was far tougher than her in every sense: any contest between them was bound to be unequal. And there was too an underlying psychological difficulty in Constant which made a clinging, stifling or constraining relationship with a woman bring out his aggression.

The rift had now been mended and reopened several times between Constant and Isabelle: each time resentment and hatred had surfaced in both of them. It is hardly surprising that, whatever the rights and wrongs of the situation, Constant was ready for something different, for a new friendship with Germaine de Staël and the new beginning it seemed to offer. He told Isabelle in a bitter ending to a letter: 'Even the mirage of literary fame that you went out of your way to rid my mind of has now returned and brightens the future for me' (letter of 26 September 1794).[9] He went to Coppet on 26 September to see Germaine de Staël again: she had left but he caught up with her, travelled in her coach to Nyon, and spent the next day and a half with her. He wrote to Isabelle on 30 September:

> I have watched her and above all listened to her carefully. It seems to me that you judge her somewhat severely. I think she does too much, is very imprudent and very talkative, but she is also kind, trusting and genuinely open. Proof that she is not simply a talking machine is to be found in the concern she shows for the people she has known and who are suffering. She has just succeeded, after three costly failed attempts, in saving from prison and smuggling out of France a woman who had been her enemy in Paris. . . . That's more than just talk. I think all the things she involves herself in satisfies a need in her as much as it is meritorious action. But she puts that need to work in doing good for others. . . . I have no plans to have a closer relationship with her: she is too surrounded by people, too

busy, too absorbed in her various activities for that. But she is the most interesting acquaintance I've made in a long time. . . . It's astonishing to hear Madame de Staehl [sic] saying exactly the same things as you on politics, word for word.[10]

During October Constant showed Germaine de Staël his work on religion, the enterprise that he thought the most worthwhile thing in his life. She praised him for it, telling her lover Ribbing on 22 October that she considered Constant to have the talent of a Montesquieu.[11] His prodigious erudition and ability to deal with complex metaphysical problems impressed her enormously – and he made her laugh a great deal into the bargain. But this was not enough for Constant who, by early October, was head over heels in love with her and wanted Germaine to feel the same. His looks were the obstacle: he was tall and awkward, with reddish hair, spectacles with green lenses, small cold eyes and a blotchy, freckled face, hardly the *beau idéal* of male beauty. On a brief visit to Colombier with his cousin Charles, Constant made Isabelle smart with his praise of Madame de Staël. Despite Charles's deep antipathy to Constant, his remarks on the visit in a letter to his family of 8 October 1794 ring true:

B[enjamin] has a different way of talking when he is with Madame de C[harrière] from with the others. He mixes a degree of emotion in with what he says. He made her very jealous of Madame de St[aël]. She is afraid he will abandon her.[12]

Perhaps it was the example of Germaine de Staël that was now bringing Constant round to a more moderate political position comparable with Isabelle's own – a backhanded compliment if ever there was one. He reported to Isabelle:

The French political scene has mellowed to an astonishing degree. . . . I see with pleasure the moderates taking a clear ascendant over the Jacobins. . . . I can feel myself growing more moderate, and it would need you to suggest an innocuous little counter-revolution now for me to return to the high ground of republican principle.[13]

Robespierre had been overthrown in July and the Terror had ended; the Revolution had, in modern terms, taken a swing to the Right, yet Constant was pleased – Isabelle must have felt bitter to see Germaine receive the credit for having been correct in her political judgement all along, and cannot but have suspected the erstwhile republican diehard Constant of sailing with the wind: she would, of course, have been fully justified. But the key was in the personality of Germaine, whom Constant now loved and admired, while at the same time he was slowly moving out of Isabelle's life. He struck a deliberately valedictory note in his letter to Isabelle of 21 October:

> Since I have got to know [Madame de Staël] better, I find the greatest difficulty in not endlessly praising her and in not showing everyone I speak to how I admire her and am affected by her. I have seldom seen such a combination of astonishing and attractive qualities, so much brilliance and right judgement; or anyone so busy doing good to others, showing so much generosity, such considerate and sustained politeness at social gatherings, and so much charm, naturalness and openness when she is with her closer acquaintances. She is the second woman I have met who could take the place of the whole world for me, who could be a world unto herself for me: you know who the first was [i.e. Isabelle]. . . . She is a being apart, a superior being such as one might come across perhaps only once in a hundred years.[14]

But the superior being who was the subject of this panegyric stubbornly refused to reciprocate Constant's feelings. Germaine was amused but unmoved by his spaniel-like devotion to her, and even thought him a little deranged. His reaction was to provoke embarrassing scenes which put her off him still more. In the meantime he was working for her, going on errands to various parts of Switzerland, probably in aid of French *émigrés*, while writing to her several times a day to declare his love for her. He began work again on his book on religion, telling Isabelle on 3 December 1794:

> What you say about your reasons for wishing that I would undertake to write a book that was less vast in its scope is very pertinent and very sensible. But the only thing for which I have ever felt any really sustained interest is the very thing that you have never been able to get interested in yourself, and if I don't finish this one, I don't think I'll ever write another.[15]

In December 1794 they corresponded on the subject of Kant's notion of duty, which was to be the unusual starting point for Isabelle's novel *Trois femmes*,[16] but henceforth their letters were to be about intellectual or literary matters rather than personal. Meanwhile the curious comedy went on day after day with Madame de Staël, with Constant watching and adoring, and Germaine gradually more and more touched by such attention, despite her calling him 'singularly ugly' in a letter to the absent Ribbing.[17]

In February 1795 Constant moved into Madame de Staël's house at Mézery, but he was still without any tangible reward for all his despairing love and daily histrionics. Germaine continued to find him physically repulsive. Matters came to a head at the end of March when one night the servants at Mézery were awoken by screams of pain from Constant's room. They found him writhing on his bed and foaming at the mouth. Constant asked one of the house guests, mostly French *émigrés*, to tell Germaine that he was dying for love of her. She rushed to his side and pleaded with him to live: he kissed her arm and by the time a doctor arrived he was already recovering.[18] The attempted suicide by poisoning, whether genuine or bogus, marked a turning point in Constant's fortunes, although Germaine was no doubt aware that she had been duped. He gradually assumed greater and greater importance in the household, in the continued absence of Germaine's official lover Ribbing; he even aroused the jealousy of her temporary lover, the *émigré* Mathieu de Montmorency. When Isabelle saw Constant again at the end of April 1795 she found he had altered, as she told her friend Henriette L'Hardy:

> He had lunch and dinner here. I find him very much changed. . . .
> He seemed somehow mysterious and self-important and occupied
> with weighty matters, and all that has replaced his former cheerful-
> ness, naturalness and youthful sense of fun. . . . He has plans for the
> future, journeys to make, services to render.
>
> (Letter of 2–5 May 1795[19])

His resignation from the service of the Duke of Brunswick had become official by early May 1795. The political situation in France had now returned to something approaching normality under the Thermidorians, and Germaine judged it was safe to return to Paris. When she left on 17 May Constant was at her side.

In *Cécile* the narrator describes his impressions on arriving in Paris as Constant did on 25 May 1795:

> With all the impetuosity of my character and with a mind that was
> even younger than my years I enthusiastically embraced revolution-
> ary ideas. Ambition took hold of me and I could see only two things
> in the world that I wanted: to be the citizen of a republic and to
> be at the head of a political party.[20]

Isabelle was right in seeing a change in Constant. At 27 he had finally reached where he really wanted to be. He was independent of his father and at last far from his family and from Switzerland; indeed he was now centre stage in the only place that mattered for a French speaker, Paris, and had the determination and ambition to make his mark there. For that he could thank the woman he loved. Madame de Staël now introduced him to the political thinkers Barras and Sieyès, and in her salon at the Swedish Embassy in the Rue du Bac – which soon became an important political meeting place once again – Constant was exposed to all shades of opinion. He soon realized how lacking in sophistication his thought was, and began to listen and learn, as he was to tell his friend J.-J.

Coulmann later in his life, and attended sittings of the Convention every day.[21] He and Germaine had in fact by chance caught the aftermath of the insurrection of 1 Prairial (20 May 1795) against the Thermidorians when they had arrived in the capital, and were there when the six deputies sympathetic to Jacobinism who had supported the insurgents were condemned to the guillotine.

Throughout June and July 1795 while his passion burned incandescent for Germaine, or 'Minette' as he came to call her, she continued to say no. He was visited by Juste who was looking for ways of being rehabilitated in Holland, and again wrote documents to help him in his cause.[22] But French politics was now Constant's obsession and he lost no time in publishing three 'letters to a Convention deputy', *Lettres à un député de la Convention* in Suard's journal, the *Nouvelles politiques*, of 24, 25 and 26 June 1795, denouncing the Convention for its recent actions.[23] The letters caused a considerable stir and his father and friends feared that his rashness might put him in gaol. The Convention was meanwhile busy drawing up a new Constitution to consolidate the Republic: there was even talk in some quarters of reviving the monarchy in some form. This was indeed a momentous and exciting time for Constant to be in Paris, but there was a price to pay. His friend the former *émigré* Camille de Malarmey de Roussillon, brother of Pierre, visited Constant and Germaine and reported what he had seen to Isabelle de Charrière on 11 July, perhaps with mocking echoes of Germaine's way of speaking. He had been present the previous evening at 'the Delightful One's home', ('chez la délicieuse', i.e. Madame de Staël) when a long and animated discussion had taken place between her and Constant:

The love of liberty has not diminished in the Lover's [Constant's] heart and he loves liberty to nearly the same extent that he loves his adored Royalist divinity [Germaine], but whom he will not adore for long – the dear young boy! (for he is truly lovable as long as he is seen when he has a lot of other people with him. . . .) The salon of the Embassy [home of Germaine's husband] suits him much better than the little study at Colombier. . . . If he spent only two hours a day in the salon, it would be an excellent study for him, but unfortunately he spends eighteen hours a day there. All he does is live in the salon, and the salon tires him, he can't stand it any more. His health is deteriorating and his body which was already painfully thin is beginning to suffer. With that height of his he had suddenly begun to look elegant, but once again he is beginning to stoop in the manner that Mademoiselle Moula caught so well [in a silhouette of him made in 1792]. His forehead is covered in pimples. He says he's thinking of withrawing from society completely. He longs for the sweet solitude of Germany.[24]

On 24 July Constant wrote an article for *Le Républicain français* hostile to the reactionary elements among the *émigrés*, urging all Frenchmen to rally to the support of the Republic and to stand by the present government, despite its shortcomings, at the cost of their lives if necessary.[25] Constant's greatest fear was a return of the *ancien régime* with a vindictive monarchy and aristocracy seeking retribution against the regicides and their sympathizers, and the Catholic church once again all-powerful in France. Indeed an attempted invasion by *émigrés* with British support had been defeated by General Hoche at Quiberon Bay in Brittany (June–July 1795) and *émigré* prisoners taken had been massacred. Constant now attracted the attention of the novelist and politician Jean-Baptiste Louvet de Couvray (1760–97), and at Louvet's invitation collaborated with him in writing a speech which the deputy delivered to the Convention on 20 August 1795.[26]

All of Constant's activity, in the complex and shifting political scene of that summer of 1795, was directed to two ends: impressing and winning over Germaine – who continued to refuse to become his mistress and was now taking an interest in an old acquaintance, François de Pange; and giving support to the setting up of a legally established Republican government with a new constitution, a government that would resist both Royalist and Jacobin extremism. The Constitution of Year III, adopted in August 1795, enshrined the respect for private property which had been challenged during the Terror. Through it the Convention abolished universal suffrage, and limited the franchise to the propertied classes. This move may appear shocking to modern eyes, but to eighteenth-century eyes – and especially to those of people who had witnessed the excesses of 1793–4 – it was absolutely logical: the government needed to be elected by those with the best education and who, because they owned property, obeyed the laws and had a vested interest in ensuring a stable future for the country. Such was, indeed, the principle which Constant himself held to throughout his political career. To prevent any return to a pre–1789 situation, priests and former *émigrés* were disenfranchised, and the 'law of the two-thirds' decreed that in any case two-thirds of the members of a new legislative body would have to come from among the members of the outgoing Convention. That last item was eventually to be the Convention's undoing: such a blatant attempt to perpetuate its own power led to an uprising on 13 Vendémiaire (5 October 1795) by moderates and royalists, which was crushed by the army under an energetic young general by the name of Bonaparte.

At about this time Constant began to plan a future for himself in his adopted country, and bought three properties in France in order to become an enfranchised citizen, farms near Rouen (only five hours travel from Paris) and near Dreux, and land at Vaux.[27] Juste, showing his usual lack of understanding of his son – but also, it has to be said, fearing Benjamin's eventual financial ruin – wished him to take up his post in Brunswick again. Germaine de Staël left the capital in September for Mathieu de Montmorency's château at Ormesson not far away lest she be accused of using her salon to interfere in the elections that were currently taking place.[28] Needless to say Constant accompanied her there, but he was back in Paris at the Convention during two all-night sittings (26–7 September and 3–4 October 1795) with Louvet ready to defend it against a threatened royalist revival.[29] In a tragicomic misunderstanding Constant found himself caught up in a street disturbance following the failed 5 October monarchist insurrection and spent the night of 7–8 October in prison with François de Pange, both of them accused of having spoken in pro-royalist terms.[30] In Constant's case the accusation was patently absurd. However, the experience of prison, though very brief, was a valuable one that Constant never forgot, in particular the shocking contrast between the sound of free people going about their business in the street outside and the prisoner's confinement and humiliation.[31] It can only have reinforced in him the profound love of – and need for – personal freedom he had always felt.

One major liberation came at last to Constant on 18 November 1795: his divorce from Minna finally became legal.[32] He had left the Duke of Brunswick's service and a page had now been turned in his personal history. Or almost: at the end of the year, according to *Cécile*, he received a letter from Charlotte which had taken some months to find him. The sight of her familiar handwriting gave him a shock, and he sent an affectionate letter of reply which seems not to have reached her.[33] There were, however, other more immediate threats to his liberty than Charlotte's desire to marry him: as a result of his earlier arrest, his apartment in Paris had been searched;[34] and the whole city was plunged into a ferment of unrest and uncertainty as the rule of the Directory began in November 1795. Constant left for Switzerland with Germaine on 20 December,[35] interrupting his political activities for her sake, and stayed in Lausanne and at Coppet with her until mid-April 1796. At the end of their stay he was at last rewarded for eighteen months of waiting and became Germaine de Staël's lover. It was not physical attraction, but the slow development of a friendship and real affection between them that had led to this consummation of all Constant's wishes. There exists a document, drawn up possibly at this time to seal the relationship, in which the lovers promise 'to devote our lives to each other', considering themselves 'indissolubly joined together' and undertaking never to contract another relationship. Constant for his part adds:

> I hereby state that I am entering this commitment out of heartfelt conviction, that I know no one on earth as lovable as Madame de Staël, that I have been the happiest man on earth during the four months I have spent with her, and that I consider it the greatest

happiness of my life to be able to make the years of her youth happy ones, to grow old gradually by her side and to reach the end of my life with the one who understands me and without whom there would be no interest and no emotion left for me on this earth.[36]

During his stay Constant maintained his contact with Louvet and expressed concern at the activities in Switzerland of William Wickham, the British government envoy whose job it was to send secret agents into France among the returning *émigrés* and to pay them well for their work.[37] This was not only a threat to a France now ruled by the Directory, a government of which Constant increasingly approved: Wickham's activities also risked drawing the neutral Swiss cantons into the European conflict. Constant also took the opportunity while in Switzerland to visit Ludwig Ferdinand and Therese Huber who were living at Bôle near Neuchâtel, and sent a note on 26 January 1796 to Isabelle de Charrière asking if he could go and see her since he was so near. By return he received the following tart reply:

> I like neither your way of life nor your friends, neither your politics nor the politics of those with you, and I have no wish to argue with you any more. Now I've said it. I'm obliged to you for a delightful winter. Two years ago this winter and earlier I was grateful to you for very pleasant hours, days, months. They cannot come back again. I wrote to you at the beginning of the Revolution, 'If you go to Paris and if you become involved in some clique or other, it will be the end of our friendship'. Eighteen months ago I begged you not to let yourself get recruited by anyone in Germany. Now you have joined someone's ranks, or rather you are under her wing, and there you reason and write articles. You are no longer my kind of person, and since you have no need of me, we'd better leave things as they are. Be happy – that is what I wish for you with all my heart.[38]

Why did Constant invite such a rebuff? Earlier in the same letter Isabelle says:

> I've heard you say sometimes, 'I never finish with anybody'. On other occasions it was, 'I feel like writing to Madame de M[arenholtz, i.e. Charlotte]. Did you say to yourself today, 'I feel like writing to Madame de Charrière'? 'But what is the point?', I used to ask you apropos of Madame de M. 'I tell you I *want* to write to her', you said, 'I never finish with anybody'.[39]

Isabelle de Charrière's remark takes us once again to the heart of Constant's personality, and to his horror of any final separation which would be something akin to the ultimate separation of death. Although more vulnerable than Constant in other respects, Isabelle did not at least have this particular Achilles' heel. He could never finally close the door on his relationship with her, even in the letter of farewell he sent her on 26 March 1796:

> I shall never stop loving you. . . . I may have wronged you by my behaviour towards you because I am both sharp-tongued and disorganized by nature, but my feelings for you have always remained the same. . . . I am linked to you by all manner of memories, regrets, and I might add, in spite of you, by many hopes. Farewell, you who have made eight years of my life more beautiful; despite some painful experiences with you, I can never imagine you posturing or feigning; farewell, you whose true worth I appreciate better than anybody ever will, farewell, farewell.[40]

They continued to correspond in spite of such a letter, and indeed were at this time taking a common interest in the English radical William Godwin's political novel *The Adventures of Caleb Williams, or Things as They Are* (1794).[41]

On 19 February 1796 Juste de Constant was rehabilitated and received an annual allowance of 2,400 Dutch florins.[42] He expressed gratitude to his son for his help over the years.[43] The legal victory was as yet only partial, however. And Juste was increasingly concerned at the rate at which his son was spending money, at Benjamin's wasting his time, as he saw it, with Madame de Staël and failing to find a secure post, at his continuing to dabble in the risky game of French left-wing politics. Unmoved by his father's concern, Constant was now working side by side with Germaine as they would so often in the future, Constant on a defence of the Republic under the Directory, *De la force du gouvernement actuel et de la nécessité de s'y rallier* (*On the Strength of the Present Government and the Need to rally to it*), and Germaine on an essay on the influence of the passions.[44] Constant's pamphlet was completed around 22 March 1796. When he returned to Paris alone in mid-April, he was to find that his pamphlet was meeting with some success and attracting the approval of the Directory, although his motives and sincerity were also being called into question – not for the first or last time in his political career. He even inspired a spirited and stylish rejoinder by Adrien de Lezay-Marnésia (1769–1814) in the form of a pamphlet entitled *On the Weakness of a Government that has only just come to Power, and its Need to rally to the Majority of People in the Country*.[45]

Constant found life on his own in Paris very tiring and became somewhat dispirited, despite having plenty of friends to talk to. He wrote to his aunt Madame de Nassau on 8 May 1796:

> It's a sad thing to have tastes as narrow as mine. Loving and thinking are the only things I am capable of. What others call amusements,

distractions, or letting oneself go don't exist for me. The countryside depresses me, and I wilt when I'm in the company of other people. In order for me to be able to live life to the full, I need a heart that loves me or an idea that completely absorbs me.[46]

He did, however, have one important new friend to support him in Paris, Julie Talma (1756–1805), wife of the celebrated actor François-Joseph Talma. Constant and Julie Talma appear to have become acquainted the previous August, possibly through Louvet. A highly intelligent woman and staunchly republican, Julie greatly admired Constant's wit and intellect. They saw each other regularly in the early summer of 1796 and a firm friendship came into being.[47] Although their relationship appears never to have become a sexual one, there is little doubt that Julie – who was twelve years Constant's senior and was unhappy with her unfaithful husband whom she would divorce in 1801 – loved Constant, and there is perhaps something of a parallel here with Isabelle de Charrière. In the meantime Germaine de Staël who was still in Switzerland was banned by the Directory from setting foot on French soil, being considered politically meddlesome and suspect, and Constant himself had to appeal to the government against a law requiring all foreigners to leave Paris. Indeed he was active all summer trying to *cease* being a foreigner and to obtain French citizenship by the best means available to him – by drawing attention to his rights under a new law that had recently allowed his father to take French citizenship as a descendant of Huguenot exiles.[48] His request was finally to be granted on 21 March 1797, although the question of his nationality would dog him intermittently for the rest of his life. Germaine herself, who was of Swiss Protestant ancestry, was to claim the same privilege, and would be helped in drawing up the required documents by Constant.[49]

The repercussions of Constant's pamphlet continued, and in July 1796 he felt his honour to have been impugned by a vitriolic article from the pen of a journalist Louis-François Bertin ('Bertin de Veaux') calling him a 'discourteous little Swiss' and accusing him of being a Jacobin terrorist. Never afraid of a fight, Constant challenged Bertin to a duel with pistols on 14 or 15 July, and wrote a will leaving his house in Lausanne, La Chablière, to Germaine and other effects to his aunt, Anne de Nassau.[50] Fortunately the promise of a published apology by Bertin made on the field of combat prevented any bloodshed, and in later years the two men became friends. But the shock Germaine experienced when looking back on this whole affair and its possibly fatal consequences deepened her feelings for Benjamin so that when he rejoined her at Coppet in Switzerland on 4 August 1796 he found that she had now fallen passionately in love with him.[51] There was talk of a divorce from her husband, the Baron de Staël, and some speculation about a possible remarriage to Constant.

By the time Constant left Germaine to return to Paris on 7 October she was pregnant.

In France Constant tried to secure citizenship for Germaine and published a favourable review of her essay on the influence of the passions which appeared in Le Moniteur on 26 October 1796.[52] But he did not neglect his own future and, partly on money borrowed from Germaine's father, Jacques Necker, bought Hérivaux, a ruined abbey and estate near Luzarches, 20 miles north of Paris, for 50,000 francs on 1 November,[53] sold two of his French farms and prepared to sell La Chablière in Lausanne. It was a grandiose gesture which also had a practical objective, that of enabling Constant to stand for election at some future date. His efforts on Germaine's behalf had meanwhile borne fruit, and in December Constant was able to go to Coppet and accompany her back into France with the prospect of her taking up residence there permanently. The couple stayed at Hérivaux on and off from January to May 1797, receiving many distinguished visitors including Talleyrand, before Germaine was finally allowed to return to live in Paris at the end of May. On 30 March Constant's political ambitions began to be realized in a minor way when he was elected chairman of the municipal administrative body in Luzarches. He told Anne de Nassau:

> The people of the canton have elected me chairman of their administrative committee, which gives me the opportunity to make sure the laws which I cherish are respected in a small community, and to protect republicans against the malevolence of priests who are stirring up fanaticism in our countryside.
>
> (Letter of 14 April 1797[54])

In March 1797 Constant's pamphlet Des réactions politiques came off the press. Once again he gave his support to the legal Directorial government, and this time his venom was aimed particularly at journalists such as the Catholic Jean-François de La Harpe. In a Preface Constant stressed that it was impossible to be more French than he was, on account of his birth, his principles, the properties he owned and by legal right.[55] Once more his pugnaciously dogmatic anti-monarchist and anti-Catholic tone attracted attention, bringing him hostile reviews and making him unwelcome in some salons. Perhaps the most unexpected response – and one which has considerably outlived Constant's ephemeral brochure – came from the philosopher Immanuel Kant who published a famous essay entitled 'On a supposed right to lie out of love of humanity' in Berlinische Blätter on 6 September 1797 in which he sharply contested a passage about the defensibility of telling a lie in order to save a human life.[56] Constant brought out a second edition of Des réactions politiques in late May or early June, accompanied by a new essay, Des effets de la Terreur (On the Consequences of the Terror), intended, he wrote 'to prove that the Terror

146

was not necessary to save the Republic . . ., that the Terror did nothing but harm, and that its legacy to the Republic of today is all the perils which threaten the Republic even now'.[57] Citizen Constant, the scourge of priests and *émigrés*, was now becoming an established figure on the political stage after only three years in Paris, and in mid-June delivered the opening address at the Club de Salm[58] of which, together with Talleyrand, M.-J. Chénier, P.-L. Ginguené, P. Cabanis and other distinguished names, he was a founder member. The Club, which met at the Hôtel de Salm (former home of the German Prince Frederick III of Salm-Kyrburg who had been guillotined during the Terror), was dedicated to opposing the royalist Club de Clichy, to furthering the republican cause and supporting the government of the Directory. The elections of 20 May 1797 had returned a counter-revolutionary majority and the Directory, racked by economic and foreign-policy difficulties, looked distinctly shaky. Things appeared rather less than promising for Constant himself at Luzarches where, after a long investigation, his election to the chairmanship of the municipal administration was declared null and void because at the time of his election he had not been resident at Hérivaux a full year.[59]

On 8 June 1797 Albertine de Staël was born. A well-known passage in the *Mémoires* of Barras, a left-wing member of the Directory, says that her looks, hair and everything about Albertine suggested she was Constant's daughter.[60] With Madame de Staël it would be difficult to say any such thing with certainty, of course, but Constant always felt a strong attachment to Albertine, and she may have been one of the reasons why Constant was reluctant to leave Germaine in the later stormy stages of their liaison.

Another happy moment for Constant and Madame de Staël was to see their friend Charles-Maurice de Talleyrand (1754–1838) appointed Minister for Foreign Affairs on 16 July 1797, but it was to be mingled with disappointment: despite a strong letter of recommendation from Talleyrand to General Bonaparte in Italy, Constant was not made Secretary of the Ministry for Foreign Affairs, and the press took pleasure in reporting his discomfiture.[61] However this was soon overshadowed by the prospect of civil war in France during August, and on the night of the 3–4 September 1797 the three left-wing members of the Directory – J.-F. Rewbell, L.-M. La Revellière-Lépeaux and Paul Barras – set up a committee which claimed they had uncovered a royalist conspiracy. Constant and Madame de Staël were with their friend Paul Barras (1755–1829) the evening before the bloodless *coup d'état* of 18 Fructidor (4 September 1797), according to the *Souvenirs historiques et parlementaires* of the Comte de Pontécoulant:[62] they must have been embarrassed by his subsequent actions. General Augereau had been sent from Italy by Bonaparte and his troops now occupied Paris; the Law of 19 Fructidor cancelled the unwelcome election results of the previous May which had returned right-wing deputies; priests and politicians were deported to Cayenne; and Barras was left with the reins of power, unchallengeable.

Constant's reaction is inclined to leave an unpleasant taste in the mouth, a little like Cicero's defence of the murder without trial cf the Catiline conspirators. The former Club de Salm had now been renamed the Cercle constitutionnel, and in a speech he made to it on 16 September 1797 Constant hailed the *coup d'état* as a triumph for the Republic, while at the same time expressing regret at the means used to eliminate the Republic's enemies – deportation to Cayenne, which was known as 'the dry guillotine' because it was tantamount to a death sentence.[63] It is not easy to resist the feeling that Constant was behaving opportunistically, currying favour with an administration in the hope of eventually gaining political office.[64] His defence against such a charge – as on later occasions – would undoubtedly have been that the right course lay in defending the gains of the Revolution, in strengthening the Republic which enshrined them, in holding firmly to the ideals of freedom and democracy, but being flexible in the means to achieving them. He detested royalism, but he also feared a return of Jacobin terrorism, anarchy, and the confiscation of private property: he deplored the arbitrary exercise of power, but on this occasion he was willing to tolerate it. It is perhaps not too early to speak of Constant's developing political position as liberal – a notoriously difficult one to maintain without exposing oneself at times to accusations of trimming or of having one's cake and eating it. Constant's speech to the Cercle constitutionnel, which was widely commented on in the press, was entitled 'For the planting of a Tree of Liberty' – a reminder of the curious secular ceremonies characteristic of France in the post-revolutionary period. He had no doubt had to preside in his official capacity at Luzarches at other stranger rites recently invented by the Republic to replace earlier religious ones. In fact on 5 November 1797 Constant was reinstated to an honorary post there, and took up his seat having sworn the customary oath of hatred of royalty and anarchy and fidelity to the Republic and the Constitution of Year III.[65]

In early January 1798 Constant accompanied Germaine de Staël to the Swiss border, then returned to Hérivaux. At this stage Germaine was a fervent admirer of the hero of Italy, the young General Bonaparte and on his return to Paris in December 1797 she had succeeded in meeting him.[66] Now on 28 January 1798 French troops entered the Pays de Vaud, which was annexed by France. Such an invasion by the government he was supporting was not likely to endear Constant to his family in Switzerland, but he wrote confidently to his aunt de Nassau on 19 February 1798 about the Vaudois's liberation from the yoke of Berne:

If the overthrow of everything that was founded on simply privilege and prejudice was inevitable, all one can hope is that this change takes place in an atmosphere of calm and good order. That is the nature of your revolution, and one could call it more a series of reforms.[67]

Whether Constant was really quite as sanguine about the prospects for his native canton as he appeared to be is perhaps doubtful, but he could hardly afford to lose his nerve now that there was a distinct possibility of his being elected to the Legislature in the forthcoming elections. He took a step along that road when on 22 March he was made an elector for the canton of Luzarches and wrote to the Director Barras on 27 March to ask for his support in now being elected a deputy.[68] He made a desperate bid at electoral meetings in Versailles to have himself nominated for the Department of Seine-et-Oise, but he had acquired too many enemies and was unsuccessful. One outcome was a duel in the Bois de Boulogne with Georges Sibuet, one of the owners of *L'Ami des lois*, a newspaper which had campaigned against him; it resulted in Constant's receiving an apology.[69]

For some time now Constant had felt that his relationship with Germaine de Staël was becoming a burden to him. Bored and in low spirits after his failure to be nominated, he let slip the truth when he wrote to Anne de Nassau from Hérivaux on 15 May 1798 and confided in her:

A tie which I have respected out of duty, or if you prefer out of weakness, but which I am sure I shall honour until such time as a more genuine duty frees me from it; a tie which I could break only by admitting I am terribly weary of it – something I am too polite to say; a tie which, by plunging me into a world I no longer like [i.e. salons] and tearing me away from the countryside I love, makes me profoundly unhappy and greatly threatens the limited amount of money I've managed to acquire only by a miracle in my nomadic existence; a tie finally that can only be broken by a massive upheaval which I cannot bring about – this tie has held me in bondage for two years.

I am isolated without being independent; I am completely subordinate to her without being at one with her. I see the last years of my youth slipping away with neither the peace of solitude nor that sweet affection which comes from a legal union. I have tried in vain to finish with her. It is not in my nature to resist the complaints of another human being. . . . And once this tie is broken I shall find myself alone again, and that solitude will add to the pain, genuine or false, that people will say I have caused. To console myself I need to make someone happy.[70]

All the pain of Adolphe's dilemma is already present in this letter, the inability to take decisive action, the fear of causing pain, the sense of life slipping by. In the same letter Constant asks his aunt to look for a suitable wife for him, just as the fictional Adolphe will long for a calm and steady relationship in marriage after his burdensome relationship with Ellénore has ended. In June Constant's father suggested that he marry his cousin Angletine de Sévery: she would also make him financially secure with her dowry.[71] It was to come to nothing.

By the end of June Germaine was back at Hérivaux and Constant felt guilty at his plans for an 'insurrection', as he told his aunt Anne de Nassau. Such ingratitude would only lead to painful regrets in the future (letter of 28 June 1798).[72] Face to face with Germaine, as he had foreseen, his resolution crumbled – indeed by Christmas 1798 there was to be talk in Lausanne of her divorce and marriage to Constant. Constant's finances stood to benefit handsomely, as Madame de Charrière told Huber that December.[73] He now retreated into study, took up the threads of his book on religion, long since laid aside, and at Isabelle de Charrière's request no doubt read her new novel *Trois femmes*.[74] Despite a feud with the local Catholic priest, Father Oudaille, Constant also continued to make speeches and preside in Luzarches at the extraordinary *fêtes* of which the republican calendar was full, such as the *Fête* of Married Couples, of the Sovereignty of the People or that of the Fall of the Throne. It may well be that at about this time Constant finally learnt that his father had married Marianne years before and had kept it secret from him.[75] This was to have serious financial consequences for him, since eventually Juste would have to provide for Benjamin's half-brother Charles and half-sister Louise. Altogether it was not proving a good summer for Constant, who must more than ever have felt that his life was leading nowhere.

Constant needed a focus elsewhere, in his work. In common with Isabelle de Charrière, he had become interested in William Godwin and probably from September or October 1798 until January 1800 worked on a translation of his *Enquiry concerning Political Justice* (1793).[76] Constant shared some, though not all, of Godwin's views expressed in a work which at its publication had been considered dangerous and incendiary, notably Godwin's belief in human perfectibility – the notion that mankind is capable of improvement and is gradually doing so – and his profound libertarianism. Madame de Staël was working on her essay *Des circonstances actuelles* about the current political situation, and it may be that Constant collaborated with her in its composition, although this is by no means certain.[77] At the end of October 1798 the couple left for Switzerland where Constant dealt with financial matters and continued to work on his translation of Godwin. They visited Constant's cousin Rosalie in Lausanne, who reported to her brother Charles on 4 December 1798:

In all that [Madame de Staël] and our cousin say about France one can see that everything is going very badly there, although it is not their design to discredit it. They assure us that all will go much better for our grandchildren, that they will profit by all our misfortunes. That is no consolation to me.[78]

Constant also spent two days with Isabelle de Charrière, around 20–21 November 1798 and again in January 1799, reading her works and telling her that while translating Godwin he had discovered the *Enquiry* to be 'mediocre, that is full of commonplaces'.[79] (In fact the translation would never be published in Constant's lifetime and was destined to remain in manuscript until 1972.[80]) He returned to Hérivaux in early February 1799 and resumed his republican duties in Luzarches, but larger political projects were on the horizon. With the support of Madame de Staël he now planned to stand for election as deputy for Geneva, which had recently been annexed by France: he did research into his ancestral connections with the city in order to strengthen his claim to be its representative. He was unsuccessful once again.[81]

At the same period Constant's friendship with and admiration for Emmanuel-Joseph Sieyès (1748–1836), the former pamphleteer and now one of the Directors – or members of the Directory – was at its strongest: foreseeing political change in France as inevitable, he hoped that Sieyès had the theoretical *nous* to be able to ensure the country's future as a republic by formulating one of the constitutions of which he was a noted inventor. Sieyès, whose hatred of the nobility was undiminished since the time of his *What is the Third Estate?*, written at the outbreak of the Revolution, replaced Rewbell in the Directory in May 1799. Constant wrote to this man whom history now judges as a vain, narrow and sometimes cynical schemer on 18 May 1799 using the terms of hero worship and telling him that he saw in him the guarantor of the Republic's future:

> I give you now the expression of my unchanging feelings for you: friendship, devotion, admiration, hope, the conviction that you alone can finish the work you began, and a deep resolve to devote ... all the means at my disposal, all my intellectual resources and all my strength to your service.[82]

As with his earlier defence of Barras and 18 Fructidor, it is difficult to judge whether what looks like repellent sycophancy is motivated by Constant's desire for personal advancement or by a genuine love of the Republic: in Constant's rather desperate circumstances in 1799 the honest answer is probably both. In *Mémoires de Madame Récamier* (1815)[83] Constant was to write a scathing account of Sieyès's character and career that shows he had by then come to judge the Director in a similar way to posterity. Possibly in order to support the Director Sieyès's views and certainly to consolidate a Republic which was constantly threatened by both royalist and Jacobin (as well as by recent Austrian and Russian successes in the continuing war), Constant published *Des suites de la contre-révolution de 1660 en Angleterre* (*On the consequences of the Counter-révolution of 1660 in England*) in July 1799, one of his most effective and, in the circumstances, courageous works.[84] It was a reply to a royalist pamphlet by Boulay de la Meurthe which had praised the restoration of the English monarchy after Cromwell in 1660 for having brought general well-being to the nation. Constant's rejoinder pointed to vindictive confiscations and reprisals against supporters of the previous régime in England. The message was clear: if the Bourbons were ever to return, their revenge would be still more terrible than this.

War was now raging in Switzerland where the French Republic was fighting against the Austrians of the anti-French coalition and where the French gained a victory at Zurich on 26 September 1799. Across the Mediterranean the Egyptian campaign was in progress. Constant's friends Talleyrand of the Foreign Ministry and the devious Sieyès were in secret contact with General Bonaparte with a view to using the army to overthrow the Directory, on the spurious grounds of an alleged Jacobin plot. On 9 October 1799 the young general landed at Fréjus, travelled to Paris and over the next five weeks worked on his future strategy. Constant maintains in his *Souvenirs historiques* that he only knew about the impending *coup d'état* of 18 Brumaire (9 November 1799) the day before.[85] On the day itself, towards evening, Constant entered the capital which was now under military control accompanied by Germaine de Staël who could hope to see an end to her (intermittent) exile if Bonaparte did come to power. He witnessed the dramatic events at the Orangery in Saint-Cloud where the Council of Five Hundred fled as grenadiers entered the building, and he sent reports of what was happening to Germaine. The next day he wrote to Sieyès warning him of the extreme danger for the Republic of such a man as Bonaparte, unaware of Sieyès's part in the affair: 'In everything [Bonaparte] does, he looks only to his own elevation. But for him he has the generals, the soldiers, the part of the populace that has aristocratic [i.e. counter-revolutionary] sympathies, and everyone who enthusiastically surrenders to a show of force'.[86] As Constant recalls ruefully in his *Souvenirs historiques*: 'A spectator rather than a participant, I hurried over to Saint-Cloud, not without some pain and uncertainty, and there I saw the collapse of representative institutions in France for the next fourteen years.'[87]

For a time there was hope that something good might emerge from 18 Brumaire, and Constant wrote to Sieyès on 15 November:

> The post of deputy was the only one I wanted, because I believed that through it I could serve the cause of liberty. But since it is now

being said that, as of the next elections, it will be necessary to have been the administrator of a Department or a *commissaire*, I have felt obliged to apply for appointment either in the Léman [Lake of Geneva] Department where I was born, and where I could be of help to Geneva which suffered a great deal under the Directory, or in that of Seine-et-Oise where I have lived for several years, and where I have been *administrateur municipal* for three. I would prefer the latter as it would not take me so far away from you.[88]

On 25 December 1799 a new constitution came into force, the Constitution of Year VIII, originally the idea of Sieyès, which provided for four separate bodies to run France under the three Consuls, Bonaparte, Cambacérès and Lebrun: the Senate, consisting of sixty senators appointed for life by the Consuls; the *Corps législatif* or Legislative body; the Tribunate, whose members were appointed by the senators; and the *Conseil d'Etat* or Council of State whose councillors were nominated by the First Consul, Bonaparte, who would address them directly. It was soon to become clear that this elaborate pyramid inaugurated a new age of dictatorship, one in which the sovereign people of France were in fact to have very little say through the electoral process. Bonaparte now had the fullest executive authority, with the other two consuls playing a minor auxiliary role. A popular vote on the new Constitution confirmed his position, and by a massive majority. The Tribunate consisted of 100 members, each receiving a salary, whose function was to examine proposed *projets de loi* or bills, to accept or reject them, and to express a view on them. It could not, however, change a bill. To this toothless and essentially advisory body Constant was appointed on 24 December 1799 thanks to the support of Sieyès. Constant recommended a friend, the Genevan lawyer J.-M. Pictet-Diodati (1768–1828), to Sieyès to represent Geneva on the Legislative body, and the friend was duly appointed.[89]

Constant's appointment was the culmination of an ambition stretching back more than six years, the satisfaction of which had so often eluded him. His father had in the meantime become embittered, seeing Benjamin reject a salaried post in Brunswick in order, as Juste saw it, to squander his fortune and his talents with Germaine de Staël in France. Lately their relationship had deteriorated still further in a lengthy, acrimonious and complicated wrangle over monies which father and son both felt were due to them from the estate of Benjamin's mother. The rift between them was to last until Juste's death. But now, finally, Constant had the chance to prove he had been right: he immediately resigned from his post in Luzarches and on the first day of the new century attended the first sitting of the Tribunate, making it his special concern to represent the interests of Geneva. He also continued work – begun possibly under the Directory – on a political treatise now known as *Fragments of an Abandoned Work concerning the Possibility of a Republican Constitution in a Large Country*.[90] Constant's deep distrust of Bonaparte and of the military led him, with the encouragement of Germaine, to use his very first speech to the Tribunate on 5 January 1800 to demonstrate the possibility of using it as a platform for independent opposition to the Consulate and to warn the public of the threat of tyranny in France.[91] It was a bold high-risk gesture: it made his name as an orator and won him the respect of his fellow tribunes. Bonaparte never forgave him for it, nor did the press which the First Consul controlled. Constant recalls the occasion in an entry in his *Journaux intimes* dated 6 January 1805:

> I was due to have many, many people to dinner at my house, all rallying around the fledgling government, and gathering around me as around a favoured candidate. But I had shown too much independence when I had spoken the previous day. Only two turned up and they couldn't avoid me because they were my colleagues and met me at the Tribunate. It was from that moment that my tribulations began, the attacks by my enemies, and Biondetta's [Germaine's] despair.[92]

Germaine recalls in her *Dix années d'exil* (*Ten Years in Exile*) being summoned by Bonaparte's sinister chief of police Joseph Fouché (1759–1820) and being told of his master's displeasure at her involvement in Constant's opposition. It was suggested to her that she spend some time in the country.[93] Constant, after years of angling for a position and behaving rather shabbily on occasion in the process, now had a clearly identifiable enemy and the solid conviction of having right on his side. The Tribunate was his natural element: like an actor who has found exactly the right role, he was in character at last. And that role brought out the very best in him, both in eloquence and bravery. He wrote to his uncle Samuel on 20 January 1800: 'Whatever fate may have in store for us, we must serve the cause of freedom to the very end. . . . To follow one's conscience and be answerable to it alone is the only way not to be eaten up by uncertainty.'[94] He was visited during early March at the Tribunate by Isabelle de Charrière's nephew, the Dutchman Willem-René van Tuyll van Serooskerken, who reported back to her favourably. Her reply to him on 8 June 1800 was stern as well as being perceptive:

> Constant was fine when you saw him, from the little you saw of him, but elsewhere than in Paris, here, with me, you would see him as he really was. He is a true chameleon, without ever wishing to be one – although he is not without being aware of the fact, because he is surprised when he notices he's changed his position, having completely forgotten what he was like just a few days before. That

is how he has often forgotten both me and Colombier when he was with Madame de Staël.[95]

Constant no longer needed to put up with the habitual sniping of Madame de Charrière, now in her sixtieth year: he had the backing not only of Germaine but also of a truly sympathetic friend, Julie Talma, who wrote to him on 6 March 1800:

> Each time I read a new work by you, I have the feeling that your remarkable talent has found in my own heart everything that it expresses so well. That is because it is the natural vehicle of expression for every truly republican heart. I consider you to be the voice and mind of the Republic. . . . Having read your work carefully, and seeing all the friends and all the enemies it will make for you, I think you very fortunate.[96]

The work Julie was now reading in manuscript was the *Principes de politique* (*Principles of Politics*), a *summa* of Constant's political thought up to this point in his life on which he worked from early 1800 to April 1803.[97]

The political climate was meanwhile growing consistently more antipathetic to all of Constant's most cherished ideals. By the military victory of Marengo (14 June 1800) Bonaparte enhanced his reputation as a military leader. All the while, by his charm and the favours he bestowed on those who supported him, he was consolidating his hold on power; his government was making overtures towards the Catholic church; the prosecution of the war was an excuse for repressive measures, for increased police surveillance of opposition groups, for closing down newspapers, for attempting to limit the freedom of the Tribunate. The unsuccessful royalist bomb plot of the Rue Nicaise against him on 24 December 1800 only strengthened his hand. (Significantly the whole Tribunate, including Constant, went to see the First Consul to express its indignation on hearing the news of the attempted assassination.) Constant's own life was now dominated by the serious duties of his position as a tribune – resisting as best he could the abuse of executive power by Bonaparte, questioning the ambiguous wording of draft bills and representing the interests of Geneva. In spare moments he read Isabelle de Charrière's manuscript novels and plays and tried to find a publisher for her, or listened to those trying to persuade him to sell La Chablière in Lausanne. All of this was interspersed with ferociously hard work on his political treatise, particularly during October 1800 while he was at Hérivaux. In the middle of a stay in Switzerland with Germaine between July and September his uncle Samuel de Constant, Juste's brother, died during the night of 12–13 August 1800. Benjamin's relationship with him had often been strained, and the hypersensitive Samuel had felt that he showed him neither sufficient respect nor affection: as a final act of piety Benjamin wrote an obituary of Samuel (who had published novels and a moral treatise) which appeared in newspapers in October.[98]

By the autumn of 1800 Constant's existence was becoming thoroughly worthy and not a little dull. No doubt aware of this, Julie Talma introduced him to one of her friends, Anna Lindsay, on 20 November 1800.[99] Constant's relationship with Germaine de Staël had grown stale; they were frequently apart for long periods, first under the Directory because of the decree of expulsion of 1794, and now at the whim of the Foreign Ministry (although Talleyrand had lately been kind to Germaine); when they were together Constant often smouldered with resentment at her domineering and possessive manner; and Constant did not plan to remain unmarried for ever. For her part Germaine may well have resisted the idea of marriage to Constant because she was afraid of his alarming propensity for gambling and running up debts – something that must have been an unpleasant reminder of her spendthrift husband the Baron de Staël. Her remaining fortune might not last long in Constant's hands. Thus Anna Lindsay entered Constant's life, if unexpectedly, at a moment when he was ready for a new emotional experience. When it came, that experience was to be one of the most intense of his life.

7

'THE INTERMITTENCES OF THE HEART' (1800–1806)

Anna Lindsay (1764–1820), *née* O'Dwyer, the daughter of an Irish Catholic innkeeper from Calais, had been educated at the expense of the Duchess de Fitz-James and, in order never to return to poverty, had accepted a number of male 'protectors', the first, a Monsieur de Conflans, described by Julie Talma as 'mediocre' in a letter to Constant of 8 July 1802.[1] Conflans was followed by a British officer, Louis Drummond, who went through a form of marriage with her when she was 20 and lived with her in Paris for two years. It was he who encouraged her to change her name to Lindsay. In 1788 she gave him a son, Charles. In 1789 Drummond abandoned her and returned to Scotland, whereupon Anna began an eleven-year liaison with a married man, Auguste de Lamoignon, whom Julie Talma thought 'pitiful'.[2] Anna bore him two children, followed him to London during the Terror – where her drawing-room became the meeting place of a distinguished circle of *émigrés* – and showed him exceptional loyalty and devotion. Her reward was to see Lamoignon later seek a rapprochement with his wife for purely financial reasons. And it was at this precise moment in her life that she was introduced to Constant by her close friend Julie Talma. As the result of her upbringing and the injustices she had suffered at the hands of men, Anna showed an unusual mixture of character traits: she was intelligent, well read in French and English literature; she was a devout Catholic with royalist leanings – quite the opposite of her friend the free-thinking republican Julie, and of course of Constant; she was ambitious, passionate, sensitive, and had a strong sense of her own worth; she was also beautiful and had gained considerable sexual experience.

Within a few days of their first meeting Constant was in love with Anna, and his love was returned. They began corresponding in both French and English, and became lovers. In an undated letter to Constant Julie Talma remarked, 'When [Anna] is in the room, you lose all common sense',[3] and it was the same for Anna with Constant: they lost their heads in a delirium of physical passion, Constant visiting her between Tribunate meetings which in his impatience he now found tedious. They were seen together at dinners, at the theatre, at balls. At the height of their affair, on 14 December 1800, Constant wrote a letter to Anna full of praise of her. She had remained pure in a world of corrupt men, and her lofty, noble and generous nature was unsullied:

> For me you are more than a mistress and more than a friend. You are the only person my heart desires and the only one who can fill my imagination. You are are everything that is pure, noble and good. . . . I love you with my whole soul because I understand you, because I am like you, because I too have travelled through life alone, relying only on my strength of character in the midst of the battles I have fought and the failings I have been accused of. . . . I love to see you, hear you, make love to you because you are the object of my love, respect and veneration. What you need is your independence, you can be sure of everything else. Be patient just a few more days and you will reach your objective. You will only find peace of mind and the sympathy of others when unnatural ties with people who are unworthy of you [i.e. with Lamoignon] no longer impose a state of agitation on you.[4]

Anna had translated an English novel, *Marcus Flaminius* (1792) by Cornelia Knight which was set in Imperial Rome, and Constant searched for a publisher for her. (When Buisson published it in 1801, Constant took the credit for having contacted him.) On 28 December Constant wrote to Anna: 'Remember that each hour that passes brings nearer our complete and eternal union, that in a few months we will be united for ever.'[5] It seemed that nothing could now stand in the way of their relationship becoming a permanent one, each having found the perfect partner in the other. In the same letter, however, Constant explained that he would have to spend part of the evening with 'her' so as to counter 'her perpetual complaints'. 'She', of course, was Germaine, who had returned to Paris.

It is tempting for the biographer to see in Anna Lindsay Constant's greatest lost opportunity for happiness, a chance missed out of weakness or cowardice or some deeper flaw of character on his part. Tempting but perhaps wrong. There is in fact a parallel here with our response to his novel *Adolphe*. There can be little doubt that the character of Ellénore owes a great deal to Anna Lindsay: her Catholicism, her foreignness (Ellénore is Polish), her sense of being worthy of something better than what fate has given her, her passionate and impetuous nature, even the two illegitimate children she has had by an aristocrat whose attitude towards her is rather condescending. Adolphe likewise resembles Constant in his two most characteristic traits: an obsession with himself and his own welfare, and a passionate desire for independence, the two factors raising insoluble dilemmas for him in the course of his relationship with Ellénore. The problem of comprehending why Constant eventually left

Anna is akin to that of understanding Adolphe's complex feelings towards Ellénore. In the novel Adolphe and Ellénore believe that they have much in common: both are somehow marginal to society, restless and discontented with their lot and looking for an intense and emotionally fulfilling love. However, this surface similarity hides deep and fundamental differences resulting from their social positions, their sex and the intellectual disparity between them: above all Ellénore is as fiercely possessive as Adolphe is fiercely attached to his freedom and independence.[6] The challenge which Constant's great novel offers to its readers is to our sympathy and our intelligence. We are forced to see how a relationship looks and feels *from within* – at least from Adolphe's point of view – and to guard against any easy apportioning of blame. Likewise with Constant and Anna Lindsay we must resist hasty judgements or condemnations.

Germaine de Staël's return understandably brought out Anna's jealousy and resentment. Constant's characteristic response was to ask for time: in the long term they would be together for ever. He also felt his usual annoyance at any woman presuming to think that she owned him, an irritation that was to grow stronger apropos of Anna just as it had alienated him from Germaine, and perhaps from Isabelle before her. As in *Adolphe* the impasse was to remain without there being any prospect of a solution until the passage of time or some unforeseen event or intervention by a third party brought about a separation: even then that separation was not to be complete. By early January 1801 a note of acrimony had entered their correspondence, and by 19 January, despite seeing each other frequently, they were at loggerheads. On that date Constant, while still referring to their being happy and together for ever at some point in the future and saying that Anna was his ideal woman, nevertheless made it clear to her that she must not finish with Lamoignon and that he could not yet finish with Germaine: Anna would be criticized in society, while Constant's enemies would rightly be able to charge him with ingratitude and heartlessness.[7] Anna was devastated, but their affair continued into May 1801.

Constant meanwhile plunged himself into work in the Tribunate, bravely attacking a proposed law drafted in the aftermath of the failed bomb plot against Bonaparte which would set up special courts to try suspects. He denounced such courts without juries as unconstitutional and paving the way for the arbitrary exercise of power. Anna was present in the public gallery on one occasion to hear his speech on another bill.[8] At the end of April 1801 she reported to Julie Talma that Constant had asked for another ten days in which to make up his mind between her and Germaine de Staël:

He doesn't want to finish with her before she leaves, as if I were asking him to cause a pointless scene with her. . . . It's my future I want him to guarantee. I want to be sure that he won't use the time he claims to be devoting to an old friendship to have arguments with her that will end with her being infatuated with him again.[9]

Not surprisingly no decision was forthcoming from Constant, who left Paris with Germaine de Staël on 19 May for three days on the Marquis de Lafayette's estate at La Grange. Anna's contempt for his weakness and perfidy now knew no bounds: she left Paris for Amiens to be as far away as possible from both him and the equally unreliable Lamoignon. There she began copying out all his letters with the intention of returning the originals to him so that he could be confronted with the evidence of his treachery.

Constant returned to Paris on 23 May 1801, while Anna remained in Amiens, feeling guilty at the effect of her feelings for Constant on Lamoignon. At this point Julie Talma tried to play the honest broker between her two warring friends. Anna issued an ultimatum through her on 28 May:

Ask Benjamin whether he wants me to admit [to Lamoignon] that I love him [Constant], whether he wants to give up everything for me. Without being false or hypocritical I shall then ask Auguste [de Lamoignon] to end our relationship, and I shall not return to Paris until he has accepted.[10]

It was to be Germaine or Anna, but not both, and Anna's affair with Constant was at an end until a decision was made in her favour. Faithful to his usual policy when faced with two alternatives – that of choosing both – he refused to give any such undertaking in his letter to Anna of 31 May,[11] saying that they should both retain their independence but remain friends. He thereupon left Paris for Hérivaux, saying that he could no longer face being in a city where everything reminded him of the woman he was losing.

Anna's pride thus left her in the most invidious position possible: remaining the mistress of a married man who had become reconciled with his wife, or losing the man she loved to Germaine de Staël. And Constant's unwillingness to leave Germaine lost him a woman he still passionately loved and desired. In early June he received the following lines from Anna:

Now receive my eternal farewell. . . . It remains for me now to begin a new life. I hope that in a few days I shall be calm enough to set out in a new direction. I shall never see you again. . . . Give yourself over to that tender friendship which you have no desire and feel no obligation to give up, and which I would not have asked you to sacrifice if you had remained only friends [i.e. with Germaine]. Naturally I wanted you to finish with her, but it would have been enough to know you had done so if you did not accompany her to Geneva this year and did not live in the same house as her this coming winter. But that was more than you could manage, and I was not worthy of such an effort. I would refuse it now if you offered to make it.[12]

However, Anna did indeed resemble Constant, as he had remarked in an early letter to her, to the extent of stopping at his request at Hérivaux on her return from Amiens to Paris. And when she returned to the capital in mid-June there was a stormy scene between her and Lamoignon which resulted in a rift between them.[13] Whatever Constant had said to her – no doubt out of weakness or to make Anna happy – had brought her to the brink of disaster, and all he could do afterwards was to advise her to go back to her 'protector' Auguste de Lamoignon. By July she was understandably in despair, and full of hatred for her tormentor. Julie Talma wrote to Constant on 9 July: 'Anna is furious with you. She swears that she will never go back to Auguste. The surest way to make such a reconciliation odious to her was for you to advise it.'[14]

Meanwhile, in almost comic contrast to these painful dramas, Constant had been badgered by Isabelle de Charrière over the past few months into taking on a Neuchâtel boy named Rivière as a copyist.[15] She had also chivvied him into action to find publishers for the many creations of her seemingly unstoppable pen.[16] Out of touch with his life as she manifestly now was, she was nevertheless still capable of hitting the nail on the head when it came to his character, as her remark in her letter of 13 July 1801 shows: 'I have noticed that when you express a feeling, it is on the point of disappearing.'[17] Isabelle was more perceptive than she could have known, not being informed of the imbroglio with Anna Lindsay. For, despite his reassurances of love, Constant was about to leave Anna for Geneva and Madame de Staël. He was roundly told off by Julie Talma on 17 July for mincing his words with her friend and prolonging her agony.[18] That pain was to last for a very long time, and not in Anna's heart alone: their correspondence continued sporadically for many years (despite Anna's being forced to return to Lamoignon in September 1801); their passion for each other flared up again from time to time – a manifestation of what Proust in our own age would memorably call 'les intermittences du cœur' – and there were short-lived reconciliations.

Constant left for Switzerland around 19 July 1801. During August he finally sold La Chablière, and while resuming work on his political treatise, watched from a distance as Bonaparte and Pope Pius VII negotiated their way towards a Concordat, ratified by the Pope on 15 August 1801, which would lead to the restoration of the Catholic church in France. Julie Talma, rationalist and republican, was full of contempt for these developments.[19] Constant for his part was to find the enormously popular quasi-religious writings of Chateaubriand not to his taste, although he recognized his talent: *Atala* (1801) and the like were all too strong a reminder of how powerfully the current was now flowing back in the direction of organized religion in France,[20] as Constant discovered on his return to Paris towards the end of October 1801. In the Tribunate he resumed his opposition to the wording of bills, objecting also to the speed at which they were being processed, and in particular on 7 and 8 December 1801 to the highly significant word 'subjects' applied to citizens of France in a treaty with Russia.[21] The Revolution had theoretically done away with that kind of language, but now Frenchmen found themselves under the personal rule of the First Consul, Bonaparte, who was gradually increasing his quasi-mystical appeal to the soul of the French nation in a way that would soon bypass representative institutions completely, and culminate in the re-establishment of a dynasty. In such a political climate, Constant's spirited and barbed interventions in the Tribunate sounded increasingly like those of an unreconstructed Jacobin, especially to the man who now ruled France and believed that he embodied the will of the people. In January 1802 Bonaparte therefore saw to it that Constant was expelled from the Tribunate, together with a number of other troublesome colleagues, although Constant continued as a tribune until 21 March 1802.[22] Constant had written on 14 January to tell Isabelle de Charrière about what was going to happen, and she reported it gleefully to Constant's friend Ludwig Ferdinand Huber on 26 January:

> It was a sensible letter and written in quite a noble style, that is to say he was showing he was a man of moderation and too high-minded to be affected by his downfall. I suppose that by now the tribune is no longer a tribune. Madame de Staël will not love him any the more for it.[23]

She was to be even more cruel on 12 February 1802 in a further letter to Huber:

> Constant must now have woken up from his dream, during which he imagined he was a kind of statesman, a man whose talent, reputation and fate were henceforth linked to the destiny and the renown of the French Republic. . . . In France Constant will only ever be a clever and witty man who is not very highly thought of generally. The French are too distrustful of foreigners, there will always be too many competitors in France, and that will ensure that outsiders like him will always be left on the sidelines. The very word 'foreigner' gives ammunition to those who are jealous of him, to his rivals and to his enemies.[24]

For once his father showed more sympathy and understanding, perhaps for having himself experienced injustice in Holland, and urged him to turn his talents to writing: that would be the best means of revenge.[25] Even Anna Lindsay felt mortified for him.[26] In March 1802 when Constant finally left the Tribunate, he could tell himself that the struggle against tyranny had been an unequal one, but that he had acquitted himself honourably, putting behind him the years of career calculation under the Directory.

During the weeks between his expulsion from the Tribunate and his actually ceasing to be a tribune, Constant had been a guest at a dinner party given on 18 January 1802 at the home of the widow of the *philosophe* Condorcet with Julie Talma and General Laclos – that is Pierre-Ambroise-François Choderlos de Laclos (1741–1803), author of *Les Liaisons dangereuses* (1782). The occasion is recorded with tantalizing brevity by another of those present, the Genevan Etienne Dumont: 'Dinner at Madame de Condorcet's with Benjamin Constant, Madame Talma and General Laclos who told us how he had written his novel – which he seems very pleased with.'[27] It was not the first time that Constant had heard Laclos on the subject: he had met him in Paris during the 1780s, and in one of Constant's funniest letters to Isabelle de Charrière, that of 9–14 March 1788, he recounts a conversation with a Belgian from Brussels, François-Louis-Charles Boutmy (1739–1817), Professor of French Language and Literature at the Collegium Carolinum, a technically orientated university in Brunswick where Jakob Mauvillon also taught.[28] Hopelessly confused but very stubborn, Boutmy had insisted that *Les Liaisons dangereuses* was the work of a 'Monsieur Constant d'Avranches' – that is Constant *d'Hermenches*, Benjamin Constant's late uncle – to which Constant had replied, 'But Monsieur, I have had dinner with Monsieur de Laclos' and everyone in Paris knew that he *had* written the book. Neither of these meetings is recorded by Laclos's most recent biographer Georges Poisson.[29] Whether Laclos and his great novel were later a stimulus to Constant in his own writing is open to conjecture. Certainly Adolphe sets out to be a seducer in the mould of a Valmont, and then discovers too late that his finer feelings prevent him from abandoning Ellénore: the real story of *Adolphe* begins, in a sense, where *Les Liaisons dangereuses* leaves off.[30] Sadly Laclos was soon to meet a very unpleasant death while on military service in the heat of southern Italy. He died of exhaustion, dysentery and malaria at Taranto the following summer.

In March 1802 the Treaty of Amiens was signed, bringing a temporary peace to Europe: on 1 April there were English guests at Madame de Staël's dinner table.[31] From time to time Constant and Anna Lindsay met each other and corresponded, in spite of all that had happened. Constant read Chateaubriand's five-volume *Génie du christianisme* (*The Genius of Christianity*) (1802) and disliked its imprecise Romantic style and sentimentality intensely.[32] Its subject matter continued to interest him, however, and even in the midst of work on his political treatise, Constant's long and unfinished book on the history of religion was never entirely forgotten. He was depressed and discontented when he arrived in Switzerland in mid-May 1802 to visit relatives: General Bonaparte was seeking election as Consul for life and France was moving inexorably from military dictatorship to Empire. Under Bonaparte's bullying personal rule censorship and surveillance were flourishing, the press had become routinely sycophantic – advancement now being dependent on flattering the régime – and war was everywhere glorified. (The parallels with twentieth-century dictatorships are striking, though Bonaparte's was of course mild and amateur by our standards.) There was little Constant or liberal-minded friends could do but become, like dissidents in Soviet Russia, 'internal exiles', members of the intellectual *maquis*. And that is precisely what Madame de Staël's Coppet was to symbolize in the years to come: a focus not just of French but of European resistance to the Emperor's warmongering and to his authoritarian rule.

The sense of an impending real exile cannot have been far from Constant's mind during his summer in Switzerland. Germaine's active political intriguing added to the risk that his return to France might be unwelcome to the régime. Hard work on his political treatise and considerable background reading made his thoughts turn to travel during the coming winter, perhaps to Scotland or Germany, both countries being inextricably associated in his mind with study.[33] In the meantime he filled his letters to Anne de Nassau that August with satirical – and prophetic – wit concerning Bonaparte's supposed claims to North Africa,[34] and was warm in support of a new book by Germaine de Staël's aging royalist father, Jacques Necker, *Dernières vues de politique et de finances* (*Last Thoughts on Politics and Finance*) which appeared the same month. As Henri Grange has demonstrated,[35] Necker's influence on Constant has generally been underestimated: in the long run he may have won Constant over to accepting the idea of a constitutional monarchy.

Constant decided not to return to Paris at the end of October as he had in the past, perhaps judging that there was an element of risk in being so close to the centre of power. Letters were read, informers now reported on conversations, there was a general atmosphere of suspicion everywhere, and Constant's known hostility to Bonaparte might have brought retribution. He stayed in Switzerland and continued, despite ill health, severe eye troubles and financial worries, to work on *Principes de politique*, constantly rewriting and recasting it – his usual method of work with non-literary material. From November 1802 he was based in Geneva, and tried to avoid all political discussion. Then, in December 1802, Madame de Staël's epistolary novel *Delphine* was published in Paris in three volumes. The novel, set during the Revolution, concerns Delphine d'Albémar, an unconventional and articulate woman who comes into conflict with society's rules and conventions. Although it achieved considerable popularity, Bonaparte objected to views expressed in it which indirectly called into question his rule and his policies. Constant wrote to his friend the historian and critic Claude Fauriel (1772–1844) on 28 December 1802 asking his opinion of the work and adding: 'I have seen few novels in which there are so many new and perceptive observations, such truth in the depiction of character, and such lofty sentiments.'[36] But even as he praised *la dame de Coppet* and her talent, Constant was planning his escape from her, this time by marriage to Amélie Fabri (1771–1809), a full account of which is to be found in the first of Constant's *Journaux intimes*, *Amélie et Germaine* (16 January–10 April 1803).[37] In January 1803 he decided he needed marriage so that he would have someone to love and look after him: no outstanding intelligence was required of the fortunate woman, but she needed to have money and good sense. Amélie, a member of Genevan society, had some of the necessary qualities, but Constant was concerned that she lacked *mesure* in her conversation; she was forever indulging in inane humour and repartee, and as a wife she might bring ridicule upon her husband. Constant's breathtaking condescension – expressed, of course, in candid diary entries never intended for publication – was not only part of the age he lived in, it was also a fundamental part of him· he needed a housekeeper and companion, that was what marriage was about. But there was too a side of him that must invite sympathy even from the most censorious observer: he needed mothering, although he would never have put it in those terms. Intellectual and sexual satisfaction he could always find elsewhere: what he needed was a continuity of calm, uncritical affection, of the kind that he had all too rarely experienced.[38] Marriage would have the advantage of enabling Constant to continue his friendship with Germaine de Staël, while no longer being tied to her as her lover in a humiliating secondary role or having to endure frequent stormy scenes with her. Moreover, although they both were fiercely opposed to the despotic rule of Bonaparte, Germaine was taking brave but foolish risks in that area. There was now a proposal from Bonaparte to his advisers that he be crowned Emperor: Germaine might step on the lion's tail once too often. In any case the official lover Constant had been temporarily supplanted by a handsome married Irishman named O'Brien whom Madame de Staël was currently pursuing.[39] Nevertheless during March 1803 her jealousy on learning of Constant's plans became as violent as ever, and she used all of the very considerable means at her disposal to prevent the marriage, possibly enlisting Constant's father to her cause as well as ensuring that the whole of Genevan society was hostile to the union. At that point Constant seems to have begun to lose interest in Amélie, a woman about whom he had in any case never been enormously enthusiastic – it was the escape and the change which she had seemed to offer that had been important.

Constant's *Principes de politique* were now complete,[40] but it was impossible to publish the treatise in the current political climate where even a novel like *Delphine* was likely to be objected to by the authorities. Instead he began a history of the reign of Frederick the Great, hoping to be able surreptitiously to slip in some political observations relevant to the present time: this history was likewise destined to remain unfinished and unpublished in its entirety in his lifetime.[41] He returned to Paris in the first half of April and thence to a new property, Les Herbages, which he had bought in September 1802. It was within a couple of miles of Hérivaux (which he had now sold), but much smaller and more manageable. From Les Herbages he now wrote to Bonaparte on 15 April 1803 asking that Madame de Staël be allowed to live in France, the country where she was born, while he himself undertook to abstain from political activity and to concentrate on his scholarly activities. His request was ignored.[42] Germaine continued to write Constant letters of complaint about his treatment of her, but although his conscience was uneasy, his days and nights were now at least his own. During the summer of 1803 he was able to lead the agreeably quiet existence of a country gentleman at Les Herbages, riding, seeing neighbours, supervising the refurbishment of the house, rarely visiting Paris, reading German lives of Frederick the Great, writing (though with no certainty that Bonaparte would ever permit him to publish what he wrote), annotating the manuscript of his friend Claude Fauriel's essay on the last days of the Consulate[43] . . . and meeting Anna Lindsay again, the latter event leading Julie Talma to fear[44] – with some justification – that he might mislead Anna and hurt her again. War broke out with Great Britain in May 1803 after the year-long truce. Germaine was still in exile in Switzerland, though she had been finding some consolation in the company of visiting Englishmen. Constant's wish to be free was undiminished, and he was now firmly supported in it by his cousin Rosalie's letters to him.[45]

In the midst of this, according to *Cécile*, Constant received a letter from Charlotte on 7 August 1803, the first for several years.[46] Having remarried, to a penniless French royalist, the Vicomte Alexandre Du Tertre (or Dutertre) in 1798 (on learning the news Constant had felt a pang of regret and annoyance), she had been in Paris for three months and had heard that Constant was living alone and in penury, in a hovel in the country: she generously offered him money. Again according to *Cécile*, Constant wrote back declining to accept anything.[47] Smiling no doubt at this reminder of Charlotte's endearing and at times infuriating obtuseness, he went to Paris to meet her, but she had already left for Geneva. They nevertheless corresponded during August and September 1803. In September Madame de Staël returned to France and Constant dutifully went to meet her at Nangis, near Fontainebleau. He had advised her it was imprudent to return to Paris and, predictably, on 3 October 1803 Bonaparte ordered her to leave France. It was possible that Constant himself might soon be exiled as well. He left with Germaine and two of her children for the east of France at the end of October, with the intention of finding a haven in Germany: as he would recall in *Cécile*, he could not now abandon such a close friend who had been proscribed by the First Consul.[48] One might add that one of the children accompanying them was Albertine, in all probability Constant's own daughter. And Germaine's German, though she had been learning the language since 1799, was not as fluent as Constant's.[49]

By way of Châlons-sur-Marne and Metz the couple and their retinue made for Frankfurt, the derision of Bonaparte's tame Parisian press in their ears. While in Metz between 26 October and 8 November 1803 Constant and Madame de Staël met Charles de Villers (1765–1815), a philosopher and important intermediary between German and French literature and thought, who had lately published an essay in French on the spirit and influence of Luther's Reformation.[50] This and Villers's known enthusiasm for Kant were recommendation enough, and after being a correspondent of Madame de Staël he now also became a friend. Constant and Germaine reached Frankfurt on 13 November 1803. There he attempted to remain incognito as tutor to Germaine's children while acquiring German books for the work on religion which he was now resuming.[51] On 3 December they set out again for Weimar, travelling via Fulda and arriving on 14 December. As Constant's journal entry for 7 December 1804 reveals,[52] what he at first considered an enormous sacrifice for a woman he no longer loved – abandoning Paris and his studies at Les Herbages – was to prove an infinitely valuable opportunity to learn from German writers and philosophers in an atmosphere of intellectual freedom that had now disappeared in France. Above all it would give a much needed stimulus to his work on religion. He seems to have planned to leave Germaine after a while and to go to Geneva to find Charlotte. Nothing of the sort happened: Constant was in his second homeland once again, surrounded by erudition and unflagging intellectual curiosity, his morale boosted by the familiar German atmosphere of unprejudiced tolerance and enlightened liberal attitudes. He found he was in no hurry to leave.

But first Constant went through the curious charade of absenting himself in Gotha briefly around the New Year in order to drop his incognito and return, as it were, officially to Weimar on 4 January 1804.[53] Both the flamboyant Germaine de Staël and the slightly less conspicuous Constant were well received by the Duke and Duchess of Saxe-Weimar. Germaine wrote to A. Necker de Saussure on 31 January 1804:

[Constant] is invited to the Court twice a day, every day; the literary people here value him highly. He has a place here because people have opinions but aren't partisan in Weimar, and because the love of literature and of things of the mind are taken extremely seriously here.[54]

Then as now the city was small, peaceful and delightful, with its green meadows by the River Ilm. Under the benign rule of Duke Karl August (1757–1828) it had become home to some of the greatest figures of German literature – a literature which had yet to gain due recognition elsewhere in Europe – and was destined to become the byword for a golden age in German culture. Constant was fortunate once again, as he had been in Edinburgh. One piece of bad luck, however, was that Herder, the one man in Europe who might have helped him most in his work on the history of religion, died in Weimar on 18 December 1803, just four days after Constant's arrival. Nevertheless throughout his stay of two and a half months Constant worked for many hours each day on his unfinished book on religion. On 5 January 1804 the couple were introduced to the Court and met Schiller. Either then or shortly after they also met Wieland, and Madame de Staël was able to report to her father: 'Wieland told Benjamin that I was the person whose genius in both writing and speaking had impressed him most in his whole life.'[55] There were visits to the theatre, suppers, balls, conversations with historians and philosophers, French play readings at Court, there were even open lectures to attend: Constant's spirits rose and he became generally good-humoured. He too was much appreciated – in the end considerably more so than Germaine whose overbearing questioning of literary figures could be exhausting. Through Karl August Böttiger (1760–1835), director of the Weimar Gymnasium, the couple were introduced to Henry Crabb Robinson (1775–1867), an English lawyer who was a friend of both Schiller and Goethe, and an expert on Goethe's thought.

We are exceptionally well informed on the later part of Constant's stay in Weimar because on 22 January 1804 he began a series of diaries or *journaux intimes* which were to run for the next three years.[56] They contain frequent references to chapters of his book on religion now being completed or revised in Weimar, ideas found in his reading of Herder that had helped him in discussing the relationship between religion and ethics – now the real subject matter of his book: they also contain this important observation on German attitudes to religion, written on 4 February 1804: 'In Germany the Protestant religion becomes each day more a matter of feeling than an institution: no forms, no symbols, nothing obligatory, almost no ceremonies, only gentleness in its ideas and a morality based on feeling.'[57] This perception would become a central one in *De la religion* many years later, where Protestantism is presented as the highest point of perfection so far reached by mankind, both in its morality and in its lack of priestly authority or coercion.

In the midst of his patient labours on obscure musty tomes devoted to such recondite subject matter as fetishism in Greenland, Egyptian animal worship and Zoroastrianism, Constant also found time to record in his journal the gradual change in his attitude to Goethe. The first mention in the diary, 'Seen Goethe', is dated 23 January,[58] although they may have met earlier than this. They had dinner together on 27 January, when Constant commented 'Difficulty of having any conversation with him. What a pity he has been swept away by the mystical philosophy of Germany'.[59] After this unpromising start they had an 'interesting conversation' on 15 February about Homer and the Greek classical painter Polygnotus on whom Goethe was working,[60] and the following day: 'Quite remarkable supper with Goethe. He is a man full of wit, outbursts of high spirits, profundity, new ideas. But he is the least good-natured man I know.'[61] Shortly before leaving Weimar he spent the evening of 28 February with Goethe and Schiller and had supper with them. Constant's final remark is very positive: 'I know of no one in the world who has as much gaiety, subtlety, strength of mind and breadth of thought as Goethe.'[62] Goethe's own comment on Constant, written in 1822 in the light of Constant's subsequent political career, was to be no less appreciative:

> I spent many instructive evenings with Benjamin Constant. Whoever recollects what this excellent man accomplished in [later] years, and with what zeal he advanced without wavering along the path which, once chosen, was for ever followed, realizes what noble aspirations, as yet undeveloped, were fermenting within him.[63]

On 1 March 1804 Madame de Staël and Constant left Weimar for Leipzig, travelling through snow storms and atrocious weather. They arrived two days later and stayed for a week. Once again Constant found scholars with whom he could discuss questions relating to his research on religion. Germaine went on alone to Berlin where she received a triumphal welcome, while Constant returned to Weimar to be with some of the friends he had made there, not least Schiller and Goethe (10–18 March 1804). His ultimate intention was to make for Geneva where he might meet Charlotte again: during the whole of his stay in Germany Constant had been in correspondence with her, and had received warm and encouraging replies. Not for one minute had Charlotte forgotten him – though he might have forgotten her – and her hopes of their being together again one day had never been extinguished. In the meantime Constant spent evenings in Weimar with Sophie von Schardt (1755–1819), wife of an official at the ducal Court, with whom he seems to have had a brief flirtation,[64] and on 17 March attended the first night of Schiller's *Wilhelm Tell* with Goethe, which Constant found somewhat chaotic and inferior to his other plays.[65] On 18 March he set out for Geneva, knowing that he was leaving behind friendship and hospitality for a very uncertain future.

The journey back took Constant through Gotha, Fulda, Frankfurt and Ulm where on 31 March he spent the day with Ludwig Ferdinand Huber and his wife. En route he had plenty of opportunity to take stock of his life, coming to the conclusion that only writing could bring him lasting contentment. As far as 'Minette' – Germaine – was concerned, the diary entries show him to have been far less decided. When he reached Lausanne on 7 April 1804 he was informed that Germaine's father, Jacques Necker, had been taken ill. As he prepared to go to see him, Constant learned to his great shock that Necker was dead. Germaine had always had the closest of relationships with her father, Jacques Necker had treated Constant like a son-in-law, and Constant had great affection and respect for him. If Madame de Staël were alone in the depths of Germany when she received the news, in exile and without the support of a friend, her grief and despair would be unendurable. Constant deserves all credit for doing the noble thing: after three weeks on the road back from Germany he did not hesitate to return there, travelling day and night, hoping to be with her before she received the news.[66] He reached Weimar at midnight on 20 April 1804, and broke the news to Germaine when she arrived in the town on 22 April. Her distress was as intense as Constant had foreseen, and he himself was physically exhausted from his difficult journey. Nothing however had changed in their relationship, and Constant felt his longing to be free after nearly ten years with her more keenly than ever. They discussed their position and neither party expressed the wish to marry the other: Constant wanted to live apart from Madame de Staël. On 3 May they set off for Switzerland together via Würzburg and Ulm, where Constant saw the Hubers once again. Constant and Germaine were accompanied to Coppet by the austere and dogmatic August Wilhelm von Schlegel (1767–1845), with whom Constant argued all the way about contemporary German philosophy.

Germaine's grief was only increased by being in her father's château at Coppet. Constant kept out of the way in Lausanne, wrote to Charlotte, worked on Greek religion and ancient mythology while despairing of ever finishing his book when so far from the peace and calm of Germany. When as a distraction from her mourning Germaine began planning a tour of Italy, Constant declined to accompany her, knowing such a trip would delay his book even further. On 11 June 1804 Constant consulted a Genevan doctor about his health and recorded the following conclusion in his diary: 'Butini has confirmed what I have felt for a long time: that being deprived of women ruins my health. Within the next six months I must make a suitable arrangement in that regard.'[67] It was, it must be stressed, not only Constant's sexual appetite that needed satisfying. He could and did have frequent recourse to prostitutes, often at this time riding to Geneva for that sole purpose according to his diary. Nevertheless as he grew older – he was now 36 – he needed more and more a secure, stable atmosphere in which to study without interruption. That was his ideal: solitude and independence, but with a woman friend somewhere else in the same house. He did not need another grand passion, but rather the companionship of marriage. Germaine was unique in being the only woman he knew who was clever enough to criticize his style and ideas. Her guests at Coppet were a continual stimulus to Constant's thought – Schlegel or the historians Charles-Victor de Bonstetten (1745–1832) and Simonde de Sismondi (1773–1842), for example. Constant always enjoyed being with Albertine de Staël, now aged 7 (who had, incidentally, now grown to resemble him even more). There was, however, a permanent shortage of peace and quiet in the household. Marriage to his cousin Antoinette de Loys – rich, young, beautiful and agreeable in character – was a possibility, but in July he spent some days in Solothurn with Julie Talma, where Julie's son was ill, and there he had reason to reflect on a marriage he was now grateful to Madame de Staël for preventing – to Anna Lindsay:

> [I] have seen a few letters from the woman I used to call 'my Anna' two years ago. It is an example of the blunders which my relationship with Minette has prevented me from making. If it were not for [Minette], it's almost certain that I would be burdened down by that woman and her two children. I would have turned my life upside down and condemned myself out of a sense of duty to look after her. I'd have lost everything – my money and my independence. I need to remember the advantages of my ties [with Germaine] as well as their disadvantages. But that Anna is a distinguished woman, with great nobility of character and sound judgement. She is unsubtle, however, and rather narrow, and the prejudices that she has adopted with the highest of intentions all run counter to her own self-interest. There is a fieriness, a violence and a meticulousness in the way she runs her house that make her a veritable domestic demon. She is probably the woman who has loved me the most, and who has made me the most unhappy. But I owe to her everything I know about the ecstasy of physical and emotional love in a woman.[68]

The passage is echoed in the well-known description of Ellénore at the beginning of *Adolphe*.

He spent August 1804 in Geneva with Germaine, dictating chapters to his copyist and trying to put some order into a book that frequently threatened to overwhelm him with its multiple drafts and numerous sections, his study of religion. Planning to leave as soon as possible himself for Germany, he marked time until Madame de Staël left for Italy. On 21 August he described himself under Germaine's domination as 'a shade, conversing with other shades, but no longer able to make plans for the future'[69] – 'shade' (*ombre*) was a fashionable word and concept at this time – and in similar mood, while watching his 2,000 books being packed for despatch to Les Herbages, remarked in his diary on 22 October:

> This library . . . which because of all its travels has cost me more than it's worth, especially since half of the books are worn through having been moved about so much without even having had their pages cut, this library really is emblematic of the existence of a man who has never known what he wanted to do with his life.[70]

In France Pope Pius VII was about to crown Napoleon emperor; repression had become generalized and any political activity was out of the question. Scholarship appeared to be the only worthwhile pursuit left open to Constant, and, seeing so many apparently wasted years behind him, he was understandably desperate to make his mark through it. His attitude to religion had gradually changed and he now felt himself at a considerable distance from his earlier self and the age in which he had grown up:

> What a strange philosophy, in truth, was that of the eighteenth century, poking fun at itself and other philosophies, setting out to discredit not only received prejudices, not only the consoling or moral ideas that it could have separated from them, but also mocking its own principles, taking pleasure in sparing nothing from ridicule, in degrading and cheapening everything! When you read the works of that period carefully, you are surprised neither at what came after nor its consequences today [i.e. Napoleon]. They were men who lived for the moment, limiting their existence and influence to that moment, writing only to encourage the next generation in selfishness and degradation, a generation which has certainly profited from their lessons.[71]

His critique of Napoleon's age for its systematized baseness, its rapacity, selfishness and indifference to suffering was taking shape and had a historical and philosophical foundation. On religion he was to write in his journal on 19 February 1805:

> There is something coarse and blasé in irreligiousness which I find repellent. And besides there is a part of me that is religious. But that religion is entirely a matter of feelings, of vague emotions. It cannot be reduced to a system.[72]

Worries and distractions now crowded in upon Constant. His father and Marianne were in continual and serious dispute with him about the money that would be needed to bring up his half-brother and half-sister. Constant commented on this marriage and its consequences: 'Strange man, who never considered the wrong he was doing to me, even as regards my feelings, or to himself.'[73] It is a remark that sums up their unhappy relationship, and shows how far Constant had advanced in his understanding of it since defending him in Holland in the early 1790s. But more unsettling still was Germaine de Staël's imminent departure: separations usually filled Constant with anguish, and for days beforehand he was upset by this one. He left for Paris on 26 November 1804, spending a few days at Dole with his father on the way, and then a few more in Lyon with Madame de Staël (6–12 December 1804). Then she left on 11 December for Turin, and Constant reached Les Herbages on 21 December. In Paris he saw Claude Fauriel, the historian Claude Hochet (1773–1857)[74] and other friends, but was profoundly disappointed by the superficiality of French people's attitudes when he described his book on religion, and now found the obligatory socializing and late nights exhausting. He saw Anna Lindsay, who still loved him, but had still to meet Charlotte. He noted on 28 December 1804 in his diary: 'I hope to see [Charlotte] again, the woman who changed my whole life and whom I loved so passionately for a few days. I am quite curious about meeting her after twelve years of separation.'[75] In the event he was too cool with Charlotte, at least that was his feeling afterwards: he was afraid of becoming involved again lest his writing suffer. He saw her again, met her 'cold but polite' husband, the Vicomte Du Tertre, and she once more offered him her fortune: her feelings for Constant were still as strong as ever. He found both Anna and Charlotte with similar feelings towards him – of desire mingled with resentment – and he straightaway retreated. He even considered the commercial alternative which was available in Paris – that of hiring a mistress to spend three months at Les Herbages with him so that he would have agreeable company when he wanted it, but could also work without distraction – but the arrangement fell through. The problem, as in *Adolphe*, was not so much the risk of falling in love again himself as someone else falling in love with him – and all the pain that might bring them both.

January 1805 was spent at Les Herbages, with frequent trips to Paris, sometimes to visit prostitutes, as Constant's diary candidly records. He was still wrestling with the problem of shaping his book, abandoning plan after plan and studying Roman polytheism – thereby forming the nucleus of what would eventually become his study *Du polythéisme romain*. On 9 January he learned that Ludwig Ferdinand Huber had died, and on 19 January he confided to his journal: '[I am filled with] a kind of terror about Fate. I never draw a line under my journal entry for the day without a feeling of anxiety about what that next unknown day will bring.'[76] It was to be a year marked by illness and loss, one which revived Constant's death obsession and threatened to plunge him into depression. As he remarked on 25 January: 'Suffering, whether genuine or simulated, will for ever be all-powerful over me.'[77] Nothing was settled in his life: he saw Charlotte and Anna regularly in Paris; Charlotte's husband became jealous and Constant felt pity for Charlotte, forced to live in the dispiriting company of the ignorant and bigoted provincial French gentry. As for Anna, Constant's feelings for her were liable to catch fire at any moment, and the same was true for her. He contemplated writing to Germaine de Staël in Italy to propose marriage and, if she refused, leaving alone to settle in Weimar or Berlin. He was more than ever engaged in the continuing financial dispute with his father, and remarked in his diary on 20 March: 'There is always something hurtful in the style [of his letters]. Anyone would think that I am the only one of his children who has no right to his money.'[78] Above all, perhaps, literary fame continued to elude him, making any praise he received for small achievements unbearable. Small wonder that as a consequence he was frequently overcome that winter with bouts of extreme melancholy. Nevertheless, to the outside observer it is clear that a strange thing was slowly happening: Constant's entries in his *Journaux intimes* were becoming the matrix of feelings, striking observations and aphorisms out of which *Adolphe* would shortly grow. Indeed on the strength of his diaries alone, had he wished to publish them, he need have had no reason to fear about his literary talent.

To that complex matrix of thought and emotion was to be added another essential ingredient in *Adolphe*, the idea of the final separation of death, the most powerful of all Constant's obsessions. Julie Talma, who had always given Constant unstinting sympathy and support, lost her one remaining son Félix de Ségur on 10 February. Grief made rapid inroads in her own health. By mid-March it was clear that she was dying, and Constant, appalled at the prospect of being without the most honest and loyal of all his friends, listed in his diary on 15 March 1805 all those of whom he had been robbed by death – Jakob Mauvillon, Ludwig Ferdinand Huber, Jacques Necker and most recently the Marquis de Blacons, a disreputable but amusing companion and habitué of Coppet who had committed suicide. Then there was the brilliant John Wilde of Edinburgh who was now as good as dead, having lately lost his reason completely. Constant reflected bitterly that wherever he walked it was as if it were over the graves of his friends, while his enemies were all still alive and flourishing. Who was there left to think, write or live for?[79] To his horror he watched as Julie Talma grew inexorably weaker with the progression of her illness while her character remained fundamentally unchanged. In a manner entirely alien to his usual way of thinking, he fell to speculating on whether some part of a human being might survive death.[80] Julie died on 5 May and was buried two days later. Constant's grief was such that he discontinued the detailed journal he had kept since January 1804 and reverted to an abbreviated and coded form, considerably less informative than hitherto, for several months to come.

Madame de Staël had proposed a secret marriage which offered the advantage of ensuring Constant's financial security and the possibility of being with 'my delightful Albertine', as he called her. Germaine was not only his intellectual equal, able to understand his work on religion and offer useful comments on it: as he recognized in his diary entry for 1 May 1805 there was a part of him that was prone to depression, and Germaine's company was the only effective antidote.[81] There were, however, enormous drawbacks to the remedy, not least Germaine's fearsome temper. Charlotte was the milder alternative, and indeed she now offered to divorce Du Tertre in Germany and marry Constant. Constant noted in his diary on 4 May 1805:

> She [would bring] me her delightful character, a degree of intelligence
> – more indeed than I had thought, a distinguished family, enough
> money for me to be no poorer married to her than I am now, and
> an attachment to me that has survived ten years of separation as well
> as my own indifference. . . . Heaven has shown me an unexpected
> haven in Charlotte: I must make for it.[82]

But the shock of Julie's death inevitably made an early reunion with Germaine more likely now that she had returned from Italy. Charlotte left for Germany to spend some time with her relatives, and in July 1805 Constant travelled to Geneva with Claude Hochet and Prosper de Barante (1782–1866), all three friends involved in journalism and sharing a passionate interest in politics and history. They reached Coppet on 10 July. Once more Constant slipped back into a repetition of the kind of life he had led three years earlier: visits to his family in Lausanne, visits to prostitutes in Geneva (his sexual drive was undiminished, and he notes in his diaries how essential frequent sexual intercourse is for his morale), frustration at making little progress with his book amidst the gossip, late nights and distractions of Coppet, inability to make a final break with Germaine – his coded numerical journal showing rapid alternation between the desire to leave and the desire to stay with her. Entirely preoccupied with plans to travel and finally to break his 'éternel lien' – his unending bondage to Germaine de Staël – and with the political situation in Europe (Napoleon was now planning an invasion of Britain across the Channel), Constant failed to notice what was happening right under his nose: Madame de Staël had fallen passionately in love with Prosper de Barante, and Constant became aware of the fact on 18 September 1805. It produced in him a predictable mixture of desire, resentment and paralysis as to which course to follow. As he asked in despair in his journal on 3 October 1805, 'Was there ever a man more undecided?'[83]

Napoleon's success on land at Ulm (15 October) and Austerlitz (2 December) – despite a spectacular naval defeat at Trafalgar (21 October) – induced Austria to sign a humiliating peace, and promised a widening of imperial tyranny in Europe. To complete this year of dispiriting news and bereavements Constant learned on 30 December of the death of Isabelle de Charrière during the night of 26–7 December 1805. The last letter she ever wrote was to Constant, on 10 December 1805, urging him to take a spa water cure for his recurrent eye troubles. In spite of everything they had maintained contact by letter. Constant wrote in his diary on 30 December:

> Death of Madame Charrière de Tuyll. I have lost in her another friend who tenderly cared for me, a refuge if ever I needed one, a heart which, though hurt by me, never turned away. How many deaths I have already recorded in this book! The world is becoming depopulated. Why go on living?[84]

At Coppet, meanwhile, Germaine had decreed that it was time for amateur theatricals, and Constant was coerced into learning the part of Zopire in Voltaire's tragedy *Mahomet*: as he remarked in desperation in his diary on 5 January 1806, out of the previous 714 days, he had devoted only 259 to work. He was wasting his life with Germaine, he would never have any peace with her. He debated the alternatives with himself – marriage to Charlotte, if she would still have him; staying with Madame de Staël but on the understanding that for sex he was allowed to go elsewhere (sexual relations between Constant and Germaine had long since ceased, no doubt because of mutual physical antipathy); or keeping a mistress who could also take dictation and copy out his writings. Again he plunged himself into his work as best he could, beginning on 4 February a political essay which would become the beginning of his *Principes de politique*, and continuing, despite illness and quarrels with Germaine, through March and April 1806. By 16 April the manuscript was 469 pages long, and Madame de Staël liked it. Three days later the restless Germaine left for Lyon, tired of Geneva and Coppet and full of hope that her exile would soon be at an end, that Napoleon would relent and allow her to return to her beloved Paris. It was not to be: she was kept at a distance of 40 leagues from the capital and stayed near Auxerre, at the château of Vincelles, where she was visited by friends, notably the unfortunate Prosper de Barante, a new victim of her cataclysmic love, and from whom on 30 March 1806 she had demanded – and received – a written statement 'ceding himself entirely' to her.[85] Left behind in Geneva, Constant tried to continue his studies but even without her the social life there was a distraction, and in any case he found he missed the intellectual stimulus of Germaine. Boredom was being without her; there was always excitement in her vicinity – and always a price to pay. The problem lay of course in Constant himself and in the contradictions of his character: needing peace and quiet for the one thing that he believed really mattered to him, his writing, yet also craving the stimulation of company, especially the company of women.

On 1 June 1806 Constant began the journey from Geneva to Auxerre knowing full well how bad things would be. He would find Germaine discontented, bored, angry with Barante – who wished to end their affair – and with himself. As he observed in his diary on 5 June:

All the volcanoes in the world are less fiery [*flamboyants*] than she is. What can I do about it? Fighting against her tires me. No more plans. I shall lie down in my boat and sleep through the gales. No more working: the fact that I have the talent to is pure chance anyway, and illness might have destroyed it. I'll pretend that illness has destroyed it. [Worked] for the last time in my present circumstances.[86]

It was a notion that had a particular appeal for Constant, the idea of being rocked in the well of a boat, like a child in the womb, sleeping through storms raging around him, and no doubt called up associations with his earliest years.[87] But he was an adult and sleep was no longer an option available to him; he must face the emotional bedlam of *la dame de Coppet* and her entourage. He paused at Dole to visit his father who was ill, and reached Auxerre on 9 June to find Germaine's rented château in complete turmoil. The purpose of his visit was to decide with her whether they were to stay together. Ghislain de Diesbach in his shrewd and lively biography of Madame de Staël describes the scene thus:

By 15 June the usual circle of friends had assembled around Madame de Staël without her finding in them the slightest remedy for her agitation. There was Don Pedro de Souza [whom Germaine had met in Italy], Benjamin Constant, complaining all the time and tormented by his need for a Venus of the streets (a difficult need to satisfy in a place as remote as this), Elzéar de Sabran [the poet], [August Wilhelm] Schlegel, jealous of everyone else, and Prosper de Barante who had come [from Paris] for only twenty-four hours – which had made Madame de Staël furious. 'I feel like raising a little altar to Unreason', noted Constant ironically, a man who was no longer capable of being astonished by anything.[88]

During July things were calmer amongst this curious *ménage* of Germaine de Staël's lovers, ex-lovers and would-be lovers. Constant went to Paris (30 June–15 July) to see Fouché in a vain attempt to persuade the government to revoke the order exiling Madame de Staël from the capital. He visited Les Herbages briefly, saw old friends – and was to his relief at last able to visit brothels regularly again, as his diary records. (Despite his best efforts he had been unable to rid himself of unruly desires at Auxerre.) On his return he found being exhibited as one of Germaine's subservient possessions no longer acceptable. The result on 30 July was: 'Terrible scene, terrifying, insane. Appalling things said. She is mad, I am mad. How will it all end?'[89] The scenes lasted until he left for Paris again on 24 August. In spite of everything he had managed to do some work on his political treatise, completing a draft of it on 3 August. While in Paris Constant arranged with Fouché for Madame de Staël to be allowed to live in Rouen, a rather more attractive prospect than Auxerre, and on 18 September he took up residence there with her, determined to complete his work on politics. For Germaine there was now the possibility of evenings at the theatre, and Constant was once again able to find prostitutes to satisfy his own priapic cravings.

Fully expecting the final defeat of Napoleon by the Prussians in the forthcoming battle, Constant wrote in English in his diary on 30 September 1806, misquoting Addison's *Cato*: 'The dawn is overcast, the morning lowers, and heavily on clouds brings on the day – big with the fate of Cato and of Rome.'[90] In the event it was Prussia that was to be humiliated at Jena (14 October) as Russia would be in 1807 at Eylau and Friedland. The whole of Europe, it seemed, would soon be under the yoke of the Corsican tyrant and his family. Constant could not yet know that the Prussian defeat would also mean the end of the Weimar he had known under Duke Karl August: after the battle even his friend Goethe's house was invaded by French soldiers intent on plunder and indeed the great man was saved only by the intervention of his wife! Under French military occupation the civilized and humane Duke of Brunswick would be deposed too, and an entire constellation of small eighteenth-century German courts would be swept away. Constant still hoped one day to return to Germany, whatever the circumstances there might be, and on 10 October 1806 he received a tangible reminder of his life there in the form of an affectionate letter from Charlotte who had now returned to Paris:

> Without knowing the reason for your uncharacteristic silence, I am making a third attempt to obtain news about you. If it proves as fruitless as the previous ones it will be the last. But I cannot believe you are indifferent, and I will prove it by speaking to you with confidence. I am alone here: Monsieur Du Tertre thinks I am still in Germany, he is not due to return before the end of the month. You must believe that I am doing nothing that has not been authorized by my whole family and that my stay here has no impropriety about it whatsoever. . . . It has never been more important that I talk to you than now when, of the three possible courses of action before me I must choose one. If you can return to Les Herbages and if you prefer to see me there rather than here, I shall go there. We shall spend the day together and decide on our future. I beg you to write immediately saying either that you have lost interest in me or that you are still fond of me. I hope to have a reply in the next six days. If I receive none, I shall know where I stand. I shall

finally separate two lives which until now have always been united in my heart.

(Letter of 8 October 1806[91])

Constant replied and, touched by her unchanging attachment to him, went to Paris on 18 October. On 20 October, after 'thirteen years of resistance' as Constant noted in his journal, they became lovers. At first Constant seemed unaffected by their new intimacy, but by 22 October he was writing: 'Evening with Ch[arlotte]. That woman is an angel of gentleness and charm. What a prize I have missed in my life!' (followed by codes indicating 'love for Charlotte' and 'physical [i.e. sexual] pleasure').[92] Charlotte had grown tired of a jealous husband heavily reliant on her money. There had only ever been one man in her life and her patience had now been rewarded. As for Constant, this was a full-blooded passion such as he had not known for years. He took Charlotte to see his estate at Les Herbages then returned to Paris, amazed at ever having failed to realize the happiness she could bring him, and more resolved than ever to be free from Madame de Staël. The entries in his *Journaux intimes* now become fuller as he records the change in him:

> The contrast between [Madame de Staël's] impetuousness, her egoism, her constant obsession with herself and Charlotte's calm, gentle, modest, self-effacing ways makes Charlotte a thousand times more dear to me. I am tired of the masculine woman [*l'homme-femme*] whose iron hand has kept me in chains for ten years. Now a truly feminine woman is intoxicating and enchanting me (26 October).[93]

On 28 October Charlotte bade him a tearful farewell, and the next day he returned to Rouen. On 30 October 1806 he noted in his diary 'Wrote to Charlotte. Began a novel which will be our story. Any other work would be impossible for me.'[94]

8

'ITALIAM, ITALIAM'
(1806–1812)

Constant was not a natural novelist in the way that he was a natural diarist, historical scholar or master of invective. Apart from one attempt at novel-writing in collaboration with Isabelle de Charrière – the *Lettres de d'Arsillé fils*[1] – he had hardly ever touched the genre. But now something out of the ordinary, an event of the greatest importance in his life compelled him to write the narrative of how he had found, lost and found again the perfect woman companion. We no longer possess the text that he wrote that autumn in Rouen, which doubtless underwent transformation after transformation through multiple drafts. Critics and scholars have examined minutely the evidence of entries about it in the *Journaux intimes* and have often come to conflicting conclusions as to whether this unknown work, this *Urroman* was an early version of *Adolphe* or of *Cécile*.[2] What seems most likely is that the first draft began – as do both *Adolphe* and *Cécile* – at a small German court in the late eighteenth century, and that as Constant retraced mentally the events of his life at Brunswick and his first infatuation with Charlotte, the misery of his subsequent years and his present unhappiness with Germaine de Staël crowded in upon him. From a factual, historical account of separation and eventual reunion – in all probability something along the lines of the beginning of the *Cécile* we know – it became a less serene and altogether more tragic story about a man unable to finish with a woman he no longer loves. As Constant wrote that November and read his autobiographical novel aloud to Germaine – herself of course a novelist and currently completing *Corinne*, her best work – his text undoubtedly underwent the wholesale changes and rearrangements all of Constant's works were to know. On 7 November he discovered that the Vicomte Du Tertre had burnt a letter he had sent Charlotte: in panic and disarray he told Germaine of his feelings for Charlotte and perhaps more.[3] Madame de Staël's anger was terrible. It then emerged that Du Tertre might be prepared to consider a divorce on condition that he was financially rewarded, and Constant saw Charlotte again in Paris at the end of November. By 1 December his novel had begun to bore him, and he returned, after having laid it aside ten months before, to his book on religion: then he turned back once again to his work of fiction, improving it.[4] By the end of December the novel now contained an 'Ellénore episode' within the story and an account of Ellénore's death: this now sounds more like the *Adolphe* we know, although it was still contained within a separate autobiographical framework. Whatever its nature, it cannot but have reflected closely the impasse of his relationship with Madame de Staël, for it caused a terrible scene with her when Constant read it aloud on 28 December: he himself was physically ill and spat blood.[5] It was now to be the story of Ellénore alone, not of a man caught between two women: *Adolphe* now seems to have taken on a separate existence from *Cécile* in Constant's mind.

And there our knowledge of the two texts at this period ends. On 2 January 1807 Constant began work again in earnest on his projected study of religion.[6] Charlotte's husband was unreconciled to the idea of losing her and indignant at her continuing sporadic affair with Constant: there was the possibility of a duel, but the storm eventually blew over. Constant's resolve wavered from time to time as he recognized Charlotte's limitations: 'Walk with Charlotte: in her character sensitivity, extreme uprightness, kindness, love, touchiness and a little monotony' (10 January 1807).[7] In fact marriage to Charlotte in Napoleon's newly Catholic France might not be without its complications. Quite apart from the social stigma of Charlotte's double divorce, which made it likely that she would be snubbed in some Parisian circles, a considerable legal problem existed. Constant was a Protestant divorcee from a wholly Protestant marriage to Minna; Charlotte's first husband by a German Protestant marriage, Baron von Marenholtz (whom she had divorced on 15 August 1794), was still alive, and therefore the practising Catholic Alexandre Du Tertre ought never to have married her in Brunswick in June 1798 – in the eyes of the Catholic church that second marriage was invalid. But the problem could be simplified: Du Tertre could ask to have his marriage to Charlotte declared null and void by the Catholic Archbishop of Paris, and then the two Protestant divorcees could simply enter into a new marriage using any Reformed church that tolerated divorce and remarriage.

Madame de Staël was putting the finishing touches to *Corinne* during January 1807 at the château of Acosta, 12 leagues from Paris, where she was now allowed to live. Her novel reflects through its gifted Italian poet heroine Germaine's own disappointment with weak-willed and unreliable men, personified in the Scotsman Oswald. It has understandably been viewed as a reply to Constant's own portrayal of the tragic predicament of a man very like himself through the character of Adolphe, a man who out of a sense of loyalty and responsibility stays with a woman, Ellénore, whom he no longer loves and whose possessiveness torments him.[8] As Germaine saw *Corinne* through the press during February and wondered whether to marry the poet Elzéar de Sabran, Constant became more and more set on marrying his 'sweet angel' – as his diary repeatedly calls Charlotte – as a means of liberation from Madame de Staël. But the idea of marriage to a woman whose reputation might be judged scandalous in the social circles in which they would wish to move gave him pause. Extraordinarily – given his genuine feelings for Charlotte – he once again seriously considered taking his father's advice and marrying his cousin Antoinette de Loys instead.[9] Matters were taken out of his hands at this point by the reckless actions of Germaine who defied Napoleon by breaking the terms of her exile and spending 20–2 April in Paris: her punishment was an enforcement of the order of banishment to no less than 40 leagues (160 kilometres) from the capital.[10] The character of such an imprudent dreamer as Germaine with her conspicuous lack of common sense could hardly have presented a sharper contrast with the steady level-headed Charlotte, a woman who would, he thought, make an undomineering helpmate for him. Constant accompanied Madame de Staël along the road to Lyon as far as Mongeron, on 25 April, then returned to Paris. He showed loyalty to her by publishing a fine review article on *Corinne* in three issues of *Le Publiciste*, on 12, 14 and 16 May, a fortnight after it had been published.[11] Attacks on the novel had come from reactionary quarters which Constant lambasted for, in accordance with corrupt contemporary taste, preferring sentimentality to naturalness in art, and for expecting literature unrealistically to show virtue being rewarded with happiness. Nevertheless Constant was very relieved to have some peace now the fretful Germaine had gone, and felt sorry for Albertine, tied to the tail of such a comet.

Good news came on 6 May 1807 when Du Tertre consented to a divorce, saying that as a Catholic he was uneasy in his conscience about the status of a marriage which he now wished to have declared null and void by the Church.[12] Constant continued to feel protective towards Charlotte, despite his occasionally offhand and aggressive manner: that was a normal alternation for him, and deeply rooted in his personality. In fact that unusual personality greatly puzzled even his friend Fauriel when on 28 May 1807 Constant read to him from his autobiographical novel: perhaps the reading was prompted by his seeing a similarly indecisive character with ambivalent feelings towards women the previous evening – Hamlet, in a superb performance by the actor Talma.[13] In June Charlotte and Constant left Paris for different destinations, she for Germany to seek a divorce from Du Tertre (who on 5 June 1807 had signed an authority to Heinrich Christoph Samuel Niemeier, a lawyer in Brunswick, empowering him to seek to bring about a legal end to his marriage, but on 10 and 11 June had threatened out of pique to revoke his consent[14]), he for his father's house near Dole and thence, inevitably, to Coppet. Not only Juste but also his relatives in Lausanne continued to reproach him for prolonging his relationship with Madame de Staël, but were soon to be equally disapproving of his friendship with a twice-divorced woman. Constant for his part felt guilt at concealing his marriage plans from them. During stormy scenes at Coppet Germaine de Staël began threatening suicide by swallowing opium. She forced him once more to act in one of her own amateur productions, and to play the role of Pyrrhus against her Hermione in Racine's tragedy *Andromaque*. The situation on stage was, of course, ironically appropriate: Hermione loves Pyrrhus . . . who loves Andromaque.[15]

Throughout August 1807 Constant's diary continues to reflect his ceaseless hesitation, self-doubt and back-tracking on earlier decisions, behaviour which at times clearly borders on the neurotic. In the middle of it all came a curious interlude in Lausanne where he and Germaine came into contact with a Pietistic or Quietist group led by Constant's cousin Charles de Langalerie (1751–1835), who was helped by François Gautier de Tournes (1755–1828), by coincidence a relative of Madame de Staël.[16] The sect, which followed the writings of Madame Guyon (1648–1717), the French mystic, rejected religious dogmas and sought peace of mind through bringing the believer into harmony with God's wishes. Constant took an interest in the circle, to which his cousin Lisette, Samuel's daughter, belonged, both on account of his still uncompleted book on religion, but also because of the *Gelassenheit* or tranquility of mind (akin to that of the German mystics), the calm fatalism, passivity and openness to the will of God it encouraged in its members. Here indeed, to use one of Constant's favourite images, one could 'sleep sound in one's boat in the middle of a storm'. No doubt because he came across it at this particular troubled moment in his life, the philosophy touched a chord in his heart, and in years to come his interest in the *Mystiques* or *Ames intérieures* was to deepen, as the so-called 'quietistic episode' in *Cécile* makes clear.[17] On 21 August, after talking to Langalerie, he noted in his diary 'I am very struck by this new way of thinking'.[18] Although he was never in any sense 'converted', he could write to his aunt Anne de Nassau on 20 April 1813, on learning that Langalerie was ill again:

> I'm really sorry to hear about the Chevalier de Langalerie's relapse. It's one intelligent man less in the world – or it will be; a man who had very original ideas on interesting subjects and a very persuasive way of expressing them. In the last analysis his system of belief is something each individual alone must judge for himself; but it has a comforting side to it and, at certain moments, does one's soul good.[19]

Indeed in September 1815, during another crisis in his life caused by his love for Madame Récamier, he was to know comparable moments of mystical exaltation under the guidance of the Russian Madame de Krüdener.

Charlotte's continued absence in Germany left Constant with the ever more possessive Madame de Staël demanding – and getting, it seems – conjugal rights once more. Constant remarks somewhat pathetically in his diary on 13 October: 'The life I lead here [at Coppet] and the enforced extra 1 [= sex] will end up killing me or driving me mad.'[20] (The next day he adds: 'I must have grown older, I never felt this tired before'.[21]) He began to worry about Charlotte's safety in Germany after Prosper de Barante arrived bringing horrific stories from the battlefields of Europe where he had spent some time as an observer, all of which confirmed Constant in his detestation of 'the monster', that is Napoleon. Perhaps to maintain some link with Germany, he began a major literary project in September 1807, a verse translation/adaptation of Schiller's long drama *Wallenstein*, a task with which he persevered until November, giving readings from it and feeling justly proud of his achievement.[22] Yet still he longed for Charlotte and felt guilty whether he stayed or contemplated leaving Coppet. He put the contrast succinctly in his journal on 6 October 1807:

> I cannot live with a person who is perpetually taking the pulse of her own sensibility and who gets cross when I don't always show enough interest in her self-analysis. Charlotte is less complicated, life with her is plain sailing.[23]

On 4 December 1807 Germaine de Staël at last left on the first stage of a journey to Vienna she had planned with Schlegel, and Constant, having said farewell to her in Lausanne, joined Charlotte in Besançon on 6 December after a nightmare coach journey over the snow-covered Jura mountains.[24] What exactly happened thereafter is a mystery that we may never get to the bottom of: it is a black hole, as it were, deliberately created by Constant – or perhaps by Charlotte – in the middle of his biography for reasons it is hard to fathom. What we know for certain is that Charlotte had returned from Germany, had travelled from Paris to Besançon where Constant had arranged to meet her; Constant did join her but was his usual vacillating self and asked her for time in which to make up his mind. On the coach journey to Dole Charlotte was taken violently ill, and by the time she reached there she was close to death, with stomach cramps and cold stiff limbs. She recovered and convalesced at Dole, and then at Juste's house at Brevans nearby, until 2 February 1808. A page is missing from the *Journaux intimes* for that crucial period of 20 November to 10 December 1807 – indeed the journal itself, even in its coded and abbreviated form stops altogether on 27 December 1807 and only recommences on 15 May 1811;[25] and the narrative of *Cécile* breaks off inexplicably with Cécile/Charlotte hovering between life and death in Besançon, and with an anxious narrator/Constant at her bedside.[26] The possible explanations for such gaps and silences open a rich field for speculation: did Charlotte panic in Besançon, issue threats, even try to commit suicide? Constant dreaded her reaching Besançon, as his journal shows, and he felt pangs of guilt at still being in Switzerland when she arrived. Charlotte had now sacrificed everything – two husbands and her reputation – for a man who was too spineless to leave a woman he no longer loved: suicidal despair would be all too understandable. But there is no hard evidence, and Constant and/or Charlotte (who was eventually to inherit his papers after his death) seem to have wished things to remain that way.

While Charlotte recovered from her illness at Brevans, Constant continued to work on his manuscript, now entitled *Wallstein* (Schiller's original title had been *Wallenstein*). They arrived in Paris together on 9 February 1808, where he made further improvements to the play and began to think about finding a publisher for it. He also returned to his researches on religion. While Germaine de Staël led a life of extreme brilliance in the best circles of Viennese society that winter, meeting that epitome of *ancien régime* cosmopolitanism and sophistication the Prince de Ligne and falling passionately and unhappily in love with Count Maurice O'Donnell, an officer in the Austrian army, Constant's life was as humdrum and domestic as he could wish now that the crisis seemed to have passed. With Madame de Staël hundreds of miles away, he could in her absence now contemplate an altogether quieter future life with his 'angel'. During March he became fascinated by phrenology – a branch of science which was to have an enormous following later in the century – and attended a course of lectures by its German inventor, Dr Franz Joseph Gall (1758–1828), whose serious attempts to understand the workings of the human mind, Constant told his aunt Anne de Nassau on 7 March 1808, had met with the customary arrogance and scorn which the French reserved for new and original ideas, especially when they came from Germany.[27] Under Napoleon the idea of the superiority of the French over other nations had become yet more deeply entrenched, and the generosity of Madame de Staël towards Britain and Italy in *Corinne* and later towards Germany in *De l'Allemagne* (and the respect for differences between cultures which characterized her friends at Coppet) was attracting more and more official disapproval in France.

This period of marking time came to an end for Constant on 11 April 1808 when the Reverend Pierre Boislesve, Doctor of Canon Law to the Archbishopric of Paris, declared Alexandre Du Tertre's marriage to Charlotte von Marenholtz, which had taken place in Brunswick on 14 June 1798, null and void in the eyes of the Catholic church because Baron von Marenholtz was still alive in 1808 (he was to die on 18 December 1808). In addition Du Tertre was fined 30 francs to be given to the poor of the parish of Notre Dame.[28] The way was now clear for Constant to marry Charlotte, and at the end of May the couple went to Juste's house at

Brevans to make the necessary arrangements. On 5 June 1808 they were married in secret in a Protestant ceremony performed by Pastor Jean-Henry Ebray (1769–1840) of the French Reformed church in Basle, although the religious ceremony and accompanying marriage certificate had no legal validity in France until a civil ceremony was performed.[29] With any ordinarily constituted man this might have meant the end of his relationship with another woman. With Constant, however, things were seldom so simple. Germaine de Staël had left Vienna on 22 May and was returning to Coppet: Constant felt compelled to see her again in order to bring things to a satisfactory end. On 27 June 1808 Constant and Charlotte left Brevans and travelled together as far as Concise in the Pays de Vaud. There they parted for the time being and Constant went with Auguste de Staël to meet Auguste's mother. By the beginning of July Constant and Germaine de Staël were in residence again at Coppet. Charlotte patiently spent the summer travelling within Switzerland before returning to Brevans at the end of September. She was not to have Constant to herself again until December.

During that summer of 1808, which perhaps marked the highwater mark of the Coppet group and its intellectual activities,[30] Madame de Staël worked on the book about Germany which she had been planning since her stay in Weimar, and for which her visit to Vienna had been a further stimulus.[31] She also tried to get over her unreciprocated love for Maurice O'Donnell. At the same time Constant was on the point of finishing *Wallstein* and profited whenever he read it aloud to them from the comments of Madame de Staël and several German speakers at Coppet – the playwright Zacharias Werner (1768–1823), the visionary poet Adam Oehlenschläger (1779–1850) and Franz Tieck, the sculptor brother of the prominent poet Ludwig Tieck (1773–1853). The pressure was off Constant, and indeed during August Germaine was away at Unspünnen, near Interlaken in German-speaking Switzerland, for the picturesque shepherds' festival, allowing him to finish an essay on German theatre[32] and to prepare *Wallstein* for the Genevan printer. When it appeared in Paris on 26 January 1809, *Wallstein* achieved some measure of critical acclaim, despite its being too lengthy for a stage production.[33] By 25 March 1809 the first edition was sold out and a second was planned. Constant sent a copy of the adaptation to Chateaubriand, whose letter of thanks was full of admiration.[34] (Constant for his part was to be strongly critical of Chateaubriand's *Les Martyrs* later that month, privately confessing his dislike of its overblown Romantic language which he told Anne de Nassau in a letter of 30 March 1809 he found monotonous.[35]) The publication of *Wallstein* provided the perfect excuse for Constant to return to Paris so as to be present when it reached the bookshops, while Germaine took up residence in Geneva for the winter. On 15 December 1808 he reached Juste's house at Brevans and was reunited with Charlotte.

In all the time he had been at Coppet Constant had been unable to summon up the courage to tell Madame de Staël that he was married to Charlotte. In fact he had not even dared to tell his relatives in Lausanne, not even his aunt, Anne de Nassau, although they all knew of his close friendship with her. On the day he arrived at Brevans he wrote to his aunt telling her of the frosty reception he had received from his father – their differences over money had now poisoned their relationship irretrievably – and summarized his situation thus:

> I am nearing the goal I have aimed for doggedly and with such effort for so long; there are moments when I am happy with it. In Madame D[u Tertre] there is gentleness and the capacity for self-sacrifice, her feelings for me are uncomplicated, and all of this soothes me. But often I am overcome by my memories: my heart has grown accustomed to being with someone else, and the roots I need to tear up are very deep and bleed secretly. My hope lies in the passage of time, in the things that will happen, in an unknown power that has seemed on occasion to be protecting me. Then I shall no longer have to struggle against public disapproval, against the false and distressing situation I find myself in, against feelings that are wearing me out. I shall no longer be forced to blush at a pretence I find degrading.[36]

But yet again there was no hint of a firm decision to make a final break with Germaine, indeed there was still every reason to believe that he would be drawn back sooner or later into the whirlwind of her emotions, as Prosper de Barante aptly described it.[37] The precautions Constant took in Paris during January 1809 to prevent anyone from suspecting that he had married Charlotte were extraordinary. He left her in the city while he himself stayed at Les Herbages, visiting her discreetly from time to time, just as, not so long before, he had visited the brothels of the capital, and taking Charlotte with him to gaming houses where he sometimes lost large sums of money. Meanwhile he very probably took out again the manuscript of his as yet untitled autobiographical novel and rewrote it in such a way as eventually to create the *Adolphe* we now know. It is certain that during the winter of 1808–9 and later in the summer of 1809 he reworked the manuscripts of his book on the religions of Antiquity to produce a book on polytheism – the belief in many gods as opposed to monotheism, belief in one god – for on 12 February 1809 he wrote to Prosper de Barante:

> I'm working a great deal on my Polytheism with a zest that delights me. I'm copying it all out myself to avoid any long encyclopaedia-like sections. If I'm not disturbed by any unexpected storms, internal or external, I shall have finished copying it out this spring.[38]

As the letter suggests, Constant knew the exeat he had been granted by

Madame de Staël was necessarily finite: one day soon he would be recalled to Coppet.

At some point during those early months of 1809 a decision was made by Constant and his wife that Germaine must be informed of the marriage by Charlotte. There was certain to be a scene of apocalyptic proportions, but telling her could no longer be put off. Accordingly, at the beginning of May 1809 husband and wife arrived on the outskirts of Geneva. Charlotte took a room alone at the village inn at Sécheron while Constant awaited the result of her interview with Madame de Staël at nearby Ferney. On 8 May 1809 Charlotte sent a note to Germaine signed 'Charlotte Constant de Hardenberg' asking to see her the next day at Sécheron. Realizing the situation Germaine ordered a coach and was there the same evening. She burst into Charlotte's room as Charlotte was washing her feet and preparing for bed, and exclaimed 'I have come to see you because you are a Hardenberg!' Summoning up more dignity than the tragicomic circumstances might have allowed anyone less resolute, Charlotte remained calm and polite, every inch the *grande dame* like her adversary, but refused to reveal Constant's whereabouts or to renounce her marriage to him. Charlotte's only concession was to agree to keep the marriage secret until after Germaine had realized her current intention of leaving for the United States where she owned land around New York. Nevertheless when Madame de Staël finally left at 4 o'clock in the morning, Charlotte was sad in the knowledge of the extent of Constant's perfidy: he had repeatedly told each woman that he could only be happy with her alone. He used what one might call his customary Adolphean defence, believing that duplicity which spares pain is preferable to honesty which only causes more pain.[39]

Constant's punishment was to be obliged to spend the summer with Germaine; only then, after three months, could he return to his wife: those were Madame de Staël's terms. He would be forced to witness Germaine's near-suicidal grief and fury while Charlotte was required to withdraw as far away as possible, preferably back into the depths of Germany. Yet again Germaine had achieved a kind of victory. All she had to do now was quietly drop the idea of going to America and she could prolong her hold over Constant indefinitely. But Charlotte had her pride too, and despite her husband's pleading with her to leave Switzerland for fear of angering Germaine still further, she stayed on at Sécheron: Madame de Staël might be able to browbeat and bully Constant, but Charlotte need have none of it. From 13 May 1809 Constant was resident at Coppet again, and eventually Charlotte decided – but in her own good time – to return to Brevans. In early June Madame de Staël left for Lyon to see the great Talma act in *Hamlet*: Constant slipped away to see his wife in secret, but was then summoned to join Madame de Staël in Lyon, and meekly left. The courageous Charlotte, unintimidated by *la dame de Coppet*, her court or her renowned eloquence in vituperation, and never afraid of looking ridiculous, arrived at the Hôtel du Parc where they were staying and asked for her husband back – to the great embarrassment of that husband who immediately ordered her to return to her lodgings. It seemed to Charlotte that she had lost him for good, and she thereupon decided to take her own life the same day, 9 June 1809, sending him a letter explaining why:

> You have abandoned me; this did not come from your heart, your heart is probably broken too by what you have done. I am more sorry for you than for myself. I love you. I am, I think, the only woman in the world who has ever really loved you. The woman who has caused my death is hard, and only capable of feeling what she calls humiliation. The only pain I feel now is my pain at leaving you. Pray that God may forgive me. Before I die, I shall pray for you, for my dear son, for the good Du Tertre who will grieve when he learns of my death. Endure what you still have to suffer on this earth.[40]

Constant and Germaine rushed across to Charlotte's hotel and found her writhing in pain, having probably taken poison. She recovered in a few days and was sent to Paris. Constant accompanied her there but promised to return to Coppet to serve out the rest of his three-month 'sentence' under the terms of the extraordinary agreement of 8–9 May. He had in any case left his irreplaceable manuscripts at Coppet at the mercy of a possibly vengeful woman. Thus, having arrived in Paris around 15 June 1809, he was already on the road back to Switzerland by 24 June.

During Constant's enforced residence at Coppet from late June to 19 October 1809 he began surreptitiously sending his precious manuscripts off in batches for safe-keeping to his aunt, Madame de Nassau. He knew an exceptionally turbulent period lay ahead of him: Juste had informed the rest of the Constant clan of his son's marriage. News of Constant's marriage had gradually filtered out and was now generally common knowledge, putting both Madame de Staël and himself at the mercy of hostile public opinion. Constant now appealed to his ever loyal and much loved aunt Anne de Nassau to write to Madame de Staël pointing out the wrong she was doing him and asking her to give him his freedom. The Comtesse de Nassau's letter was copied out by Rosalie de Constant and has thus been preserved:

> It gives me great sorrow to be obliged to write to you, Madame, now that my nephew's position vis-à-vis yourself, which has for long been an unhappy and humiliating one, has become reprehensible. I feel it is the duty of his nearest relative and best friend to help him and to lead him out of the situation in spite of himself: I can no

longer tolerate my sister's son adding to his own unhappiness the grievous wrong of making the woman who has joined her destiny to his unhappy as well.

I therefore wish to inform you, Madame, that I know all about your treatment of my nephew. I know that for several years he has asked in vain for his freedom, freedom of which you have no right to deprive him. Out of delicacy and his high regard for your feelings, he wanted you to give him that freedom yourself, and remained with you fearing your unworthy threat to end a blameworthy liaison by a criminal act [i.e. Germaine's suicide]. Finally, after enduring scenes as violent as they were shocking and base, he used his right to live his own life and made sacred vows; he informed you of them, and you, in mockery of human and divine laws, have kept him in miserable servitude. He has been weak enough to put up with that servitude out of consideration for the pain you claim to be suffering and your histrionic grief.

It is my duty to do everything in my power to bring such a scandal to an end; it is ruining my nephew's reputation, it has reduced his father to despair as well as such virtuous relatives and friends as he has left. Since I also know that, while forcing my nephew to maintain a guilty silence about his marriage, you are having the rumour spread about that that marriage never took place but was merely planned, and that you are painting his legitimate spouse in the most odious colours, I wish to make clear to you, Madame, that the whole of Europe will learn of your iniquity. You enjoy fame, Madame: to that of your writings will now be added that of your actions so that your moral standards can be judged for what they are.[41]

Germaine's reply has not been preserved, but it is likely that in it she would have accused Constant of treachery, of having using the time he kept the marriage secret in order to stay on at Coppet and improve his *Wallstein* with her help and that of her guests.

While all this was happening in Switzerland, Charlotte remained in Paris and seems to have rallied for a while. Things were beginning to move in her direction at last, and it had always been in her nature to be patient. Although she was the victim of a whispering campaign in Paris – she was known as 'the woman with three husbands' – and although legal expenses and the yearly allowance she gave Du Tertre[42] had reduced her income, she was still a wealthy woman. Once her husband had rejoined her the future looked promising. Only she was able to offer the domestic calm which at 42 Constant now needed so desperately. There was one small cloud on the horizon, however: Constant had become jealous of the German doctor and man of letters who was looking after her in Paris,

David Ferdinand Koreff (1783–1851) – perhaps as the result of an idea put in his mind by Germaine de Staël – and he asked her to leave her rented apartment in the Rue d'Anjou and return to Brevans. Juste's gloomy and uncomfortable house had too many unhappy memories associated with it and she refused. Her counter-proposal was that, despite the dangers of travel in a war-ravaged country, they should leave for Germany. They could both be happy there. Germaine de Staël – whose power and influence, supported by considerable wealth, Constant had always feared – was a continuing threat as she intrigued, spread calumny and planned her revenge. As a result he was being pilloried in the gossip of fashionable circles as the man who betrayed his wife with his mistress and his mistress with his wife. Madame de Staël even sent Juste de Constant the document promising fidelity to one another which she and Constant had drawn up many years before, and she was triumphant when the old man replied that he could not decide between the two women in his son's life. She later promised to see if she could give some financial help to Juste's children by Marianne, Charles and Louise. Juste could no longer be relied on to stand by him, as Constant now realized.[43]

Constant left Coppet on 19 October 1809 and went via Brevans to Paris. After five months apart there was at first considerable tension between husband and wife. Sharp words as well as letters were exchanged. Then there was peace. They went through a civil marriage ceremony in Paris in mid-December 1809[44] and spent the subsequent weeks at Les Herbages, with regular visits to the capital. Constant began to get to know his extensive new family: Charlotte's cousin, for example, Count von Fürstenstein, who was minister to King Jerome of Westphalia, Napoleon's younger brother who now ruled over what had once been Brunswick and Hesse-Kassel. Constant enjoyed the company of the Count and his wife who were in Paris to prepare for the arrival of King Jerome for the Emperor Napoleon's forthcoming marriage to Archduchess Marie-Louise of Austria. Constant was also trying to disentangle his finances from Madame de Staël's, but there were some unresolved problems. On 27 January he left Paris, visited his father who was ill at Brevans (and now thoroughly won over to Madame de Staël's cause), and by 1 February 1810 was back in Switzerland with Germaine, having promised Charlotte he would return to Paris in a fortnight. Now that their marriage was official and public, Charlotte became fearful of scandal, not only in France but also in Germany, especially in Kassel to which the von Fürstensteins would shortly return – Kassel was a major centre of social life in the region and much frequented by the von Hardenbergs and their circle. Her worst fears were confirmed when Constant failed to reappear in March. Apart from trips to Lausanne and Geneva he was not in fact to leave Coppet until 10 April.

What Charlotte may not have known is that either during this stay or later in 1810 or 1811 Constant was working on the most permanent tribute to his relationship with her that she could have hoped for. He was writing *Cécile*, the account of his struggle to free himself from Germaine – fictionalized in the form of Madame de Malbée – and to reach the haven of marriage to Cécile de Walterbourg, a thinly disguised Charlotte. This short unfinished novel, which was published only in 1951, was based on memories but also no doubt on diaries and letters from the turbulent years 1793–1808.[45] It probably developed from the same embryo as *Adolphe*, the untitled autobiographical *Urroman* begun in the autumn of 1806. Thanks to the remarkably precise dating of its sections or 'phases' – Constant calls them 'epochs' – *Cécile* throws light on some of the more obscure areas of Constant's biography. But it also has great literary merit. Although its style is less tightly controlled than *Adolphe*, and although it lacks the memorable aphorisms of that great novel and its affecting intensity, *Cécile* does similarly explore the psychology of a weak man unable to decide on the right course of action – in this case he has to choose between two women – and who causes suffering by his hesitations and changes of mind.[46] The narrative breaks off with Cécile on the point of dying from grief in Dole, although it is clear from its opening sentence – 'On 11 January 1793 I met Cécile de Walterbourg who is now my wife' – that she will eventually recover. That the story will end in triumph and happiness is also evident from its Virgilian epigraph, 'Italiam, Italiam' (*Aeneid* III, 523), taken from famous lines evoking the longing for a promised land that eludes the hero Aeneas.[47] In Constant's case that promised land was a peaceful and happy life married to Charlotte. Yet even after that marriage had take place, the goal proved no less elusive.

On 21 March 1810 Constant made a provision in his will whereby he left Madame de Staël or her heirs 80,000 francs. Over many years Constant and Germaine had pooled their financial resources, but Constant had also borrowed 34,000 francs from her father Jacques Necker to buy Hérivaux. A settlement was reached – albeit a humiliating one which left him in debt to Germaine for the rest of his life – and on 14 April he was back in Paris with Charlotte.[48] But after only a few weeks in the country at Les Herbages with Charlotte, making improvements to his property, Constant was thoroughly bored. When the call came from Madame de Staël, who was staying at the château of Chaumont on the Loire, his capitulation was instantaneous. In spite of everything he accepted her invitation and rejoined her. He stayed with her between 10 June and 14 July 1810 in order to help her make last-minute corrections to the text of *De l'Allemagne* (*On Germany*), a book based in part in their memories of Weimar.[49] *De l'Allemagne* was being printed by Mame for the publisher Nicolle, and Germaine hoped that it would bring about a reconciliation with the Emperor. However Napoleon was in no mood to trifle any longer with those he considered to be troublemakers, and on 3 June 1810 he replaced

Fouché, his Minister of Police, whom he considered to be too soft on enemies of the régime, with Savary, Duc de Rovigo. Fouché had generally tended towards leniency with Madame de Staël; Constant knew Fouché well and had wrung some concessions from him in the past. That would no longer be possible with the tough apparatchik Rovigo. Once again Constant's thoughts and concerns were inexorably taken over by Germaine and her world, by the pleasures of intelligent, lively conversation with her and with her usual heterogeneous collection of guests – among others the celebrated beauty Juliette Récamier with whom both Prosper de Barante and Germaine were in love, a Russian prince, a baron from a Baltic state and a young American.[50] On 1 July Charlotte escaped being burned to death in a fire at the lavish ball organized in Paris to celebrate the Emperor's wedding. When she wrote to tell Constant the news, his response was merely to prolong his stay on the Loire.[51] Eventually he returned on 14 July and husband and wife spent the rest of that exceptionally wet and dreary summer together at Les Herbages.

All summer Germaine de Staël was busy preparing her book on German culture for publication. She completed the third and final volume as she was correcting the proofs of the first volume sent to her by the publisher Nicolle. That first volume was passed by Napoleon's censors in May, the second in August. Rumour and speculation were rife in the capital that the finished work would be critical of the government. By 15 September most of Volume III was in proof and in the hands of the censors. Then, like a bolt from the blue, on 26 September 1810 Germaine's son Auguste brought her the devastating news that the Duc de Rovigo, the new Minister of Police, had ordered that the proofs and manuscript of *De l'Allemagne* be seized and that she herself leave the country.[52] Rovigo ignored the censors' approval of the work: the seizure was a punishment for her conduct in recent months, her proud refusal to bend the knee to Rovigo's master either when at what amounted to a rival court at Chaumont or in her letters. Napoleon wrote to Rovigo on 8 September 1810:

> I have sent you back Madame de Staël's book. Is she entitled to call herself 'Baroness'? Has she used that title in the works she has published up to now? Suppress the passage about the Duke of Bruns-wick, and three quarters of the passages where she praises England. Such misplaced enthusiasm has already done us enough harm.[53]

The peevish despot who had lately founded his own ersatz dynasty deeply resented Madame de Staël's flamboyant insolence and her genuine claim to nobility – nobility, one might say, in every sense of the word.

Germaine's sons Auguste and Albert fought a vain rearguard action to have the ban lifted. Rovigo demanded to know why their mother had nowhere mentioned in her book either the Emperor Napoleon's name or the eighteen years of war which France had been waging against Germany since 1792. Her book was un-French and unpatriotic for proposing another – and defeated – nation as a model, and she must now embark for America without further delay. *De l'Allemagne* did indeed praise German literature of the *Sturm und Drang* for its freedom from rules and received ideas, its freshness and reluctance to imitate the Greco-Roman classics. It not only revealed contemporary German literature and culture to the French in a way that had never been done before: it would shortly reveal Germany to the Germans. Perhaps finally that was the real danger that *De l'Allemagne* represented, rather than its implicit critique of the staleness of French culture under Napoleon – it might rally a subject people against its unworthy new master. Constant can only have felt pride at Madame de Staël's refreshing openness to another and hitherto despised culture and her praise of the freedom of expression which German culture encouraged: those were the things that Coppet had stood for.[54]

On 11 October 1810 Rovigo sent his myrmidons round to the printing shop of the unfortunate Mame and had the printing plates smashed; on 14 and 15 October the proofs were pulped. All traceable copies of the book in circulation were seized and destroyed.[55] Madame de Staël, having saved the publisher Nicolle from bankruptcy by returning his advance of 13,000 francs, had left for Coppet on 6 October, where in December she learned of another example of the Emperor's spitefulness: Prosper de Barante, Constant's friend and her lover, was stripped of his post as Prefect of Napoléon-Vendeé because of his association with Germaine.[56] On her way to Coppet and exile, Madame de Staël had met Constant and Charlotte on 10 October at Briare. Three days later, probably in some emotional disarray, Constant lost 20,000 francs in one furious evening's gambling in Paris, and was forced to sell Les Herbages, his furniture and part of his library to pay his debts.[57] He no longer had any reason or desire to remain in France where it was now the reign of Caligula: the Emperor might at any moment pick on him and for his own amusement make him the victim of another piece of gratuitous unpleasantness, such as conscripting him into the *Garde Nationale* or the *Garde Sédentaire*. On 17 January 1811 Constant left with Charlotte for Lausanne, where further difficulties awaited him. No doubt put up to it by Germaine de Staël, the increasingly senile Juste wished to take his son to court in Geneva over their long-running financial dispute. And the reception accorded to Constant and his wife by polite society in Lausanne was to be good or bad depending on the host's feelings towards Madame de Staël: as Constant had always feared, Germaine's influence was proving to be both extensive and rather effective in making life disagreeable for him. During February and March 1811 his time was largely taken up with trying to reach some agreement with his father over money. On 20 April 1811 they succeeded in patching up their differences and signed a private treaty in Geneva,[58] though things had deteriorated between them to such an extent that in January 1812 Juste was to take the extraordinary step of having an account of their financial dealings with each other printed – with his own critical observations – to circulate to other members of the family. Juste's self-righteousness and stubborn tenacity were unchanged since the days of his court martial, and even though he ratified the treaty on 28 April 1811, some weeks later he found it unsatisfactory and unacceptable.

It is no wonder that Constant's *Ma Vie* – also known by the more romantic but bogus title of *Le Cahier rouge*, from the red notebook it is written in[59] – which was composed in all probability in the same year, possibly during the summer of 1811, reads like an indictment of Juste for his incompetence as a father. *Ma Vie* is an irresistibly comic, picaresque and sometimes bitter-sweet account of Constant's life from his birth in 1767 up to the quarrel with François du Plessis-Gouret in November 1787. The narrator in middle age sympathizes with the scatterbrained young man he once was but maintains an ironic distance from his follies. The underlying theme which that ironic tone disguises is the young Benjamin's complete dependence on his father and Juste's inability either to choose good tutors for him or, more important, to communicate face to face with his son or show him the affection he genuinely felt. *Ma Vie* may have been begun as early as 1793 during the first phase of his relationship with Charlotte,[60] but the single unfinished manuscript of it which has survived dates from this later period of conflict with Juste, and had to wait until 1907 for publication. It is a matter for regret that, as with *Cécile*, there is no readily available English translation of a work which throws valuable light on *Adolphe*, particularly on the father–son relationship portrayed there.

Madame de Staël was at Coppet that spring of 1811 under the watchful eye of Napoleon's new, zealous and thoroughly unscrupulous Prefect of the Lake of Geneva region, Baron Capelle. Capelle would have had little to learn from the methods of modern totalitarian régimes: not only was Germaine kept under permanent surveillance as usual, she was also urged by him to write a work in praise of her tormentor, the Emperor. Her inevitable refusal was then publicized by Capelle in order to blacken her name still further.[61] She was confined to within a radius of 2 leagues of the château, and the devoted August Wilhelm von Schlegel was ordered to leave. Although Capelle probably did not know it, Schlegel was not all that sorry to be going, since he had taken umbrage at Germaine's latest passion, John Rocca (1788–1818), who was something of a rough diamond when compared to her many other conquests. Despite his English Christian name, Rocca was of Piedmontese origin and from Geneva: it was there that she had met this handsome 23-year-old hussar when he had been recovering from a wound he had received in Spain in the Emperor's service. He had beautiful brown eyes, was slight of build and walked with the aid of crutches because of his injury. His experiences in the Peninsular Wars had aligned his feelings about Napoleon with those of Germaine. Rocca was uncultivated and quick-tempered, and idolized the woman he was set on marrying. Young and probably consumptive, he made an odd but rather touching match for Madame de Staël, now in her mid-forties, aware not only that she was losing her looks but also putting on weight. She was greatly flattered by his attentions, even though he was quite incapable of understanding most of her intellectual enthusiasms. She invited Constant to supper at Coppet on 18 April 1811, and Rocca, who could not bear the sight of her obvious affection for him, challenged Constant to a duel.[62] Despite the absurdity of the situation, Constant who, as we have seen, was never a coward when it came to physical combat, accepted the challenge from an experienced military man half his age. Fortunately the affair was settled honourably without bloodshed the following day, but Rocca remained intensely jealous of his Venus's former lover, and was to challenge him yet again in May when Germaine slipped away to Lausanne to bid Constant farewell on his departure for Germany. Once more the young hothead was persuaded to drop his affair of honour, and was subsequently rewarded by secretly becoming Germaine's second husband.[63]

At about this point, and very significantly, on 15 May 1811 Constant's *Journaux intimes* begin again after a long silence with his departure from Lausanne, and they run through to 1816.[64] At 11 a.m. on 8 May 1811 on the staircase of the Hôtel de la Couronne in Lausanne Constant had said farewell to Madame de Staël: she had told him she did not expect that they would ever see each other again. The next day he had written to Claude Hochet:

> People judge [Madame de Staël] more severely than she deserves, and she enjoys less pleasure than she thinks. Everything to do with her, now that my life is beyond her control, is a source of deep melancholy to me and it is the only sadness to trouble my life which from other points of view suits me more and more as each day passes.[65]

As he travelled north by coach his thoughts were also with his father from whom he had not heard and to whom he wrote one of his most moving pleas on 18 May 1811:

> My dear father, I beg you to give me back your affection, to allow me still to consider myself a friend to Charles and Louise. . . . Do not make me despair at leaving you once more without being able to hope that your heart has found once again its former kindness towards me.[66]

The poignancy of the letter is increased by Constant's obvious feeling that he might never see his ailing but intractable father again, a premonition which was to be fully justified.

As Constant and Charlotte neared Germany, he returned to his *Polythéisme* which he seems not to have touched for several months. Via Berne, Basle and Freiburg they reached Strasbourg on 10 June and halted for a week, then travelled on at a leisurely pace, arriving in Göttingen on 18 August 1811. In the various cities they passed through on the way Constant's gambling mania took hold of him again – possibly a response to hidden emotional stresses – and he and his wife appear to have lost a considerable amount of money. But his intellect was fired again by the polytheism project which he decided in Strasbourg to divide up into forty-four books:[67] this was to be the basis of the version of *Du polythéisme romain* which would finally be published. Once in Göttingen he renewed his friendship with Charles de Villers whom he had met in Metz eight years before. Villers taught French literature at Göttingen University and Constant shared with him a fascination with German thought: through him Constant was slowly to come to know members of the university staff, a university which at this time rivalled Edinburgh as the finest in Europe and which boasted a magnificent library. The town itself, furthermore, was the perfect image of quiet, provincial Germany, with its half-timbered houses and watermills. Its tranquility was rarely disturbed by anything but the sound of livestock being herded through the streets in the early morning. The cuisine might be considerably more basic than Constant had been used to at Coppet, but if peace was what he was really looking for, it was to be found in plenty in this bucolic haven. On 2 December 1811 he described some of the inhabitants to Claude Hochet:

Life [in Göttingen] is entirely inward, and anyone who is not dedicated to a life of thought could not survive here. The university teachers, who are certainly the most learned and enlightened in the whole of Europe, do not even stay together as a community but live apart, each in his own home. They work from 5 in the morning until 6 in the evening, then they sit smoking with their family, with wives who are little more than housekeepers. There they forget their studies and listen to the gossip these housekeepers tell them, judging it a better distraction from their labours than more serious conversation. The students follow the courses at the University quite diligently, then they gamble, drink, sing and fight each other.[68]

Between 19 August and 2 November 1811 Constant stayed at Charlotte's family home, Schloß Hardenberg, just outside the town, then took rooms in Göttingen itself to be nearer to the University Library, at Jüdenstraße 12 (now the Centralhotel) where the landlord also kept fowl and pigs.[69] In such rustic surroundings his work suddenly started to proceed rapidly again, but as always with Constant that process was one of interminable recasting and rewriting. And gradually – although it was not easy at first – he was finding acceptance with some members of the University. He met the aged Christian Gottlieb Heyne (1729–1812), Professor of Philology, author of a Latin dissertation on Hesiod which had been useful to him, and of course father of his late friend Huber's wife Therese. Later he came to know, among others, Friedrich Bouterwek (1766–1828), Professor of Philosophy, Johann Friedrich Blumenbach (1752–1840), Professor of Medicine, Baron Seckendorf (1775–1823) who taught aesthetics, Gustav von Hugo (1764–1844), a famous Professor of Civil Law, and Georg Friedrich Benecke (1762–1844), Professor of German Philology and University Librarian. When reading the writings of Georg Christoph Lichtenberg (1742–1799), late Professor of Mathematics at Göttingen – but of course better known as a humorist and satirist – Constant soon recognized the accuracy of Lichtenberg's caricatures of the serious and earnest German academic.[70]

News of Napoleon's unrelenting persecution of Germaine de Staël continued to reach and upset him: the link was never broken, they corresponded, and Constant missed her. Life was not as easy as he had hoped with Charlotte: she was undeniably intelligent, but not always intelligent enough. They quarrelled from time to time, and sheer boredom and frustration must have played their part in such disagreements: Constant missed the wit and brilliance of Germaine's Coppet. At the end of the year he was shaken by a claim for 50,000 écus made against him by Juste, who in late November 1811 sought to have their private treaty of 20 April 1811 made invalid.[71] Constant was unable to work properly for a week with the shock. He told his aunt Anne de Nassau in December 1811 that his father seemed bent on his complete ruin; he would not even have enough left to honour his obligation towards Germaine under the terms of his will:

> What a strange destiny is mine: at the age of 23 I was put in possession of a fortune I was told was mine. I was prevented from earning money, which I would have done if I had thought I was poor. And now at 45 I am asked for money which I had thought I didn't owe anyone, in order to make the children of a peasant girl rich. It is not, my dear Aunt, that I think I am likely to lose this cruel court case if it takes place, but it is so painful to fight it that I am devoid of life when I am occupied with it, and yet in spite of myself it is on my mind day and night. I have never been so unhappy in my life. Göttingen is a bad place to be when one is in this state of mind. There are no amusements here: work alone makes life here bearable, and when one is in no fit state to work, as I am, I have only one depressing thought on my mind, which also bores me with

its unchanging monotony. My wife is an angel and sometimes shakes me out of my mood of dejection, and I owe her the only good moments I enjoy. Perhaps we will go and find some distractions in Kassel for two or three days.[72]

It is difficult to resist passing a somewhat harsher judgement on Juste than Constant could ever bring himself to do, even in *Ma Vie*: quite apart from his treatment of Benjamin in his childhood, his behaviour during Constant's mature years was characterized by a lack of consideration that almost defies belief. For years he failed to tell his son about his marriage to Marianne, or about Benjamin's blood relationship to Charles and Louise, yet he had demanded months – indeed years – of his son's time to defend him in legal actions in Holland, some of which were ill-advised, and which may have helped destroy Constant's marriage to Minna von Cramm. Juste then asked for money back to support his new family from a son who admittedly had by now lost much of it through reckless gambling and extravagant living with Germaine, but who had at least honestly believed that the money was his to lose. He betrayed Benjamin at a crucial moment in his life by siding with Madame de Staël, probably in the hope of obtaining money for Charles and Louise from her, then set in motion a process of legal harassment that would have meant Constant's almost certain ruination. On 4 January 1812 he began an action in Paris to have Constant's possessions there seized.[73] Fate stepped in, however, and Constant was saved from disaster by Juste's death on 2 February 1812, news of which reached him in Brunswick on 19 February.[74]

He was spending some time there with Charlotte (4–23 February 1812), and had been overcome by memories of his youth, of Minna and of Mauvillon. He saw Minna again at a soirée, and spent an evening with Mauvillon's widow Marie Louise. The Duke of Brunswick had long since been deposed by Napoleon, and the old city was now part of the newly created Kingdom of Westphalia – but in an Empire in which cracks were already visible and in which resistance was increasing. (The Emperor, meanwhile, was turning his attention to Tsar Alexander's Russia, one of the few countries of Europe not to be under his sway. It was of course to prove one of the greatest mistakes in modern history.) Constant's stay in Brunswick had been a melancholy affair even before the devastating news about Juste reached him. On 12 February there was an angry scene with Charlotte and he wrote in his diary, 'I would not put money on our living together for the rest of our lives'.[75] Three days later they argued bitterly over politics and Constant was appalled at the quality of her intellect. When he finally learned that his father was dead and that there was now no possibility of a reconciliation, he packed and returned to

Göttingen with Charlotte. There he fell to looking through his old papers, wondered whether after all he had been in the wrong with Juste – then wrote in his diary on 28 February 1812: 'Worked. My father would have been pleased with my book.'[76]

9

THE END OF AN EMPIRE
(1812–1816)

Constant's life gradually slipped month by month into a calmer routine, interspersed with the occasional treat, such as five days on his own in Kassel (29 March–1 April 1812) or getting so drunk he could not stand up (3 April).[1] But always there was work, or the thought of work, and of course an unending series of quarrels and reconciliations with the often domineering Charlotte. He managed to contain and hide the boredom he felt with her better as time went by, but regularly confided it in his diary (for example on 24 June 1812: 'Charlotte is the most boring creature who ever walked the earth'[2]). In his complete isolation a letter from Madame de Staël became a longed-for event, much as his own letters had been to Isabelle de Charrière years before. Unbeknown to him, Germaine gave birth in secret to a son, Louis-Alphonse Rocca (1812–42), during the night of 7–8 April 1812.[3] On 23 May she slipped past her guards and, having obtained passports near Berne, travelled as quickly as possible via Zurich and Bavaria to Vienna. Although Austria was now subject to the wishes of France, and the Austrian police had her under constant surveillance, she was left unhindered. Her objective now was to reach England and freedom.

Napoleon's Grand Army had crossed the Niemen and was massing for the assault on Russia. There was absolutely no time to lose: by mid-July Madame de Staël was across the Russian border and on the road to Moscow. She found the sheer vastness of the landscape around her awe-inspiring. She reached Moscow, the 'Rome of the Tartars', as she called it, on 2 August – a city of gleaming domes arrayed in a Byzantine glory that was so soon to be destroyed by fire. She was generally well received there, though essentially as a curiosity. In any case she could not afford to linger in Moscow as the French were advancing towards the city, and on 13 August she reached the relative safety of St Petersburg in whose Europeanized elegance she felt rather more at home, and where she spoke to the British Ambassador about her wish to cross to England. She was also granted an audience with Tsar Alexander I. Madame de Staël's political objective was now the future establishment of a constitutional monarchy in France under Bernadotte, Crown Prince of Sweden, as an alternative to a Bourbon restoration; it was a subject she no doubt broached with the Tsar. While she was in St Petersburg, Napoleon's army had taken Smolensk and was about to occupy Moscow: Madame de Staël now crossed to Sweden and by 24 September she was in Stockholm where she put herself, her family and even Schlegel at the service of Prince Bernadotte's cause. She is credited by historians with having had some small influence in bringing about Sweden's alliance with England and Russia to form the 1813 coalition against France.[4]

Compared with such a life as Germaine's, Constant's existence was humdrum indeed during 1811–12. Never before had he worked so uninterruptedly, while thinking all the time of 'la voyageuse' – the nomadic Madame de Staël – and praying for her safety. God in fact makes a frequent appearance in his journal at this period for the first time: Constant's brief daily observations often contain the abbreviation 'L. v. d. D. s. f.', 'La volonté de Dieu soit faite', 'God's will be done', a memory of the passively fatalistic outlook of the *Mystiques* of Lausanne which had so marked him during 1807. When he attended a student supper party on 14 January he felt with regret that he was growing old, and when on 8 January he had opened his 'novel' again – by which he probably now meant *Adolphe* – he remarked: 'How one's impressions fade when circumstances change! I should no longer be able to write it today.'[5] The following November his reaction was very similar: 'Read my novel. I am amazed at myself' (diary entry for 9 November 1812[6]). Constant's feelings about his new place of residence were somewhat ambiguous. Göttingen was rather too remote and primitive for his taste: only the sophisticated company of Charles de Villers made it tolerable. And yet his work was profiting enormously from his stay there. On 11 November 1811 he had been invited to an academic reception, and he became a member of the *Gelehrten-Club* at some point during his stay.[7] This was a drinking and dining club for academics which seems to have met every week or fortnight. More significant was his being nominated on 14 December 1812 as a Corresponding Member of the Academy of Sciences of Göttingen on the recommendation of his friend the Professor of Medicine Johann Friedrich Blumenbach. He wrote to his aunt Anne de Nassau on 20 April 1813:

> I have not received recognition from the University, but from the Göttingen Academy of Sciences. It is only an honorary title which the scholars here have been kind enough to bestow on me; it brings me no stipend and I am not obliged to do anything on account of it. I owe my being elected to a book which is not yet finished; I hope it comes up to the expectations some of them have of it.[8]

In a letter of thanks to Blumenbach of 23 December 1812 he referred to his work on religion as 'the purpose of my whole life and its consolation'.[9]

All that summer and autumn he had worked, getting bored with everything he had (Charlotte), and missing everything he did not have (Germaine), and feeling he must be mad, as he remarked in his diary on 16 September.[10] In October he and Charlotte moved lodgings, while continuing to row with each other. He thanked God when he heard that Germaine had disembarked in Stockholm, and now entered enthusiastically into her plans for Bernadotte.

On 5 October 1812 in one of his characteristically long letters to Claude Hochet – some of the most informative in the whole of his correspondence – Constant wrote:

> We received news today of the destruction of Moscow. It is difficult not to be greatly moved when one thinks of the sum total of evils now spread across the face of the earth. This event may prove to be of some considerable moment, quite independently of its importance for those it is affecting directly. But here people are so immersed in their study and research that, with [Charles de] Villers out of town, I have been unable to find anyone to talk to about it. A city of 500,000 inhabitants can be blown up without a Göttingen professor lifting his eyes from his book.[11]

Constant could hardly have been more prescient: when Napoleon reached Moscow the enemy, who had already cost him 30,000 men at Borodino in September, had abandoned the city and melted into the countryside. When in October the expected Russian peace emissaries never came and fires broke out, the looted city was relinquished and the Grand Army retreated westwards, first through mud, then snow. After they crossed the Beresina on 27 November 1812, Napoleon's troops were decimated by cold and hunger, and by December the whole huge military machine and the Empire it supported looked broken. Although the Emperor clung obstinately to power for a further fifteen months, the end was in sight for him. News of the retreat from Moscow reached Kassel where Constant was staying with Charlotte on Christmas Day 1812. 'Important news' is his laconic comment in his diary that day.[12] The exact reasons for his first stay in Kassel (5 December 1812–18 January 1813) are unclear, as are those for his brief return alone to Göttingen where on 19 January 1813 he noted in his diary, 'Arrangements. To stay or not to stay, that is the question, perhaps that of my [whole] life.'[13] Certainly Charlotte was there to collect money which was owed to her by various members of her family, but Constant's writing was seriously disturbed by the social life of Kassel. Were his mysterious and lengthy stays in Kassel, a busy cosmopolitan city and one of the crossroads of northern Europe, prompted by some clandestine contact with friends of Bernadotte and perhaps an invitation to join him, and no doubt Germaine, in Sweden, as has been suggested by Kurt Kloocke?[14] Constant had been politically inactive for so long: he knew that such an opportunity, if it came, was unlikely to present itself twice. There is no firm evidence, however, and naturally Constant would not mention anything so dangerously seditious in a journal.

Sedition of a literary kind was, however, on his mind. On 15 March 1813 Constant began a poem, an allegorical anti-Napoleonic satire *Le Siège de Soissons* (*The Siege of Soissons*). Although the verse is mediocre – as he himself implies on 23 March in his diary, he no longer had Germaine's excellent critical judgement to guide him[15] – it shows that Constant's thoughts were beginning to return to both politics and literature after his long sojourn in the realm of history and theology. On 7 and 25 March he 'read [his] novel'[16] (it is not clear whether this was aloud to friends in Kassel or alone), and waited as parties of Russian cossacks crossed the Elbe in the wake of the French retreat. In one of her rare letters to survive the destruction of her correspondence with Constant, Madame de Staël wrote from Stockholm on 17 April 1813, as if intuiting his discontent with himself:

> What I cannot understand is how it can be that your love for literature has not manifested itself sooner and why indeed it is not showing itself now. I am not talking about myself but you. How can you not be tempted by the Doxat [i.e. England and the English, from the name of her bankers Messrs Doxat and Divett of London]? And what are you actually doing with your rare genius? You lack decisiveness. Since I found mine, I'm better for it.[17]

The letter took months to reach him. All that summer Constant worked and hoped that if Napoleon were deposed he could be in Paris by the end of the year and perhaps even able to publish part of his *Polythéisme*. Germaine left Stockholm for London on 9 June 1813, Schlegel and her son Albert de Staël having joined Bernadotte's Swedish forces now moving south against the French. Tragically Albert was to be killed in a duel on 12 July: communications now having become extremely difficult through opposing armies, Constant was for a long time unaware of what had happened.

A family visit which Charlotte now made with him north to Brunswick on 19 September 1813 put Constant – either by chance or design – within striking distance of Bernadotte's forces. On 20 September the couple began a five-week stay at the Von Marenholtz family residence of Groß Schwülper, 7 miles outside the city of Brunswick, with Charlotte's son Wilhelm who was the heir to his father's estate.[18] As the opposing armies gained and lost ground successively, Constant worked on his manuscripts on religion and continued to bide his time, confessing in his diary on 2 October, 'I am agitated by foolish ambition once again'.[19] General Chernychev and his cossacks passed through Brunswick during the build-up to the battle of Leipzig (17–19 October 1813) in which Napoleon was decisively defeated by the armies of the coalition. Word of the Allied victory reached Brunswick on 25 October, and on 2 November Constant made his move. He left for Hanover to declare his support for Prince Bernadotte. He was followed by Charlotte and her son. His diary entry for 6 November 1813 reads:

> Dined with the man from Béarn [Bernadotte]. He was extremely friendly. Tomorrow or never. I have perhaps stupidly put him off me by being polite but familiar with him. Tomorrow we shall see, and in any case if I decide not to follow him, I must choose which alternative course to follow and have no regrets about it. Even if I am successful, there will be painful consequences.[20]

Over subsequent days he saw Bernadotte again several times and, in a surge of self-confidence, on 22 November resumed work on an essay which was soon to become perhaps his finest and best-known piece of political analysis and polemic, *De l'esprit de conquête et de l'usurpation dans leurs rapports avec la civilisation européenne* (*On the Spirit of Conquest and Usurpation in their Connection with European Civilization*). It was finished in record time: by 30 January 1814 his 'bombshell' as he called it was already printed and ready for publication.[21]

De l'esprit de conquête, based on political manuscripts accumulated over a decade or more such as the *Principes de politique* and the *Fragments of an Abandoned Work concerning the Possibility of a Republican Constitution in a Large Country* written many years earlier, is a savage philippic against the despotism of Napoleon. Its importance, however, far transcends its original purpose. The psychology and mechanisms of what we would now call totalitarian rule by a dictator are described with extraordinary and prophetic perceptiveness, so that Constant, although unaware of the prodigious sophistication which methods of surveillance and coercion would attain in the modern police state, seems at times to have anticipated the internal conditions of Hitler's *Reich* and Stalin's Soviet Union. The book marks a decisive development in Constant's thought and links his writings on religion and politics with his autobiographical fiction. For by now he had come to the conclusion that there was a strong parallel between the historical growth of oppressive priestly government among religious groups and that of tyrannical rule based on military conquest and enslavement. The former ran counter to the natural modern aspiration to freedom in religious belief, just as the latter belonged to the violent world of distant Antiquity.

In Constant's view what characterizes our modern world are commerce and the production of goods, activities which need peace among nations and the maximum personal liberty to be carried out successfully. The rights of individuals to self-expression, to property and to privacy have therefore become essential in modern societies. An intimidating priestly caste or rigidly imposed dogmas are as out of place in the religious life of nineteenth-century Europe as Napoleon's military dictatorship is in its civil life; it is a dictatorship moreover which perpetuates itself by waging expansionist wars and suppressing all opposition. Constant sees that guaranteeing the freedom of the individual against the encroachments of the wider group or of society as a whole must henceforth be the chief concern of politicians and legislators. Similarly *Adolphe*, *Cécile* and *Ma Vie*, each in their different ways, explore the obstacles, internal and external, which the modern individual encounters when aspiring to be free.[22]

The originality of Constant's distinction between the ancient and modern worlds, with Napoleon being firmly placed in the first category and the individual's rights dominating the second, brought him literary success at last, and *De l'esprit de conquête* appeared in several revised editions. His purpose was to show that a form of government must be in keeping with the spirit of the age: not only Napoleon but also a restored Bourbon dynasty bent on revenge and all too likely to slip back into *ancien régime* absolutism were anachronisms. Constant believed that an English-style constitutional monarchy under Bernadotte was what best suited France now. It was an illusion on his part to imagine such a thing could come about: the crowned heads of Europe who had led the victorious Allies would not contemplate anything less than a Bourbon on the French throne. But while that illusion lasted Constant had a new purpose in life. Despite disagreements with Charlotte and his own uncertainty, he joined Bernadotte at his headquarters in Liège on 7 March 1814 just as a second edition of *De l'esprit de conquête* by Murray – thanks to whom Germaine de Staël's *De l'Allemagne* had at last been published the previous year – was appearing in London bookshops. For the next five weeks he waited in Liège, having been joined there by Auguste de Staël, Germaine's son. Meanwhile Bernadotte's prospects grew ever dimmer. On 11 March Constant was already writing in his diary: 'I must jump onto a different branch.'[23] His dealings with the Prince had in any case proved to be less cordial than he had hoped. By 6 April the Bourbon Louis XVIII was being proclaimed King in a newly liberated Paris, and on 11 April 1814 Napoleon abdicated. Bernadotte's cause was lost.

For a few days Constant was unsure what to do next and accompanied the Prince's party to Brussels. He wrote in his *Journaux intimes* on 11 April that the waters were muddy in France and that he would stay put until they cleared – then characteristically decided the next day that he would leave for Paris.[24] He left Brussels on 13 April and arrived in the French capital with Auguste de Staël on 15 April 1814 after an absence of just over three years. His first visit was to his faithful correspondent Claude Hochet, and over the next few weeks he renewed other friendships, with Talleyrand, for example, but also with members of the Göttingen *Gelehrten-Club* among the German forces occupying Paris.[25] The day after his arrival the *Journal des Débats* published the following brief report: 'Monsieur Benjamin Constant, Private Secretary to His Royal Highness the Crown Prince of Sweden, is accompanying the Prince and arrived this evening in Paris.' Constant was understandably furious at being publicly compromised by this exaggeration of his closeness to Bernadotte and insisted that on 18 April the journal publish a correction written by him:[26] he could hardly serve the cause of liberty in France, as he now fully intended to once more, if he were seen as supporting a rival to the monarch now in place. As it was things would look bad enough to an incoming conservative, Catholic and very probably repressive administration: Constant was a Swiss Protestant divorcee and ex-Thermidorian with known libertarian tendencies who was rather too fond of England and Germany and who had wished to prevent the rightful heir from ascending the French throne.

Constant was impatient to be involved in politics under the Restoration and was drawn back into writing political journalism while Parisians waited with little enthusiasm for their new King to enter the capital. After Louis XVIII's arrival on 3 May, Constant finally succeeded in obtaining an audience with Tsar Alexander I, one of the architects of the new political order which the Allies had drawn up for France: it seems that little came of the interview, and certainly no appointment for Constant. Indeed he was now totally eclipsed by Madame de Staël who arrived in Paris from London on 12 May 1814. Germaine was already a friend of the Tsar and highly thought of by all those influential in shaping the future of France – British members of parliament, the Bourbons (had she not risked everything to rescue *émigrés* from France during the Terror?) and enemies of Napoleon everywhere. Constant, however, though no less an enemy of the Corsican tyrant, had burnt his boats with her – the one person who could help him most to re-enter French political life. When he visited her on 13 May and on subsequent days she was understandably cool with him, still resentful no doubt at the humiliation she had suffered as a result of his marriage.[27] On 18 May Constant wrote in his journal:

> Dined with Madame de Staël. She has changed completely. She is absent-minded, almost offhand with people, thinks only of herself, hardly listens to others, only bothers with people – even her daughter – out of a sense of duty, hardly bothering with me at all.[28]

He was galled by her treatment of him, as he had been by her treatment of his *De l'esprit de conquête* when she had been in London. She had written to him on 8 January 1814 apropos of a memoir he had drawn up for Bernadotte:

It was written in the manner of everything that flows from your pen. I don't believe that that style, that firmness of control, that clarity of language can be found anywhere else. You were born for high office, if only you had been able to be faithful to yourself and to others.[29]

She had been in London with Constant's old friend Sir James Mackintosh who told her of the regard Constant was still held in by his former fellow students at Edinburgh University, a fact she passed on to Constant to remind him none too subtly of how little he had so far achieved in his life.[30] She was visibly savouring her revenge. Then, when she had received *De l'esprit de conquête* for John Murray to publish, she expressed her own and Mackintosh's admiration for it before proceeding to tell him that he was endangering France:

Is this a time to be speaking ill of the French, when the flames of Moscow are menacing Paris? . . . It is no longer the moment to whip up people's feelings against the French, they are already hated enough. As for the man [i.e. Napoleon], could any freedom-loving heart wish him to be overthrown by cossacks? . . . He must sign a humiliating peace treaty and France must demand a representative parliament. But while foreigners are still occupying the country, should we be helping them? The Opposition here is of my opinion, and you know how much I hate Napoleon. Think carefully about what you are doing. It is possible to say everything in a great work of literature; but to do so in a pamphlet, which is akin to an action, it is necessary to choose the right moment. You must not speak ill of the French when the Russians are at Langres. May God banish me from France rather than allowing me to go back there with the aid of foreigners!

(Letter to Constant of 23 January 1814[31])

She finished by telling Constant that she was as completely captivated by reading the pamphlet as she would have been by reading a novel: 'It's saying a lot when I am *that* impressed by ideas. I give myself as an example of its likely effect on the masses.'[32]

Reading such a letter to Constant – and it will always be a matter for regret that so few survived subsequent destruction – one's sympathies are with him. He had frequently been inept in the conduct of his life and sometimes vain, but here was punishment indeed: to be patronized with meagre praise – written in Germaine's style at its most prolix and illogical – for his best work yet, and then told that he should have written it differently or not at all because he was being unpatriotic – this from a fellow Swiss, who was shortly to arrive back in Paris in triumph alongside the conquering Allies.

Constant was now unable to look for any help or encouragement from Germaine de Staël, even if he were to become submissive to her once again. To add to his humiliation he made the mistake of reading her the awful burlesque epic poem of which he was so inexplicably proud, *Le Siège de Soissons*, on 24 May and reported glumly in his diary:

> Read my poem to Madame de Staël. It's easy to see she no longer loves me because she hardly had a word of praise for me. She only praises people who are part of herself, the man she is currently keeping [i.e. Rocca] for example. It's a great weight lifted from my life now that I've seen her. There is no uncertainty now about the future, because there is no trace of any affection for me left in her. Linon [i.e. Charlotte] is worth so much more than her. Why doesn't she come [to Paris]?[33]

Feeling abandoned and isolated, and chafing at the fact that for all his talents he seemed destined for oblivion while Germaine could look forward to enduring literary fame, Constant looked on helplessly as Louis XVIII prepared to issue the Charter which was finally granted to the French people on 4 June 1814. In the hope of being noticed Constant wrote a pamphlet of a general kind on the basic principles of constitutional monarchy *à l'anglaise* – a free press, religious toleration, and so forth. He did attract attention, that of the government censor who indicated to him firmly that he should write nothing about the contents of the Charter – if indeed the monarch was gracious enough to grant one – either before or after it was made public. Comment of any kind was unwelcome. Constant therefore fired off two more squibs, on the freedom of pamphlets and newspapers and on a speech made by the Minister of the Interior, in which he boldly attacked the imposition of limits on freedom of expression.[34] At last people began to register that he was back on the scene. In the meantime he had become associated with François-Jean-Frédéric Durbach (1763–1827), deputy for the Moselle, who was hostile to the Bourbon royal family and for whom Constant began to write speeches on the liberty of the press. But this was hardly enough for a former member of the Tribunate, a man who desperately wanted to write and deliver his own speeches and to be at the centre of political controversy.

During the spring and summer of 1814 Constant was frequently without any word from Charlotte. There was depressing news from Göttingen where his friend Charles de Villers had been unjustly stripped by the Allies of his Professorship of French Literature which had been given him by the Napoleonic puppet Kingdom of Westphalia (Villers was to die the following year), and then on 3 June he heard that his dearly loved aunt, the Comtesse Anne de Nassau had died the week before. She left him very little in her will, and now both Madame de Staël and his half-brother and half-sister (he took to calling the last two 'the bastards' in his diary) wanted money from him. With his morale and self-esteem at their nadir he wrote on 17 July 1814:

> Miserable morning. I shall never be anything in this country if I do not succeed by way of its government, and that is no easy matter. I must devote my whole mind to it. Letter from Charlotte. She is not coming [to Paris]. I must become somebody in the next six weeks. Dined at Madame Récamier's.[35]

That last phrase marks the beginning of perhaps the last genuinely grand passion in Constant's life. He was now 46 and had known Juliette Récamier (1777–1849) for many years. She had been Germaine's close friend at Coppet, and a friend of his too, though he had never really taken a great deal of notice of her. After all, despite her extraordinary beauty and grace, immortalized by the painters Gérard and Jacques-Louis David, she was not particularly intelligent when seen by the side of Madame de Staël, and had always appeared rather insipid and devoid of interest. While the *châtelaine* of Coppet had been drawn to Juliette in an intense *amitié amoureuse*, in which Juliette was like a younger sister or perhaps something more to Germaine (there may have been homoerotic undertones to the relationship), and while Prosper de Barante had pined for her, Constant had remained immune to Madame Récamier's mysterious power to disturb people's lives.[36] She was now 37 and although she had kept her good looks, her intellect had not developed noticeably over the years. Not only that, but she was instinctively a royalist and moved in political circles with which Constant had little sympathy. She now asked a favour of him, that of using such influence as he had to ensure that her friend Joachim Murat remained on the throne of Naples where Napoleon had put him, together with his consort, Caroline. Although, as Françoise Wagener's recent biography of Madame Récamier has pointed out (redressing the traditional estimate of her somewhat), Juliette was a woman of good sense and refined taste, there was little about her to suggest that she might make a suitable partner for a man like Constant. Which is perhaps why the 'explosion' of passion in him when it came (Ephraïm Harpaz's term and hardly an exaggeration[37]) was of such cataclysmic force in his life.

In the calm which preceded it, Constant's life went on as before: a pamphlet was revised and printed, and he began to give public readings of his novel, the as yet untitled *Adolphe*:

> 23 July 1814: Read my novel to Madame Laborie. The women who were there all burst into tears. . . .
> 24 July 1814: Reading at Madame de Catelan's. Success.[38]

On 11 August to his great dismay the government passed a law limiting press freedom. Nevertheless, despite the threat now looming of what in effect was a counter-revolution in France, Constant's diary is full of dinner parties and discussions with friends and political figures – Guizot, with whom he argued, Talleyrand, Barante, Garat, and on 29 August a heart-warming reunion with Sir James Mackintosh. Then on 31 August it happened: 'Madame Récamier. Really! Have I taken leave of my senses?'[39]

During early September 1814 Constant attempted to make light of his infatuation: Juliette in no way corresponded to his type, this was an amusement, no more. He gambled to take his mind off her, and unusually he won two days running. At this stage he was still confident of success with her:

> 7 September 1814: A day entirely given over to Juliette. She doesn't yet love me but she likes me. There are few women who can remain indifferent to my way of being obsessed and dominated by them. All this is a powerful new source of interest in my life. I can feel an unaccustomed warmth in my veins.[40]

He felt guilt at deceiving Charlotte and decided to leave Paris: he was unable to and found himself slipping into the familiar maelstrom of desire, indecision and deception that he had no doubt believed he would never experience again. His journal entries grew longer as each day he was shaken by conflicting emotions of great force. On 13 and 14 September he wrote a *mémoire* to defend Joachim Murat's right to remain King of Naples, as Madame Récamier had asked him to: there even seemed to be the possibility of a post in his service if he would go on a secret mission to Vienna, where preparations were being made for the Congress of Vienna on the future shape of Europe. The mission came to nothing because the government of Naples refused to give Constant the full diplomatic status he wanted, though the real reason had more to do with his still unrequited passion: he needed to be with Juliette every day.

For three months, from September until the end of November 1814 he was in a state of adolescent love-sickness, a fact he himself realized but was powerless to change: he could not work or concentrate on anything but her, nor could he resolve to leave her and rejoin Charlotte in Germany. In fact his mind was now set on living in Paris permanently, and his recent large winnings at the gaming tables enabled him to buy a house, No 6 Rue Neuve-de-Berry, on 12 November, and subsequently some land around it: as a property-owner he was legally entitled to vote and perhaps one day to be voted for. He felt that he had become the slave of a heartless, shallow coquette, like the many other men who had been captivated by Juliette Récamier's beauty over the years. Of course, as Françoise Wagener's spirited 'défense et illustration' of Madame Récamier suggests, Juliette knew Constant rather too well, had witnessed years of argument and bitterness in his relationship with Germaine and was not anxious to become seriously involved with him herself:[41] in all probability she had no real love for him. But it must also be said that she made no effort to spare his feelings when she encouraged Constant and three aristocratic rivals, the painter, the Comte de Forbin, the Marquis de Nadaillac and the Comte de Montlosier to court her simultaneously. Beside himself with jealousy as a result of her treatment of him, Constant challenged all three of the other unfortunate suitors to duels on different occasions: Forbin on 27 September 1814 (the matter was settled without bloodshed), Montlosier on 28 May 1815, who was wounded in the hand (afterwards combatants and seconds all went off to a restaurant to continue what was ostensibly a political argument there) and Nadaillac in early August 1815, when the matter was settled peacefully.[42] Constant's diary records sleepless nights, panic, tears, elation, anguish, thoughts of suicide; the word *paroxysme* frequently marks the sudden resurgence of passion after fruitless attempts to tear himself away from Juliette. He visited a prostitute in order to exhaust himself, in the hope, as he put it, that he would no longer be able to bear a woman's touch, but to little avail.[43] He knew that his love for this enigmatic woman who so often appeared to him hard and frivolous was both absurd and self-destructive, but as with Adolphe his will was paralysed and rational knowledge could do little to affect his feelings or actions. On 17 October 1814 he confided in his journal:

Oh God, I give up. She has put me through another appalling day. She is a linnet, a cloud, without memory, discernment or preferences. Her beauty has made her the object of many homages from men, and all the romantic talk she has listened to has given her the appearance of having feelings but in fact that is purely superficial. The next day she is never as she had been the day before. Her memory is not good enough when she has had one enjoyable conversation for her to want to seek another. She is the same with everyone as she is with me.[44]

As the year came to an end his *extravagances* prompted him to write in his diary on New Year's Eve: 'I must think carefully and lead a sensible life. I am so tired and so unhappy because of all my follies. I must get a grip on myself, it is high time that I did.'[45] But 1815 was to prove a still more disastrous year for him.

Despite the late nights which were always bad for his health, despite the gambling, the obsession with Madame Récamier and his endlessly postponed departure for Germany, on 13 December Constant began a pamphlet which was to earn him respect: on the responsibility – and answerability – of government ministers. But all the consideration and praise in the world meant little if it did not also come from Juliette Récamier, and that was never to be. On 23 and 31 January 1815 he gave two public readings in Paris salons of the novel that was soon to be called *Adolphe*, on the second occasion with great success,[46] yet still his ambitions lay elsewhere, above all in politics. In that particular area he could be certain of receiving no help whatsoever from Germaine de Staël who not only deeply resented the fact that the man who had publicly rejected her was now pursuing her closest woman friend, but was also demanding money from him – no less than 40,000 francs – as a contribution to Albertine's dowry on her marriage to Victor de Broglie. Fate – in the form of major political developments – was shortly to step in once again and spare Constant the penury that such a claim might have reduced him to. But he was soon to lose something more precious than money – the hard-earned reputation resulting from his many years of steadfast opposition to Napoleon's tyranny.

On 1 March 1815 Napoleon landed at Fréjus with 1,050 troops, having made good his escape from the isle of Elba and slipped past the British navy. He marched north, gathering support as he went. There was general dissatisfaction with the Bourbon King, there were even stirrings of the old revolutionary spirit which the young Bonaparte had capitalized on in his early days. Word of the landing reached Constant in Paris on 6 March. For days as Napoleon moved nearer – Grenoble, Lyon, Autun, Auxerre – the government dithered. On 8 March Constant wrote a stirring denunciation of the ex-despot. By the time it was published on 11 March in the *Journal de Paris*,[47] it was clear that Paris would soon be in the hands of the Bonapartists and his life was at risk. The royalists were frightened and ironically it was the former republican Constant who was standing up for the Bourbon King – admittedly with some prompting from the royalist Juliette Récamier. Madame de Staël fled Paris for Switzerland the same day, but Constant stayed on, hoping that some resistance could be mustered against the return of a tyrant. On 18 March, the day after news had come that Napoleon was in Auxerre, he wrote another courageous and hostile article for the *Journal des Débats* which appeared the next day[48] likening the ex-Emperor to Attila the Hun and Genghis Khan, and defending constitutional monarchy under Louis XVIII. Then a strange thing happened. Constant went into hiding in Paris (21–2 March), then fled to Angers and the Vendée, before immediately returning (23–7 March); after two days of hesitation he went to see Joseph Bonaparte, the ex-Emperor's brother but nevertheless an old friend of Madame de Staël, and wrote in his diary on 30 March: 'Hopes. Might there really be a chance of freedom?'[49] From that moment he began to swing towards the person he had recently so vehemently denounced. A reformed Napoleon – who had, after all, been a man of the Revolution and who had abolished so many feudal institutions across Europe – might just be preferable to the Bourbons who had clearly learnt nothing in the past twenty-five years and manifestly believed that they had a God-given right to carry on exactly where they had left off in 1789.

Constant now put his pen at the service of Napoleon, writing *mémoires* on the Congress of Vienna and on Germany. The former, which appeared in the *Journal de Paris* anonymously on 4 April 1815[50] saying that, given the public support Napoleon enjoyed, the Emperor now represented the will of the French nation. It was an astonishing *volte-face*, written just days before new decrees were issued against the Bourbons and forbidding armed assemblies. But Constant had chosen his new course and was ready to meet accusations of opportunistically seeking office – accusations which were not long in coming. Madame de Staël wrote to him expressing her scepticism and disapproval when on 5 April it was made public that Constant was working on a new constitution for a France ruled by the restored Emperor.[51] On 14 April 1815 he was granted an interview with the man he had so recently denounced and wrote in his diary: 'Long conversation. He's an astonishing man. Tomorrow I'll bring him a draft constitution. Shall I finally be a success? Should I wish to be? The future is black. God's will be done.'[52] Constant was not the first person to succumb to the unique mixture of confidence, energy, magnetic charm and bullying in Napoleon's character. But there was more to it than that, for Constant still had the unshakeable conviction that he was destined for high office if only circumstances would allow it: once there he could use all his talent in the cause of building a free and just society whoever the ruler might be. Once again what looks like self-serving had a less ignoble side to it.

The Emperor rejected Constant's first proposals – Constant observed drily, 'It's not exactly freedom he wants'[53] – but after amendments were made the 'Additional Act to the Constitution of the Empire' was ready by the end of April 1815. It came to be known familiarly as 'la benjamine', a nickname that was to haunt Constant's later political career as a reminder of his apostasy. He was made a member of the Emperor's Council of State and became in effect a courtier. Yet despite criticism – his article of 19 March denouncing Napoleon was reprinted and circulated as a fly-sheet to embarrass him – he remained proud of the work he had done on the 'Additional Act'. It had been a genuine effort to ensure that the Emperor became a constitutional monarch and its intention was to guard against a return of his despotic tendencies. To answer those who accused him of being without principle in politics Constant drew on his manuscript treatise written in 1806 and published in late May 1815, *Principes de politique*, 'Political principles applicable to all representative governments and particularly to the present constitution of France'.[54] Of course no instant conversion of the former tyrant could be guaranteed, but at least Constant could feel that he was on the side of right. It looked like a gamble worth taking.

The gamble failed and, as so often, Constant lost heavily. On 18 June 1815 Napoleon was defeated by Blücher and Wellington at Waterloo, his 'Hundred Days' of power were soon to be over. He asked to see Constant on 21 June who noted in his journal: 'He is still calm and making jokes. He will abdicate tomorrow, I think. The wretches, they served him with enthusiasm when he crushed liberty, they are abandoning him when he is establishing it.'[55] All of Constant's plans for personal, religious and press freedoms in France were now destined to come to nothing. Whether Napoleon would have honoured the liberal *Acte additionnel* is open to doubt – Constant himself was uncertain. But having taken the risk of collaboration, he now faced the consequences. At the end of June and the beginning of July 1815 he went to eastern France as part of a delegation representing the defeated Emperor's administration: their mission was to negotiate with the Allies. On his return to Paris he wrote a memoir defending his conduct under Napoleon and sent it to Louis XVIII: it convinced the King who thereupon had Constant's name struck off the list of those – including several of Constant's friends such as Durbach – being punished with exile from France. On 10 August he then began a longer version of his apologia, a 'history of these past three months' which was eventually to culminate in his celebrated *Mémoires sur les Cent-Jours (Memoirs concerning the Hundred Days)*.[56]

All this time, during all the upheaval since March, Constant's passion for Juliette Récamier had continued to burn fiercely. He was frequently irritable and touchy, and ready to fight duels over her as we have seen. The new government proved to be as reactionary and vengeful as Constant had feared it would be, but Madame Récamier kept him in Paris when wisdom dictated that he should leave France altogether. In September 1815 Madame de Krüdener (1764–1824), the novelist and celebrated Pietistic mystic of Russian origin, came into contact with Madame Récamier and Constant. He liked the simple basis of Madame de Krüdener's beliefs – which were not far removed from his own since his encounter with the Lausanne *Mystiques* of 1807 – although he found their expression sometimes embarrassing and absurd.[57] Seeing Constant's hopeless and near-suicidal pining for Juliette, Madame de Krüdener took pity on him and offered to try to forge a 'spiritual bond', a 'lien d'âme', between him and Madame Récamier. He began praying with Juliette, on 4 October wrote her a religious letter, and even gave money to the poor like a latter-day Valmont – but all in vain. As always with a man as complex as Constant these were not simply the actions of a *roué* who has gone through a simulacrum of conversion in order to be a more successful seducer: his religious aspirations, though vague, were now nevertheless genuine. By 31 October, however, the political situation had deteriorated to such an extent that he reluctantly bade Madame Récamier farewell and began a period of self-imposed exile in Brussels. There he continued to give occasional readings of his novel as he had in Paris, worked on the *Memoirs concerning the Hundred Days* and waited for Charlotte to join him. When she did, on 1 December 1815, he noted grimly in his diary the following day:

Sad but important day. Positive developments: 1. my wife hardly cares for me any more; 2. she came here out of what is left of her friendship for me, but she would have done better to stay in Germany without me; 3. she is German and fanatically anti-French, and would be my ruination if ever she came to France. It's fortunate that she didn't come. Hence these two rules: 1. don't take her to France at any price and 2. resettle her gently in Germany.[58]

As Madame de Charrière had once perceptively remarked, as soon as Constant expressed a feeling it meant that it was already about to vanish. And indeed by Christmas he was entirely reconciled to 'le Linon' as he called his wife. On 21 January 1816 his long-planned departure for England could take place.

10

ADOLPHE
(1816–1819)

Constant and his wife reached Dover from Ostend on 25 January 1816. By 1 February he had found a suitable house to rent in London, and was relieved to be generally better received than a recent courtier of Napoleon had any right to be. To the usual round of dinners, visits to the houses of friends and acquaintances in and near London, and trips to the theatre, Constant added public readings in French of his novel, soon to be entitled *Adolphe*, to the appreciative audiences of the capital. Perhaps his aim was to deflect attention from his political past. These readings were extraordinary affairs, and the several accounts of them that have survived suggest that they very literally filled the function of Freud's 'talking cure', that they were some form of dramatic therapy for Constant. Victor de Broglie, Albertine de Staël's husband and generally hostile to Constant, says the following about one such occasion in Paris in his memoirs:

> Benjamin gave several readings [of *Adolphe*] during the Hundred Days, one of which I was present at in Madame Récamier's house, which deserves to be recorded here, since it was not reported at the time.
>
> There were twelve or fifteen people present. The reading had been going on for nearly three hours. The novelist was tired; as he approached the dénouement his feelings were more and more evident, and fatigue added to his emotion. Finally he could no longer contain himself; he broke into sobbing; everyone present, already very moved, began crying as well; soon the room was full of weeping and moaning; then suddenly, as the result of a psychological mechanism which is not unusual according to doctors, his convulsive sobs turned to nervous and irrepressible laughter, so that if anyone had entered the room at that moment and chanced upon the writer and his audience they would have been hard put to know what to think, or to deduce the cause from its effects.[1]

The London literary hostess, Miss Mary Berry (1763–1852), tells a similar story in her journal entry for 14 February 1816:

In the evening at the Bourkes where there had been a dinner. Lady
Holland, Princess Lieven etc. and where Benjamin Constant read his
romance or history; I do not know what to call it as he has not
given it a name. It is very well written – a sad and much too true
story of the human heart, but almost ridiculously so with the company before whom it was read. It lasted two hours and a half. The
end was so touching, that it was scarcely possible to restrain one's
tears, and the effort I made to do so made me positively ill. Agnes
[her sister] and I both burst into tears on our return home.[2]

There can be few examples of prepublication performances like this, comparable in their impact with those of Dickens many years later. What has
too often been overlooked is the effect which *Adolphe*'s nature as a
performance text seems to have had on its content and structure: sub-
plots were necessarily excluded, the story was kept short, simple and
linear, the number of characters minimal.[3] The narrating voice of Adolphe
was taken by Constant himself, allowing him to re-experience the distilled
emotions of the past thirty years. In *Adolphe* were his experiences at
Edinburgh and Brunswick, his friendship with Madame de Charrière and
his difficult relationship with his father, his passion for Madame de Staël,
Anna Lindsay and Charlotte and its inevitable decay; perhaps too an
implicit critique of the values of eighteenth-century society to which the
Napoleonic age had given a new and artificial lease of life.[4] It is hardly
surprising that a work which was both a summary of his life and its
highest achievement should have produced such emotional anguish and
the *fou rire*, the hysterical laughter that such stress can trigger. But such
an ordeal was clearly very necessary to him, not merely to allow him to
explain publicly his much discussed behaviour, but also to enable him
relive his past in the hope of one day being free of it.

Adolphe, which ironically Constant never valued as highly as his work
on religion or political theory but which now belongs to the canon of
great French novels, epitomizes his mastery of French prose. Its style is
clear, direct, elegant and concise, its narrative intensely felt, its tone plan-
gent but with no trace of the mawkish sentimentality which the accounts
of its performance might suggest. The many memorable aphorisms which
emerge naturally in Adolphe's account of his sudden passion for Ellénore
and his inability to end their relationship when that love has died bear
comparison with the *moralistes* of seventeenth-century France. And the
exceptionally complex account which Adolphe gives of his changing
emotions within the space of the mere hundred or so pages the novel
occupies both invites the reader to share in the task of passing judgement
on his treatment of Ellénore and precludes our reaching any easy conclusions. The Preface and framing letters add to that richness and com-

plexity, and these appear to have been added at the last moment in London.[5]

By late February 1816, after giving several public readings, Constant decided to have his novel published. It might bring him money and establish his reputation on a terrain rather less embarrassing than the political one. He found Henry Colburn of 50 Conduit Street, London, who was as yet little known in England as a publisher but who had already brought out works by Madame de Staël. Colburn offered him 70 *louis* for the manuscript. On 9 and 13 May Constant noted in his diary that he was writing a preface to the novel,[6] and on Monday 27 May he wrote to Colburn:

> Mr Constant's complts to Mr Colburn – informs him that he sends to-day the last proofsheet corrected, and that he supposes the little publication will be finished to-morrow. He wishes that the sale may begin at the latest on Saturday.[7]

As C. P. Courtney has established, a copy of this first edition of *Adolphe* was entered under copyright regulations at Stationers' Hall on 7 June 1816,[8] the novel was therefore published no later than that date. A Paris edition was published almost simultaneously. *Adolphe* was an immediate success in London, though Constant was upset that English newspapers pounced on the similarity between Adolphe's relationship with Ellénore and his own with Madame de Staël. On 23 June he had a letter published in the *Morning Chronicle*:

> SIR, Various papers have given the public to understand that the short novel of 'Adolphe' contains circumstances personal to me and to individuals really existing. I think it my duty to disclaim any such unwarrantable interpretation. I should have thought it foolish in me to describe myself, and surely the very judgment I passed upon the hero of that anecdote, ought to have screened me from that suspicion; for no one can take pleasure in representing himself as guilty of vanity, weakness and ingratitude. But the accusation of having described any other person is much more serious. It would fix on my character a stain I can never submit to. Neither Ellenore, nor Adolphe's father, nor the Count de P—, have any resemblance to any person I have ever known. Not only my friends, but my acquaintance [*sic*] are sacred to me.[9]

Constant was fortunate enough to find a good English translator for *Adolphe*, the Edinburgh-educated Alexander Walker, whose translation was entered at Stationers' Hall on 3 September 1816.[10]

The disclaimer in the *Morning Chronicle* was disingenuous, and among Constant's family and friends no one was taken in, though of course it was understandable that he should issue such a denial in the circumstances.

His cousin Rosalie wrote to her brother Charles de Constant on 5 July 1816 saying that Ellénore was *la dame de Coppet*, Madame de Staël; Charles replied on 8 July that Adolphe was Benjamin but that Ellénore was really Anna Lindsay. Whereupon Rosalie told him on 12 July that the Anna Lindsay story was a red herring deliberately trailed by the Coppet clique to protect Germaine. Rosalie was on the whole sympathetic to the novel: Charles, who had always detested his cousin, was hostile, telling Rosalie for good measure that to sell one's life to the public for money was the lowest form of degradation.[11] Others likewise reacted in accordance with their feelings towards Constant. His friend Prosper de Barante was full of admiration, and another approving reader, Simonde de Sismondi, wrote to the German Comtesse d'Albany on 14 October 1816 giving information that was inaccurate in detail but broadly true in spirit:

> Benjamin's father was exactly as he has described him. The older woman with whom he lived in his youth, whom he very much loved and whom he saw die is a certain Madame de Charrière, the author of several delightful novels. The busybodying woman friend who, while claiming to be trying to bring about a reconciliation between the couple, drives them further apart is Madame Récamier. The Comte de P*** is a complete invention and indeed, although he at first appears to be an important character, the novelist didn't bother to give him distinctive features, and doesn't let him play any real role in the story.[12]

While in London Constant found time to devote to other projects apart from *Adolphe*: he discussed letters which were destined eventually to become his *Mémoires sur les Cent-Jours* (*Memoirs concerning the Hundred Days*) with Lord Byron's friend, John Cam Hobhouse (1786–1869), who had recently published *The Substance of Some Letters written by an Englishman resident at Paris during the Last Reign of the Emperor Napoleon*. Constant briefly considered entitling them *Lettres à Hobhouse* (*Letters to Hobhouse*), then abandoned the idea. The letters were subsequently to undergo many transformations in manuscript before being published in 1819–20.[13] And then there was something he considered far more lasting as a monument than his 'anecdote' *Adolphe*: his book on polytheism. So many years of work had now gone into it that before leaving England he took the extraordinary step of entrusting the voluminous manuscript 'to God's safekeeping' ('à la garde de Dieu'), as he put it in his diary, that is, to the care of the Reverend Nathaniel May, his tutor in the early 1780s whom he had not seen for thirty-five years. May was now a clergyman at Leigh, near Tunbridge Wells in Kent, and Constant went to visit him there on 22 and 23 July[14] before taking ship to Ostend with Charlotte on 27 July: his life's work was too precious to risk either leaving it in an

empty house in London or taking it to France where there was a reactionary government hostile to him. (He returned to Leigh on 25 July to give
May his preface to the second edition of *Adolphe*.[15]) Once in Belgium
Constant spent two weeks writing steadily at Spa, then decided to risk
returning to Paris via Brussels. He must now have felt that he had reached
some kind of turning point in his fortunes for he seems finally to have
abandoned keeping a journal altogether on 26 September 1816.[16] From
that date onwards we must rely on other sources of information.

It is always a temptation to divide a writer's life into neat phases, as
Sir Harold Nicolson did in his lively but occasionally inaccurate *Benjamin
Constant*. For Nicolson, the years 1816 to 1830 'were comparatively
sedate' now that Constant had 'found at last the protective tenderness [of
Charlotte] for which (without knowing it) he had always yearned'.[17] It is
certainly true that there were to be no more extraordinary public scenes
like the salon readings of *Adolphe* – and, whether Constant was conscious
of the fact or not, those performances do seem to have enabled him to
understand and come to terms at some deep level with his past behaviour
and relationships. But in the rest of his life as in the preceding years there
were to be no tidy divisions between happiness and restlessness, stability
and anxiety. Everything we have seen of Constant's character would in
any case tend to make the likelihood of any sudden and lasting conversion
to a calm acceptance of his lot extremely remote, and this was indeed the
case. He was often bored with Charlotte and embarrassed by her when
in company, and despite his increasing successes in politics, a glance at
the unpublished literary fragments from his later years suggests that his
days and nights were often suffused with melancholy – even more than
one might expect in a man who knew that he had not many years left to
live.[18] And to scotch finally the notion that after *Adolphe* was published
Constant settled down contentedly with Charlotte, there is the fact that
he had at least one more relationship with another woman during those
last fourteen years of his life, a relationship of which Sir Harold Nicolson
had no knowledge.

While in Spa, Constant wrote to his cousin Rosalie to thank her for
what she had written to him about *Adolphe*. On 14 July 1816 she had
written:

> You can imagine how *Adolphe* brought me back close to you again.
> It is so completely you that it made me suffer something of what
> the actual events had put me through. All my feelings about you
> were revitalized, as were my regrets at your failure to achieve results
> with the gifts you have been given, and my grief at the pain you
> have suffered, and my ardent desire to see you reconquer what ought
> to be yours by right. I said to myself: with such talents it is never
> too late; with that goodness of heart, that delicacy of a conscience

so keenly aware of the suffering it is causing, with that sensibility sharpened by the power of thought – whereas in other people it is only diminished – it may still be possible to be loved and enjoy being loved.[19]

In his earlier letter Constant had told her that the thought of death which had always obsessed him prevented him from making the most of his life and abilities. He now replied to Rosalie on 17 July:

What you say about *Adolphe* gives me great pleasure. I think there is a measure of truth in the details and observations in the book. But I've never thought it a very important work, and it was written ten years ago. I only published it so as not to have to read it aloud any more, as I had fifty times in France. Since some English visitors had heard it in Paris, I was asked to read it in London, and after having given four readings in a week, I thought it would be better if people took the trouble to read the novel for themselves.[20]

With *Adolphe* out of the way, Constant was getting on with what really mattered to him, the *Memoirs concerning the Hundred Days*, written in the form of letters, as well, of course, as his work on religion. He added:

I would like to believe that I have as bright a future before me as you describe, but my heart is little inclined to hope, and I find looking on the black side more tolerable at the moment. If that need to write which people call talent didn't force me to work, I would tend towards complete inactivity. But since nothing in everyday life inspires the slightest interest in me, and since I'm permanently ill at ease, I'm obliged to keep busy, just as a sick man keeps taking his medicines.[21]

It was in such a state of mind that he returned to Paris on 27 September 1816, having decided that any long-term stay in England, where the cost of living was relatively very high, was out of the question. During October he and Charlotte took a rented apartment in the Hôtel Vauban, and at the urging of Germaine de Staël he set about writing a pamphlet which – with his usual taste for long titles – he called *A Political Doctrine which would bring together All the Parties in France*. It was published in December 1816 to some acclaim.[22] The Second Restoration of Louis XVIII after Waterloo was a very different affair from the First, and Constant had had a brief taste of it before leaving for Belgium in the autumn of 1815. The King, despite having been an exile in England, had never truly been converted to the notion of parliamentary government. The *Charte* or Charter he had given to his people recognized Roman Catholicism as the official religion of France, and the Hundred Days and its aftermath had reinforced what to Constant were illiberal tendencies in the King and his government. The separation of church and state and the freedom of the individual, two of Constant's central political principles, were under threat. Before he had left France in 1815, Constant had visited Count Charles de Labédoyère in prison. Labédoyère had been condemned to death for having rallied to Napoleon with his regiment on the road to Grenoble in March 1815, and was executed by firing squad on 19 August 1815. In the south of France a White Terror had raged, Napoleon's loyal general Marshal Ney had been executed in December 1815, and a staunchly royalist Chamber of Deputies, known as the *Chambre introuvable*, had been elected. There was, however, a small chink of light ahead. In September 1816 the reactionary *Chambre introuvable* was dissolved and a new government with a working majority was elected under a competent administrator, the Duc de Richelieu. Between September 1816 and December 1818 when he resigned Richelieu restored the finances of France. Richelieu was to draw his support from the Centre and Right of the French political spectrum, but he was able to achieve what he did only as long as he enjoyed the monarch's favour. The extent to which France was slipping back into *ancien régime* ways was underlined when Louis XVIII replaced Richelieu with a personal favourite of his, Count Decazes, in December 1818. Ironically Decazes, despite being the King's man, was to draw his support from the Left.

With Constant's name gradually becoming respectable once again in France, during the winter of 1816–17 he had a house in Paris made ready for him to occupy the following summer (he was never in fact to live in it himself[23]), and began a very active career in political journalism with the relaunched newspaper the *Mercure de France*. Still his expectations and morale were not high, and he told Rosalie on 6 December 1816: 'The future is still doubtful and sometimes sombre, the present is monotonous, the past somewhat depressing. And besides, life is running out and death profiting from everything.'[24] But the *Mercure de France* which began appearing from 4 January 1817 was to prove a lifeline for Constant. Signed articles by him which appeared every week soon established him as a respected liberal commentator not only on the activities of the Chamber of Deputies, but also on wider political and literary matters.[25] In the midst of these positive omens for his career he received a severe blow: Madame de Staël was taken ill while climbing a staircase at a ball held at Count Decazes's residence on 21 February 1817, and was left partially paralysed. Thanks to her doctor's efforts she was able to leave her bed a month later, but all who saw her knew she was a changed woman. It was obvious to them, as it was to Germaine herself, that she was dying. As the paralysis spread – according to Ghislain de Diesbach possibly the result of a disease of the spinal marrow[26] – she took to a wheelchair. Among her visitors were Chateaubriand and Madame Récamier: Chateaubriand was shortly to succeed where Constant had failed and to begin a celebrated liaison with Juliette. Madame de Staël died in her sleep in the early morning of 14 July 1817. During the later stages of her illness she had refused to let Constant see her, and he had also sensed a new degree of antagonism towards him among her entourage, even in Albertine, who had married Victor de Broglie the previous year. Constant was allowed to sit with the family by her body, but their hostility to him was to be undiminished not only during the rest of his lifetime but also the rest of the nineteenth century.

As a final tribute to Madame de Staël, Constant wrote her obituary in the *Mercure de France*,[27] and twelve years later composed a longer and more impressive memorial to her, 'De Madame de Staël et de ses ouvrages' ('On Madame de Staël and her works'), paying tribute to her long struggle against Napoleon and her dedication to the cause of political freedom. Despite their having grown apart in recent years, Germaine's death deeply affected Constant and revived his despairing sense of futility in the face of the certainty of death. He wrote to Madame Récamier at the beginning of August 1817:

> I am sad and above all indifferent to everything. In vain I urge myself to get interested in things, it doesn't work. I am unmoved either by successes or setbacks. I can't get angry about those who are working against me or feel gratitude to those who are on my side, other than by being forced to do so by my reason. I cannot be said to be still living.[28]

That same month he twice failed to secure election to the Académie française: despite his remarkable powers as a writer and polemicist and the excellence of his French style, Constant was sadly never destined to wear the green uniform of one of the *Immortels*, although he was a candidate again in 1828 and 1830. Then an opportunity arose for him to return to active politics during September 1817. The French political scene was by now divided among the pure diehard royalists, known as the Ultras, who supported not the King but his brother the Comte d'Artois (and among whom Chateaubriand was numbered); the political Centre, who supported Louis XVIII, with Richelieu on its right wing and Decazes on its left; and then the real Left, supporters of liberal principles and parliamentary monarchy, who called themselves Independents. It was as a member of this last group that Constant stood for election, and wrote several pamphlets to defend his position. Although he was defeated, he now at last had friends and allies, and a precise cause to struggle for.

From that autumn of 1817 books, articles and pamphlets began to flow from his pen in numbers that are scarcely believable. As the government fought back with repressive measures, so Constant's natural zeal in pursuit of liberty drove him on to ever greater activity. In November he and others formed the Society of Friends of Press Freedom (Société des Amis de la Liberté de la Presse) in solidarity with an imprisoned publisher: as a result of police harassment the Society would be dissolved on 18 December 1819.[29] Then in December 1817 Constant took up the cause of one Wilfrid Regnault whom he believed to have been unjustly condemned to death for murder on flimsy evidence. Thanks to open letters in 1818 to the Court of Appeal, Regnault's sentence was reduced to twenty years imprisonment – a triumph for Constant who was now following in the campaigning and humanitarian footsteps of Voltaire defending the Chevalier de la Barre or clearing the name of the innocent Calas. As a consequence he rose considerably in the public's esteem.[30] The year was rounded off with the closure by the government of the *Mercure de France* by order of the Minister of Police: Richelieu had been enraged by an article which had appeared in it concerning the Concordat. Almost immediately the *Mercure* was to be replaced by a new newspaper, *La Minerve française*, launched in February 1818 by a group of liberal journalists including Constant. Nor was Constant's work on religion forgotten: from November 1817 he began planning a course on the history of religions at the Athénée royal – the successor to La Harpe's Lycée, a hall where by payment of a subscription the public could attend open lectures. The first lecture took place on 6 February 1818.[31] It is possible that in the audience was an admirer whose name we do not know, a woman who used the pseudonym of 'Eliane', and who was about to disturb the calmer rhythm of his life.

Among the papers of the Von Marenholtz family kept in the archives of Lower Saxony, in the Niedersächsisches Staatsarchiv in Wolfenbüttel near Brunswick, is a remarkable series of unpublished letters addressed to Constant from August 1818 to February 1819 and running to 172 pages in all.[32] The letters are not originals but copies made in a careful secretarial hand, perhaps on the instructions of Charlotte, who had always taken a generous and selfless interest in the other women who, like herself, had loved Constant over the years.[33] One letter is signed 'Eliane', and from the letters' contents it seems that this unknown admirer, now living in Paris, is older than Constant and knew him many years before, perhaps in Germany. Her French style at times suggests that she may have been German, some such figure, perhaps, as Sophie von Schardt (1755–1819) with whom Constant may have had a brief liaison in Weimar in 1804, or even an acquaintance from Brunswick or Erlangen thirty or more years before. Her manner is that of a confident emancipated woman, forthright, often witty and teasing: she numbers her letters, and Constant is required to send his replies via a Polish woman of their acquaintance. Although we do not possess Constant's replies, we gain glimpses of the relationship, and of Constant's feelings of despair at this time – he was 51 in October 1818 and beginning to show signs of physical frailty. 'Eliane' writes, for example:

Despite my sadness at reading your letter in which you liken yourself to a man sitting by the sea which separates him from his homeland, I felt inclined this morning to tease you about your notion. . . . Will you tell me why the man who writes with a kind of melancholy about the distance between himself and happiness seems to be afraid of getting nearer to it? Why has he exiled himself from it voluntarily? Why is he so sad? Why when he remembers the homeland he loved does he feel its charms? . . . You also say that my letters are like waves breaking at your feet. Oh, let me get nearer to your heart, I beg of you, and sacrifice to me your philosophy of indifference! Cross quickly that gulf which you are staring at, come to me when I give the sign.[34]

More than once 'Eliane' mentions *Adolphe* and understandably does not wish to share the fate of Ellénore. She appears to have met Constant at a masked ball in 1818, and at first does all she can to maintain the air of mystery surrounding herself. A rendezvous is eventually arranged; it seems that there is an affair; and the correspondence ends with a note of sadness entering 'Eliane's' letters.

Thus, despite making his mark in French politics, there is evidence that during 1818 Constant was often gloomy and nostalgic for past times, particularly no doubt for the scholarly life of Germany, with which his course of lectures on religion at the Athénée royal in February was a tangible link. He continued to defend his political beliefs, publishing in March the second volume of his collected essays on representative government.[35] Then, on 25 June during a visit to his friend, the banker Baron Davilliers, Constant fell – reportedly while jumping in Davilliers's garden to show he was still physically agile – and permanently injured a leg.[36] The next two months were spent gradually recovering from the accident, and despite medical treatment he thereafter walked with the aid of a stick, and later of crutches. ('Eliane' begins her correspondence on 26 August [1818] by expressing her concern about his health since his 'cruel accident'.) Despite this handicap he stood for election as an Independent deputy in the Seine department, where he encountered unfair interference in the electoral process by the government which supported its own candidate.[37] As if that were not already sufficiently dispiriting, there was factional squabbling among his liberal political allies, and the Friends of Press Freedom were also opposed to his candidature, thinking him more useful outside the Chamber. When yet again Constant failed to be elected in October 1818 – in spite of his articles in the *Minerve* revealing the machinations of his enemies[38] – he was understandably bitter. This time, however, though he did not know it, success was not very far off.

In November 1818 Constant was written to by Charles-Louis-François Goyet (1770–1833), a lawyer in Le Mans with his own newspaper, a political activist and leader of liberals in the Département de La Sarthe, the area around Le Mans. Goyet invited Constant to stand as a liberal candidate at the forthcoming by-election in the Sarthe.[39] Constant naturally seized the opportunity with both hands, especially since, through Goyet's powerful influence in the region, his friend General Lafayette had already been elected a deputy in the Sarthe. He wrote immediately to his cousin Charles in Geneva for documentary evidence that the Constant family had fled France in the sixteenth century to avoid religious persecution for their Calvinism: he was anxious to reinforce his claim to French nationality and to refute the accusation of being a foreigner which persistently hindered his acceptance in France.[40] From December 1818 to March 1819 he fought hard, using all of his journalistic skills in the *Minerve*, and with the help of Goyet he was elected on 25 March 1819. After seventeen years in the political wilderness he was back once more where he knew he belonged.

11

APOTHEOSIS
(1819–1830)

Electoral success meant fame for Constant, of that he could be sure: he was as aware of his strengths as he was of his personal weaknesses, and the greatest of them was his skill with the French language. Apparently without effort he could produce polished, elegant and highly persuasive prose – rhetoric in the best sense of the word, not vacuous but tightly argued and carefully constructed with the aim of convincing the reader or listener. (*Adolphe* is, of course, among other things, the putting forward of a strong case for the defence.) Political success was also inevitably to reduce the time that he had for longer projects and force him to concentrate on journalism and pamphlets. But even Constant's contributions to the *Minerve* became less numerous as his time was filled with preparing for debates, carrying out the necessary research and writing his speeches.

There is an interesting pen-portrait of Constant at about this period of his life written by an American who had lately settled in France, Augustus Lucas Hillhouse (1791–1859) and published for the first time by C. P. Courtney in 1985:

> Mr Constant is of a sanguine complexion with white eye-lashes & brows & reddish flaxen hair. His features are not bold, except his high & noble forehead which gives an expression of greatness to his physiognomy. He lisps very much, is not uncommonly fluent in conversation, & is unassuming in his demeanour.
>
> While he was gone into his closet to fetch me a book upon England I had leisure to examine his apartment. A folding paper screen surrounded his table, on wh[ich] & on the desk & secretary books & papers were heaped in disorder. I noticed on the table a pile of blank cards, & others written on one side: in another part of the room an amanuensis was copying a heap of these cards upon a sheet of paper: I suspect that it was the manuscript of some work of Mr Constant, & that this is his manner of composing.[1]

Hillhouse's succinct and valuable observations complement what is known from other sources about Constant's appearance, manner of speaking and method of work at this time.[2] Baron de Loève-Veimars (1801–54) gives a lively picture of the parliamentarian in action:

One saw him arrive at the Chamber always a few minutes before the sitting, dressed in his gold-embroidered deputy's uniform so as to be ready to address the House from the tribune where it was obligatory to wear this formal dress. His hair was blond and turning white, and on his head he wore an old round hat. He carried under his arm a coat, books, manuscripts, printer's proofs, a copy of the budget and his crutch. Once he had got rid of all these impedimenta and was seated on his bench, on the far left, he began to write and to send off an unbelievable quantity of letters and notes to people, to the great annoyance of the gentlemen ushers of the Chamber. Then – or rather at the same time – he corrected the proofs of his latest book, took notes to enable him to reply to the person speaking from the tribune, answered the questions of all those crowding around him to ask for information on different subjects, and tried to attract attention so as to be allowed to speak himself. And when it was his turn to address the Chamber, he picked up seemingly at random a few scraps of paper from the mass of documents around him and he made his way slowly up to the tribune.... His pale forehead and long face, so like that of a Puritan, were not well suited to expressing emotion, and his slow and monotonous delivery at first surprised those whom his reputation for eloquence had drawn to the Chamber. But gradually his voice grew louder, became impassioned and filled the room. His great blue eyes flashed with sudden brilliance, and the most lucid reasoning, irony, wit and well-chosen quotations all poured forth in abundance in his improvised speeches. One could listen to him for hours without tiring of hearing him speak. It was a delight to see him calmly drive his opponents into a fury and then, as if it were merely an amusement for him, meet the paroxysms of rage on the right-wing benches with cold and cutting politeness – which only exasperated his adversaries all the more. He was quite untroubled by other deputies insolently calling him a blackguard, a fomenter of sedition, a revolutionary, or by the loud shouts of many of them claiming that he was out of order. He carried on speaking as if he were in a quiet drawing room, and more than once he disconcerted his enemies by a witticism so apt that it completely disarmed them by provoking their laughter.[3]

Unfortunately the Deputy for the Sarthe now had little time left to devote to writing of anything but an ephemeral kind. This is posterity's loss, since no longer would he be able to lecture at the Athénée royal, where on 26 December 1818 he had given a speech in praise of the life and liberal principles of the Englishman Sir Samuel Romilly, who had recently committed suicide,[4] and had begun a course of lectures on the British constitution which would end in June 1819:[5] in fact his third lecture, on freedom in ancient and modern times, given on 13 February 1819, was an important summary of his political thought, drawing the distinction he had made in *De l'esprit de conquête* in 1814 between the collectivistic view of freedom in Antiquity, in the Greek city states for example, and the modern world's stress on the individual's right to privacy.[6] Henceforth much of Constant's work is regrettably of interest only to the specialist parliamentary historian, and appears either in the volumes of *Discours à la Chambre*, the French equivalent of Hansard,[7] or in newspapers. He himself was aware of this self-imposed limitation on his talents, and told Rosalie in September 1820:

> Despite all the interest which politics must and do inspire in me in my present situation, I sometimes get terribly tired of my job as a schoolteacher, having to repeat again and again the same ideas. I have just finished a pamphlet, which will be my last, judging by how much it's bored me.[8]

Some of his campaigns still stand out amongst long-forgotten arguments about budgetary policy, such as that against the slave trade in Senegal which began in August 1819 with an article by Constant in the *Minerve*,[9] or the following year in favour of individual and press freedom. But it is to Constant's extra-parliamentary work that one now generally turns for interest, such as his long-awaited seventeen letters on Napoleon's Hundred Days, serialized in the *Minerve* between September 1819 and March 1820,[10] at which date the newspaper was closed down by the government.

On 13 February 1820 the Duc de Berry, who was to succeed Louis XVIII to the throne, was assassinated by a saddler named Louvel while leaving the Opera. Although his murder was the work of a fanatic, it resulted in a sea change in French political life. The relatively liberal Decazes was replaced by the Duc de Richelieu, and an already reactionary and repressive government became considerably more so: censorship was strengthened (hence the demise of the liberal *Minerve*), suspected persons could be rounded up by the police, and richer members of the electorate were given a double vote. Such severity gave birth to a secret insurrectionary movement, parallel to the *Carbonari* in Italy, and the centre ground of French politics was increasingly eroded. There was a simultaneous polarization to Left and Right. All spring and summer of 1820 Constant resisted attempts to muzzle the press and the 'double vote' as best he could with brilliant speeches in the Chamber and at considerable risk to himself as the country appeared to be drifting towards civil war. He continued to produce pamphlets even as the régime seized letters he had sent to Goyet during July; then in August he rested for a while at a country house he was to rent from this period of his life onwards at

Montmorency, just outside Paris. The following month he went to Normandy with Charlotte to visit his electorate in the Sarthe for the first time in two years, and became the focus of a near riot in Saumur on 7 and 8 October where he was threatened by officers from the cavalry school. The incident not only produced a pamphlet from him; it is not impossible that it may also have inspired an incident in *Lucien Leuwen* (1834–5), Stendhal's wryly comical account of the perils of political ambition.[11]

The year 1820 ended as inauspiciously as it had begun with a massive influx of royalist deputies into the Chamber after elections in November. The only lasting piece of work Constant had to show for the past twelve months was the first volume of his *Memoirs concerning the Hundred Days*, begun in fact in Paris in August 1815 when it was called *Mon Apologie* (*My Apologia*), briefly entitled *Lettres à Hobhouse* (*Letters to Hobhouse*) in 1816, first published in letter form in *La Minerve française* in 1819–20, and now appearing as a book. During his stay in London in 1816 Henry Colburn of Conduit Street who had published *Adolphe* agreed to publish the *Mémoires sur les Cent-Jours* and now generously considered the agreement null and void so that the Parisian publisher Béchet could bring it out.[12] As André Cabanis and Kurt Kloocke have demonstrated in their critical edition of the *Mémoires*,[13] the purpose of the work went beyond a mere *apologia pro domo*, a defence of his own conduct in 1815. In its various editions from 1819–20 up to 1829, Constant took the opportunity to contrast the situation in France with constitutional arrangements in Britain – now quite unmistakably his ideal – and pointed indirectly to the dangers posed by the continuing royalist extremism, vindictiveness and repression. Urging forgiveness and tolerance on the Ultras, he indicated that Napoleon had failed to win the hearts of the French people in 1815 because they had not forgotten his suppression of personal freedoms: extreme monarchists bent on revenge against supporters of the Revolution, Consulate and Empire might now also find that they were alienating the majority of the nation too.

The year 1821 was to be a little more productive of new work than 1820. Debates in parliament became heated and unpleasant as the newly reinforced Right attempted to bury the Revolution of 1789 and its consequences for good. Constant's eloquence was marshalled in argument against them, despite a further injury to his leg which rendered walking more and more difficult. His physical and moral courage drew high praise from Goyet and other liberals during the spring and summer as free speech came under ever greater threat. He condemned the slave trade in Senegal from which the government appeared to be profiting, and denounced the censorship of newspapers, but he was vastly outnumbered in the Chamber. Perhaps realizing the hopelessness of the struggle – though never once weakening in his efforts or resolve – he took out once again his manuscripts on religion in September 1821, and was pleased to see how far he had advanced with them. He was still not yet ready to publish, however. Instead, he prepared the second volume of his *Memoirs on the Hundred Days* for Béchet, and began a new work, a *Commentary on Filangieri's Work* (*Commentaire sur l'ouvrage de Filangieri,*) an essay which accompanied the French translation of the Italian social theorist Gaetano Filangieri's *Science of Legislation*.[14] It was an opportunity for Constant to restate his opposition to the eighteenth century's idealization of the Greek city state and its institutions. Behind Filangieri was Constant's old intellectual adversary Jean-Jacques Rousseau whose concept of the General Will he had always seen as opening the way to a totalitarian popular democracy where power was concentrated in the hands of the few and the individual was stripped of all freedom of action, expression or belief.[15] Social engineering on the part of a legislator figure like the Greek Lycurgus which Filangieri suggested could open the way to the moral regeneration of society Constant viewed as leading inevitably to an anachronistic tyranny. Not for the first time Constant seems to have seen beyond Robespierre and Napoleon to the horrors of twentieth-century totalitarian states.

The commentary on Filangieri was published on 9 January 1822.[16] The first six months of 1822 were to prove a period of ceaseless and exhausting conflict in the Chamber for Constant. The second Richelieu ministry had fallen at the end of 1821, and an ambitious intriguer, the Comte de Villèle, now presided over what seemed to be a creeping, if bloodless, counter-revolution. It was indeed the best of times and the worst of times for Constant: he found fulfilment in being no longer regarded as a political *arriviste* but as the great hero of liberalism in France, and his enemies on whom he poured his brilliant sardonic eloquence were self-evidently misguided reactionaries. Although hopelessly outnumbered, he had never shrunk from a fight (except, of course, from verbal ones with women). Indeed in June 1822, though now crippled, Constant fought yet another duel, this time with the ultra-royalist deputy Forbin des Issarts (1770–1851) after a public disagreement in the newspapers.[17] Unable to stand, Constant sat in an armchair and the two adversaries fired their pistols at each other from close range. As a result of the duel Constant found he had alienated Charles Goyet and members of his constituency in the Sarthe. His resilience was to be tested still further in August. The ultra-royalist Villèle attempted to implicate Constant in the Berton plot against the Bourbons. He was tried and eventually fined. While protesting his innocence, he secretly tried to negotiate for the conspirators' lives, offering not to stand at the forthcoming elections if the King would pardon Caffé, one of the plotters.[18] In the event, Caffé killed himself, Berton was executed and Constant, who did stand for re-election in the Sarthe in October 1822, was defeated by a royalist, despite Goyet's continued support. Constant was still under a cloud as a result of the trial, and although he was in the middle of an appeal against the judgement, the circumstances doubtless counted against him in the eyes of the electors.

At the end of 1822 Constant withdrew from what were often the intolerable stresses of parliamentary life, satisfied in his own mind that his honour was intact. He was now 55, his hair was turning white, his eyes were weak and no less vulnerable to bright light than in his younger days, his health was generally poor. He had been effectively a cripple since his leg injury, despite courses of hydrotherapy involving frequent tiring baths and, whenever possible, visits to spas. Charlotte was 53 and, to his amusement (and sometimes his embarrassment), she was growing gradually more absent-minded. As old age began to weaken Constant's long resistance to humdrum domesticity, he does now at last appear to have found some measure of peace and consolation in the company of a devoted wife, whether when they were in Paris or out at Montmorency. Not surprisingly, by the end of 1822 he had returned to his manuscripts on religion. However he still had to face further wearying confrontations with Villèle's government and its tame judiciary, who were now intent on breaking Constant for good. On 6 and 13 February 1823 he lost two appeals he had made against different judgements and was fined 2,000 francs.[19]

Villèle's Ultra government appeared to be going from strength to strength. It was not only financially successful, but had now involved itself, albeit somewhat reluctantly, on behalf of another Bourbon monarch, Ferdinand VII, in the civil war which had broken out in Spain in 1820. In April 1823 an expeditionary force was sent into Spain. Although according to all the laws of military strategy the campaign ought to have proved a disaster, it was a complete and remarkable success. Virtually unopposed, indeed welcomed by the Spanish people who had so recently fought a bitter guerilla war against Napoleon's troops, the French army restored the Bourbon King of Spain to his throne. Chateaubriand, now Foreign Minister to Villèle, had advocated the successful policy; Villèle was furious and, on the grounds of Chateaubriand's opposition to a government finance measure, dismissed him. It was a serious error of judgement, for Chateaubriand went straight over to the opposition and henceforth, after having been Constant's political adversary, became in effect a royalist ally. Constant, excluded from parliamentary activity for the foreseeable future, worked all spring and summer of 1823 on the history of religion, recasting his manuscript for the last time. On 7 July 1823 he wrote to his friend Simonde de Sismondi thanking him for sending him the most recent volumes of his *Histoire des Français* (*History of the French People*):

> I never write to anyone any more. . . . I can't get used to the idea of my letters being read publicly before they reach my friends, and even now when I have good reason to write, I have got so used to

silence that I couldn't bring myself to break it and talk about His-pano-European affairs. I can only say that nations ought not to attack others since they cannot even defend themselves. I have decided to attempt to publish my book, even though we live under Jesuit rule, but I shall publish it in instalments, because the first, which I don't think will alarm anyone, will I hope establish its reputation sufficiently for no one to dare stop me later on. I enclose some prospectuses.[20]

The Jesuit order was believed to have been responsible for all the recent government legislation in favour of the Roman Catholic church, a view echoed by Constant. The general atmosphere of suspicion and repression comes through clearly in the letter, as does Constant's uncertainty as to whether, after forty years of work, his great book will ever finally see the light of day. Nevertheless he signed a contract in August 1823 and on 30 March 1824 the first of five volumes was printed.[21]

De la religion, considérée dans sa source, ses formes et ses développements (*Concerning Religion, considered in its Source, Forms and Development*) which was only part of his work – the rest would appear posthumously in *Du polythéisme romain* (*Concerning Roman Polytheism*) – shows a parallel with Constant's political beliefs. As it traces the gradual development of religious feeling through history and examines the various outward forms which that belief has adopted and later discarded, a permanent law of historical change is shown to be operating. Change in all human affairs is inevitable and to be accepted, in the outward shape of religious belief as in political institutions. But that change must be gradual and continuous: any sudden attempts at a radical transformation either in the political or religious sphere is likely to produce a violent reaction, just as trying to halt all change and bring about fixity and stasis may provoke no less of a revolt. Throughout history the permanent and precious human instinct to believe and to sacrifice oneself because of that belief has assumed many outward guises, and has reached its greatest perfection in modern Protestant Christianity, freed from the oppressive burden of a priestly caste.[22] Constant could not hope to win many friends in France with such a book: rationalists would reject it as vaguely mystical and obscurantist; Catholics and many Protestants would see it as as anti-clerical and devoid of dogmatic content. That indeed was to be the case. Just as in politics Constant was an instinctive member of the opposition rather than of government, so on matters of religion he was an independent and critical voice, a permanent minority of one.

The military operation in Spain ended in September 1823. At about the same period Constant told a new friend, Jean-Jacques Coulmann – an enthusiastic young liberal admirer from Brumath near Strasbourg whom he had met in 1822 through Baron Davilliers[23] and who was destined in his *Réminiscences* to play Boswell to Constant's Johnson[24] – that he was interested in one day returning to the Chamber as the representative of Alsace. It was an obvious choice of constituency: Constant spoke German almost as well as he did French, and his life's work, one might say, had been to effect some kind of intellectual synthesis between Germany and France. But first he stood for a seat in Paris in February 1824, and in March was elected deputy. Challenged yet again about his nationality, he visited Switzerland in April 1824 to collect historical family documents to prove his claim, and on this last visit of his life he also saw again his cousin Rosalie in Lausanne.[25] After two months of argument Constant was finally allowed to take up his seat in the Chamber, and immediately set about launching attacks once again on the ultra-royalist government. Although parliamentary activity took up most of his time, the publication of *De la religion* at the end of May 1824 involved him in considerable controversy, in particular with the Catholic apologist Baron d'Eckstein (1790–1861),[26] and on 7 August a third edition of *Adolphe* appeared in the bookshops which contained passages which had been left out of the earlier editions, possibly to spare Madame de Staël's feelings.[27]

Life seemed to be returning to something like normal after the hiatus of 1823, and it may have been at about this time that he wrote one of the very few letters to Charlotte to have been preserved. Its tone gives a valuable – perhaps unique – insight into the nature of their relationship:

> [our financial affairs] are not desperate: and there are three courses we can follow – but we must take one of the three. Lafitte [Constant's banker] won't be placated for ever by polite words, and if he wanted to he could ruin me completely by suddenly calling in his loan.
>
> At the moment this is our position: you have an annual income of 15,000 francs; the income from my three houses is entirely taken up by what I owe: but it is enough to cover those debts, and my house in the Rue d'Anjou should bring me in 6,000 francs net. So that's 21,000 francs clear income we have between us, assuming I manage to let the house. I give you the whole amount on condition that you cover all our expenses without exception. If you don't want the house to be let, we shall have only 15,000 francs income but we shall at least have a roof over our heads. It's an extra 3,000 francs, we shall have 18,000 francs including the rent. Arrange for us to be able to live on that amount in Paris. There are many people who live on less. I'm not very demanding. If we can't afford to travel by carriage, I shall go on foot. If we can't afford wine, I shall drink water: but at least I shall be able to repay what I owe. I shall devote any money I make from my publications to clearing my debts, and my mind will be at rest.

The second possibility is for each of us to live on our own income. As I say, if I rent out my house, I shall have 6,000 francs when I have paid my expenses, that's more than I need. So I can manage quite easily if we do that.

The third alternative, which I only mention in case you should reject the other two, is for you to arrange to spend your winters more agreeably than in Paris, and that I come to see you there every summer. I would live in a flat in Paris costing 400 francs and I'd save – which is always easy for a single man, and it would do me more good than harm if, as I very much wish to do, I give up salon life, and if I've not got a carriage which suggests I have wealth – something the people I'm not repaying find inexplicable.

Think about all that and make your mind up. I love you with all my heart and I've proved it to you. I've made sure quite scrupulously that your money cannot be affected by my financial embarrassment: my feelings for you demanded that I should do so, even though the law would have allowed me to act differently. I am at the mercy of the slightest change of expression on your face, and when you get here you will be able to make me take back everything I'm writing now. But once again I must say that the effect you have on me in no way changes the facts themselves, and if I go beyond the financial limits I've now reached, my creditors will be unmoved by my excuses. So think about it and decide.

Farewell, dear Linon. I love you more than you think and sometimes more than I think myself. If by adopting the first course of action I've outlined you save me from financial difficulty, my love for you and for life will be reborn. My reputation will be strengthened, I shall no longer have a serpent gnawing away at me, and I shall be the most cheerful and best of Ouffys.

My best wishes to your son. I am, believe me, your

Ouffy.[28]

The letter, from the Von Marenholtz papers in Wolfenbüttel, is more intimately revealing than any other of the state of Constant's marriage in his later years. By 1829 his gambling debts to the banker and liberal Jacques Lafitte (1767–1844) would total 102,580.75 francs,[29] though Lafitte was always shrewd enough to allow almost limitless credit to a politician who might one day hold high office. Charlotte had more than enough income for both herself and Constant, despite the money she had given Du Tertre, but he felt embarrassed at asking her to keep him – no doubt in view of his foolishness in continuing to gamble. But he also knew that she would never accept the idea of their living apart. As for their emotional rapport, Constant appears to have settled into an affectionate if somewhat condescending relationship with Charlotte, and long before this date had adopted with her the nickname 'Ouffy' which may possibly in some way have been linked to the name 'Adolphe'.

The Irish novelist Maria Edgeworth (1767–1849) has left us a memorably unflattering description of the older Constant in a letter she wrote from France to a cousin in July 1820:

> I do not like him at all. His countenance, voice, manner and conversation are all disagreeable to me. He is a fair whithky-looking [*sic*] man, very near-sighted with spectacles which seem to pinch his nose. He pokes out his chin to keep the spectacles on, and yet looks over the top of his spectacles, squinching up his eyes so that you cannot see your way into his mind. Then he speaks through his nose, and with a lisp, strangely contrasting with the vehemence of his emphasis. He does not give me any confidence in the sincerity of his patriotism, nor any idea of his talents, though he seems to have a mighty high idea of them himself. He has been well called *le héro[s] des brochures*. We sat beside each other and I think felt a mutual antipathy.[30]

Of course if Maria Edgeworth had known the tribulations that Constant's eyes had caused him since adolescence, she might perhaps have been a little less censorious. Another witness, Thureau-Dangin, in his study of liberals during the Restoration, gives a somewhat more sympathetic portrait of the redoubtable parliamentary debater in action:

> At first sight one would never have said that he had the usual qualities necessary to make an orator. He seldom improvised without having a pen in his hand; but his pen had the quickness of speech, and sometimes he wrote out his reply in full while still listening to the harangue he was to refute. He normally read his speeches from little pieces of paper which he was constantly obliged to put in order. His voice was high like a woman's, sometimes had difficulty in making itself heard and its intonation could be monotonous. He lacked the powerful lungs and strength of emphasis that are needed for great eloquence. But despite these disadvantages, he was always a tricky adversary to have in the Chamber, sometimes a formidable one. With his clever rather than highly coloured speeches, subtle rather than powerful in their delivery, he showed great skill in argument, rare presence of mind, he had a way of saying everything, despite legal restrictions, so that even the most intolerant audience understood what he was implying, and he was nimble enough to slip through his opponent's fingers and to stand up for himself even in the tightest corner.[31]

In September 1824 Louis XVIII died and was succeeded by Charles X. Under Louis the power of the Catholic church had returned to something like that which it had enjoyed under the *ancien régime*. Secondary and even university education was placed under church supervision, and legal penalties were introduced for printing anything offensive to the Church in the press. In the country at large there was also something of a religious revival, although the rationalism and anti-clericalism inherited from the eighteenth-century *philosophes* and the Revolution remained strong in many quarters. Something like the tense opposition between socialist rationalism and the Catholic church which occasionally persists in French towns and villages even today was already coming into being at this time. Constant anticipated being caught again in the crossfire between the two sides as he worked that September on the second volume of *De la religion*: for the rationalists he took religion too seriously and for Catholics he was too relativistic in his views and too critical of the Catholic church's structures and beliefs. On 22 September 1824 he wrote to Rosalie:

> Thank you for approving of my book. I am hard at work on the second volume which is more shocking than the first. It's impossible to foresee or calculate today what it will be permissible to print or say, but I must work on in the meantime.[32]

Then serious illness struck, and during the last three months of 1824 Constant, perhaps for the first time, came to the realization that he probably did not have long to live. The nature of that illness, possibly the result of a seizure or minor stroke, is not clear, and it has been suggested by one modern medical commentator, Dr Michel Folman, that Constant, like so many of his contemporaries, could have been suffering from the later stages of syphilis, of which the failure of his leg injury to heal was a possible sign.[33] In the absence of other evidence there can, of course, be no certainty about this. Constant wrote to Rosalie on 9 December 1824:

> I see from your letter, my dear Rosalie, that Constance did not tell you that I was ill when she left Paris. She probably didn't consider my illness serious. But it was, and probably still is. This is the sixth week that I've been unable to leave my bedroom. Everyone, including my doctor, says I'm better. I don't feel it, but I let them say so, because it amuses some and reassures others. I do believe that I shall get better, but the axe has struck the roots of the tree, and the blow has shaken its whole interior. It is nature's first warning, it is the beginning of infirmity. I shall live for another ten years, twenty perhaps, but it's no longer like living, and I consider myself struck off the list of those who have a firm grasp on the world and a future. I shall take advantage of my good spells to finish my book if I can.[34]

During that winter of 1824–5, as he gradually regained his health, Constant made tentative contact with the secretary of Louis-Philippe and the Orleanist camp. It became clear that a government as regressive and reactionary as Charles X's Ultras, in which the King was keen to involve himself, would sooner or later be brought down by the very extremism of its measures. Among those measures were laws to compensate former *émigrés* and their heirs for property they had lost through confiscation under the revolutionary land settlement. The indemnity to former *émigrés* enraged not only Constant, who made speeches in January, February and March 1825 against it; it incensed many others in France including property owners who resented these privileges which were now being accorded to a small and arguably parasitic group when many thousands more had also suffered. In its zeal to roll back the consequences of the Revolution, the ultra-royalist government of Charles X also brought in a law on sacrilege which only added to the anti-clerical and anti-Bourbon feeling that was mounting in France. It took no small degree of courage on Constant's part to attack such a measure – which he viewed as interfering with the citizen's right to hold private opinions – and then to carry on working as he did throughout the summer of 1825 on the second volume of *De la religion*.[35] And by the time his book went on sale in October 1825 he was already involved in yet another new campaign, this time in favour of Greek independence from Turkish rule. Word had reached France of Greek Christians being massacred or sold into slavery by the Muslim Turks. Despite its recent readiness to intervene in Spain on behalf of the Catholic Bourbon king, the French government showed itself slow to react in defence of the Orthodox Greeks. In September Constant had published a pamphlet entitled *Appel aux nations chrétiennes en faveur des Grecs* (*Appeal to Christian Nations on behalf of the Greeks*):[36] his instinctive abhorrence of religious fanaticism and his longstanding opposition to slavery and to all infringements of individual liberty made his defence of Greece as natural as his resistance to those moves which now threatened to take France back towards the world of the Inquisition.

Perhaps the most remarkable development, however, in Constant's pamphlets and speeches in 1825–6, is the expression of a growing unease at the way society was now evolving among the advanced nations of Europe, an uneasiness shared by his fellow novelist Stendhal who in December 1825 published his anti-Saint-Simonian pamphlet *D'un nouveau complot contre les industriels* (*Concerning a New Plot against the Productive Members of Society*). Seeing the very considerable Luddite unrest in Britain, Constant made a speech to the Chamber on 9 May 1826 in which he condemned the concentration of large tracts of land in the hands of a few people, a development which was driving the poor into despair and revolt:

> Will people tell me that [the dispossessed] are rising up against industry; that they do not attack the châteaux but the looms and machines which threaten to deprive them of their means of existence?

No doubt: they are attacking what appears to be the immediate cause of their impoverishment. But who does not feel that this impoverishment stems from a more distant source, the system of concentration [of property] which leaves thousands of proletarians at the mercy of circumstances, and makes even mechanical inventions and improvements work to the detriment of mankind?[37]

As Kurt Kloocke points out, Constant's far-sighted analysis of the sources of social change and friction anticipates that of Karl Marx two decades later.[38] Constant was never a proto-socialist, but by 1826 he was beginning to distance himself somewhat from the bourgeoisie and to consider the good of society as a whole, including the proletariat. Nevertheless he still placed his faith in the importance of the property-owning class to whom at this period the franchise was limited under the arrangement known as the *cens*. People of independent means were the best guarantee of independence of thought at elections: an employee, on the other hand, might be bullied into voting as directed by his employer. In accepting the so-called *régime censitaire* whereby ownership of property governed one's right to vote or otherwise, Constant was, of course, simply thinking and behaving like any man of his time. His hope was in a constitutional monarchy, in the development of a range of institutions comparable to those in Britain – a free press, well-informed public opinion, an impartial judiciary, and so on – and in the gradual spread of *les lumières*, of education and enlightened attitudes, through society as a whole, and for the good of all. His political thinking had its limits which were those of his time: unlike ours, however, it was dominated less by economics than by more general philosophical and moral considerations.

In the summer of 1826 Charlotte fell ill, which prevented a trip to Switzerland that Constant had been planning. His parliamentary activity had lately seemed increasingly futile and more tiring than ever to him, and in the latter half of the year he concentrated his remaining energies on work on the third volume of *De la religion*, the last to appear during his lifetime.[39] On 23 October 1826 he wrote to Sismondi from the château of the liberal General Marquis de Lafayette at La Grange-Bleneau where he had been invited to stay:

I am working on my third volume as much as my rather poor physical shape allows me to – I don't know why it should be so. Or rather I do know: it's because the day after tomorrow is my fifty-ninth birthday.[40]

To add to his worries, a large chest full of papers – legal documents concerning his lengthy financial wrangle with his father, letters to cherished friends and relatives and perhaps even the manuscript of *Cécile* – which he had left in Göttingen in the care of a friend was now on its way to Rosalie in Lausanne from whom Constant was to have collected it when he was in Switzerland. Sadly he was never to see the chest or its contents again; Rosalie seems to have given it to her cousin Auguste d'Hermenches when Constant died, and subsequently at least some of the documents went into d'Hermenches's family archives.[41]

After an autumn spent partly in Paris and partly in the country, Constant returned for the parliamentary session of January to June 1827 and to its familiar themes for debate, including the slave trade in Africa and the government's continuing attempts to curb the press. Despite his age and clear signs of a physical decline in him, he remained an active speaker in the Chamber, and from this point until his death was considered a sufficiently serious threat to Villèle's ultra-royalist ministry to be spied on by the government's secret police.[42] Constant's eloquence was to have a more fitting and permanent memorial than police reports, however, for in June 1827 a subscription list was opened for the first volume of his collected speeches to the Chamber from April 1819 to May 1827: the first volume appeared in July 1827, the second in March 1828.[43] This was followed in mid-August 1827 by the publication of volume III of *De la religion*.[44] Still followed everywhere by police spies, he made a triumphant visit to Alsace between August and November 1827 in order to court the electorate, having been invited there by Coulmann.

By an irony that Constant would have appreciated, we are better informed than we otherwise would have been about his activities and movements thanks to the copious private correspondence of Esmangart – Prefect in Strasbourg and particularly ill-disposed towards him – with the Minister of the Interior in Paris. From 23 May 1827 when Constant was still in Paris, Esmangart was sending reports of the effect of Constant's speeches to the Chamber on Catholic–Protestant relations in the Bas-Rhin department, losing no opportunity to blacken Constant's name for having suggested, for example, that Protestants were being unfavourably treated in Alsace. Once Constant reached Esmangart's own region after having taken the waters at Baden-Baden, the Prefect's small-minded and malevolent zeal in compiling his dossier became worthy of the KGB or Stasi in our own time. Biased reports went off almost daily to Paris saying that Constant had been seen at the roulette wheel while in Baden-Baden, that Constant's audience in Alsace was made up mostly of students and tradesmen, that people only turned up at meetings to hear the band play, and so on. Yet Esmangart was unable actually to stop his enemy's royal progress through Alsace or prevent a banquet from being given in his honour in Strasbourg, though Constant's every move was noted, even during his stay out at Brumath with Coulmann. Indeed even in Baden-Baden there had been no escape from his fervent admirers. A group of *Alsaciens* had arranged a dinner there in Constant's honour on 23 August

1827: the text of the song written and printed in praise of him has been preserved.[45]

Towards the end of October 1827 Constant returned to Brevans near Dole, where his late father Juste and late step-mother Marianne de Constant had made their home. His plan was to visit his cousin Rosalie in Lausanne, something he had been unable to do the previous year. Once again he was prevented from doing so by the surprise announcement that the Chamber of Deputies had been dissolved and there were to be elections the following month. He immediately returned to Paris and there learned of the death of Madame de Staël's son Auguste. It prompted the following lines to Rosalie in December 1827:

> Life is hard, and when I remember I am 60 years old, I'm delighted. I have kept only one illusion, that of being famous when I'm dead, but as God is my witness I don't know why. It's a habit of mind I've had since my childhood. But I can't say I'm tempted by what the future holds: there is virtually nothing but public and private tribulation awaiting me.[46]

In fact virtually nothing but public adulation lay in store for Constant. For he had suddenly become a much admired symbol to the rising generation of young liberals, and achieved re-election very easily in Paris. He was also elected for the first time in Strasbourg, which he now chose to represent, and by mid-December 1827 was active in a new Chamber of Deputies where Villèle's men were in a minority.

Villèle in fact was seen as too moderate by more extreme Ultras, despite his having achieved a naval victory at Navarino on 20 October 1827 in an expedition to help the Greeks in their War of Independence. The Chamber was now made up of Villèle's government with 160 to 180 supporters; the liberal opposition with about the same, and sixty to eighty disgruntled extreme royalists who were henceforth opposed to Villèle. The government was clearly unable to govern, and Villèle soon resigned, in January 1828. A stop-gap government, effectively under the leadership of Martignac, the new Minister of the Interior, was to last for the next year and a half while Charles X looked for someone more to his own extreme – one might say crackpot – taste. Between January and August 1828 Constant made forty-nine speeches to the Chamber which were documented in the volumes of the *Archives parlementaires*.[47] The tide was at last running the way of the liberal opposition – a curious sensation for Constant who now saw a limited degree of liberalization being successfully forced upon Martignac's government. When the Chamber went into recess, Constant left Paris in August 1828 for Baden-Baden, once again in an attempt to mend his failing health. He rested, bathed, took the waters, gambled; crossed back into France to visit Coulmann at Brumath in September and once again in October; and spent a month in Alsace at

Munster where he appears to have worked on the fourth volume of *De la religion*. Information on this period of Constant's life is relatively scarce, and for what we do know we have the ever suspicious Prefect Esmangart and his spies to thank. What is beyond doubt is that in Alsace Constant was popular and fêted wherever he went. Charlotte looked on Alsace as part of her homeland, to her husband's occasional embarrassment, and Constant himself was happy in its Franco-German cultural atmosphere, while privately regretting the general humourlessness there at times. Cultivating the electorate was therefore no real hardship for either of them.

In November 1828 Constant was bitterly disappointed when his friend Prosper de Barante, now a distinguished historian and diplomat, was elected to the French Academy instead of himself. He had written despairingly to Rosalie from Baden-Baden on 18 September 1828, more and more overwhelmed by the idea of his own impending death, something he had bravely kept at bay until now by ceaseless activity and hard work:

> Yes, my dear Rosalie, the years rush by, carrying away our strength and bringing infirmity in their wake. Little by little they take away every means of pleasure from us. They leave us with the past to sustain us, which is sad, and offer the prospect of a future which will be brief. Thank you for what you say about how I have used my life. I have not done a quarter of what I ought to have done, and if I were not secretly very ashamed of having wasted my time and energy, I would be proud of the good things people say about what I have done despite that waste. But what does it matter? The grave awaits the hard-working man just as it does the idler, awaits fame as well as obscurity, and it is happy to close over them without worrying about who and what it is covering up. I would like to see you again before I am lowered into mine, but I can no longer make plans. I see so many people dying around me who had reckoned on having a future that I can hardly believe I'm still alive myself. I'm working in order to leave, as they say, something behind me when I'm gone. When I'm gone – that 'I', what will become of it and what will that 'I' have in common with what I've left behind? No matter – I'm working out of force of habit, and because time is weighing heavily upon me. My fourth volume – the last, thank Heaven – will be published, I think, this winter. I feel it is more unusual, more original than the others, but sad too, because reaching the end is always sadder than being on the journey when one is constantly being distracted by the objects one passes.[48]

Rosalie, an intelligent and devout Calvinist, replied on 18 October 1828 with a letter and two parallel texts on the theme of death, one from a meditation on death in volume III of Constant's *De la religion* and the other her own reply. For Constant death was a dark and terrifying night which left all of our questions unanswered and our regrets without consolation; for Rosalie death was a release from suffering, often bringing a sense of well-being to the person who was dying and the feeling that separation from loved ones would not be eternal.[49]

Yet all was not entirely gloom for Constant: he still had loyal friends who were very much alive and who considered that his life had not been a failure: indeed who strongly supported everything he was doing. One such was Sir James Mackintosh, a treasured link with the Whig optimism of Edinburgh in the 1780s. The bond formed between them then had never been broken, despite many years of separation. While waiting in Liège in March 1814 for Bernadotte's fate to be decided, Constant had written an important and little-known letter to Mackintosh which was printed in Mackintosh's *Memoirs* and written, it seems, in English. In it he set out his political credo, which at that time was governed by 'the necessity of overturning the most systematical and baneful tyranny, that ever weighed, with iron weight, on mankind', that of Napoleon. He continued, referring to the recently published *De l'esprit de conquête*:

My last publication, a copy of which I hope you have received, has already explained to you, I suppose, what are my notions on modern patriotism. It cannot, like that of the ancients, be irrevocably confined within the narrow bounds of a particular territory. Liberty, religious feelings, humanity, are the general property of our species; and when the government of a nation attempts to rob the world of all that ought to be dear to every inhabitant of the world – when it tramples on every idea, every hope, every virtue – that nation, as long as it consents to be the tool of that government, is no longer composed of fellow-citizens, but of enemies that must be vanquished, or madmen that must be chained.

After these prophetic observations, Constant concluded:

I have often boasted of your friendship, when your literary and political eminence were my only mode of communicating with you, unknown to yourself, and when I had but very faint hopes of your remembering me. You may, therefore, well believe that the renewal of that friendship has been one of the greatest pleasures I have ever experienced.[50]

During the next fourteen years Constant's fame overtook that of Mackintosh who, despite his wide experience – Recorder of Bombay, Professor of Law and General Politics at the East India Company College, Hailey-bury from 1818 to 1824, Member of Parliament, political writer – and despite his brilliance in so many fields, notably philosophy and history, had never really achieved greatness in any one. On 29 May 1828 Mackintosh wrote thanking Constant for his 'occasional Remembrance' of him and congratulating him 'on the Strength gained & gaining' by him, that is his success as a politician in the liberal cause.[51] Now on 2 July 1829 he wrote again, enclosing a speech he had lately composed and had the letter delivered by hand by his son-in-law who was passing through Paris: 'The Speech I send you only as a Proof that after an Acquaintance of more than Forty Stormy Years We continue to think alike. – especially on Questions of Faith and Justice.'[52] Constant marked the letters 'à conserver' – 'to be kept'.

During the French parliamentary session which ran from January to August 1829 it became more and more evident that Martignac's efforts to govern were proving ineffective. Constant was as busy as ever, not only writing speeches but resuming the journalistic work he had tended to neglect the previous year. According to C. P. Courtney, between April and June 1829 Constant published twenty-four articles in the *Courrier français*. In the period 1829–30 he is also known to have contributed unsigned articles to *Le Temps*, though it is more difficult to identify these with certainty.[53] In addition he now brought together a miscellaneous collection of articles he had written over many years under the title *Mélanges de littérature et de politique*, and these appeared in June 1829. They included, among mostly political essays, his *Lettre sur Julie* – an article on Julie Talma, his study of Madame de Staël and her work based on earlier essays including the 1817 obituary, and his thoughts on German theatre which had appeared in a slightly different form alongside *Wallstein*.[54] He was to develop his ideas on the theatre further in two articles which appeared in October 1829 in the *Revue de Paris* entitled 'Réflexions sur la tragédie' ('Reflections on tragedy').[55] According to Kurt Kloocke Constant had met the German Jewish playwright Ludwig Robert (1778–1832) (brother of the celebrated Berlin literary hostess Rahel Varnhagen von Ense (1771–1833)) in Paris in May 1826, and may have seen him again at Baden-Baden between August and October 1829 where Constant's poor health took him once more:[56] the 'Réflexions' on tragedy were inspired by Robert's play, *Die Macht der Verhältnisse* (*The Force of Circumstance*) (1819), about a man who defends the social prejudices and institutions by which he is oppressed. Such a paradoxical situation, of course, had also been close to the heart of *Adolphe*.

Constant may have written his important 'Réflexions' while at Baden-Baden. It was from there that he wrote to Rosalie on 7 October 1829:

I was sent back from Paris to take the waters. I have been here for two months, having been quite ill when I arrived. I'm slowly recovering, without the cause of my illness having been in any way cured by the remedies I have been given. Old age is making itself felt in every part of me: it's attacking my eyes, my stomach, my kidneys, my bowels, my feet. I observe it as it happens, just as I might watch a heartless cat tormenting a mouse. I'd rather not be the mouse, but what can I do about it?[57]

In October 1829 Constant made a brief visit to Coulmann's house at Brumath and attended a banquet given in his honour in Strasbourg, before returning to continue his treatment at Baden-Baden. His welcome was as enthusiastic as ever in Alsace, but he now found the number of requests coming from his constituents a drain on his time and on his low reserves of energy. And he had another difficult parliamentary session to face in January 1830, for which the opposition had been bracing itself for some months.

While Constant had been in Germany in August 1829, Charles X had replaced Martignac's ministry with a new one under his favourite, Prince Jules de Polignac, which was guaranteed to be yet more fanatical than its predecessor. A final confrontation between a stubborn Bourbon king unable to learn or to adapt to nineteenth-century realities and his opponents was becoming unavoidable. Political societies were being formed, the Left was being mobilized, and all the while the Orleanists were waiting in the wings. A new liberal newspaper financed by Lafitte and inspired by Talleyrand, the *National* began to appear. Polignac's cabinet was composed entirely of new and inexperienced men, and on 21 March 1830 the Chamber of Deputies was dissolved and new elections called. In June Constant was re-elected deputy for Strasbourg, despite attempts at the usual *tripotages*, or electoral chicanery. The King issued a plea to all electors to support his government's candidates, but to no avail: Polignac's ministry was defeated very decisively. Electoral defeat coincided with Charles X and Polignac's flexing France's military muscles in North Africa and the founding of a French colony in Algeria. Word of a military victory in Algiers reached Paris on 9 July 1830: the King and Polignac believed they were in a strong enough position to be able to ignore the unwelcome election result. On 25 July 1830 Polignac issued the so-called Four Ordinances: no journal or pamphlet could be published without official authorization; the newly elected Chamber was dissolved; only the richest 25 per cent of the existing electorate were henceforth allowed the franchise; and new elections to the Chamber were called for mid-September.

Such measures were widely seen as outrageous and amounting in fact to a *coup d'état*. The *National*, edited by the liberal historian Adolphe Thiers (1797–1877), called for civil resistance. Discontent with the King's unpopular minister soon turned into a revolution. On 26 July 1830 shops and workshops in Paris remained closed. On 28 July there were riots in the streets, and by 29 July, after 1,800 rioters and 200 soldiers had been killed in the fighting, deputies were already forming a provisional government. Both the King and Polignac had distinguished themselves during the 'Trois Glorieuses' – the 'Three Glorious Days' of what would come to be known as the July Revolution – by almost unbelievable fecklessness. For example, their victory in Algiers had meant that their best troops were still on the other side of the Mediterranean and unable to be of any assistance when they needed them. There was no question of a Republic being created: such an idea was anathema to the well-to-do conservative supporters of the uprising. Instead, the deputies invited the Duke of Orléans to become king, and on 1 August 1830 temporary ministers were appointed. Charles X now abdicated in favour of his grandson, but Orléans was already on the throne. The legitimate Bourbon line had been replaced by the Orleanist line.

Constant's direct role in these dramatic events was minimal: in late July he had been out in the country at Bagneux and suffering again with his leg. On 29 July, at Lafayette's invitation, he arrived back in the capital. The following day he drew up a declaration in favour of the new king, Louis-Philippe, with Count Sébastiani and, carried in a litter, accompanied the King to the Hôtel de Ville, the town hall of Paris. The editor of *Le Temps*, Coste, had written inviting him to 'bring his head as his stake in the revolutionary game'. Despite his frailty, it was not the kind of challenge or excitement that an inveterate gambler like Constant was likely to ignore, nor, given his immense popularity with young liberals, would he have been allowed to. When Charles X had gone back on the *Charte* in his Ordinances, depriving much of the commercial class of the franchise and reimposing censorship, the intransigent monarch had finally forfeited Constant's support. Constant now pledged allegiance to Louis-Philippe, the deposed king's cousin, who offered him the post of President of the Legislative Committee of the Council of State. According to Louis de Loménie, a contemporary observer, the King also made him a gift of 200,000 francs to pay off his gambling debts to the banker Lafitte 'in the name of Liberty'. Constant accepted the money but reserved his right to be independent, warning him that he would be the first to oppose the government if it made mistakes. Louis-Philippe generously allowed him to keep the money and do as he wished.[58]

Constant was not in fact offered a position in the government. His reputation with conservative French Catholics was not high: he was after all a Swiss Protestant divorcee with a German divorcee wife and a dubious revolutionary past, an incurable gambler who had failed for years to repay his debts, and had been highly unconventional in matters of sexual morality. And so he remained where it suited him best, as an outsider and occasional sniper in the Chamber and an adviser on drawing up new legislation. He was re-elected deputy for Strasbourg in October 1830 and continued defending individual freedom of thought and belief against all assailants. But it was not to be for long. The excitement of the July

Revolution and what had followed had brought him back to life but it had also exhausted him. In November two disappointments possibly brought the end much nearer: a rather poorly thought-out proposal of his on the regulation of printing and bookselling was overwhelmingly rejected by the Chamber of Deputies.[59] And on 18 November he felt crushed when he failed yet again in his candidature to the French Academy, even though this time he had been supported by Chateaubriand. He must have realized that this was his last chance to wear the *habit vert* of the *Immortels*, but thanks to the intriguing of a fellow liberal, Pierre-Paul Royer-Collard, who detested the unconventional and individualistic side of Constant, he lost to Viennet, a writer who is now forgotten.

On 27 September 1830 Constant had written what was to be his last letter to Rosalie. After expressing hopes about the new King's liberal sentiments, he had said:

> What is sad for me is my state of health. I have been moving about rather too much since 25 July and I am suffering for it. My legs are swollen, all I can face is a little soup. Finally I've been forced to take refuge in the Tivoli Baths to take douches and try to gain a short reprieve from nature. I don't know if I'll be granted one. Among the causes of my illness is the army of people seeking favours who descended on me after our victory. Working people and young people are admirable. But the hordes of people with requests are brazen and greedy. They arrive with claims and pitiless determi- nation. For five hours I was tormented right up to midnight, then awoken again at 5 in the morning by people asking for posts I was in no position to give.[60]

He added as a postscript that creeping paralysis now affected his feet, his tongue and sometimes other parts of his body. He wrote to his friend Prosper de Barante on 18 October 1830:

> My health is so bad that I have been unable to sustain an hour's conversation. I'm better now, and perhaps I'll be granted an exten- sion to my lease of life of two or three years again. Some things are so intriguing that one wants to see – I don't say how they turn out in the end, but at least what happens next.[61]

By December he was unable to climb a staircase, and now divided his time between his house, 17 Rue d'Anjou, and the Tivoli Baths, which were in effect a kind of nursing home. Nevertheless, faithful in spirit to a personal hero he had cited more than once in his letters, a knight in battle described by the poet Ariosto, he fought on, unaware that he was already dead.[62] Volume IV of *De la religion* which had been due for publication in July 1830 had been held over because of the Revolution, and would appear with the final volume, volume V, in April 1831:[63]

Constant was working on the proofs of volume V on 8 December 1830 shortly before he died in the early evening. Dorette Berthoud, in her study of the life of 'the second Madame Benjamin Constant', says the following about that final day:

> What were Constant's last moments like? Afraid of reviving emotions that were too painful to bear, Charlotte refused to write about them, even to Rosalie who had asked her to. 'Ever since that dreadful 8 December my life has become a torment. . . . The details about him then, about those last hours of a life so cruelly cut short weigh heavily on my heart. . . . Nevertheless I will give them to you, but have pity on me. You cannot imagine how painful it is to recall a happiness which is lost for ever with words which sum up a whole life.' The two women took their secret with them to the grave.[64]

But thanks to Constant's secretary Beaune we have an eye-witness account of that last day:

> The day of his death I brought him early in the morning the last printed page of his book. 'I'm glad', he said, 'I was afraid of dying before I had finished it. Don't talk to me about money, don't even bring me the newspapers. . . . I feel I am very ill, and I don't think I shall get through the day'. . . . His mind was unaffected, and his ideas were as lucid as when he was in good health. . . . At the end of the day, when he was dying, he called me to him. He asked me for his folder, it was next to him on his bed. I gave it him, he put it under his pillow. A quarter of an hour later he passed away.[65]

The reference to the folder concerns a dispute between Beaune and Charlotte: the secretary maintained that Constant had promised to leave him money in his will; Charlotte, however, said there was nothing about such a bequest among Constant's papers in the folder. Jean-Jacques Coulmann records in his *Réminiscences* that Constant's death occurred at 5 o'clock in the evening in his room at the Tivoli Baths, and that the numerous doctors who subsequently examined his body found no visible specific organic illness and attributed his death to the 'progressive weakening . . . exhaustion and fatigue of a nervous system which was no longer working'.[66]

The funeral on 12 December 1830 amounted to a lavish state occasion, the biggest event in Paris since the Revolution the previous summer. Enormous crowds lined the streets, detachments of guards accompanied the body; many different organizations were represented in the cortège, and students and young people were particularly numerous. The whole Chamber of Deputies turned out, with the Prime Minister and Constant's old colleague General Lafayette. The service was held at the Protestant church in the Rue Saint Antoine, and then Constant's coffin was carried by students towards the Père Lachaise cemetery. On the way the cry went up from the students 'To the Panthéon!' – the Church of Sainte Geneviève in the Latin Quarter which had become a cemetery for national heroes after the Revolution of 1789 and where Mirabeau had been interred – but the police ruled otherwise. The cortège continued to its destination, speeches were made, one by the aging Lafayette who was now so unsteady on his feet that he almost fell into the grave himself, and then the body was laid to rest at the Père Lachaise cemetery, where it still lies.[67]

EPILOGUE

Constant was a haunted man, pursued by the nightmare of death and oblivion. Jean-Jacques Coulmann, who knew him well during the last seven or eight years of his life, observed:

> The thought of death remained one of the most indestructible and permanent ideas in his mind. Everything brought it back to him: pleasure and pain, fame and obscurity, gratefulness and ingratitude, love and hate. It weakened his links with other people, it made all his passions grow lukewarm, it made him detached from everything. It was the ultimate reason for that indifference which many people considered scandalous, or reproached him for, thinking that it was the result of egoism, whereas he himself was one of the people he was least concerned about. He knew by heart the finest verses on death by English, German, Italian and French poets, languages which were all equally familiar to him.[1]

Edouard Laboulaye, drawing on the memories of Constant's friends and enemies, attempted in 1861 to suggest a solution to *le cas Constant*, the enigma of his personality:

> Benjamin Constant never had a mother to bring him up: in the cutting irony which characterized his style one can tell that that early happiness was missing from his life. During his childhood he was unable to open his heart to anyone. The Colonel remarried a few years after his first wife died, and by this marriage had children, one of them a daughter for whom Benjamin always had great affection. But, rightly or wrongly, it does not appear that the son of the first wife felt at home in his new family. As a young adult he speaks about it with bitterness. As a child he appears only to have loved his grandmother. His father frightened him, and that fear, as we shall see, had a fateful influence on the rest of his life. . . . [2]

In the early part of this book it was my contention that the experiences of those early childhood years for Constant – the long-term effects of losing his mother, the rivalry between his female relatives to compensate for that loss, his arbitrary removal from that circle in order to be entrusted to Marianne Magnin whom he detested, and Juste's subsequent unpredictable and often wrong-headed treatment of him – produced a number of characteristic traits which remained with him to the grave, among them those to which Coulmann and Laboulaye allude. True, he seems to have inherited from Juste some of his restlessness and changeableness, as well as his intellect and sharp tongue. Nevertheless the effects of a haphazard upbringing from which maternal love was signally absent left an indelible mark on him. Laboulaye's comment is obviously true: 'This child who had no mother and who was consumed by a need to love, had not found in his father that maternal tenderness, that warmth of affection that he needed in order to become a fulfilled human being.'[3] And Laboulaye goes on to rehabilitate Isabelle de Charrière's role in Constant's life, so often decried by commentators and, curiously, by Constant himself:

> In my opinion Madame de Charrière did not play the kind of part that has been attributed to her. She was something better: the intelligent and devoted friend of a young man who had no mother and who was looking around him for the affection he could not find in his father's house. . . . One can understand how Constant, having found the happiness he had missed, allowed himself to be caressed by a mother's hand while continuing to show all the egoism and thoughtlessness of a child.[4]

The Dutch Freudian critic Han Verhoeff, in his 1976 study of Constant and *Adolphe*, saw the source of Constant's behaviour towards women in his sense of having been 'abandoned' by his mother.[5] What Verhoeff sees as almost the flow of an alternating current of affection and aggression, attachment and the desire for separation vis-à-vis the women in his life stems from that early loss. It is a theory which at first reading gives one a sudden shock of deep recognition, the feeling that here at last is the key to all of Constant. But one only has to step back a few paces to realize that it offers only a much reduced and simplified part of the whole picture. Constant's attachment and aggression could be on occasion exercised as readily in non-sexual friendships with men as in sexual ones with women – his journals show this. But, more important, Verhoeff does not take full account of other facets of Constant's personality which were as fundamental to him – his deep and passionate love of liberty, for example, not simply freedom from a mistress but freedom in *all* its aspects, political, religious, the right to privacy, and so on. But still more important, Verhoeff hardly gives sufficient credit to Constant for the exemplary triumph that his life represents of Eros over Thanatos, the positive life wish over the death wish.

For against that nightmare of death which filled him with such stark terror even in the brightest noonday of his life, and against the temptation of despair and suicide, Constant marshalled all the resources of humour, hard work and commitment to a political or moral cause. He seldom surrendered to the overtly Romantic and only in a few private fragments to morbid Gothic melancholy,[6] unlike his contemporary Chateaubriand. His written style at its best – as in *Adolphe*, *Ma Vie*, in many of his letters or *De l'esprit de conquête* – is concise, direct and luminous. (For the benefit of the non-French speaker, it would be no exaggeration to liken its hypnotic power to the experience of listening to one of Schubert's late piano sonatas.) Through all the struggles, adventures and sufferings recounted in his letters and diaries Constant's overriding urge was to see himself clearly, to understand himself and to improve his behaviour. And to confide some of the disobliging things he knew or might suspect posterity would read took more than self-obsession: it took courage. Perhaps the contrast which Alfred Fabre-Luce makes between Chateaubriand and Constant comes closest to what, despite his many faults, remains fascinating and appealing about Constant. He imagines first a visitor being received in Viscount Chateaubriand's impeccably well-ordered salon with starchy politeness, and then the visitor's relief at being welcomed like a friend into the chaotic disorder of Constant's study.[7]

If there can ever be such a thing as the right moment to die, then Constant appears to have found it. He was fortunate not to see the idealism of 1830 evaporate entirely[8] and Louis-Philippe preside over a society of harsh *laissez-faire* capitalism and greed. In 1831 Stendhal's *Le Rouge et le Noir* marked the beginning of a new kind of French novel, the third-person novel painting a vast fresco of social life, so unlike the intimate scale of *Adolphe* – although Stendhal's wit and irony had much in common with that found elsewhere in Constant's writings. Death also spared Constant disappointment at the reception accorded to the fruit of a lifetime of work on the history of religion: the ever-faithful Charlotte, who jealously watched over her husband's reputation, saw to it that in April 1831 the last two volumes of *De la religion* were published, and then at last in April 1833 *Du polythéisme romain* in two volumes,[9] intended by Constant to complete the work begun in *De la religion*. They pleased neither the scholars – being already outdated and superficial in some areas – nor any of the Christian churches: his ideas were vague and lacking in precise commitment. One by one Constant's friends and loved ones died, Sir James Mackintosh in 1832, Rosalie de Constant in 1834, Albertine de Staël in 1838, and finally Charlotte in 1845.

Charlotte had continued to receive literary figures in her salon, where a bust of Constant by Bra had pride of place.[10] She had kept his memory alive, treasuring the death mask made of her husband by the sculptor Gois and even planning a monumental frieze to be carved by Théophile Bra, probably for Constant's tomb. Lack of money, however, seems to have prevented the latter project from being realized. Many tributes had been paid to Constant after his death, and of these she had kept one of the most moving – a letter still in the Von Marenholtz family archives at Wolfenbüttel, sent from Fort Royal, Martinique in the French West Indies, dated January or February 1831 and bearing thirteen signatures. It refers to Constant's campaign to end the slave trade, and in particular his attempts in July 1829 to obtain civil and political rights for the coloured peoples of Guadeloupe and Martinique:

> How could we forget the Honourable Deputy who by his efforts did so much to abolish, at least in part, the revolting ill-treatment of which we were the victims? ... The entire family of coloured peoples [*la famille entière de Couleur*] dares to hope that in your justifiable grief you will deign to accept the expression of the regrets which his loss inspires in us – the loss of a man who was always the staunchest supporter of our rights.

Charlotte's own death occurred on 22 July 1845 and was a particularly painful one. She was in bed one night when somehow the strings of her bonnet caught light from the lamp or candle she was using. She sustained terrible burns from which she died some days later. Her beloved son Wilhelm von Marenholtz was at her side during her last hours. He subsequently inherited her papers, which returned to the family home at Groß Schwülper near Brunswick.[11]

Constant's literary reputation suffered the usual decline that follows on a writer's death, recovering towards the end of the nineteenth century with a revival of interest in the self-analysis of *Adolphe*, perhaps the most quintessential French *roman d'analyse*, on the part of Anatole France, Paul Bourget and others.[12] The twentieth century saw the establishment of *Adolphe* as one of the acknowledged classics of French literature, a renewal of scholarly interest in Constant's life and very many books and articles on his work. In the 1970s and 1980s the reaction against Marxism and the growth of interest in the origins of liberalism gave further impetus to research into Constant's political writing. It is fair to say that at the end of the twentieth century his reputation rests on his work as a novelist and introspective – a fact which would have genuinely surprised him – and on his work on political theory, which would have perhaps been some consolation to him for the neglect into which his writings on religious history have fallen. Among the great literary figures of nineteenth-century France, Constant remains nevertheless one of the least explored. Proof of this is in the continued discovery year by year of hitherto lost or unknown documents and letters that have lain hidden in various parts of Europe and beyond – a process now hastened by preliminary surveys in preparation for the publication of Constant's complete works and correspondence.[13] For any given year of Constant's life information is likely to surface about an obscure area that may confound the biographer's speculations. The author of this very provisional biography will be happy to see his speculations give way to the truth when that truth is finally uncovered.

LIST OF ABBREVIATIONS USED
IN THE NOTES

ABC	*Annales Benjamin Constant*, 1980– , Lausanne: Institut Benjamin Constant (annual journal of the Association Benjamin Constant, 12 vols to 1991).
Adolphe, ed. Paul Delbouille	Benjamin Constant, *Adolphe. Anecdote trouveé dans les papiers d'un inconnu*, ed. Paul Delbouille, Paris: Les Belles Lettres, 1977.
Anna Lindsay	*L'Inconnue d'Adolphe. Correspondance de Benjamin Constant et d'Anna Lindsay*, ed. Baronne Constant de Rebecque. Préface de Fernand Baldensperger, Paris: Plon (1933).
Cécile, ed. Paul Delbouille	Benjamin Constant, *Amélie et Germaine – Ma Vie – Cécile*, ed. Paul Delbouille, Paris: Librairie Honoré Champion, 1989.
Charrière, *Œuvres*	Isabelle de Charrière/Belle de Zuylen, *Œuvres complètes*, ed. Jean-Daniel Candaux and others, Amsterdam: G. A. van Oorschot, 1979–84, 10 vols.
Constant, *Correspondance I (1774–1792)*	Benjamin Constant, *Correspondance générale I (1774–1792)* (*Œuvres complètes, série II, vol. I*), ed. C. P. Courtney et Dennis Wood, Tübingen: Max Niemeyer Verlag, 1993.
Constant, *Œuvres*	Benjamin Constant, *Œuvres*, ed. Alfred Roulin [et Charles Roth], Paris: Gallimard (Bibliothèque de la Pléiade), 1957.
Jasinski, *L'Engagement*	Béatrice W. Jasinski, *L'Engagement de Benjamin Constant: amour et politique (1794–1796)*, Paris: Minard, 1971.
Ma Vie, ed. C. P. Courtney	Benjamin Constant, *Ma Vie (Le Cahier rouge)*, ed. C. P. Courtney, Cambridge: Dæmon Press, 1991.

Melegari (1895)   *Journal intime de Benjamin Constant et lettres à sa famille et à ses amis*, ed. Dora Melegari, Paris: Paul Ollendorf, 1895.

Menos   Benjamin Constant, *Lettres à sa famille 1775–1830*, précédées d'une introduction, d'après des lettres et des documents, par Jean-H. Menos, Paris: Librairie Stock, 1932.

Rudler, *Jeunesse*   Gustave Rudler, *La Jeunesse de Benjamin Constant 1767–1794. Le disciple du XVIIIe siècle. Utilitarisme et pessimisme. Mme de Charrière*, Paris: Armand Colin, 1909.

Staël, *Correspondance générale*   [Germaine] de Staël, *Correspondance générale*, ed. Béatrice W. Jasinski, Paris: Jean-Jacques Pauvert (vols I-IV); Paris: Hachette (vol. V), 1960–85.

As in the main body of the text, all translations given in the notes are my own unless otherwise indicated.

NOTES

INTRODUCTION

1. The international conference – the second on Constant, the first having taken place in October 1967 – was held in Lausanne on 15–19 July 1980, and its proceedings were published under the title *Benjamin Constant, Madame de Staël et le Groupe de Coppet*, ed. Etienne Hofmann, Oxford: The Voltaire Foundation; Lausanne: Institut Benjamin Constant, 1982. Also in 1980 the first issue of the annual journal *Annales Benjamin Constant* appeared, and a committee was set up to plan the publication of Constant's complete works and correspondence, of which the first two volumes appeared in 1993. On 12 December 1980 France Culture broadcast a programme devoted to Benjamin Constant who was described as 'one of the founders of French liberalism'. It was the twentieth in the radio series 'Relectures', and consisted of a discussion chaired by Hubert Juin (now deceased) with Pierre Manent, Philippe Raynaud and Marcel Gauchet, with readings from Constant's works. Marcel Gauchet's selection of Constant's political writings, *De la liberté chez les Modernes. Ecrits politiques* appeared in the same year, published by Livre de poche, Paris.

2. Isaiah Berlin, *Four Essays on Liberty*, London: Oxford University Press, 1969, p. 126. There are several illuminating observations on Constant's political thought later in the book (pp. 162–6).

3. Constant, *Œuvres*, p. 835. The passage occurs in the preface to the *Mélanges de littérature et de politique* published in June 1829.

4. Beatrice Camille Fink, in 'The Idea-World of Benjamin Constant as expressed in his Political Philosophy', University of Pittsburgh Ph.D., 1966 (reprinted by University Microfilms, Inc., Ann Arbor, Michigan, 1987), p. 5, notes:

> The reasons for Sainte-Beuve's hostility are not entirely clear. Perhaps it was because of a difference of political opinions, or perhaps mere jealousy. In all likelihood, it can be traced to the fact that he obtained a good deal of his information on Constant by word of mouth via the de Broglie family, related to Mme. de Staël and unfriendly towards Constant.

5. Stephen Holmes, *Benjamin Constant and the Making of Modern Liberalism*, New Haven and London: Yale University Press, 1984; Benjamin Constant, *Political Writings*, trans. and ed. Biancamaria Fontana, Cambridge: Cambridge University Press (Cambridge Texts in the History of Political Thought), 1988; and Biancamaria Fontana, *Benjamin Constant and the Post-Revolutionary Mind*, New Haven and London: Yale University Press, 1991. It is only fair

to add that regrettably both books by Biancamaria Fontana contain numerous factual inaccuracies, especially on biographical matters.

6. Quoted from Constant's *Esquisse d'un essai sur la littérature du dix-huitième siècle (Outline of an Essay on the Literature of the Eighteenth Century)* in Beatrice Camille Fink, *op. cit.*, p. vi.

7. On the historical context of Lausanne in the eighteenth century, see Charles Burnier, *La Vie vaudoise et la Révolution. De la servitude à la liberté*, Lausanne: Bridel, 1902.

8. May wrote to his sister Jane at some date before 19 February 1781: 'Young Constants passions are sometimes very strong it is only the presence and authority of his Father that can govern him. If he will not conduct himself well with me I shall not stay with him long' (Benjamin Constant, *Correspondance I [1774–1792]*, Appendice A.21).

9. Beatrice Camille Fink's neat summary, *op. cit.*, p. 161. In *De la force du gouvernement actuel et de la nécessité de s'y rallier* (1796) Constant stated that 'le grand art est de gouverner avec force, mais de gouverner peu', 'the great art is in governing firmly but governing very little' (ed. Philippe Raynaud, Paris: Flammarion [Champs], 1988, p. 64).

10. On this, see Dennis Wood, *Benjamin Constant: 'Adolphe'*, Cambridge: Cambridge University Press (Landmarks of World Literature), 1987.

11. In such books as *Benjamin Constant muscadin, 1795–1799*, Paris: Gallimard, 1958, *Madame de Staël, Benjamin Constant et Napoléon*, Paris: Plon, 1959, and *Pas à pas*, Paris: Gallimard, 1969.

12. Benjamin Constant, *De l'esprit de conquête et de l'usurpation*, ed. Ephraïm Harpaz, Paris: GF Flammarion, 1986, Chapitre XIII, 'De l'uniformité', p. 122: 'La variété, c'est la vie; l'uniformité, c'est la mort.'

13. Quoted in Kurt Kloocke, *Benjamin Constant: une biographie intellectuelle*, Geneva: Droz (Histoire des idées et critique littéraire, 218), 1984, p. 296.

14. Quoted in Beatrice Camille Fink, *op. cit.*, p. 188, from Constant's manuscript 'Du moment actuel et de la destinée de l'espèce humaine, ou histoire abrégée de l'humanité' ('Concerning the present moment and the destiny of the human race, or a short history of humanity').

1 'THE GRIEF THAT DOES NOT SPEAK': CONSTANT AND HIS FATHER (1767–1783)

1. On the circumstances surrounding Benjamin Constant's birth, see *Ma Vie*, ed. C. P. Courtney, pp. 3 and 71; Rudler, *Jeunesse*, pp. 31–5; and the correspondence in Appendice I to Constant's *Correspondance I (1774–1792)*, 'La mort de la mère de Benjamin Constant'. Pierre Cordey established that Benjamin Constant was born in the house of his maternal grandfather, Benjamin de Chandieu, now 7 Place Saint-François (premises currently occupied by the Lausanne Cercle littéraire) opposite the church where he was shortly to be christened (*Mme de Staël et Benjamin Constant sur les bords du Léman*, Lausanne: Payot [collection 'Paysages de l'amour'], 1966, p. 233). Although he was christened Benjamin-Henri, from an early age he always signed himself Henri-Benjamin Constant. The significance of this might be worth exploring. John E. Jackson, in his *Passions du sujet. Essais sur les rapports entre psychanalyse et littérature*, Paris: Mercure de France, 1990, pp. 94–6, elaborates an intriguing Freudian hypothesis concerning Stendhal's autobiographical *La Vie de Henry Brulard*, Stendhal's own Christian name Henri (Henri Beyle) and that of his mother Henriette who died in childbirth when he was 7, and the 'couple imaginaire Henri–Henriette'.

One might ask whether the positioning of the name Henri was of importance to Constant, and why.

2. See for example, Rudler, *Jeunesse*, p. 33, note 2.

3. Letter from Catherine de Charrière de Sévery to Angletine-Charlotte de Chandieu of 20–1 November 1767, quoted in Appendice I to Constant, *Correspondance I (1774–1792)*.

4. See in particular Michael Rutter, *Maternal Deprivation Reassessed*, Harmondsworth: Penguin Books (Penguin Modern Psychology), second edition 1981, and John Bowlby's trilogy *Attachment and Loss*, consisting of vol. I, *Attachment*, Harmondsworth: Penguin Books, second edition 1982, vol. II, *Separation: Anxiety and Anger*, Harmondsworth: Penguin Books, 1975, and vol. III, *Loss: Sadness and Depression*, Harmondsworth: Penguin Books, 1981. Bowlby's *A Secure Base: Clinical Applications of Attachment Theory*, London: Tavistock/Routledge, 1988, was the final summary of his views before his death in 1990.

5. Rudler, *Jeunesse*, p. 33.

6. Jean-Jacques Rousseau, *Les Confessions*, ed. Jacques Voisine, Paris: Garnier Frères (Classiques Garnier), 1964, pp. 6–7. See Pierre-Paul Clément's *Jean-Jacques Rousseau. De l'éros coupable à l'éros glorieux*, Neuchâtel: A la Baconnière (Langages), 1976, for a psychoanalytical study of Rousseau which in places suggests interesting parallels with Constant.

7. John Bowlby, *Charles Darwin. A Biography*, London: Hutchinson, 1990, p. 77. (The title given on its cover, as opposed to on the title page, is *Charles Darwin. A New Biography*). Whether Constant's problems produced any somatic symptoms is an interesting question that has to the best of my knowledge never been raised by other biographers of Constant: one thinks immediately, for example, of the recurrent eye troubles which plagued him all his life and which often seem to have coincided with an emotional crisis. It is a subject worthy of further investigation.

8. See Rudler, *Jeunesse*, pp. 38–45.

9. John Bowlby, *Attachment and Loss*, vol. III, *Loss: Sadness and Depression*, Harmondsworth: Penguin, 1981, pp. 288–9.

10. Dominique Verrey, *Chronologie de la vie et de l'œuvre de Benjamin Constant*. Avec la collaboration du professeur Etienne Hofmann. Tome I: *1767–1805*, Geneva: Editions Slatkine, 1992.

11. *Ma Vie*, ed. C. P. Courtney, p. 3.

12. Constant, *Œuvres*, p. 1455.

13. Rudler, *Jeunesse*, p. 33.

14. Henri Troyat, *Tolstoy*, Harmondsworth: Penguin Books (Pelican Biographies), 1967, p. 26.

15. *Ma Vie*, ed. C. P. Courtney, p. 72. It seems likely that Constant had one or several tutors before Ströhlin, but Ströhlin is the first he professes to remember.

16. [Michel de] Montaigne, *Œuvres complètes*, ed. Albert Thibaudet et Maurice Rat, Paris: Gallimard (Bibliothèque de la Pléiade), 1962, [Essais], I, XXVI, pp. 174.

17. The best introduction to the sometimes forbidding world of Lacan's thought is Malcolm Bowie, *Lacan*, London: Fontana Press (Fontana Modern Masters), 1991.

18. Harold Nicolson, *Benjamin Constant*, London: Constable, 1949, p. 5.

19. On this and Freud's Irma dream, see James Hopkins's chapter 'The interpretation of dreams' in *The Cambridge Companion to Freud*, ed. Jerome Neu, Cambridge: Cambridge University Press, 1991, esp. pp. 101 ff.

20. See Constant, *Œuvres*, p. 1479.

21. Constant, *Œuvres*, pp. 295–6.
22. See Dennis Wood, 'Constant and the case of Ann Hurle', *French Studies Bulletin*, 5 (Winter 1982/3), pp. 6–8.
23. Quoted in the Introduction to Charles Dickens, *David Copperfield*, ed. Trevor Blount, Harmondsworth: Penguin Books (The Penguin English Library), 1966, pp. 18–19.
24. Rudler, *Jeunesse*, p. 37.
25. *Ibid.*: 'L'éducation de son fils lui donna beaucoup de peine; il se ressentit du malheur d'avoir perdu sa mère.' The 'il' appears to refer to Juste.
26. Ian D. Suttie's usefully provocative critique of Freudian theory *The Origins of Love and Hate*, London: Kegan Paul, Trench, Trubner, 1935, pp. 80 ff.
27. Constant in a letter to his aunt Anne de Nassau of 7 July 1795, quoted in Rudler, *Jeunesse*, p. 61, note 1.
28. *Adolphe*, ed. Paul Delbouille, pp. 110 and 276.
29. Once again Rosalie de Constant in her valuable *Cahiers verts*, quoted in Rudler, *Jeunesse*, p. 41.
30. Ian D. Suttie, *op. cit.*, p. 89.
31. John Bowlby, *op. cit.*, p. 304.
32. *Ma Vie*, ed. C. P. Courtney, pp. 24–6.
33. Charrière, *Œuvres*, III, p. 31.
34. *Ma Vie*, ed. C. P. Courtney, p. 62.
35. John Bowlby, *op. cit.*, p. 304.
36. *The Letters of John Keats*, ed. Maurice Buxton Forman, London: Oxford University Press, 1947, p. 72, letter of 21 December 1817 to George and Thomas Keats.
37. See John Bowlby, *op. cit.*, especially chapter 21, 'Disordered variants and some conditions contributing', pp. 350–80.
38. John Bowlby, *op. cit.*, especially pp. 28–9, 170–2, 202–6, 218–19, 343–6, 370–6.
39. Han Verhoeff, *'Adolphe' et Constant: une étude psychocritique*, Paris: Klincksieck, 1976.
40. See Han Verhoeff, *op. cit.*, p. 84, note 10.
41. Constant, *Œuvres*, p. 296.
42. Constant, *Œuvres*, p. 495.
43. One of Constant's favourite images which occurs in his letters several times was drawn from the Italian poet Ariosto (1474–1533): that of the knight who is so busy fighting that he does not notice that he has already been killed.
44. Han Verhoeff, *op. cit.*, p. 104.
45. Dominique Verrey, *op. cit.*, p. 3, entry 14.
46. See Rudler, *Jeunesse*, chapitre II, 'Marianne', pp. 50–6.
47. Rudler, *Jeunesse*, pp. 51–2.
48. Dominique Verrey, *op. cit.*, p. 4, entry 19.
49. See later, Chapter 6.
50. Rudler, *Jeunesse*, p. 55, note 3.
51. Charrière, *Œuvres*, III, p. 480.
52. Rudler, *Jeunesse*, p. 34.
53. Harold Nicolson, *op. cit.*, p. 10.
54. Rudler, *Jeunesse*, p. 43.
55. See Christine Chicoteau's sympathetic study *Chère Rose. A Biography of Rosalie de Constant (1758–1834)*, Berne, Frankfurt am Main, Las Vegas: Peter Lang (Europäische Hochschulschriften: Reihe 13, Franz. Sprache u. Literatur, Bd. 65), 1980.

56. Benjamin et Rosalie de Constant, *Correspondance 1786–1830*, ed. Alfred et Suzanne Roulin, Paris: Gallimard, 1955, p. 81, letter of September 1808.
57. *Ibid.*, p. xiv.
58. William [et Clara de Charrière] de Sévery, *La Vie de société dans le Pays de Vaud à la fin du dix-huitième siècle. Salomon et Catherine de Charrière de Sévery et leurs amis*, Lausanne: Georges Bridel; Paris: Fischbacher, 1911–12, 2 vols, vol. I, p. 303.
59. C. P. Courtney, 'Benjamin Constant seen by his father: letters from Louis-Arnold-Juste to Samuel de Constant, 1780–96', *French Studies* XXXIX (1985), pp. 277–8.
60. Benjamin Constant, *Correspondance I (1774–1792)*, lettre 11: 'mais je ne sai par quelle magie ces airs si lents finissent toujours par devenir des prestissimo; il en est de même de la danse, le menuet se termine toujours par quelques gambades. je crois ma chere grand-mere que ce mal est incurable et qu'il résistera a la raison même'. There is a facsimile of the letter in Paul L. Léon's excellent *Benjamin Constant*, Paris: Editions Rieder (Maîtres des littératures), 1930, pp. iv-v of the illustrations.
61. Rudler, *Jeunesse*, p. 55.
62. *Ma Vie*, ed. C. P. Courtney, pp. 3–4 and 72–3.
63. *Ma Vie*, ed. C. P. Courtney, p. 4.
64. Gobert has not been identified by editors of *Ma Vie*.
65. *Ma Vie*, ed. C. P. Courtney, p. 5.
66. Duplessis remains unidentified by Constant scholars.
67. *Ma Vie*, ed. C. P. Courtney, p. 6.
68. *Ma Vie*, ed. C. P. Courtney, p. 5.
69. Rudler, *Jeunesse*, p. 97. The 'Epistle' is reproduced in facsimile in Paul L. Léon, *op. cit.*, p. vii.
70. C. P. Courtney, *op. cit.*, p. 278.
71. On Nathaniel Bridges and Nathaniel May, see C. P. Courtney, 'Benjamin Constant et Nathaniel May: documents inédits', *Revue d'histoire littéraire de la France*, LXVI (1966), pp. 162–78. Bridges is mentioned several times in J. S. Reynolds, *The Evangelicals at Oxford 1735–1871. A Record of an Unchronicled Movement*, Oxford: Basil Blackwell, 1953, esp. p. 162. On p. 49 he is described by a contemporary as 'distinguished by [his] compass of mind, . . . vivacity of thought, and . . . strength of memory'.
72. On May's career, see Constant, *Correspondance I (1774–1792)*, Appendice VI, 'Nathaniel May, précepteur de Benjamin Constant' and the notes to letter A14.
73. *Ma Vie*, ed. C. P. Courtney, pp. 6–7.
74. Letter of Nathaniel May to his sister Jane May of 23 May 1781, Constant, *Correspondance I (1774–1792)*, Appendice A24.
75. The same to the same, before 19 February 1781, *op. cit.*, Appendice A21.
76. The same to the same, 23 May 1781, *op. cit.*, Appendice A24.
77. See Constant, *Œuvres*, p. 819, journal entries for 22, 23 and 25 July 1816.
78. *Ma Vie*, ed. C. P. Courtney, pp. 6–7.
79. *Ibid.*, p. 7.
80. Rudler, *Jeunesse*, p. 158. The record of matriculation is catalogued in Erlangen University Library, Matr. Ms. VI, Abt. 2, p. 119 verso: 'd. VI Febr. MDCCLXXXII Henricus Benjamin L. B. de Constant Rebecque/Lausanno Helvetia anno aetatis XIV'. The catalogue entry notes: 'Beigeheftet ist das Wappen der Familie mit dem von Heinrich IV. verliehenen Spruch "In arduis constans"'. The punning motto of the Constant family, meaning 'steadfast in

adversity', is engraved on Constant's tomb in the Père Lachaise cemetery, Paris.

81. See C. P. Courtney, 'An eighteenth-century education: Constant at Erlangen and Edinburgh (1782–85)', in *Rousseau et le dix-huitième siècle: Essays in Memory of R. A. Leigh*, ed. M. Hobson, J. Leigh and R. Wokler, Oxford: The Voltaire Foundation, 1992, forthcoming.

82. William [et Clara de Charrière] de Sévery, *op. cit.*, vol. I, pp. 150–1. The editors of Constant's *Correspondance I (1774–1792)*, state that the letter probably dates from April 1783.

83. Rudler, *Jeunesse*, p. 118.

84. An interlinear entry in *Ma Vie* reads, enigmatically : 'Mes duels. Olivayra' ('My duels. Olivayra'), *op. cit.*, p. 8.

85. Benjamin Constant, *Correspondance I (1774–1792)*, Appendice VII, A25.

86. Edouard Laboulaye, article in the *Revue nationale et étrangère*, V (1867), p. 327: 'son père lui faisait peur; et cette peur . . . eut une influence fatale sur le reste de sa vie'.

87. Quoted by Laboulaye, *op. cit.*, p. 346: '[La pensée de la mort] était enfin la cause de cette indifférence que beaucoup de gens considéraient comme un outrage, ou lui reprochaient comme de l'égoïsme, tandis qu'il était un de ceux à qui il s'intéressait le moins.'

2 'THE CHARMS OF FRIENDSHIP' (1783–1785)

1. *Ma Vie*, ed. C. P. Courtney, p. 9.

2. *Matriculation Roll of the University of Edinburgh*, vol. II, 1775–1810, Edinburgh, University Library.

3. Rudler, *Jeunesse*, especially pp. 121–3 and 163–73.

4. On Constant's period in Edinburgh, see the following articles by C. P. Courtney: 'Autour de Benjamin Constant: lettres inédites de Juste de Constant à Sir Robert Murray Keith', *Revue d'histoire littéraire de la France*, 67e année (janvier-mars 1967), pp. 97–100 – henceforth: Courtney (1967; 1); 'New light on Benjamin Constant: three unpublished letters from Juste de Constant to J.-B. Suard', *Neophilologus*, LI (1967), pp. 10–14 – Courtney (1967; 2); 'Isabelle de Charrière and the "Character of H. B. Constant": a false attribution', *French Studies*, XXXVI (1982), pp. 282–9 – Courtney (1982); 'Benjamin Constant seen by his father: letters from Louis-Arnold-Juste to Samuel de Constant, 1780–1796', *French Studies*, XXXIX (1985), pp. 276–84 – Courtney (1985); and 'An eighteenth-century education: Constant at Erlangen and Edinburgh (1782–5)', in *Rousseau et le dix-huitième siècle: Essays in Memory of R. A. Leigh*, ed. M. Hobson, J. Leigh and R. Wokler, Oxford: The Voltaire Foundation, 1992, forthcoming – Courtney (1992); and by Dennis Wood: 'Constant's *Cahier rouge*: new findings', *French Studies*, XXXVIII (1984), pp. 13–29 – henceforth: Wood (1984); 'Constant in Edinburgh: eloquence and history', *French Studies*, XL (1986), pp. 151–66 – Wood (1986); and 'Constant in Britain 1780–1787: a provisional chronology', *ABC*, no. 7 (1987), pp. 7–16 – Wood (1987). A good introduction to the intellectual atmosphere in eighteenth-century Edinburgh and in Scotland generally is provided in *A Hotbed of Genius. The Scottish Enlightenment 1730–1790*, ed. David Daiches, Peter Jones and Jean Jones, Edinburgh: Edinburgh University Press, 1986.

5. Courtney (1967; 1), p. 99, note 5. It seems that Constant made other living arrangements later. In an entry in his *Journaux intimes* for 1804 he says: 'Twenty years ago today 9 August I was in Scotland, quite happy, living by turn with

friends and with an excellent family in the country, three miles from Edinburgh'
(Constant, *Œuvres*, p. 351). Constant lived with the Wauchope family at Niddrie, a little to the south-east of the city, during the vacations, it seems. In *Ma
Vie* Constant records returning to Niddrie in August 1787 to see 'the Wauchopes
who had been so hospitable to me when I was a student' (Constant, *Œuvres*,
p. 156). James Wauchope was, perhaps, one of the 'friends' Constant shared
lodgings with during term, and during the summer recess he stayed with Wauchope's family in the country. James Wauchope was the same age as Constant,
was enrolled as an undergraduate in 1783–4, 1784–5 and 1788–9, and in 1789
was called to the Scottish Bar. He was a member of the Speculative Society
from 1787 to 1789, and died at the early age of 30 in 1797. When Constant
wrote in the *Journaux intimes* 'several of my friends are dead', he must have
had James Wauchope in mind, for he added: 'The Niddrie family has renewed
itself. The new generation doen't know me' (Constant, *Œuvres*, p. 351). See
Matriculation Roll and *History of the Speculative Society of Edinburgh from
its Institution in M.DCC.LXIV.*, Edinburgh, 1845, p. 181 (henceforth: *HSSE*
followed by page number).

6. From 1791 to 1793 (*HSSE*, p. 29).
7. *Ma Vie*, ed. C. P. Courtney, p. 9.
8. Courtney (1967; 1), p. 98.
9. Courtney (1967; 1), p. 99.
10. Courtney (1985), p. 283, note 3.
11. Courtney (1967; 1), p. 100.
12. *Dictionary of National Biography*, ed. Sir Lesley Stephen, London: Smith, Elder,
    1908, vol. VI, p. 163. See also Courtney (1992) on Duncan and other Edinburgh
    'characters'.
13. Richard Kentish is dealt with later in Chapter 4, 'Escape', in connection with
    Constant's *escapade d'Angleterre* of 1787.
14. Constant does not mention Charles Hope in *Ma Vie*. Prominent in the Speculat-
    ive Society's debates in 1783–5, Hope went on to become Lord Advocate of
    Scotland in 1801, MP for the City of Edinburgh and a Privy Councillor. His
    eloquence as a judge was considered outstanding.
15. Another survivor from the eighteenth century is the Royal Medical Society, still
    active in the University, to which Richard Kentish was admitted on 30 Novem-
    ber 1782, and which several members of the Speculative Society also joined:
    Thomas Addis Emmet, Thomas Skeete, James Mackintosh and John Ffrye
    (*General List of the Members of the Medical Society of Edinburgh*, Edinburgh,
    1877, pp. 19–21).
16. *Minutes of the Speculative Society*, p. 274, kept in the archives of the Speculative
    Society (henceforth: *Minutes*, followed by page number).
17. *Minutes*, p. 277.
18. See Sir Alexander Grant, *The Story of the University of Edinburgh*, 2 vols,
    London: Longman's, Green, 1884, vol. II, pp. 486–9.
19. *HSSE*, p. 167. Thomas Macknight, in a manuscript memoir kept in the archives
    of the Speculative Society, remarks that he was 'a Russian of great distinction'
    (Biographical Letters III A-Z, Drafts of History 1845, f. 157 verso. Henceforth:
    Macknight, followed by folio number).
20. *Ma Vie*, ed. C. P. Courtney, p. 9.
21. *Memoirs of the Life of the Right Honourable Sir James Mackintosh*, ed. Robert
    James Mackintosh, London: Edward Moxon, 1835, 2 vols, vol. I, pp. 26–7
    (henceforth: *Memoirs*, followed by volume and page numbers).
22. *Memoirs*, vol. I, pp. 29–30.

23. *Memoirs*, vol. I, p. 24.
24. *Memoirs*, vol. I, p. 24.
25. It was in these terms that the Society's aims were described when a proposal was made to establish a connection with the Historical Society of Trinity College, Dublin on 18 November 1783 (*Minutes*, p. 278).
26. Wood (1986), pp. 152–3 and 155.
27. *Memoirs*, vol. I, p. 20.
28. See *Memoirs*, vol. II, *passim*.
29. *Memoirs*, vol. I, p. 25.
30. *Memoirs*, vol. II, pp. 271–2.
31. *Memoirs*, vol. I, p. 28.
32. *Minutes*, p. 284.
33. Wood (1986), p. 162.
34. *Ma Vie*, ed. C. P. Courtney, p. 9.
35. *Memoirs*, vol. I, p. 26.
36. *Memoirs*, vol. I, p. 27.
37. Macknight, f. 156 verso. Thomas Macknight (1762–1836) was, according to Lord Cockburn, 'a man of great simplicity of manners, of greater science, and of the greatest possible worth' (*HSSE*, p. 146). Although Macknight does not appear to have been particularly close to Constant, his general account of the Speculative Society's activities can, I believe, be relied on.
38. Macknight, f. 156 verso, and *Memoirs*, vol. I, p. 27.
39. See Leon ó Broin, *The Unfortunate Mr. Robert Emmet*, Dublin: Clonmore & Reynolds, 1958.
40. Macknight, ff. 156 verso and 157.
41. For details of Dr Emmet's career, see Richard R. Madden, *The United Irishmen*, London: Catholic Publishing and Bookselling Co., 1860, p. 32.
42. *Memoirs*, vol. I, p. 27.
43. *Ma Vie*, ed. C. P. Courtney, pp. 9–10.
44. Edinburgh, Speculative Society archives, Biographical Letters III A–Z, Drafts of History 1845, f. 90.
45. *The History of the Speculative Society 1764–1905*, Edinburgh: T. & A. Constable, 1905, p. 73.
46. *Memoirs*, p. 27.
47. Macknight, ff. 159 verso and 160. The *Minutes* record that Macknight, an infrequent visitor to the Speculative Society, was present with Wilde and Mackintosh at the meeting of 4 May 1784.
48. Published for the first time in Wood (1987), pp. 17–19.
49. See Courtney (1982), and Dennis Wood, 'A propos de Constant et John Wilde', *Lettre de Zuylen et du Pontet*, 7 (1982), pp. 8–9.
50. Courtney (1982), p. 285.
51. Georges Poulet, *Benjamin Constant par lui-même*, Paris: Du Seuil (Ecrivains de toujours, 78), 1968, p. 43. It is remarkable that Poulet, who could have had no knowledge of the existence of the pen-portrait of Constant by Wilde, should have written in exactly the same terms, e.g. p. 43:

> In these obsessive images what strikes us is a central stillness, with movement taking place out at the periphery. Benjamin Constant represents himself to himself as a motionless point at the centre surrounded by a mobile circumference. All the superficial happenings of life in the world outside, all external pressures and determining factors are pushed out to that periphery.

52. Patrice Thompson, *La Religion de Benjamin Constant. Les Pouvoirs de l'image*, Pisa: La Goliardica, 1978, p. 40: 'Gambling, the temptation of suicide, perhaps sodomy are symptoms of his difficulty in being with other people, something from which his relationship with Belle de Charrière saved him.' The question of Constant's friendship with the homosexual Johann Rudolf Knecht is dealt with in Chapter 3, 'Isabelle de Charrière'.

53. *Ma Vie*, ed. C. P. Courtney, p. 14.

54. *HSSE*, p. 147.

55. *Adolphe*, ed. Paul Delbouille, Chapitre VII, p. 173. This image of physical or intellectual strength unjustly imprisoned and helpless seems to have had peculiar force for Constant (one is also reminded of the Ann Hurle story discussed earlier, in Chapter 1). The idea occurs again – significantly in connection with Johann Rudolf Knecht and linked to that note of regret about the misfortune of Constant's friends that is very close to the tone of *Ma Vie*, which indeed he was composing at around this time – in a letter to Rosalie de Constant of 24 May 1811:

> I was greatly saddened in Berne. I learnt that a man I had been a good friend of twenty-five years ago, who had been very well off then, was quite clever, widely read and extremely keen to improve his mind, is now locked up in the hospital for the rest of his life, in a room with no light in it and bars on the window. I had seen him again in Geneva, his reputation ruined because of his reprehensible conduct and all of his money gone. But the mental picture of him in that dungeon pursued me for the rest of the evening. For several days afterwards it was if I had a heavy weight on my heart. Of all the friends I've had, nine-tenths at least are dead, have gone mad or have turned out badly. Anyone would think I had chosen them deliberately in order to be able to prove that, for all the stupid things I had done, I was still the wisest of all of them.
>
> (Benjamin et Rosalie de Constant, *Correspondance 1786–1830*, ed. Alfred et Suzanne Roulin, Paris: Gallimard, 1955, p. 140)

56. See *HSSE*, especially pp. 7–13.

57. Wood (1987), p. 17.

58. Macknight, f. 157 verso.

59. *Lettres de Madame de Staël à Benjamin Constant* publiées pour la première fois en original par Madame la Baronne de Nolde avec une introduction et des notes par Paul L. Léon. Avant-propos de Gustave Rudler, Paris: Kra, 1928, p. 53.

60. Courtney (1967; 2), p. 11.

61. Courtney (1967; 2), p. 11, letter to J.-B. Suard of 16 June 1784.

62. Gustave Rudler, working on the information given to him by the then Secretary of the Speculative Society, Sir David Mackenzie, about the Society's debates, came to the conclusion that Constant left Edinburgh 'during the half-yearly holidays, since Easter fell on 10 April that year' (*Jeunesse*, p. 169, note 1). However, Sir David Mackenzie gave Rudler information about those meetings at which Constant *spoke*, the last of these being that of 5 April 1785. The Society's *Minute Book* gives Constant as present at the meeting of 19 April 1785. It is clear, therefore, that he left Edinburgh between 19 April and 26 April 1785.

63. *Ma Vie*, ed. C. P. Courtney, p. 39: 'We had never been particularly close when we were in Edinburgh, but occasionally we had got drunk together.'

64. In the 'Character of H. B. Constant' quoted above.

65. Charrière, *Œuvres*, IV, p. 563, letter of 13 September 1794 from Isabelle de Charrière to Constant. On this point, see Wood (1984), p. 22.
66. *Adolphe*, ed. Paul Delbouille, p. 109.
67. *Library Borrowings Record* for the years 1783–5, Edinburgh, University Library.
68. RENATI DES CARTES MEDITATIONES *De Prima* PHILOSOPHIA, In quibus Dei Existentia, & Animae humanae à corpore Distinctio demonstrantur. *His adjuncta sunt variae objectiones doctorum virorum in istas de Deo & Anima demonstrationes*; CUM RESPONSIONIBUS AUCTORIS. *Editio ultima prioribus auctior & emendatior.* [vignette] *AMSTELODAMI*, Apud DANIELEM ELSEVIRIUM, [1678]. The title page bears the inscription 'James Praig prael 2^L 8^{s}:^{d}'. This second-hand copy was probably bought in Edinburgh.
69. Enrico Caterino Davila (1576–1631) is one of the historians singled out for discussion, along with 'De Thou, – Machiavel, – Bentivoglio, – Rawleigh, – Clarendon', in the lectures of Alexander Fraser Tytler (see later note).
70. *HSSE*, p. 147.
71. Several other hypotheses are possible, including schizophrenia, alcoholism and tertiary syphilis. Syphilis brings with it a gradual change in personality, insanity and eventual death. However Wilde lived on for another forty years after the onset of madness, and this would be unlikely if he were syphilitic. At least two other of his Edinburgh friends lost their minds: Lewis Grant (1767–1840) whose 'last thirty years of life were passed in seclusion, owing to incurable mental derangement' (*HSSE*, p. 168) and another member of the Speculative Society, Robert Urquhart who, according to Macknight's memoir, 'figured for a while in the highest style of the fashionable world, then lost his mind, and was reduced to perfect beggary, an incessant pest, I believe to the Court [he was an advocate], and to all who had ever know[n] or heard of him' (f. 155 verso). Knowledge of the insanity of some of his friends and the death of others must have contributed greatly to Constant's periods of pessimism and despair. And yet it is Isabelle de Charrière – in many ways a remarkably vigorous and positive personality – who generally gets the blame for Constant's pessimism: much of Rudler's biography is taken up with proving her guilt. The fact that Constant turned to writing and especially to scholarship may have had something to do with an increasing awareness of the possible long-term consequences of his early promiscuity. Something like this, however, could underlie the 'feeling of uncertainty about fate' (*Adolphe*, ed. Paul Delbouille, p. 112) which Constant shared with Adolphe and the fatalistic lassitude which, we are told, had diminished in Adolphe as he had grown older. It would be anachronistic, however, to suggest that Constant could have had any *precise* knowledge about the connection between the first stage of syphilis (local infection) and its third stage (madness, paralysis, death), which is a discovery of the twentieth century. On this, see Roger L. Williams, *The Horror of Life*, Chicago: University of Chicago Press, 1980, esp. pp. 48–51.
72. *HSSE*, p. 147.
73. On this, see David Daiches, *Sir Walter Scott and his World*, London: Thames & Hudson, 1971, pp. 35–6.
74. Courtney (1985), p. 281, letter from Juste to Samuel de Constant, 16 February 1786: 'He's followed courses in physics and chemistry but he never paid much attention, he's taken lessons in mathematics but without getting very far. All he likes is metaphysics, together with languages.' It is likely that Constant had private tuition from Edinburgh University teachers, as he did not formally register for such courses. He may possibly have been taught mathematics by

the eminent Professor John Playfair FRS (1748–1819), whom he appears to have met again in London in May 1816, something which gave him the wish to revisit Scotland – a journey he was never to make. See Wood (1986), p. 166.
75. Rudler, *Jeunesse*, p. 165, note 2.
76. Quoted in Sir Alexander Grant's *The Story of the University of Edinburgh* (see above, note 18), p. 326.
77. Alexander Fraser Tytler, Lord Woodhouselee, *Plan and Outlines of a Course of Lectures* . . . , Edinburgh, 1782, pp. 21 and 24.
78. *Ibid.*, p. 19
79. Charrière, *Œuvres*, IV, p. 573, letter to Isabelle de Charrière from Lausanne dated 26 September 1794: 'I must go to Germany to continue work on my book, which is the only thing in life that interests me.'
80. Alexander Fraser Tytler, *Plan and Outlines*, p. 3.
81. See Pierre Deguise's fundamental study *Benjamin Constant méconnu. Le Livre 'De la Religion'*, Geneva: Droz, 1966, pp. 42 ff.

3 ISABELLE DE CHARRIERE (1785–1787)

1. Constant, *Œuvres*, p. 474.
2. Apart from isolated passages in longer works on Constant, René Le Grand Roy's article is virtually the only treatment of an important subject, 'La passion du jeu chez Benjamin Constant', in *Benjamin Constant. Actes du congrès de Lausanne (octobre 1967)*, Geneva: Droz (Histoire des idées et critique littéraire, 91), 1968, pp. 201–14. Interestingly – and in a classic case of the poacher turning gamekeeper – Constant advocated the banning of gambling and lotteries when addressing the Société de la morale chrétienne (Society for Christian Morality) towards the end of his life (Benjamin-Nicolas-Marie Appert, *Dix ans à la cour du roi Louis-Philippe et souvenirs du temps de l'Empire et de la Restauration*, Berlin: Voss; Paris: J. Renouard, 1848, 3 vols, vol. III, pp. 75–7).
3. Benjamin Constant, *De l'esprit de conquête et de l'usurpation*, ed. Ephraïm Harpaz, Paris: GF Flammarion (Œuvres de Philosophie politique, GF 456), 1986, chapitre V, p. 96. Georges Poulet touches on the subject of gambling in *Benjamin Constant par lui-même*, Paris: Du Seuil (Ecrivains de toujours, 78), 1968, pp. 57–8.
4. Han Verhoeff, *'Adolphe' et Constant: une étude psychocritique*, Paris: Editions Klincksieck (Bibliothèque française et romane, série C: Etudes littéraires, 56), 1976, p. 99.
5. *Ma Vie*, ed. C. P. Courtney, p. 10.
6. Dennis Wood, 'Constant in Edinburgh: eloquence and history', *French Studies* XL (1986), pp. 165–6, note 42.
7. *Ma Vie*, ed. C. P. Courtney, p. 10.
8. *Ibid.*, p. 11.
9. *Ibid.*, p. 12.
10. *Ibid.*, p. 12.
11. Constant, *Correspondance I (1774–1792)*, letter 15 dating from November 1785. The three letters in question are letters 15–17.
12. *Ibid.*, letter 16.
13. *Adolphe*, ed. Paul Delbouille, p. 205.
14. *Ma Vie*, ed. C. P. Courtney, p. 13.
15. Harold Nicolson, *Benjamin Constant*, London: Constable, 1949, p. 32.
16. Charrière, *Œuvres*, III, p. 56.
17. *Ma Vie*, ed. C. P. Courtney, p. 12.

18. Quoted in Dennis Wood, 'Constant in Britain 1780–1787: a provisional chronology', *ABC*, no. 7 (1987), p. 10. See also Frédéric Barbey, *Libertés vaudoises d'après le journal inédit de Philippe Secretan (1756–1826)*, Geneva: Labor et Fides, 1953, pp. 43–4.

19. Constant, *Correspondance I (1774–1792)*, letter 16.

20. See, for example, Constant's journal entry for 8 April 1804: '[I must spend the] winter in Germany. It is only there that I shall be encouraged to finish the book which is the sole interest, the only consolation in my life' (*Œuvres*, p. 289).

21. See Benjamin Constant, *De la religion considérée dans sa source, ses formes et ses développements. Livre premier suivi d'extraits des autres livres*, Postface et notes de Pierre Deguise, Lausanne: Bibliothèque romande, 1971, p. 269. Constant claimed to 'appartenir à la confession chrétienne'.

22. See C. P. Courtney, *A Bibliography of Editions of the Writings of Benjamin Constant to 1833*, London: Modern Humanities Research Association, 1981, pp. 3–6.

23. Rudler, *Jeunesse*, p. 183.

24. Charrière, *Œuvres*, III, p. 74.

25. On the political situation in Lausanne and the Pays de Vaud at this period, see Charles Burnier, *La Vie vaudoise et la Révolution. De la servitude à la liberté*, Lausanne: Bridel, 1902.

26. See William [et Clara de Charrière] de Sévery, *La Vie de société dans le Pays de Vaud à la fin du dix-huitième siècle. Salomon et Catherine de Charrière de Sévery et leurs amis*, Lausanne: Georges Bridel; Paris: Fischbacher, 1911–12, 2 vols, vol. I, p. 154. The exact date of the 'harangue' is unclear. On Constant's connections with Lausanne, see *Benjamin Constant 1767–1830 et Lausanne* (exhibition catalogue), Lausanne: Association Benjamin Constant, 1980 and, on his complex relationship with Switzerland, Roger Francillon, 'Benjamin Constant ou la Suisse refoulée', *ABC*, no. 13 (1992), pp. 115–28. In a *Notice* on Constant's life dated April 1831, Jean-Jacques Coulmann gives a unique and valuable insight into Constant's early hatred of injustice, quoting an anecdote from a now lost manuscript by Constant:

> I was quick-tempered by nature, opposed to all injustice, and with my boyhood friends I automatically took the side of the weakest against the strongest. My father used to say to me: 'What you're doing is both a good thing and a bad thing. It's good because you are earning yourself a reputation for generosity of character, because you're so ready to get involved in disagreements for which you are the one who pays the price rather than the boy who was originally involved. At the moment it is of little consequence, being beaten by one of your playmates who stole the apples which you didn't eat, or whom the master of the house caught in the act of breaking windows, and whom he would have hit hard if you had not been there to receive the blows yourself. But as you grow older, things become more serious. If you wade in to defend a man every time you see there are two men against him, you will suffer for it, I warn you.'
> (J.-J. Coulmann, *Notice sur Benjamin Constant. . .*, Paris: Crapelet, 1831, pp. 5–6)

27. Constant, *Correspondance I (1774–1792)*, letter 21.

28. On this fascinating subject, see Patrice Thompson's article 'Pratique de la "double ironie" chez Constant' in *Benjamin Constant, Madame de Staël et le Groupe de Coppet*, ed. Etienne Hofmann, Oxford: The Voltaire Foundation; Lausanne: Institut Benjamin Constant, 1982, pp. 287–304. According to Sainte-

Beuve, Constant once told a surprised interlocutor: 'Ce que vous dites là est si juste que le contraire est parfaitement vrai', 'What you've just said is so right that the opposite is perfectly true' (see Dennis Wood, *Benjamin Constant: 'Adolphe'*, Cambridge: Cambridge University Press [Landmarks of World Literature], 1987, p. 33). Constant wrote from Weimar to his aunt Anne de Nassau on 23 January 1804:

> Why, might I ask, do you accuse me of having a weak character? It's an accusation all *enlightened* people are exposed to because they see both – or rather the thousand – sides of everything they look at, so that they find it impossible to make up their minds, and appear to be leaning now to this side, now to that. But that is good sense, it's not weakness, and you know perfectly well, my dear Aunt, that you are as indecisive as me.
>
> (Melegari [1895], p. 329)

It is not impossible that his known tendency to laugh uproariously – or hysterically – at moments of great and serious emotion was related to this ability to stand outside himself and his situation. Apropos of the pianist Glenn Gould and his capacity for laughter and irreverence, Nicholas Spice has written:

> The presence of the fool . . . not far below the surface of Gould's playing gives it an exhilarating ambiguity, in which total commitment and peals of laughter, extraordinary beauty and hilarity, seem to alternate. [He] understood that humour is not about responding to self-consciously funny things, but about laughing at those aspects of life and art which are deadly serious. Humour arises when the things we most love or fear are tested to the limit, when we allow ourselves to consider for a moment that what we regard as everything is in fact nothing. In this sense, humour is the capacity to be radical, to pull up settled things and look at their roots.
>
> ('How to play the piano', *London Review of Books*, vol. 14, no. 6 [26 March 1992], p. 7)

These comments would apply equally well to Constant, and strike me as much nearer to the reality than Han Verhoeff's view that the basis of Constant's laughter was aggression directed at his listeners (*op. cit.*, p. 92).

29. Rudler, *Jeunesse*, p. 126.
30. *Ibid.*
31. *Ibid.*
32. Benjamin et Rosalie de Constant, *Correspondance 1786–1830*, ed. Alfred et Suzanne Roulin, Paris: Gallimard, 1955, p. 3, letter of 19 March 1786.
33. Charrière, *Œuvres*, III, p. 56.
34. Charrière, *Œuvres*, IV, p. 182, letter of 25 September 1793.
35. *Ma Vie*, ed. C. P. Courtney, p. 15.
36. Rudler, *Jeunesse*, pp. 142–3.
37. *Ibid.*, pp. 143–4.
38. *Ibid.*, p. 144.
39. *Ibid.*, p. 145.
40. *Ma Vie*, ed. C. P. Courtney, p. 17.
41. Lausanne, Bibliothèque cantonale et universitaire, Fonds Constant II, 34/13, MS of *Ma Vie*, f. 22 verso.
42. Constant, *Œuvres*, p. 1458.
43. William [et Clara de Charrière] de Sévery, *op. cit.*, vol. I, pp. 151–2.
44. *Le Journal de Gibbon à Lausanne 17 août 1763–19 avril 1764*, ed. Georges

Bonnard, Lausanne: Librairie de l'Université, Lausanne, F. Rouge & Cie S.A. (Université de Lausanne, Publications de la Faculté des Lettres, VIII), 1945, p. 59. The Latin quotation is from Juvenal's *Satires*, IV, 2.

45. It is clear that they corresponded from Constant's letters of 4 August 1789 and 17 September 1790 to Isabelle de Charrière (Charrière, *Œuvres*, III, pp. 144, 236 and 648).
46. Charles de Constant's description in his *Journal*, quoted in Rudler, *Jeunesse*, p. 38.
47. Charrière, *Œuvres*, III, p. 144.
48. *Ibid.* (letter of 4 August 1789).
49. *Ma Vie*, ed. C. P. Courtney, p. 15.
50. *Ibid.*, pp. 18–20.
51. Information from Charles de Constant's *Journal*, Rudler, *Jeunesse*, pp. 150–1.
52. See Philippe Godet, *Madame de Charrière et ses amis d'après de nombreux documents inédits (1740–1805)*, Geneva: Jullien, 1906, 2 vols (reprinted Geneva: Slatkine Reprints, 1973), vol. I, pp. 339–40, where it is suggested that Constant and Madame de Charrière saw each other at Madame Saurin's.
53. On 6 March 1787 Charles de Constant wrote to his father Samuel:

> Lisette tells me that you would like to be informed about who I know here. This is how I spend my week: Monday is Madame Suard's salon, Tuesday Madame de Molé, Wednesday Madame Prévot, Thursday Madame Gaillard, Friday Madame Pauw, Saturday Madame Piscatory. I can't in fact accept all the invitations and respond to all the kindness I've been shown. I've met Madame Charrière de Zuilen, that has kept me occupied too [*jai fait connoissances avec M^e. Charrière de Zuilen voila encore de l'occupation*].
>
> (Geneva, Bibliothèque publique et universitaire, Manuscrits Constant 17, lettres de Charles de Constant à Samuel de Constant 1776–1800, f. 89)

Constant will have been with Charles at least some of the time at these various gatherings, at one of which he had in all probability recently met Madame de Charrière. The two cousins were not always at daggers drawn in Paris. Charles, who was hoping to get involved in another trading venture such as had taken him to Canton, told his father Samuel in his letter of 4 January 1787:

> I'm prepared to go to the other end of the world rather than lead the life of an idler here. I couldn't bear it at my age. Benjamin who is in pretty much the same situation as me is very miserable at the idea too. We make fine statements about our position but they don't get us anywhere.
>
> (Manuscrits Constant 17, f. 73)

Although Charles's writings on trade with China have been published (Louis Dermigny, *Les Mémoires de Charles de Constant sur le commerce à la Chine*, Paris: S.É.V.P.E.N., 1964), his letters and journal are largely unpublished and constitute a quite invaluable source of information, albeit often strongly biased, on this, a time of intense political activity in Paris with the Assemblée des notables, as well as on later periods of his cousin's life. He clearly had literary talent like his father Samuel, and this no doubt exacerbated his jealousy of Benjamin, and made his bewildered resentment at Benjamin's later success more keenly felt. In his letters to his sister Rosalie, Charles shows a marked tendency to moralize, and there would of course be no shortage of material to work on, especially during Constant's relationship with Germaine de Staël. Simone Balayé's article 'Benjamin Constant et son cousin Charles de Constant à Paris en 1796' (*Benjamin Constant et la Révolution française*, ed. Dominique Verrey et Anne-Lise Delacrétaz, Geneva: Droz [Université de Lausanne, Publications de la Faculté des Lettres, XXXII], 1989, pp. 97–118) draws on Charles's writings to throw light on the year of such events as Constant's purchase of Hérivaux and his duel with Bertin de Vaux, and on his relationship with Germaine de Staël and her circle.

54. See C. P. Courtney's recent biography *Isabelle de Charrière (Belle de Zuylen): A Biography*, Oxford: The Voltaire Foundation, 1993. A very extensive bibliography has grown up around Isabelle de Charrière in recent years, and a journal, the *Lettre de Zuylen et du Pontet*, (1976–), is published annually by the Dutch Genootschap Belle de Zuylen and the Swiss Association des Amis de Madame de Charrière. On this, see C. P. Courtney, *Isabelle de Charrière (Belle de Zuylen): A Secondary Bibliography*, Oxford: The Voltaire Foundation; Paris: Jean Touzot libraire-éditeur, 1982.

55. Charrière, *Œuvres*, I–VI, published 1979–84.

56. Charrière, *Œuvres*, X, pp. 37–9. The self-portrait gave Geoffrey Scott the title of his well-known and still useful biography *The Portrait of Zélide*, London: Constable, 1925.

57. The pastel is reproduced in colour as the frontispiece to volume I of Philippe Godet's biography (see note 52 above), and is to be seen at the Musée d'Art et d'histoire, Geneva. A superb portrait of 1777 by the Danish painter Jens Juel (1745–1802) hangs in the Bibliothèque publique et universitaire, Neuchâtel, and is reproduced in the beautifully printed and illustrated collection *Madame de Charrière à Colombier*, iconographie rassemblée et présentée par Constance Thompson Pasquali, Neuchâtel: Bibliothèque de la Ville, 1979, p. 13.

58. See Charrière, *Œuvres*, I and II. Isabelle's first letter to Baron Constant d'Hermenches dates from 22 March 1760, the last from him to her is dated 12 December 1776.

59. James Boswell wrote to his friend Temple on 19 March 1765: '[Zélide] has more genius than any other woman I ever saw, and more acquired perfections. I shall correspond with her as a *bel esprit*, but I think it would be madness to marry her' (Charrière, *Œuvres*, I, p. 594). For Boswell's correspondence with her, see vol. I of the Charrière *Œuvres*, and also Frederick A. Pottle's three books: *Boswell in Holland, 1763–1764, including his Correspondence with Belle de Zuylen (Zélide)*, New York: McGraw-Hill; London: W. Heinemann, 1952; *Boswell on the Grand Tour: Germany and Switzerland, 1764*, New York: McGraw-Hill; London: W. Heinemann, 1953; and *Boswell on the Grand Tour: Italy, Corsica, and France, 1765–1766*, edited with Frank Brady, New York: McGraw-Hill; London: W. Heinemann, 1955.

60. George Eliot, *Daniel Deronda*, ed. Graham Handley, Oxford: Clarendon Press, 1984, p. 588.

61. See C. P. Courtney, *A Preliminary Bibliography of Isabelle de Charrière (Belle de Zuylen)*, Oxford: The Voltaire Foundation (Studies on Voltaire and the eighteenth century, 186), 1980, pp. 25–32. *Le Noble, conte moral* is published in Charrière, *Œuvres*, VIII, pp. 19–34.

62. Charrière, *Œuvres*, II, p. 205, letter from Baron Constant d'Hermenches of 8 August 1770.

63. Charrière, *Œuvres*, II, p. 218, letter to Baron Constant d'Hermenches of 12 October 1770.

64. Charrière, *Œuvres*, II, p. 239, letter of 13 May 1771.

65. *Ma Vie*, ed. C. P. Courtney, pp. 20–1.

66. Vincent-Louis-Rodolphe de Saussure (1747–1826) who married Lucie-Alexand-rine – 'Alix' – Mercier (1765–1828).
67. See *Ma Vie*, ed. C. P. Courtney, Appendix, 'A note on Caliste', pp. 65–7, and his forthcoming biography.
68. Philippe Godet devotes a whole chapter to the enigma: 'Un mystère', *op. cit.*, vol. I, pp. 238–55.
69. Isabelle de Charrière was alone in Paris at the beginning of her stay, and was joined by her husband later. Charles-Emmanuel de Charrière wrote to Dudley Ryder on 25 October 1786:

> My wife spent the winter in Paris and she's still there. Her health is better. Music is her ruling passion. She has a teacher for composition and spends whole days at her pianoforte. She sends me the pieces she's com-posed which are really delightful. I've urged her not to leave Paris at the beginning of the winter in order to come and spend it in Colombier. I intend to go and join her there and we shall return together in the spring.
>
> (Harrowby Mss Trust, Sandon Hall, Stafford, Ryder Papers, 'General Correspondence Hon. Dudley Ryder 1784–1803', vol. VIII, ff. 29–30)

While in Paris Monsieur de Charrière was prevailed upon by the young Constant to lend him money, a loan which he took a long time to repay.
70. Charles-Emmanuel de Charrière's letters to Dudley Ryder contain several refer-ences to the woman he so admired, Alix de Saussure-Mercier, in particular one dated 17 April 1794 where he tells his English friend:

> My connection [*Ma liaison*] with Madame de Saussure of which you saw the beginning is now a firm friendship and for life. Your liking for her was equal to my own and certainly if you had the opportunity to see her often in England you would also become her friend.
>
> (Ryder Papers, vol. VIII, f. 54)

Charrière's friendship with her appears to date from 1785 or perhaps even earlier.
71. Charrière, *Œuvres*, II, p. 262.
72. For other examples, see Dennis Wood, 'Constant's *Cahier rouge*: new findings', *French Studies*, XXXVIII (1984), pp. 13–29.
73. Philippe Godet, *op. cit.*, vol. I, p. 249, from a facsimile page of Chaillet's *Journal*.
74. On this unusual man, see Charly Guyot, *La Vie intellectuelle et religieuse en Suisse française à la fin du XVIIIᵉ siècle: Henri-David de Chaillet, 1751–1823*, Neuchâtel: A la Baconnière, 1946. An example of the asperity of Isabelle de Charrière's wit is her comment on the hypocritical Chaillet's signing himself 'Chaillet, serviteur de Jésus-Christ' ('Chaillet, servant of Jesus Christ'): 'On ne dira pas: Tel maître, tel valet' ('No one will say: Like master, like man') (Philippe Godet, *op. cit.*, vol. II, p. 249).
75. There is a strong hint that Benjamin Constant knew of Charles-Emmanuel de Charrière's infidelity in a letter to Isabelle de Charrière from Brunswick dated 13–14 April 1788: 'How our correspondence has changed! And as long as you don't deign to let me hope that you won't go on forever punishing me for crimes you saw committed before you knew me [*des crimes que vous avez vus commettre avant de me connaître*], it will continue to have no charm for me' (Charrière, *Œuvres*, III, p. 84).
76. *Ma Vie*, ed. C. P. Courtney, p. 21.

BENJAMIN CONSTANT

4 ESCAPE (1787–1788)

1. Constant, *Œuvres*, pp. 350–1.
2. Edouard Laboulaye, article in the *Revue nationale et étrangère*, V (1867), p. 344: 'cette hardiesse d'esprit, . . . ce besoin d'aller au fond des choses, qui nous explique la lucidité de ses idées, la transparence de sa parole.'
3. *Ma Vie*, ed. C. P. Courtney, pp. 21–2.
4. *Ibid.*, p. 24.
5. *Ibid.*, p. 25.
6. See earlier, Chapter 3, note 28.
7. *Ma Vie*, ed. C. P. Courtney, p. 28.
8. Charrière, *Œuvres*, III, pp. 24–5, letter from Constant to Isabelle de Charrière of 26 June 1787.
9. *Ma Vie*, ed. C. P. Courtney, p. 34.
10. *Ibid.*, p. 29.
11. *Ibid.*, p. 21: 'des rapports plus intimes et plus essentiels'.
12. *Ibid.*, pp. 31–2.
13. [Michel de] Montaigne, *Œuvres complètes*, ed. Albert Thibaudet et Maurice Rat, Paris: Gallimard (Bibliothèque de la Pléiade), 1962, [*Essais*] III, xiii, p. 1053.
14. *Cécile*, ed. Paul Delbouille, p. 183.
15. *Cécile*, ed. Paul Delbouille, p. 182: 'bizarre d'ailleurs, et déjà vieille'; *Ma Vie*, ed. C. P. Courtney, p. 22: 'bizarre et dédaigneux que j'étais aussi'; *Adolphe*, ed. Paul Delbouille, p. 112: 'dont l'esprit, d'une tournure remarquable et bizarre, avait commencé à développer le mien'.
16. Charrière, *Œuvres*, III, p. 207, letter of 11 May 1790: 'vous serez toujours le plus cher & le plus étrange de mes Souvenirs'.
17. *Ibid.*, p. 23, letter of 26 June 1787.
18. See Dennis Wood, 'Constant's *Cahier rouge*: new findings', *French Studies*, XXXVIII (1984), p. 17, for the French text of the letter. For details of Philippe Rivier's career and family, see Théodore Rivier-Rose, *La Famille Rivier (1595 à nos jours)*, Lausanne: Imprimeries réunies, 1916, pp. 62, 78–9, 121, 130, and 212–13.
19. Charrière, *Œuvres*, III, p. 26.
20. *Ibid.*, p. 31.
21. *Ibid.*, p. 31.
22. See Dennis Wood, 'Constant in Britain 1780–1787: a provisional chronology', *ABC*, no. 7 (1987), p. 16.
23. *Ma Vie*, ed. C. P. Courtney, p. 52. Juste was making every effort meanwhile to minimize the significance of his son's act of disobedience, and wrote to his Paris banker, the Swiss Rodolphe-Ferdinand Grand (1726–94), on 27 September 1787:

> My son, having spent six weeks in the country with my friend Bridges, has returned to Switzerland where he has now been for a while. His excursion to England was undertaken without any particular purpose and has had no unpleasant consequences. He lived in very good company while he was there, and apart from the expense little harm has been done.

On this obvious tampering with the truth on Juste's part, see Henri Bressler, 'Une lettre peu véridique sur un épisode du *Cahier rouge*', *Cahiers Benjamin Constant*, série I, no. 2 (1957), pp. 43–7.
24. *Ibid.*, p. 54: 'je lui disais que comme il traitait ses amis comme des chiens, je me flattais qu'il traiterait ce chien comme un ami'. For an account of Richard

Kentish's colourful career, see Dennis Wood, 'Constant's *Cahier rouge*: new findings', *French Studies*, XXXVIII (1984), pp. 18–20.

25. *Ibid.*, pp. 57–9.
26. See *Adolphe*, ed. Paul Delbouille, pp. 110–11.
27. William [et Clara de Charrière] de Sévery, *La Vie de société dans le Pays de Vaud à la fin du dix-huitième siècle. Salomon et Catherine de Charrière de Sévery et leurs amis*, Lausanne: Georges Bridel; Paris: Fischbacher, 1911–12, 2 vols, vol. I, pp. 151–2.
28. *Ibid.*, p. 155.
29. The Duke had ruled since 1780. On his life, see Selma Stern, *Karl Wilhelm Ferdinand. Herzog zu Braunschweig und Lüneburg*, Hildesheim und Leipzig: August Lax Verlagsbuchhandlung (Veröffentlichungen der historischen Kommission für Hannover, Oldenburg, Braunschweig, Schaumburg-Lippe und Bremen), 1921.
30. William [et Clara de Charrière] de Sévery, *op. cit.*, p. 154.
31. See C. P. Courtney, *The Affair of Colonel Juste de Constant and Related Documents (1787–1796)*, Cambridge: Dæmon Press, 1990.
32. See William [et Clara de Charrière] de Sévery, *op. cit.*, pp. 153–4, Paul-Louis Pelet, 'Le premier duel de Benjamin Constant', *Études de lettres*, XXI (1947), pp. 25–6, and Charrière, *Œuvres*, III, p. 611.
33. *Lettres de d'Arsillé fils* appeared for the first time in 1981 in Charrière, *Œuvres*, IX, pp. 651–78. It seems to have been composed either in 1787–8 or during a subsequent visit to Colombier by Constant. On the complex issues raised by the manuscript which is written and corrected in the hands of both Constant and Madame de Charrière, see Dennis Wood, 'Isabelle de Charrière et Benjamin Constant: à propos d'une découverte récente', *Studies on Voltaire and the eighteenth century*, CCXV (1982), pp. 273–9, Dennis Wood, 'Isabelle de Charrière et Benjamin Constant: problématique d'une collaboration', *ABC*, no. 4 (1984), pp. 17–30, and for a brief summary in English, Dennis Wood, 'Benjamin Constant's first novel?', *Times Literary Supplement*, 6 February 1981, p. 151.
34. Charrière, *Œuvres*, VI, p. 565, letter to Baron Taets van Amerongen of February 1804.
35. Dominique Verrey, *Chronologie de la vie et de l'œuvre de Benjamin Constant. Avec la collaboration du professeur Etienne Hofmann, tome I: 1767–1805*, Geneva: Editions Slatkine, 1992, p. 64, entry 282.

5 THE BRUNSWICK YEARS (1788–1794)

1. Charrière, *Œuvres*, III, pp. 49–50.
2. Charrière, *Œuvres*, III, p. 51.
3. Charrière, *Œuvres*, III, pp. 52–3.
4. Rudler, *Jeunesse*, p. 294. See also pp. 291–301 for a description of Court life and etiquette.
5. Charrière, *Œuvres*, III, pp. 55–6.
6. Charrière, *Œuvres*, III, p. 86.
7. *Adolphe*, ed. Paul Delbouille, pp. 113–16.
8. On Constant's friendship with Mauvillon, see Rudler, *Jeunesse*, pp. 413–16, and Marcus Fontius's useful article 'Constant und die Mauvillons' in *ABC*, no. 10 (1989), pp. 9–23.
9. Melegari (1895), pp. 187–8.
10. Constant, *Œuvres*, p. 482.
11. Marcus Fontius, *op. cit.*, p. 12.

12. Marcus Fontius, *op. cit.*, p. 18.
13. Marcus Fontius, *op. cit.*, pp. 17–18.
14. 'hier Benjamin dinna ches M^de De Pailly avec M. Demirabeau' ('Yesterday Benjamin dined at Madame de Pailly's with Monsieur de Mirabeau'), Constant's cousin Charles told his father Samuel de Constant in an undated letter of January 1787 (Geneva, Bibliothèque publique et universitaire, MS Constant 17, f. 77, unpublished).
15. Marcus Fontius, *op. cit.*, p. 11.
16. Charrière, *Œuvres*, III, p. 74, letter of 19–21 March 1788.
17. Benjamin Constant, *The Affair of Colonel Juste de Constant and Related Documents (1787–1796)*, published with an Introduction by C. P. Courtney, Cambridge: Dæmon Press, 1990. See also Dominique Verrey, 'L'affaire Juste de Constant (1787–1796)' in *Benjamin Constant et la Révolution française 1789–1799*, ed. Dominique Verrey et Anne-Lise Delacrétaz, Geneva: Droz, 1989, pp. 73–81.
18. Constant, *Correspondance I (1774–1792)*, lettre 54.
19. See Constant, *Correspondance I (1774–1792)*, letter from Benjamin Constant to Samuel de Constant dated 1 November 1788.
20. 'Marié à une femme que j'avais épousée par faiblesse', *Cécile*, ed. Paul Delbouille, p. 172.
21. Lausanne, Bibliothèque cantonale et universitaire, Fonds Constant II, 34/4, unpublished.
22. Geneva, Bibliothèque publique et universitaire, MS Constant 24/1, unpublished.
23. See Elizabeth W. Schermerhorn, *Benjamin Constant, his Life and his Contribution to the Cause of Liberal Government in France 1767–1830*, Boston and New York: Houghton Mifflin, 1924, p. 96.
24. Rudler, *Jeunesse*, p. 359.
25. Rudler, *Jeunesse*, p. 296.
26. Constant, *Œuvres*, pp. 338–9.
27. Constant, *Correspondance I (1774–1792)*, lettre 64: 'Je ne vis plus que par mon père & pour mon père.'
28. Melegari (1895), p. 168.
29. Serenissimi gnädigste Deklaration für den Legationsrat Heinrich Benjamin von Constant, Braunschweig, den 27. Dezember 1788, Wolfenbüttel, Niedersächsisches Staatsarchiv, MS 3 Alt 263.
30. William [et Clara de Charrière] de Sévery, *La Vie de société dans le Pays de Vaud à la fin du dix-huitième siècle*, Lausanne: Bridel; Paris: Fischbacher, 1911–12, 2 vols, vol. I, p. 156.
31. Rudler, *Jeunesse*, p. 355. The date of Constant's marriage to Minna is confirmed by a manuscript nineteenth-century family tree of the Von Cramms as being '8/5 1789' (Wolfenbüttel, Niedersächsisches Staatsarchiv, 26 Slg Nr. 97R, 'Stammtafel der Familie von Cramm, aufgestellt von Kammerdirektor Frh. v. Löhneysen [um 1880]'). The family had four distinct branches at this period, and Minna did indeed have very numerous relatives, to whom Constant alludes on occasion. The banns were published in the Lutheran St. Blasius Cathedral in Brunswick, and the marriage took place at the Duchess Augusta's elegant Richmond Palace (*Benjamin Constant*, [exhibition catalogue], Paris: Bibliothèque nationale, 1967, p. 20).
32. *Ma Vie*, ed. C. P. Courtney, Cambridge: Dæmon Press, 1991, p. 14.
33. *Benjamin Constant, Madame de Staël et le Groupe de Coppet*, ed. Etienne Hofmann, Oxford: The Voltaire Foundation; Lausanne: Institut Benjamin Constant, 1982, p. 355.

34. One of the earliest accusations of 'défiance' Constant makes against Isabelle occurs in his letter of 9–14 March 1788: 'J'ai souvent remarqué cette défiance triste et humble, mais songez qu'elle détruit toute jouissance' ('I have often noticed that sad and humble lack of trust in you, but remember it destroys all pleasure') (Charrière, *Œuvres*, III, p. 68). Interestingly from a psychological point of view, Constant goes on to speak of the way his relationship with his father had been ruined by a similar lack of openness and trust on Juste's part.
35. Rudler, *Jeunesse*, p. 364, note 3.
36. Charrière, *Œuvres*, III, p. 152.
37. Charrière, *Œuvres*, III, p. 221.
38. *Ibid.*
39. Charrière, *Œuvres*, III, p. 251.
40. Charrière, *Œuvres*, III, p. 254.
41. Charrière, *Œuvres*, III, pp. 273–4.
42. Kurt Kloocke, *Benjamin Constant: une biographie intellectuelle*, Geneva–Paris: Droz, 1984, pp. 29 ff.
43. Lausanne, Bibliothèque cantonale et universitaire, MS Co 2848.
44. *Recueil de généalogies vaudoises*, publié par la Société vaudoise de généalogie, Lausanne: Bridel, 1923, vol. I, p. 222. *Louise*-Philippine de Rebecque, daughter of Marianne and Juste and half-sister to Benjamin, was born on 3 June 1792.
45. On this episode and, more generally, on the growing estrangement between Constant and Minna, see Kurt Kloocke, 'Benjamin Constant et Min[n]a von Cramm: documents inédits', *ABC*, no. 2 (1982), pp. 88–109. The article contains the full text of the *Narré* or account of the breakdown of his marriage which Constant was to write in March 1793.
46. Charrière, *Œuvres*, III, pp. 416–17.
47. See Kurt Kloocke, *art. cit.*, pp. 82 and 106. Dmitri Vladimirovich Golitsyn was a cavalry general and later Governor of Moscow. As a young man he was sent with his elder brother Boris to Strasbourg Military Academy where he stayed for six years. He returned to Russia at the start of the French Revolution, but was later involved in the storming of Prague in 1794. I am grateful to my colleague Professor R. E. F. Smith for his help in identifying 'le Prince Galizin' from Russian sources. The young man appears in *Cécile* in the guise of 'le Prince Narischkin'.
48. Charrière, *Œuvres*, III, p. 416, letter from Constant to Isabelle dated 17 September 1792: 'My father has just asked me to give up more than a third of my fortune to Marianne.'
49. Charrière, *Œuvres*, III, p. 480.
50. Charrière, *Œuvres*, III, p. 435, letter from Constant to Isabelle de Charrière of 5 November 1792.
51. Kurt Kloocke, *art. cit.*, p. 91.
52. Wolfenbüttel, Herzog August Bibliothek, Cod. Guelf. Nachlass Langer, MS BA II, 111, Briefe an Langer, unpublished letter, incipit: 'Monsieur/Je vous accuse le reçu de deux Volumes Beytraege'.
53. In *Cécile* Charlotte becomes the fictional character 'Cécile de Walterbourg'.
54. Despite its many inaccuracies Dorette Berthoud's *La Seconde Madame Benjamin Constant* (Lausanne: Payot, 1943) remains an indispensable guide to Charlotte von Hardenberg's life and her relationship with Constant.
55. Harold Nicolson, *Benjamin Constant*, London: Constable, 1949, p. 87.
56. The incident is recounted in his letter to Isabelle of 28 April 1794 (Charrière, *Œuvres*, IV, pp. 410–11) and is worth quoting in full:

Before I go any further I must give you quite an amusing example of

Charlottechen's stupidity. At a time when my love was only sickly and not yet moribund, I was impatient at receiving no news from her. I thought that her father – that guardian angel to whom I owe so much – was intercepting the 'sighs which were on their way from one pole to the other' [Charlotte's fanciful description of her correspondence with Constant], and I wanted to find some way of making at least one of my love letters impenetrable to his vigilant eye. I wrote to Charlotte using the name of a bookseller and saying that I had sold her books. The titles of these books were a list of the memorable moments in our chaste *amours*. I reminded her of the day, the place, the hour, the object, and finally I mentioned Henri – my *nom de guerre* at the time – and Charlotte. I dated it from *Dove-house* [i.e. Colombier, the town where Madame de Charrière lived] and signed myself *Bécé* [i.e. B.C.]. Certainly it was difficult to make things more plain. In order to have some reason for sending the letter, I ended by telling her that the books cost 32 *louis* and that I looked forward to receiving that amount from her. I knew that when he saw a bill for 32 *louis*, her worthy father would give up all claim to the correspondence and would speedily take the missive to his daughter. Since my suspicions about interception were completely groundless, the letter did go straight into the fat white hands of Charlotte. Would you believe that she didn't understand a single word of it? That she thought it really *was* a bill and that she sent from house to house asking everyone she knew to explain to her what it was all about, where was Dove-house and who was this bookseller Bécé, from whom she insisted she had never bought a thing? And thus my letter went all round the town without a soul understanding it, even though the name 'Dove-house' was clear enough for anyone who knew I was at Colombier – and everybody did know I was there – and my faulty English must have given away the fact that I was a foreigner? Finally the letter reached a man who knows some English and had guessed about my relationship with Charlotte. He explained the joke to her and she burned the fateful letter. You must admit no one was ever more stupid than that!

57. Dorette Berthoud, *op. cit.*, p.22.
58. See note 56 above.
59. Constant, *Œuvres*, p. 339, diary entry for 18 July 1804.
60. *Cécile*, ed. Paul Delbouille, p. 177. Interestingly Constant's father had indeed given him a piano – Benjamin was a good keyboard player – and in his letter of 24 August 1790 asked him: 'Are you using the piano? Is it repaired?' (Constant, *Correspondance I (1774–1792)*, lettre 97).
61. Wolfenbüttel, Herzog August Bibliothek, Cod. Guelf. Nachlass Langer, MS BA II, 107, Briefe an Langer von Féronce v. Rotencreutz.
62. Charrière, *Œuvres*, III, p. 593.
63. Rudler, *Jeunesse*, p. 402.
64. Constant, *Œuvres*, pp. 301–2, diary entry for 2 May 1804.
65. Charrière, *Œuvres*, IV, p. 209.
66. Charrière, *Œuvres*, IV, p. 67.
67. See Dennis Wood, 'Isabelle de Charrière et Benjamin Constant: problématique d'une collaboration', *ABC*, no. 4 (1984), pp. 17–30.
68. See Sabine Dorothea Jordan, *Ludwig Ferdinand Huber (1764–1804), his Life and Works*, Stuttgart: Hans-Dieter Heinz (Stuttgarter Arbeiten zur Germanistik, Nr. 57), 1978, and Jean-Daniel Candaux, 'L.F. Huber chez Benjamin Constant

(décembre 1794)', in *Benjamin Constant et la Révolution française 1789–1799*, ed. Dominique Verrey et Anne-Lise Delacrétaz, *op. cit.*, pp. 89–96.

69. Charrière, *Œuvres*, IV, p. 166.
70. Procès-verbal de comparution, Lausanne, Bibliothèque cantonale et universitaire, MS Co 4881/139, unpublished.
71. Charrière, *Œuvres*, IV, p. 266.
72. Melegari (1895), p. 205.
73. Charrière, *Œuvres*, IV, p. 350.
74. Charrière, *Œuvres*, IV, p. 386.
75. Charrière, *Œuvres*, IV, p. 395.
76. Melegari (1895), p. 211.
77. Charrière, *Œuvres*, IV, pp. 396 and 819, letter to Isabelle de Charrière of 20 April 1794.
78. Kurt Kloocke, *Benjamin Constant: une biographie intellectuelle*, *op. cit.*, pp. 47–8, note 116, letter from Constant to Langer of 26 April 1794. (It should be noted that in several places the transcription Kloocke gives is inaccurate). Mechthild Raabe, *Leser und Lektüre im 18. Jahrhundert. Die Ausleihbücher der Herzog August Bibliothek Wolfenbüttel 1714–1799* (München, London, New York, Paris: K. G. Saur, 1989, 4 vols) lists Constant's library borrowings, ten books connected with the history of religion between 29 April 1792 and 12 June 1794, correcting Kloocke, *op. cit.*, p. 48, n. 116 (vol. I, p. 76). Also listed are the borrowings of Mauvillon and others from Wolfenbüttel.
79. Charrière, *Œuvres*, IV, p. 440.
80. Charrière, *Œuvres*, IV, p. 505.
81. Constant, *Œuvres*, p. 338.
82. Charrière, *Œuvres*, IV, p. 428, letter from Constant to Isabelle de Charrière of 12 May 1794.
83. Charrière, *Œuvres*, IV, p. 429.
84. Charrière, *Œuvres*, IV, p. 456.
85. Charrière, *Œuvres*, IV, p. 553.
86. Charrière, *Œuvres*, IV, p. 457.
87. Charrière, *Œuvres*, IV, p. 546.
88. Charrière, *Œuvres*, IV, p. 553.

6 GERMAINE DE STAEL (1794–1800)

1. Charrière, *Œuvres*, IV, p. 562.
2. Charrière, *Œuvres*, IV, p. 559.
3. Staël, *Correspondance générale*, III/1, pp. 117–18, letter to Adolphe de Ribbing of 18 September 1794.
4. *Madame de Staël et l'Europe* (Bibliothèque nationale catalogue of 1966 exhibition), Paris: Bibliothèque nationale, 1966, p. 36, item no. 146.
5. The most detailed and authoritative biography of Madame de Staël to date in French is Ghislain de Diesbach's highly readable *Madame de Staël*, Paris: Librairie Académique Perrin, 1983, to which the reader is referred. In English Renée Winegarten's *Madame de Staël*, Leamington Spa: Berg, 1985, provides a succinct and largely up-to-date survey of Madame de Staël's life and work.
6. Madame de Staël had been visited at Juniper Hall by the English novelist Fanny Burney who was greatly impressed by 'the ardour and warmth of her temper and partialities' (quoted by Harold Nicolson, *Benjamin Constant*, London: Constable, 1949, p. 109). On the Juniper Hall colony see Linda Kelly, *Juniper*

Hall. An English Refuge from the French Revolution, London: Weidenfeld & Nicolson, 1991.

7. Charrière, *Œuvres*, IV, pp. 562–4, letter to Constant of 13 September 1794, and the verse letter of 18 September 1794 pp. 564–6.
8. See Constant's letter of 12 September 1794 and Isabelle's letters to him of 13 and 20 September, Charrière, *Œuvres*, IV, pp. 561–2, 562–4 and 566–7.
9. Charrière, *Œuvres*, IV, p. 573.
10. Charrière, *Œuvres*, IV, pp. 589–90.
11. Staël, *Correspondance générale*, III/1, p. 158.
12. Geneva, Bibliothèque publique et universitaire, MS Constant 16/1, letter dated 'Neuchâtel, Wednesday evening', i.e. 8 October 1794, unpublished.
13. Charrière, *Œuvres*, IV, p. 605, letter of 14 October 1794.
14. Charrière, *Œuvres*, IV, p. 620.
15. Charrière, *Œuvres*, IV, p. 654.
16. Charrière, *Œuvres*, IV, pp. 670–3, letter to Constant of 18 December 1794, and pp. 677–8, letter to Isabelle de Charrière of 23 December 1794. On reactions to Kant on the part of Madame de Charrière, Constant and the Coppet Group, see B. Munteano, 'Episodes kantiens en Suisse et en France', *Revue de littérature comparée* 15 (1935), pp. 387–459. On Madame de Charrière's *Trois femmes* see Alix Deguise, *Trois femmes: le monde de Madame de Charrière*, Geneva: Slatkine, 1981.
17. Madame de Staël, *Lettres à Ribbing*, ed. Simone Balayé, Paris: Gallimard, 1960, p. 268, letter of 3 March 1795: '[Constant] is a madman with a great deal of wit, and singularly ugly.'
18. Ghislain de Diesbach, *op. cit.*, pp. 165–7.
19. Charrière, *Œuvres*, V, p. 89.
20. *Cécile*, ed. Paul Delbouille, p. 188.
21. Jean-Jacques Coulmann, *Réminiscences*, Paris: Michel Lévy, 1862–9, vol. III, pp. 45 and 47.
22. Melegari (1895), p. 236, letter from Constant to his aunt Anne de Nassau of 7 July 1795.
23. See C. P. Courtney, *A Guide to the Published Works of Benjamin Constant*, Oxford: The Voltaire Foundation, 1985, p. 96, items D1–D3.
24. Charrière, *Œuvres*, V, pp. 123–4.
25. 'A Charles His, rédacteur du Républicain français', *Le Républicain français*, 6 Thermidor an III, i.e. 24 July 1795. See C. P. Courtney, *op. cit.*, p. 96, item D4.
26. C. P. Courtney, *op. cit.*, p. 96, item D5.
27. See Jasinski, *L'Engagement*, Appendice I, 'Les premières acquisitions de Constant', pp. 271–84. On this period of Constant's life, 1794–6, Béatrice W. Jasinski's meticulous study – and powerful refutation of the errors and wilful distortions of Henri Guillemin, Constant's most hostile modern critic – is indispensable, as is her edition of Germaine de Staël's *Correspondance générale*.
28. Staël, *Correspondance générale*, III/2, pp. 46–9.
29. Jasinski, *L'Engagement*, pp. 159–60.
30. Jasinski, *L'Engagement*, pp. 160–70.
31. See Constant, *Œuvres*, p. 387, diary entry for 7 October 1804 where Constant's memories of that night in prison are described.
32. Lausanne, Bibliothèque cantonale et universitaire, MS Co 4839/5, decree dated Wolfenbüttel, 18 November 1795, unpublished.
33. *Cécile*, ed. Paul Delbouille, p. 189.
34. Jasinski, *L'Engagement*, pp. 171–2.

35. Melegari (1895), p. 247, letter from Constant to Anne de Nassau of 10 December 1795, 'My departure is fixed for the 20th of this month'.
36. Jasinski, *L'Engagement*, p. 27.
37. Jasinski, *L'Engagement*, pp. 175–82.
38. Charrière, *Œuvres*, V, p. 197, letter of 26 January 1796.
39. Charrière, *Œuvres*, V, p. 197.
40. Charrière, *Œuvres*, V, p. 230.
41. See Isabelle de Charrière's letter to Constant of 28 March 1796, Charrière, *Œuvres*, V, p. 230.
42. Benjamin Constant, *The Affair of Colonel Juste de Constant and Related Documents (1787–1796)*, published with an Introduction by C. P. Courtney, Cambridge: Dæmon Press, 1990, p. 202.
43. Letter of 1 March 1796 from Juste to Benjamin Constant copied out by Constant, Lausanne, Bibliothèque cantonale et universitaire, Fonds Constant II, MS 34/4: 'Since it was you who prepared everything, it is to you that I owe the deepest debt of gratitude.'
44. Jasinski, *L'Engagement*, pp. 195–204.
45. *De la foiblesse d'un gouvernement qui commence, et de la nécessité où il est de se rallier à la majorité nationale.* See Christian Viredaz, 'Comptes rendus contemporains et réponses aux écrits de Benjamin Constant (1787–1833)', *ABC*, no. 6 (1986), p. 98.
46. Melegari (1895), p. 256, corrected against the manuscript in Lausanne, Bibliothèque cantonale et universitaire, MS Co 3319.
47. See *Lettres de Julie Talma à Benjamin Constant*, ed. Baronne Constant de Rebecque, Paris: Plon, 1933.
48. See Jasinski, *L'Engagement*, pp. 232–63, 'Constant et la citoyenneté française'.
49. Staël, *Correspondance générale*, III/2, p. 207, note 3, and pp. 209–10.
50. Simone Balayé, 'Un testament inconnu', *Cahiers Benjamin Constant*, 4 (juillet 1967), pp. 133–6.
51. See for example Germaine's passionate feelings for Constant expressed in her letter to Rosalie de Constant of 31 July 1796, Staël, *Correspondance générale*, III/2, pp. 224–5.
52. Benjamin Constant, *Recueil d'articles 1795–1817*, ed. Ephraïm Harpaz, Geneva: Droz, 1978, pp. 42–7.
53. Copy of document of sale, Lausanne, Bibliothèque cantonale et universitaire, MS Co 4748, unpublished.
54. Paris, Bibliothèque nationale, Nouvelles acquisitions françaises 17269, f. 57, unpublished letter dated 'Hérivaux près Luzarches Dépt de Seine & Oise 25 Germinal An 5ᵉ', i.e. 14 April 1797.
55. Benjamin Constant, *De la force du gouvernement actuel de la France et de la nécessité de s'y rallier. Des réactions politiques. Des effets de la Terreur*, ed. Philippe Raynaud, Paris: Flammarion (Champs), 1988, p. 93.
56. Immanuel Kant, 'Ueber ein vermeintes Recht, aus Menschenliebe zu lügen', *Berlinische Blätter*, I, (6 September 1797), pp. 301–14.
57. Benjamin Constant, *op. cit.*, p. 167.
58. Jean-Pierre Fabre de l'Aude [attributed], *Histoire secrète du Directoire*, Paris: Ménard, 1832, 4 vols, vol. III, pp. 13–14 and 17–18. Fabre de l'Aude is, however, frequently unreliable, and the reader is referred to Béatrice W. Jasinski's 'Constant et le Cercle constitutionnel' and Gérard Gengembre's 'Le Cercle constitutionnel: un laboratoire du libéralisme?', scholarly contributions to *Benjamin Constant et la Révolution française 1789–1799*, ed. Dominique Verrey et Anne-Lise Delacrétaz, Geneva: Droz, 1989, pp. 119–40 and 141–9 respectively.

59. On Constant's political activities at Luzarches see the important article by Maurice Déchery, 'Benjamin Constant à Luzarches. Lettres inédites', in *Benjamin Constant et la Révolution française 1789–1799*, ed. Dominique Verrey et Anne-Lise Delacrétaz, op. cit., pp. 151–68.

60. Paul Barras, *Mémoires de Barras, membre du Directoire*, ed. Georges Duruy, Paris: Hachette, 1895–6, 4 vols, vol. III, pp. 127–8.

61. See Christian Viredaz's article ' "Monsieur le Rédacteur": vingt textes oubliés de Benjamin Constant' in *ABC*, no. 6 (1986), pp. 31–80, esp. pp. 35–6.

62. Louis-Gustave-Doulcet, Comte de Pontécoulant, *Souvenirs historiques et parlementaires*, Paris: Michel Lévy, 1861, vol. II, p. 437.

63. Benjamin Constant, *Ecrits et discours politiques*, ed. O. Pozzo di Borgo, [Paris]: Jean-Jacques Pauvert, 1964, 2 vols, vol. I, pp. 115–28.

64. Such is the uncompromisingly hostile view of Henri Guillemin in *Benjamin Constant muscadin 1795–1799*, Paris: Gallimard, 1958, pp. 172–4.

65. See Maurice Déchery, op. cit., p. 161.

66. See Henri Guillemin, *Madame de Staël et Napoléon ou Germaine et le Caïd ingrat*, [n.p.]: Le Pavillon, Roger Maria Editeur, 1966. Once again the late Henri Guillemin's polemical flair, supported by an unusual mixture of genuine if selective historical research and profound antipathy to Madame de Staël and Constant makes this a book to be approached with great circumspection.

67. Melegari (1895), p. 274, where however the letter is wrongly dated 22 February 1798.

68. Quoted in Henri Guillemin, *Benjamin Constant muscadin 1795–1799*, op. cit., pp. 200–1.

69. Staël, *Correspondance générale*, IV/1, p. 135, note 1, and p. 137, note 4.

70. Benjamin Constant, *Cent lettres*, choisies et présentées par Pierre Cordey, Lausanne: Bibliothèque romande, 1974, pp. 77–8.

71. Melegari (1895), p. 269, letter from Constant to Anne de Nassau dated 'Hérivaux ce 10 Messidor An 5'. Melegari has both the day and year wrong: it is in fact 28 June (Melegari's error), and 1798 not 1797 (Constant's slip of the pen).

72. Melegari (1895), p. 268, see preceding note.

73. Charrière, *Œuvres*, V, p. 509.

74. Charrière, *Œuvres*, V, pp. 466–7.

75. The unpublished manuscript 'L'Affaire de mon Père' (Lausanne, Bibliothèque cantonale et universitaire, Fonds Constant II, MS 34/4), a notebook with 175 pages of transcribed letters, calculations and comments in which Constant chronicles the history of his financial disagreements with his father gives a number of different dates for when he learnt about Juste's marriage, but it seems likely that it was during 1798. Certainly by December 1798 he was referring to the marriage in a letter to his cousin Rosalie de Constant (Benjamin et Rosalie de Constant, *Correspondance 1786–1830*, ed. Alfred et Suzanne Roulin, Paris: Gallimard, 1955, p. 19).

76. Etienne Hofmann, *Les 'Principes de politique' de Benjamin Constant. La Genèse d'une œuvre et l'évolution de la pensée de leur auteur (1789–1806)*, Geneva: Droz (Travaux d'histoire éthico-politique XXXIV), 1980, 2 vols, vol. I, pp. 170 ff.

77. On this question see Lucia Omacini's critical edition of Germaine de Staël's *Des circonstances actuelles qui peuvent terminer la Révolution et des principes qui doivent fonder la République en France*, Geneva–Paris: Droz, 1979, p. xxiv.

78. Quoted in English in Christine Chicoteau, *Chère Rose. A Biography of Rosalie de Constant (1758–1834)*, Berne, Frankfurt am Main, Las Vegas: Peter Lang

(Europäische Hochschulschriften: Reihe 13, Franz. Sprache u. Literatur, Bd. 65), 1980, p. 232.

79. Charrière, *Œuvres*, V, p. 503.
80. Benjamin Constant, *De la justice politique. Traduction inédite de l'ouvrage de William Godwin: 'Enquiry concerning Political Justice and its Influence on General Virtue and Happiness'*, ed. Burton R. Pollin, Québec: Les Presses de l'Université Laval (Droit et science politique, 5), 1972.
81. Charrière, *Œuvres*, V, p. 546, letter from Claude de Narbonne-Pelet de Salgas to Isabelle de Charrière of 26 February 1799, and p. 889, note 14.
82. Norman King et Etienne Hofmann, 'Les lettres de Benjamin Constant à Sieyès avec une lettre de Constant à Pictet-Diodati', *ABC*, no. 3 (1983), pp. 93–4.
83. Constant, *Œuvres*, pp. 965–6, 'L'Abbé Siéyès'.
84. C. P. Courtney, *A Bibliography of Editions of the Writings of Benjamin Constant to 1833*, London: The Modern Humanities Research Association, 1981, pp. 21–2, and C. P. Courtney, *A Guide to the Published Works of Benjamin Constant, op. cit.*, pp. 6–7 and 212.
85. Benjamin Constant, 'Souvenirs historiques à l'occasion de l'ouvrage de M. Bignon. Première lettre', *Revue de Paris*, XI (février 1830), p. 119.
86. Norman King et Etienne Hofmann, *op. cit.*, p. 97, letter of 10 November 1799.
87. See above, note 85, *ibid.*
88. Norman King et Etienne, Hofmann, *op. cit.*, p. 99.
89. Norman King et Etienne Hofmann, *op. cit.*, pp. 104–5.
90. See Benjamin Constant, *Fragments d'un ouvrage abandonné sur la possibilité d'une constitution républicaine dans un grand pays*, ed. Henri Grange, Paris: Aubier (Bibliothèque philosophique), 1991. This first scholarly edition of an important political text is preceded by a valuable hundred-page introduction. Grange argues (pp. 27–8) that the *Fragments* may have been begun in the winter of 1795–6 and worked on sporadically until 1807 or even later.
91. See above, note 63, Benjamin Constant, *op. cit.*, vol. I, pp. 137–55.
92. Constant, *Œuvres*, p. 441.
93. Germaine de Staël, *Œuvres complètes*, ed. Auguste de Staël, Paris: Treuttel et Würtz, 1821, vol. XV, pp. 10–12.
94. Menos, p. 162.
95. Charrière, *Œuvres*, VI, p. 97.
96. *Lettres de Julie Talma à Benjamin Constant*, ed. Baronne Constant de Rebecque, Paris: Plon, 1933, p. 39.
97. See above, note 76, Etienne Hofmann, *op. cit.*
98. 'Extrait d'une lettre de Genève', *Le Citoyen français*, 30 vendémiaire an IX, 22 octobre 1800. Abridged versions of this obituary also appeared in *Le Journal de Paris* and *Le Publiciste* on 23 and 24 October 1800 respectively.
99. *Anna Lindsay*, p. 2.

7 'THE INTERMITTENCES OF THE HEART' (1800–1806)

1. *Anna Lindsay*, p. xv.
2. *Anna Lindsay*, p. xv.
3. *Anna Lindsay*, p. 63.
4. *Anna Lindsay*, pp. 21–3.
5. *Anna Lindsay*, p.32.
6. See Dennis Wood, *Benjamin Constant: 'Adolphe'*, Cambridge: Cambridge University Press (Landmarks of World Literature), 1987, esp. pp. 79–80. For an interesting attempt to rewrite *Adolphe* from Ellénore's viewpoint, see Eve

Gonin, *Le point de vue d'Ellénore. Une réécriture d''Adolphe'*, Paris: Librairie José Corti, 1981.

7. *Anna Lindsay*, p. 53.
8. *Anna Lindsay*, pp. 59–60.
9. *Lettres de Julie Talma à Benjamin Constant*, ed. Baronne Constant de Rebecque, Paris: Plon, 1933, pp. 161–3.
10. *Anna Lindsay*, p. 126.
11. *Anna Lindsay*, pp. 129–42.
12. *Anna Lindsay*, pp. 143–4.
13. *Anna Lindsay*, pp. 157–8.
14. *Anna Lindsay*, p. 167.
15. See, for example, Charrière, *Œuvres*, VI, pp. 351 (22 June 1801), 411–12 (5 August 1801) and 424–5 (22 August 1801).
16. Charrière, *Œuvres*, VI, p. 429, letter of 19 September 1801: 'Will you get *Les Finch* [i.e. her novel *Sir Walter Finch et son fils William*] printed? Can I rely on it?'
17. Charrière, *Œuvres*, VI, p. 380.
18. *Anna Lindsay*, pp. 172–4.
19. *Lettres de Julie Talma à Benjamin Constant*, op. cit., pp. 72–5.
20. See below, note 28. On church–state relations and the revival of religious feeling in France under Napoleon, see D. M. G. Sutherland, *France 1789–1815: Revolution and Counterrevolution*, London: Fontana (Fontana History of Modern France), 1985, pp. 369–74.
21. See Béatrice W. Jasinski, 'Benjamin Constant tribun', in *Benjamin Constant, Madame de Staël et le Groupe de Coppet*, ed. Etienne Hofmann, Oxford: The Voltaire Foundation; Lausanne: Institut Benjamin Constant, 1982, pp. 63–88, esp. p. 71.
22. Béatrice W. Jasinski, op. cit., p. 63.
23. Charrière, *Œuvres*, VI, p. 480.
24. Charrière, *Œuvres*, VI, p. 484.
25. Dominique Verrey, *Chronologie de la vie et de l'œuvre de Benjamin Constant*. Avec la collaboration du professeur Etienne Hofmann, tome I: *1767–1805*, Geneva: Editions Slatkine, 1992, p. 461, entry 1797, letter from Juste of late January 1802.
26. *Lettres de Julie Talma à Benjamin Constant*, op. cit., pp. 188–9.
27. Dominique Verrey, op. cit., p. 462, entry 1798, from Etienne Dumont's manuscript *Memorandum Book*. From entry 1784 it seems that Constant may also have met Laclos on the evening of 26 December 1801.
28. Charrière, *Œuvres*, III, pp. 60–1.
29. Georges Poisson, *Choderlos de Laclos ou l'obstination*, Paris: Grasset, 1985.
30. On the possible influence of Laclos on Constant, see A. et Y. Delmas, *A la recherche des Liaisons dangereuses*, Paris: Mercure de France, 1964, pp. 44–6, and Dennis Wood, op. cit., pp. 44–5.
31. Staël, *Correspondance générale*, IV/2, p. 483, note 7.
32. Victor Glachant, *Benjamin Constant sous l'œil du guet*, Paris: Plon-Nourrit, 1906, pp. 33–6.
33. Victor Glachant, op. cit., pp. 71–5. In the same letter of 31 July 1802 to his friend Claude Fauriel, Constant remarks 'My friends in Scotland are urging me [to go there]'. He was evidently still in contact with John Wilde and perhaps others at this date: sadly all this correspondence is now lost.
34. Melegari (1895), pp. 304–6 and 308–310.

35. Henri Grange, 'De l'influence de Necker sur les idées politiques de Benjamin Constant', *ABC*, no. 2 (1982), pp. 73–80.
36. Victor Glachant, *op. cit.*, pp. 96–8.
37. Constant, *Œuvres*, pp. 223–55.
38. Constant admired and envied his friends Ludwig Ferdinand and Therese Huber for their happy marriage, seeing in it, as Etienne Hofmann has said, 'a guarantee of peace of mind, stability, security and permanence, that is to say the ingredients of what [Constant] calls happiness' (Benjamin Constant, 'Lettres à Louis-Ferdinand et à Thérèse Huber (1798–1806)', ed. Etienne Hofmann, *Cahiers staëliens*, nos 29–30 (1981), p. 85).
39. Ghislain de Diesbach, *Madame de Staël*, Paris: Librairie Académique Perrin, 1983, p. 266.
40. See Etienne Hofmann, *Les 'Principes de politique' de Benjamin Constant. La Genèse d'une œuvre et l'évolution de la pensée de leur auteur (1789–1806)*, Geneva: Droz (Travaux d'histoire éthico-politique XXXIV), 1980, 2 vols, vol. I, p. 229.
41. Etienne Hofmann, article quoted from in note 38 above, pp. 108–11.
42. *Lettres de Julie Talma à Benjamin Constant*, *op. cit.*, p. 155–7.
43. Letter of 11 July 1803 to Madame de Nassau, quoted in Henri Guillemin, *Pas à pas*, Paris: Gallimard, 1969, pp. 52–3.
44. *Anna Lindsay*, pp. 210–12, letter from Julie Talma to Constant of 5 May 1803.
45. Benjamin et Rosalie de Constant, *Correspondance 1786–1830*, ed. Alfred et Suzanne Roulin, Paris: Gallimard, 1955, pp. 44–5, letter to Rosalie of 29 August 1803.
46. *Cécile*, ed. Paul Delbouille, p. 191.
47. *Cécile*, ed. Paul Delbouille, p. 191.
48. *Cécile*, ed. Paul Delbouille, p. 193.
49. Germaine de Staël, *De l'Allemagne*, ed. Simone Balayé, Paris: Garnier-Flammarion, 1968, 2 vols, vol. I, pp. 18–19.
50. See Kurt Kloocke, *Benjamin Constant: une biographie intellectuelle*, Geneva–Paris: Droz, 1984, p. 120, note 33.
51. Staël, *Correspondance générale*, V/1, pp. 101–2 and 109–11.
52. Constant, *Œuvres*, p. 422.
53. Staël, *Correspondance générale*, V/1, p. 181. While in Gotha Constant met the celebrated historian and biographer Adolf Friedrich Schlichtegroll (1765–1822) who lent him his *Necrolog auf das Jahr 1794* to help Constant in his work on Mauvillon's life. Evidently Constant had not abandoned his plan to write a biography of his late friend. A letter from Constant to Schlichtegroll, dated by Kurt Kloocke to 13 or 14 December 1803 (Kloocke, *op. cit.*, p. 54), has been preserved in the Niedersächsisches Staatsarchiv in Wolfenbüttel, MS 298 N 628.
54. Staël, *Correspondance générale*, V/1, pp. 212–14. On intellectual life in Weimar at this period, see W. H. Bruford, *Culture and Society in Classical Weimar 1775–1806*, Cambridge: Cambridge University Press, 1962.
55. Staël, *Correspondance générale*, V/1, pp. 184–5, letter of 6 January 1804.
56. In order to reduce the number of notes given here on this period 1804–7, the reader is referred generally to the appropriate date entry in Constant, *Œuvres*, pp. 259–674.
57. Constant, *Œuvres*, p. 264.
58. Constant, *Œuvres*, p. 259.
59. Constant, *Œuvres*, p. 261.
60. Constant, *Œuvres*, p. 268.

61. Constant, Œuvres, pp. 268–9. Constant seems to be thinking of Goethe's comment to the effect that if people commit suicide like the hero of his novel *Werther*, it is their affair, not his.
62. Constant, Œuvres, p. 273.
63. Quoted in Elizabeth W. Schermerhorn, *Benjamin Constant, his Private Life and his Contribution to the Cause of Liberal Government in France 1767–1830*, Boston and New York: Houghton Mifflin, 1924, pp. 210–11. The passage, written in 1822, is quoted in the original German in Kurt Kloocke, *op. cit.*, p. 121. Later in the passage Goethe continues:

> If it was not possible for [Constant] to consider and treat correctly my method and manner, my nature and my art; still the way in which he endeavoured to make them honestly his own, in order to bring them closer to his own conceptions, was of the greatest assistance even to me, because he set before me whatever undeveloped ideas, cloudy conceptions, inexpressible principles and impracticable designs had been allowed to remain in my exposition.
>
> (Elizabeth W. Schermerhorn, *op. cit.*, p. 210)

64. Constant, Œuvres, p. 278, entry for 17 March 1804: 'Wrote to Madame Schardt to say goodbye to her. Sad and tender reply. It's another pathetic little infatuation with me that I didn't want, and a time will come when I shall not be the object of them any more.'
65. Constant, Œuvres, pp. 278–9, entry for 17 March 1804: '*Wilhelm Tell*. It's a badly put together magic lantern show with much less poetic beauty in it than there is in Schiller's other plays.'
66. On the way to Weimar Constant read and was moved by the story of Ann Hurle, a 22-year-old Englishwoman who had been hanged in London for fraud on 8 February 1804 (Constant, Œuvres, p. 296, entry for 20 April 1804). Constant's memorable description of the silent, uncomplaining Ann has a nightmare – indeed one is tempted to say fantasy – quality to it and is tinged with disapproval: *she should have struggled harder to hold onto life*. We see Constant at once deeply troubled and fascinated by the combination of three elements: women, suffering and death, and filled – apparently in spite of himself – with both pity and contempt, tenderness and aggression, feelings he was likely then to be experiencing towards Madame de Staël. The context in which this extraordinary passage occurs is highly significant psychologically: in awe at the calamity which is about to befall the woman towards whom his feelings are to say the least ambivalent, Constant has made enormous efforts to be the one to break the news of Jacques Necker's death to Germaine, and he is shortly to witness her shock and anguish at the loss of the person she probably loved and admired more than anyone in the world. And once again we are brought close to the mystery outlined earlier in Chapter 1, ' "The grief that does not speak": Constant and his father', a mystery, I would suggest, intimately connected with the death of his mother. See Dennis Wood, 'Constant and the case of Ann Hurle', *French Studies Bulletin*, no. 5 (Winter 1982/3), pp. 6–8, and Georges Poulet, *Benjamin Constant par lui-même*, Paris: Du Seuil, 1968, pp. 34–5.
67. Constant, Œuvres, p. 318.
68. Constant, Œuvres, p. 344.
69. Constant, Œuvres, p. 357.
70. Constant, Œuvres, p. 393.
71. Constant, Œuvres, pp. 412–13, diary entry for 21 November 1804.
72. Constant, Œuvres, p. 469.

73. Constant, *Œuvres*, p. 405.
74. See Benjamin Constant et Madame de Staël, *Lettres à un ami. Cent onze lettres inédites à Claude Hochet*, ed. Jean Mistler, Neuchâtel: A la Baconnière, [1949].
75. Constant, *Œuvres*, p. 434.
76. Constant, *Œuvres*, p. 449.
77. Constant, *Œuvres*, p. 453.
78. Constant, *Œuvres*, p. 485.
79. Constant, *Œuvres*, p. 481.
80. Constant, *Œuvres*, p. 516, diary entry for 4 May 1804.
81. Constant, *Œuvres*, p. 514.
82. Constant, *Œuvres*, p. 517.
83. Constant, *Œuvres*, p. 553.
84. Constant, *Œuvres*, p. 560.
85. Ghislain de Diesbach, *op. cit.*, pp. 362 and 365.
86. Constant, *Œuvres*, p. 575.
87. See Georges Poulet's perceptive observations on this image in his *Benjamin Constant par lui-même*, *op. cit.*, pp. 40–4.
88. Ghislain de Diesbach, *op. cit.*, pp. 365–6.
89. Constant, *Œuvres*, p. 580.
90. Constant, *Œuvres*, p. 586.
91. Dorette Berthoud, *La Seconde Madame Benjamin Constant*, Lausanne: Librairie Payot, 1943, pp. 81–2.
92. Constant, *Œuvres*, p. 589.
93. Constant, *Œuvres*, p. 590.
94. Constant, *Œuvres*, p. 592.

8 'ITALIAM, ITALIAM' (1806–1812)

1. See Dennis Wood, 'Benjamin Constant's first novel?', *Times Literary Supplement*, 6 February 1981, p. 151, 'Isabelle de Charrière et Benjamin Constant: à propos d'une découverte récente', *Studies on Voltaire and the eighteenth century* (Oxford: The Voltaire Foundation), 1982, vol. 215, pp. 273–9, and 'Isabelle de Charrière et Benjamin Constant: problématique d'une collaboration', *ABC*, no. 4 (1984), pp. 17–30. The text of *Lettres de d'Arsillé fils* was published for the first time in Charrière, *Œuvres*, IX, pp. 651–78.
2. On the vexed question of the genesis of *Adolphe*, see the summary of the evidence in Paul Delbouille's *Genèse, structure et destin d''Adolphe'*, Paris: Les Belles Lettres, 1971, pp. 33–60. According to Constant's friend Jean-Jacques Coulmann, the novelist actually rewrote *Adolphe* at some point and gave it a happy ending: this version has been lost, it seems. On this subject, see C. P. Courtney, 'Benjamin Constant's projects for a revised edition of *Adolphe*, *French Studies*, XLIII (1989), pp. 292–304.
3. Constant, *Œuvres*, p. 593.
4. Constant, *Œuvres*, pp. 599–601.
5. Constant, *Œuvres*, p. 603.
6. Constant, *Œuvres*, p. 605.
7. Constant, *Œuvres*, pp. 607–8.
8. See Simone Balayé's excellent edition (Paris: Gallimard [Folio 1632], 1985), her article 'Benjamin Constant lecteur de *Corinne*' in *Benjamin Constant. Actes du congrès Benjamin Constant (Lausanne, octobre 1967)*, ed. Pierre Cordey et Jean-Luc Seylaz, Geneva: Droz, 1968, pp. 189–99, and Georges Poulet, '*Corinne* et

Adolphe: deux romans conjugués', *Revue d'histoire littéraire de la France*, 78ème année, no. 4 (juillet–août 1978), pp. 580–96.

9. See, for example, the diary entry for 20 January 1807, Constant, *Œuvres*, p. 609.

10. See Constant, *Œuvres*, p. 1542, and Ghislain de Diesbach, *Madame de Staël*, Paris: Librairie Académique Perrin, pp. 372–3.

11. See Simone Balayé, *op. cit.*, and C. P. Courtney, *A Guide to the Published Works of Benjamin Constant*, Oxford: The Voltaire Foundation (Studies on Voltaire and the eighteenth century, 239), 1985, p. 100, items D36-D38.

12. Constant, *Œuvres*, p. 632.

13. Constant, *Œuvres*, p. 635.

14. Wolfenbüttel, Niedersächsisches Staatsarchiv, MS 264 N II s. 12 Nr 23, dossier entitled 'Papiere die Erbschaft *Benjamin Constant*'s betreffend', Pouvoir donné par Mr. Du Tertre à Monsieur Niemeier, notaire à Brunswick pour faire toutes les démarches de droit afin d'obtenir la cassation de son mariage avec Dame Comtesse de Hardenberg (cause indiquée: Mr de Marenholz son premier mari dont elle est divorcée étant encore vivant), sur papier timbré, 5 juin 1807, unpublished; also Constant, *Œuvres*, pp. 637–8.

15. Ghislain de Diesbach, *op. cit.*, p. 387.

16. On this curious episode see Pierre Deguise, *Benjamin Constant méconnu. Le Livre 'De la Religion'*, Geneva: Droz, 1966, pp. 89–115; Frank Paul Bowman, 'L'épisode quiétiste dans *Cécile*', in *Benjamin Constant. Actes du congrès Benjamin Constant (Lausanne, octobre 1967)*, ed. Pierre Cordey et Jean-Luc Seylaz, *op. cit.*, pp. 97–108; and Eugène Susini, *Charles de Langalerie (1751–1835) et son entourage*, *Les Cahiers de Saint-Martin*, vol. VI, 1987. The historical background to religious movements like the Lausanne *Ames intérieures* is given in Auguste Viatte's standard work, *Les Sources occultes du romantisme. Illuminisme – Théosophie 1770–1820*, Paris: Librairie Honoré Champion, 1965, 2 vols. Vol. II contains a section on Constant (pp. 206–9).

17. *Cécile*, ed. Paul Delbouille, pp. 216–24. It must be stressed that the account of events given in *Cécile* belongs to the fictional world of an autobiographical novel and is therefore less reliable as evidence than, say, the *Journaux intimes* or Constant's correspondence. On the question of Constant's 'conversion' in 1807, as Pierre Deguise neatly puts it (*op. cit.*, p. 91), the various sources differ significantly: '*Cécile* says yes. The *Journal intime* is more vague, and Rosalie de Constant [in her correspondence] says no'.

18. Constant, *Œuvres*, p. 656.

19. Menos, p. 483.

20. Constant, *Œuvres*, p. 665.

21. Constant, *Œuvres*, pp. 665–6.

22. On the composition and publication of *Wallstein* see the critical edition by Jean-René Derré, *Wallstein. Tragédie en cinq actes et en vers de Benjamin Constant*, Paris: Les Belles Lettres, [1965], esp. pp. 1–44.

23. Constant, *Œuvres*, p. 664.

24. *Cécile*, ed. Paul Delbouille, pp. 225–7.

25. Constant, *Œuvres*, pp. 674 and 677.

26. *Cécile*, ed. Paul Delbouille, p. 232.

27. Menos, pp. 240–1.

28. Wolfenbüttel, Niedersächsisches Staatsarchiv, MS 264 N II s. 12 Nr 23, 'Papiers concernant le divorce de Mme de Constant [d']avec M. du Tertre', Extrait des Registres du Greffe de l'Officialité de Paris.

29. The marriage certificate signed by Pastor Jean-Henry Ebray was added to the Von Marenholz family papers already held at the Niedersächsisches Staatsar-

chiv, Wolfenbüttel, in 1986 by Alexander Freiherr von Marenholtz-Nolde, together with a legal document on parchment dividing up Constant's estate after his death, 'Partage de la succession de M. Benjamin Constant' dated Paris, 2 February 1831. Along with the marriage certificate there is another document, MS 264 N II s. 12 Nr 28, Document signé George Rouge Notaire public à Lausanne [certifying that the marriage certificate presented by Constant showing that he was married to Charlotte by 'Monsieur Ebray de l'Église réformé[e]'on 5 June 1808 is genuine].

30. A number of colloquia have taken place in recent years giving a long-overdue account of the wide variety of intellectual interests among the cosmopolitan membership of the Coppet Group from the late 1790s to Madame de Staël's death, for example *Le Groupe de Coppet. Actes et documents du deuxième Colloque de Coppet, 10–13 juillet 1974*, ed. Simone Balayé et Jean-Daniel Candaux, Geneva: Slatkine; Paris: Champion (Bibliothèque de littérature comparée, 118), 1977. (See also the journal *Cahiers staëliens* [nouvelle série], published since 1962 by the Société des études staëliennes, *passim*.) Among the most prominent *habitués* of Coppet or friends or correspondents of Germaine de Staël at one time or another were the historians Prosper de Barante, Simonde de Sismondi and Charles-Victor de Bonstetten; the important intermediary between French and German culture, Charles de Villers; the German philologist and anthropologist, Wilhelm von Humboldt (1767–1835); the poet and author of *Peter Schlemihls wundersame Geschichte* (1814), Adelbert von Chamisso (1781–1838); and of course the critic and scholar August Wilhelm von Schlegel.

31. On the genesis of *De l'Allemagne*, see the introduction to Simone Balayé's edition (Paris: Garnier-Flammarion, 1968), 2 vols, vol. I, pp. 17–31 .

32. *Quelques réflexions sur la tragédie de Wallstein et sur le théâtre allemand*, published as an introduction to the 1809 edition of *Wallstein* and reproduced in Jean-René Derré's critical edition (see above, note 22), pp. 47–67.

33. Jean-René Derré, *op. cit.*, p. 5, remarks:

> Although it had a mixed reception, [*Wallstein's*] success was undeniable. All two thousand copies were sold within two months, and numerous reviews appeared in the press. Even if . . . these reviews tell us more about the preferences or mood of their authors, their sheer number clearly shows the interest aroused by a work which, in France under the Empire, passed for something of a literary event.

34. Kurt Kloocke, *Benjamin Constant: une biographie intellectuelle*, Geneva–Paris: Droz (Histoire des idées et critique littéraire, 218), 1984, p. 337.

35. Menos, p. 302.

36. *Ibid.*, p. 288, letter of 15 December 1808 from Constant to the Comtesse de Nassau.

37. Ghislain de Diesbach, *op. cit.*, p. 426.

38. Kurt Kloocke, *op. cit.*, p. 337.

39. Ghislain de Diesbach, *op. cit.*, pp. 430–1.

40. Dorette Berthoud, *La Seconde Madame Benjamin Constant*, Lausanne: Librairie Payot, 1943, p. 191.

41. Ghislain de Diesbach, *op. cit.*, p. 434.

42. Wolfenbüttel, Niedersächsisches Staatsarchiv, MS 264 N II s. 12 Nr 23, dossier compiled by Charlotte's son, Wilhelm von Marenholtz entitled 'Papiers concernant le mariage de ma mère avec M^r Du Tertre et Mr B. Constant'. The dossier contains some seventeen receipts from Du Tertre to Charlotte for monies received over the period 1811–25 under the terms of the legal agreement they

had reached on 26 June 1807. One of these receipts, dated 27 May 1821, includes a brief note:

> Dear Charlotte, I have been given your letter of last night. Thank you for being so precise and for the advance you are letting me have. It will come in very handy because I'm very short of money. As for the other 400 francs, there's no hurry about that . . . I shall be in Lyon until October.

See also note 14 above.

43. Dorette Berthoud, *op. cit.*, pp. 201 and 207.
44. Kurt Kloocke, *op. cit.*, p. 339. The Von Marenholtz papers in the Niedersächsisches Staatsarchiv, Wolfenbüttel, contain a legal document dated 14 December 1809 by which Juste de Constant gives permission for his son to marry: it is presumably connected with Constant's civil marriage in Paris, the exact date of which is not known.
45. See the introduction to *Cécile*, ed. Paul Delbouille, pp. 157–69.
46. On the style of *Cécile*, see Paul Delbouille, '*Adolphe* et *Cécile*: esquisse d'une comparaison stylistique', *Cahiers d'analyse textuelle*, 17 (1975), pp. 7–22. On the literary merits of *Cécile*, see Alison Fairlie, 'Suggestions on the art of the novelist in Constant's *Cécile*', in *Literature and Society. Studies in Nineteenth and Twentieth Century French Literature presented to R. J. North*, ed. C. A. Burns, Birmingham: John Goodman & Sons, 1980, pp. 29–37, and Michel Dentan, 'Lire *Cécile*', *ABC*, no. 3 (1983), pp. 19–32.
47. Virgil, *Aeneid*, Book III, lines 521–4:

> Iamque rubescebat stellis Aurora fugatis
> cum procul obscuros collis humilemque videmus
> Italiam. Italiam primus conclamat Achates,
> Italiam laeto socii clamore salutant.

'And now the dawn had put the stars to flight and was reddening the sky when in the distance we saw the shadowy hills and the low coastline of Italy. "Italy!" – Achates was the first to cry out the name, then the rest of our companions took it up, greeting the land with joyful shouts.'

48. Kurt Kloocke, *op. cit.*, p. 339.
49. Kurt Kloocke, *ibid.*, and Dorette Berthoud, *op. cit.*, p. 222.
50. See Ghislain de Diesbach, *op. cit.*, pp. 449–53.
51. Dorette Berthoud, *op. cit.*, p. 223–5.
52. Ghislain de Diesbach, *op. cit.*, p. 455.
53. Ghislain de Diesbach, *op. cit.*, p. 454.
54. *Corinne* had given offence to Napoleon by praising the freedoms enjoyed by the British, and now *De l'Allemagne* compounded the mischief. Simone Balayé summarizes the problem in the preface to *De l'Allemagne*, *op. cit.*, p. 28:

> The central idea of the book is the freedom to think and to write, to draw one's ideas and themes from wherever one judges best, the rejection of received ideas and taboos. For Madame de Staël everything is interconnected, and literature is never far from politics. For Napoleon likewise.

55. Ghislain de Diesbach, *op. cit.*, p. 460.
56. Ghislain de Diesbach, *op. cit.*, p. 463.
57. Kurt Kloocke, *op. cit.*, p. 340.
58. Constant, *Œuvres*, p. 1551.
59. *Le Cahier rouge* was the title given to *Ma Vie* by its first editor, Adrien Constant

de Rebecque when it was first published in the *Revue des deux mondes* in January 1907. There is a recent tendency among scholars to call the work by the title Constant actually gave it.

60. Rudler, *Jeunesse*, p. 402, letter from Victor to Charles de Constant of 29 October 1809. Victor de Constant, Benjamin's cousin, recalls seeing Charlotte in Brunswick in 1794 when she showed him Constant's letters and 'the beginning of a history of his life which he had written at her house'.
61. Ghislain de Diesbach, *op. cit.*, p. 466.
62. Ghislain de Diesbach, *op. cit.*, p. 470.
63. Ghislain de Diesbach, *op. cit.*, p. 470, and Kurt Kloocke, *op. cit.*, pp. 340–1.
64. Constant, *Œuvres*, pp. 677–823.
65. Benjamin Constant et Madame de Staël, *Lettres à un ami. Cent onze lettres inédites à Claude Hochet*, ed. Jean Mistler, Neuchâtel: A la Baconnière [1949], p. 181.
66. Kurt Kloocke, *op. cit.*, p. 341.
67. Kurt Kloocke, *op. cit.*, p. 342.
68. Benjamin Constant et Madame de Staël, *Lettres à un ami. Cent onze lettres inédites à Claude Hochet*, *op. cit.*, pp. 197–8.
69. Otto Olzien, 'Benjamin Constant, Göttingen et la Bibliothèque universitaire', *ABC*, no. 3 (1983), p. 124.
70. Constant, *Œuvres*, p. 682, diary entry for 22 October 1811: 'Lichtenberg. I can recognize the people in it'.
71. Kurt Kloocke, *op. cit.*, pp. 342–3.
72. Menos, pp. 456–7.
73. Constant, *Œuvres*, p. 1552.
74. Constant, *Œuvres*, p. 687.
75. Constant, *Œuvres*, p. 687.
76. Constant, *Œuvres*, p. 688.

9 THE END OF AN EMPIRE (1812–1816)

1. Constant, *Œuvres*, p. 689.
2. Constant, *Œuvres*, p. 693.
3. Ghislain de Diesbach, *Madame de Staël*, Paris: Librairie Académique Perrin, 1983, p. 478.
4. Ghislain de Diesbach, *op. cit.*, p. 494.
5. Constant, *Œuvres*, pp. 686 and 685.
6. Constant, *Œuvres*, p. 699.
7. Otto Olzien, 'Benjamin Constant, Göttingen et la Bibliothèque universitaire', *ABC*, no. 3 (1983), pp. 125 and 137.
8. Menos, p. 483.
9. Otto Olzien, *op. cit.*, p. 126.
10. Constant, *Œuvres*, p. 696.
11. Benjamin Constant et Madame de Staël, *Lettres à un ami. Cent onze lettres inédites à Claude Hochet*, ed. Jean Mistler, Neuchâtel: A la Baconnière, [1949], p. 225.
12. Constant, *Œuvres*, p. 702.
13. Constant, *Œuvres*, p. 703. 'To stay . . . question' is written in English.
14. Kurt Kloocke, *Benjamin Constant: une Biographie intellectuelle*, Geneva–Paris: Droz (Histoire des idées et critique littéraire, 218), 1984, p. 344.
15. Constant, *Œuvres*, p. 706.
16. Constant, *Œuvres*, pp. 705–6.

17. *Lettres de Madame de Staël à Benjamin Constant* publiées pour la première fois en original par Madame la Baronne de Nolde avec une introduction et des notes par Paul L. Léon. Avant-propos de Gustave Rudler, Paris: Kra, 1928, p. 38.
18. Constant, *Œuvres*, p. 715.
19. Constant, *Œuvres*, pp. 716–17.
20. Constant, *Œuvres*, p. 718.
21. Constant, *Œuvres*, p. 724. The most recent critical edition of *De l'esprit de conquête et de l'usurpation dans leurs rapports avec la civilisation européenne* is that of Ephraïm Harpaz, Paris: GF Flammarion, 1986. On the background to its composition and on Constant's relationship with Bernadotte, see Benjamin Constant, *Lettres à Bernadotte. Sources et origine de l''Esprit de conquête et de l'usurpation'*, ed. Bengt Hasselrot, Geneva–Lille: Droz–Giard, 1952, and his *Nouveaux documents sur Benjamin Constant et Mme de Staël*, Copenhagen: Ejnar Munksgaard, 1952.
22. On this, see Stephen Holmes, *Benjamin Constant and the Making of Modern Liberalism*, Yale and New Haven: Yale University Press, 1984, and the introduction to *De l'esprit de conquête* by Ephraïm Harpaz, *op. cit.*, pp. 7–54.
23. Constant, *Œuvres*, p. 727.
24. Constant, *Œuvres*, p. 729.
25. Constant, *Œuvres*, p. 730.
26. Constant, *Œuvres*, pp. 729 and 1565.
27. Constant, *Œuvres*, p. 732.
28. Constant, *Œuvres*, p. 732.
29. *Lettres de Madame de Staël à Benjamin Constant*, *op. cit.*, p. 48.
30. *Lettres de Madame de Staël à Benjamin Constant*, *op. cit.*, p. 46, letter of 12 December 1813 from London.
31. *Lettres de Madame de Staël à Benjamin Constant*, *op. cit.*, pp. 58–60.
32. *Lettres de Madame de Staël à Benjamin Constant*, *op. cit.*, p. 62.
33. Constant, *Œuvres*, p. 733.
34. See C. P. Courtney, *A Guide to the Published Works of Benjamin Constant*, Oxford: The Voltaire Foundation, 1985, p. 12, item A12/1, *De la liberté des brochures . . .* , and item A13/1, *Observations sur le discours prononcé par S. E. le Ministre de l'Intérieur . . . .*
35. Constant, *Œuvres*, p. 736.
36. See Françoise Wagener's well-researched *Madame Récamier 1777–1849*, [Paris]: Editions Jean-Claude Lattès, 1986, and on the friendship with Germaine de Staël, Maurice Levaillant, *Une Amitié amoureuse: Madame de Staël et Madame Récamier*, Paris: Hachette, 1956.
37. Benjamin Constant, *Lettres à Madame Récamier (1807–1830)*, ed. Ephraïm Harpaz, Paris: Librairie C. Klincksieck, 1977, p. 11. A new edition by Ephraïm Harpaz giving a revised text of the letters appeared in 1992: Benjamin Constant et Juliette Récamier, *Cent quatre-vingt douze lettres*, Paris: Champion.
38. Constant, *Œuvres*, p. 736.
39. Constant, *Œuvres*, p. 739.
40. Constant, *Œuvres*, p. 739.
41. Françoise Wagener, *op. cit.*, p. 263.
42. Constant, *Œuvres*, pp. 746, 784, 790–1 and 1578.
43. Constant, *Œuvres*, p. 743, diary entry for 19 September 1814.
44. Constant, *Œuvres*, p. 752.
45. Constant, *Œuvres*, p. 763.
46. Constant, *Œuvres*, pp. 767 and 769.

47. The article began: 'For twelve years we were oppressed by one man.' It is reproduced in Benjamin Constant, *Recueil d'articles, 1775–1817*, ed. Ephraïm Harpaz, Geneva: Droz, 1978, pp. 146–8.
48. *Ibid.*, pp. 149–52.
49. Constant, *Œuvres*, p. 778.
50. Benjamin Constant, *Recueil d'articles 1775–1817*, ed. Ephraïm Harpaz, Geneva: Droz, 1978, pp. 153–6.
51. *Lettres de Madame de Staël à Benjamin Constant, op. cit.*, p. 83, letter of 10 April 1815 from Coppet.
52. Constant, *Œuvres*, pp. 779–80.
53. Constant, *Œuvres*, p. 780, diary entry for 15 April 1815.
54. See C. P. Courtney, *A Bibliography of Editions of the Writings of Benjamin Constant to 1833*, London: Modern Humanities Reasearch Association, 1981, pp. 45–7.
55. Constant, *Œuvres*, p. 786.
56. See the critical edition, Benjamin Constant, *Mémoires sur les Cent-Jours*, texte établi par Kurt Kloocke, introduction et notes par André Cabanis (*Œuvres complètes de Benjamin Constant*, série I, vol. 14), Tübingen: Max Niemeyer Verlag, 1993.
57. See, for example, Constant, *Œuvres*, pp. 798–9, diary entries for mid-September 1815. On Constant's relationship with Madame de Krüdener, see Francis Ley's *Bernardin de Saint-Pierre, Madame de Staël, Chateaubriand, Benjamin Constant et Madame de Krüdener (d'après des documents inédits)*, Préface de Jean Fabre, Paris: Aubier, Editions Montaigne, 1967, especially chapter IV.
58. Constant, *Œuvres*, p. 803.

10 *ADOLPHE* (1816–1819)

1. Quoted in *Adolphe*, ed. Paul Delbouille, p. 273.
2. Quoted in Harold Nicolson, *Benjamin Constant*, London: Constable, 1949, pp. 243–4.
3. On this subject, see the highly original article by Georges Pholien, 'Adolphe et son public', *Revue d'histoire littéraire de la France*, janvier–février 1985, pp. 18–25.
4. See Dennis Wood, 'Le Rousseauisme de Constant', in *Rousseau et le dix-huitième siècle: Essays in Memory of R. A. Leigh*, ed. Marian Hobson, John Leigh and Robert Wokler, Oxford: The Voltaire Foundation, 1992.
5. On the complexity of *Adolphe*, see Alison Fairlie, *Imagination and Language. Collected Essays on Constant, Baudelaire, Nerval and Flaubert*, ed. Malcolm Bowie, Cambridge: Cambridge University Press, 1981, pp. 3–125, and Dennis Wood, *Benjamin Constant: 'Adolphe'*, Cambridge: Cambridge University Press (Landmarks of World Literature), 1987.
6. Constant, *Œuvres*, p. 814.
7. Quoted in C. P. Courtney, *A Bibliography of Editions of the Writings of Benjamin Constant to 1833*, London: Modern Humanities Research Association, 1981, pp. 47 and 49.
8. C. P. Courtney, *op. cit.*, p. 49.
9. Quoted in Benjamin Constant, *Adolphe. Anecdote trouvée dans les papiers d'un inconnu*, ed. C. P. Courtney, Oxford: Basil Blackwell (Blackwell French Texts), 1989, pp. 126–7.
10. C. P. Courtney, *op. cit.*, p. 63. On Alexander Walker, see C. P. Courtney,

'Alexander Walker and Benjamin Constant: a note on the English translator of *Adolphe*', *French Studies*, XXIX (1975), pp. 137–50.

11. The correspondence between Rosalie and Charles de Constant is quoted in Paul Delbouille's edition of *Adolphe*, pp. 266–70.

12. *Ibid.*, p. 276.

13. Benjamin Constant, *Mémoires sur les Cent-Jours*. Texte établi par Kurt Kloocke. Introduction et notes par André Cabanis (*Œuvres complètes de Benjamin Constant*, série I, vol. 14), Tübingen: Max Niemeyer Verlag, 1993. See also Constant, *Œuvres*, pp. 810, 816, 1585–6. On 9–11 June 1816 Constant visited John Cam Hobhouse and his family at Whitton Park, Hounslow, to the west of London (pp. 816 and 1589).

14. Constant, *Œuvres*, p. 819. On Constant and the Reverend May, see C. P. Courtney, 'Benjamin Constant et Nathaniel May: documents inédits', *Revue d'histoire littéraire de la France*, 66e année, no. 1 (janvier–mars 1966), pp. 162–78. Constant wrote to May in English from Sevenoaks, Kent, on 25 July 1816:

> My dear Friend
> I had brought with me today a preface I have added to the 2^d edition of Adolphe & which I think you have not seen. But the pleasure of talking with you made me forget to leave it. I hereby inclose it in my letter & take this opportunity of repeating to you how happy I have been to find you again after so long an absence, & how much I rejoice at the hope of visiting you after my return. My wife regrets her having spent but a few minutes at Lyghe & begs to be remembered to Miss May & the other ladies whom she had the pleasure to meet this evening. If my plan of spending the winter at Edinburgh comes to execution, I shall be much tempted to bring her next summer to Tunbridge-Wells, in order that she may enjoy the climate & I the neighbour-hood, Till then I shall keep up our renewed acquaintance by correspondence. The sight of my manuscripts will likewise prevent I hope your forgetting me, & I shall be happy to remain for life
> your faithful friend
> B. de CONSTANT

Constant never did return to England, and the manuscript on polytheism was sent on to him in Paris by Nathaniel May in 1818 (Courtney, *art. cit.*, pp. 176–7.

15. Constant, *Œuvres*, p. 819.

16. Constant, *Œuvres*, p. 823.

17. Harold Nicolson, *op. cit.*, p. 245.

18. Both the extensive Fonds Monamy-Valin (Bibliothèque nationale, Paris) and, to a lesser extent, the Von Marenholtz papers (Niedersächsisches Staatsarchiv, Wolfenbüttel) contain fragments of plays and verse, some by Constant, others copied out by him from other authors, in which there seems to be a tendency towards the Germanic and the Gothic, and to dwelling on the idea of death. In particular a poem composed by Constant on the back of a speech of 1825, 'De l'heure propice sachez vous saisir', concerns the cold and darkness of the Underworld.

19. Benjamin et Rosalie de Constant, *Correspondance 1786–1830*, ed. Alfred et Suzanne Roulin, Paris: Gallimard, 1955, pp. 211–12.

20. *Ibid.*, p. 214.

21. *Ibid.*, p. 215.

22. *De la doctrine politique, qui peut réunir les partis en France*, published by Delaunay in Paris during December 1816 (C. P. Courtney, *A Guide to the*

Published Works of Benjamin Constant, Oxford: The Voltaire Foundation, 1985, pp. 49–50, item A19).

23. On the complex history of Constant's property purchases and general finances from 1814 onwards, see Kurt Kloocke, 'Les *Livres de dépenses* de Benjamin Constant. Premier article', *ABC*, no. 4 (1984), pp. 115–63, and Kurt Kloocke et Christian Viredaz, 'Les *Livres de dépenses* de Benjamin Constant. Second article', *ABC*, no. 5 (1985), pp. 105–61.

24. Benjamin et Rosalie de Constant, *op. cit.*, p. 219.

25. See Benjamin Constant, *Recueil d'articles: Le Mercure, La Minerve et La Renommée*, ed. Ephraïm Harpaz, Geneva: Droz, 1972, 2 vols.

26. Ghislain de Diesbach, *Madame de Staël*, Paris: Librairie Académique Perrin, 1983, p. 535.

27. *Mercure de France*, 19 and 26 July 1817.

28. Benjamin Constant, *Lettres à Madame Récamier (1807–1830)*, ed. Ephraïm Harpaz, Paris: Librairie C. Klincksieck, 1977, p. 261.

29. See Kurt Kloocke et Christian Viredaz, *op. cit.*, p. 126, note 1.

30. See Benjamin Constant, *L'Affaire Regnault*, textes présentés et commentés par René Bourgeois, Grenoble: Publications de l'Université des langues et lettres de Grenoble, 1979. Constant wrote in English to his former tutor Nathaniel May just before 1 June 1818:

> I have indeed been very busy & published many perhaps too many political pamphlets. I have however had the good fortune to prevent an innocent mans head from falling on the scaffold & that is certainly the best thing I have done. He was doomed to die by a noble Marquis of Normandy whose name I hope will shine in the annals of aristocratical infamy.
>
> (C. P. Courtney, *art. cit.*, p. 177)

The aristocrat involved in the Regnault affair was a local landowner, the Marquis de Blosseville.

31. Kurt Kloocke, *Benjamin Constant: une biographie intellectuelle*, Geneva–Paris: Droz (Histoire des idées et critique littéraire, 218), 1984, p. 353.

32. See Dennis Wood, 'The Von Marenholtz papers: Constant in Wolfenbüttel', *French Studies Bulletin*, 24 (Autumn 1987), pp. 5–10.

33. In Brunswick, for example, Charlotte had made Constant's former mistress Caroline her protégée when the actress had fallen on hard times. On this, see Constant's letter to Isabelle de Charrière of 12 May 1794, Charrière, *Œuvres*, IV, p. 429.

34. Dennis Wood, 'The Von Marenholtz papers', *op. cit.*, p. 9.

35. See C. P. Courtney, *A Bibliography of Editions of the Writings of Benjamin Constant to 1833*, London: Modern Humanities Research Association, 1981, p. 179, item 131a(2).

36. Kurt Kloocke, *op. cit.*, p. 353. Jean-Jacques Coulmann gives a slightly different account:

> While walking one day in 1818 at Madame Davillier's at Montalais, in the grounds of her country house situated on the hilly slopes of Meudon, he lost his footing. The path was steep and he broke his leg. In haste the surgeon Dupuytren was sent for from Paris, but first aid was given him by the local village doctor. Dupuytren decided that the leg would have to be amputated, but the patient felt his decision was a trifle harsh. Constant talked to the young doctor who was bold enough to differ in his opinion from the celebrated maestro of the operating-table. It was a

stroke of good fortune: contrary to all the predictions of medical science, the knee healed, and for the next twelve years Benjamin Constant was able to get about on crutches.

(J.-J. Coulmann, *Réminiscences*, Paris: Michel Lévy frères, 1862–9 [Slatkine Reprints, Geneva, 1973], 3 vols, vol. III, p. 67)

37. Kurt Kloocke, *op. cit.*, p. 354.
38. Constant not only published articles in the *Minerve* (C. P. Courtney, *A Guide to the Published Works of Benjamin Constant, op. cit.*, pp. 227–8), but also a short book, *Des Elections de 1818 (Concerning the Elections of 1818)*.
39. See the useful introduction to *Benjamin Constant et Goyet de la Sarthe. Correspondance, 1818–1822*, ed. Ephraïm Harpaz, Geneva: Droz (Travaux d'histoire éthico-politique, 26), 1973.
40. Menos, pp. 547–8, letter to Charles de Constant of 16 December 1818.

11 APOTHEOSIS (1819–1830)

1. C. P. Courtney, 'Benjamin Constant in 1817: a contemporary pen-portrait', *Revue de littérature comparée*, 235, 59e année, no. 3 (juillet–septembre 1985), pp. 287–90.
2. When in Paris Sir James Mackintosh had noted on 23 December 1814:

Constant called to read his pamphlet on the Responsibility of Ministers. In composing for the press, he never used paper. He writes on small cards, which are tied together by a string. He pretends that this facilitates addition and insertion; and enables him easily to change the place of his ideas till they are in what he thinks the best order. But nobody, except a writer of sententious brevity and detached maxims, could endure such a mode of writing; and it probably increases his tendency to an aphoristic style.

(*Memoirs of the Life of the Right Honourable Sir James Mackintosh*, ed. Robert James Mackintosh, London: Edward Moxon, 1835, 2 vols, vol. II, pp. 323–4.)

3. Quoted in Dorette Berthoud, *Constance et grandeur de Benjamin Constant*, Lausanne: Librairie Payot, 1944, pp. 70–1. François-Adolphe, Baron de Loève-Veimars (1801–54), was a historian and man of letters who published letters and reminiscences of Constant in the *Revue des Deux-Mondes* in February 1833.
4. Constant's *Eloge de Sir Samuel Romilly (In Praise of Sir Samuel Romilly)* (C. P. Courtney, *A Bibliography of Editions of the Writings of Benjamin Constant to 1833*, London: Modern Humanities Research Association, 1981, pp. 92–4, item 36a) appeared in January 1819. Constant greatly admired the liberal principles of Sir Samuel Romilly (1757–1818), the lawyer and Whig politician, whom he seems to have met for the first time in Paris in October 1815 (Constant, *Œuvres*, p. 799), for his vigorous championing of the rights of the individual within the legal framework of an ordered society. They no doubt met again during Constant's stay in London during the first half of 1816. (See Brian Rigby, 'Benjamin Constant and the *Eloge de Sir Samuel Romilly*', ABC, no. 7 (1987), pp. 21–38.) Constant continued to think highly of the *Eloge* and in the last weeks of his life, towards the end of 1830, appears to have been planning to republish it and to have it translated into English.
5. Kurt Kloocke, *Benjamin Constant: une biographie intellectuelle*, Geneva–Paris: Droz (Histoire des idées et critique littéraire, 218), 1984, p. 354.

6. The most convenient modern edition of Constant's lecture on freedom in ancient and modern times is in Benjamin Constant, *De la liberté chez les Modernes. Ecrits politiques*, ed. Marcel Gauchet, Paris: Le Livre de poche (Pluriel, 8346), 1980 (*De la liberté des Anciens* is to be found on pp. 491–515). Marcel Gauchet's excellent introduction to his edition was at least partly responsible for the revival of interest in Constant's political thought during the 1980s.

7. See Kurt Kloocke, *op. cit.*, p. 355, notes 237 and 238.

8. Benjamin et Rosalie de Constant, *Correspondance 1786–1830*, ed. Alfred et Suzanne Roulin, Paris: Gallimard, 1955, p. 230.

9. 'De la traite des nègres au Sénégal', *La Minerve française*, 18–23 August 1819, listed in C. P. Courtney, *A Guide to the Published Works of Benjamin Constant*, Oxford: The Voltaire Foundation (Studies on Voltaire and the eighteenth century, 239), 1985, p. 233.

10. *Ibid.*, pp. 233–7.

11. Constant's pamphlet was the *Lettre à M. le marquis de Latour-Maubourg, ministre de la guerre, sur ce qui s'est passé à Saumur les 7 et 8 octobre 1820*, Paris: Béchet aîné; Rouen: Béchet fils, 1820, which first appeared around 19 October 1820. The incident in *Lucien Leuwen* occurs during an electoral mission which Leuwen undertakes with his secretary Coffe to Blois. They distribute pamphlets, which causes a riot. Lucien receives a handful of mud in his face outside an inn and leaves Blois ingloriously and in great haste. Although Stendhal's novel is concerned with politics and political morality under the July Monarchy – that is after 1830 – there are passages in it that are strongly reminiscent of some of Constant's experiences during the previous decade.

12. See C. P. Courtney, *A Bibliography of Editions of the Writings of Benjamin Constant to 1833, op. cit.*, pp. 99–100, item 42.

13. Benjamin Constant, *Mémoires sur les Cent-Jours*. Texte établi par Kurt Kloocke. Introduction et notes par André Cabanis (*Œuvres complètes de Benjamin Constant*, série I, vol. 14), Tübingen: Max Niemeyer Verlag, 1993, introduction, *passim*.

14. C. P. Courtney, *A Bibliography of Editions of the Writings of Benjamin Constant to 1833, op. cit.*, pp. 115–18, item 50.

15. On Constant's intellectual relationship with Rousseau, see Paul Hoffmann, 'Benjamin Constant critique de Jean-Jacques Rousseau', *Revue d'histoire littéraire de la France*, vol. 82, no. 1 (janvier–février 1982), pp. 23–40. Hoffmann's sympathies are noticeably with Rousseau whom Constant is alleged to have misunderstood. For a more balanced view, see Marcel Gauchet's introduction, *op. cit.*, and Stephen Holmes, *Benjamin Constant and the Making of Modern Liberalism*, New Haven and London: Yale University Press, 1984.

16. See note 14 above.

17. Kurt Kloocke, *op. cit.*, p. 362.

18. *Ibid.*, p. 363. Constant wrote to Villèle secretly:

> You do not wish to see me re-elected, and your agents are working as hard as they can to prevent that from happening. I believe that they will not succeed, but here is what I propose: a man who compromised himself for me two years ago in Saumur, Monsieur Caffé, has very recently been condemned to death. I believe him to be innocent and I fear that the support he gave me in 1820 may have been the cause of his condemnation. Obtain a pardon for him from the King, and I will not seek re-election. I am keen to remain active in political life, but I am much more concerned about saving the life of a man who risked everything for me.

Constant added: 'If your reply is favourable, I undertake to keep the real reason for my withdrawal from the elections a secret' (quoted in Jean-Jacques Coulmann's *Réminiscences*, Paris: Michel Lévy frères, 1862–9 [Slatkine Reprints, Geneva, 1973], 3 vols, vol. III, p. 66).

19. Kurt Kloocke, *op. cit.*, p. 364.
20. Norman King et Jean-Daniel Candaux, 'La correspondance de Benjamin Constant et de Sismondi (1801–1830)', *ABC*, no. 1 (1980), p. 152.
21. Kurt Kloocke, *op. cit.*, p. 365, and C. P. Courtney, *A Bibliography of Editions of the Writings of Benjamin Constant*, London: Modern Humanities Research Association, 1981, p. 130, item 58. In the Niedersächsisches Staatsarchiv, Wolfenbüttel, there is a contract between Constant and the publisher Béchet dated 24 November 1824 concerning volume II and subsequent volumes of *De la religion* of which 2,100 copies of each were to be printed by Didot (MS 264 N II s. 12 Nr 23, 'Lettres d'affaires de Benjamin Constant').
22. The most lucid study of Constant's work on religion is that of Pierre Deguise, *Benjamin Constant méconnu. Le Livre 'De la Religion'*, Geneva: Droz, 1966. His book of selections from *De la religion* (Lausanne: Bibliothèque romande, 1971) contains an equally illuminating 'Postface' (pp. 263–74).
23. Kurt Kloocke, *op. cit.*, p. 287.
24. J.-J. Coulmann, *op. cit.*
25. Kurt Kloocke, *op. cit.*, p. 366, and Benjamin et Rosalie de Constant, *Correspondance 1786–1830*, ed. Alfred et Suzanne Roulin, Paris: Gallimard, 1955, pp. 252–3.
26. Kurt Kloocke, *op. cit.*, p. 366. Kloocke notes that Constant's correspondence with Baron d'Eckstein remains unpublished.
27. The changes are listed in Benjamin Constant, *Adolphe. Anecdote trouvée dans les papiers d'un inconnu*, ed. C. P. Courtney, Oxford: Basil Blackwell (Blackwell French Texts), 1989, pp. 101–24.
28. The French text of the letter was first published in Dennis Wood, 'The Von Marenholtz Papers: Constant in Wolfenbüttel', *French Studies Bulletin*, 24 (Autumn 1987), pp. 5–10.
29. Paul Bastid, *Benjamin Constant et sa doctrine*, Paris: Armand Colin, 1966, 2 vols, vol. 1, p. 441.
30. Quoted in Harold Nicolson, *Benjamin Constant*, London: Constable, 1949, p. 246.
31. Quoted in Victor Glachant, *Benjamin Constant sous l'œil du guet*, Paris: Plon-Nourrit, 1906, p. 548.
32. Benjamin et Rosalie de Constant, *op. cit.*, pp. 256–7.
33. Michel Folman, *Le Secret de Benjamin Constant, sa maladie, sa vie intime*, Geneva: Imprimerie de *la Tribune de Genève*, 1959.
34. Benjamin et Rosalie de Constant, *op. cit.*, p. 260.
35. Dorette Berthoud (*op. cit.*, p. 74) quotes an undated parliamentary exchange over religious affairs which gives a brief taste of Constant's irony at the expense of a reactionary régime:

   We have heard talk of a settlement reached in Toledo in the seventh century. And I thought the government was only intending to take us back to the fifteenth century. It's obvious that ambition grows with success. (Laughter).

On sacrilege he had the following to say, in similar vein:

   Sacrilege! But what is it? An affront to God Himself, miraculously contained in the consecrated host, according to the Church of Rome. . . . It is sad, gentlemen, to see the barriers going up again between two Christian churches to which the general softening of attitudes, the advances in learning, and the *Charte* seemed to have brought genuine concord. But since the language of thirteenth-century Catholic theologians is now being spoken in this Chamber, I am forced in my turn to speak that of the leaders of the Reformation to whom your respect for freedom of worship allows me to express my gratitude. I owe to those reformers the inestimable privilege of being all the more persuaded of the truth of our sacred books because they gave me the right to study the scriptures and to be convinced by them myself.

(Dorette Berthoud, *op. cit.*, pp. 86–7)

36. C. P. Courtney, *A Bibliography of Editions of the Writings of Benjamin Constant to 1833, op. cit.*, pp. 144–5, item 60.
37. Quoted in Kurt Kloocke, *op. cit.*, p. 285.
38. On the question of Constant's possible influence on Karl Marx, see Patrice Higonnet, 'Marx, disciple de Constant?', *ABC*, no. 6 (1986), pp. 11–16.
39. Kurt Kloocke, *op. cit.*, p. 369.
40. Norman King et Jean-Daniel Candaux, *op. cit.*, pp. 155–6.
41. Benjamin et Rosalie de Constant, *op. cit.*, p. 358.
42. On this see Victor Glachant, *op. cit.*, pp. 347–505.
43. C. P. Courtney, *A Bibliography of Editions of the Writings of Benjamin Constant to 1833, op.cit.*, pp. 187–9, item 132a(1), *Discours de M. Benjamin Constant à la Chambre des Députés*, Tome premier, Paris: Dupont, 1827.
44. *Ibid.*, p. 135, item 58b(3), *De la religion, considérée dans sa source, ses formes et ses développements*, tome III, Paris: Béchet aîné, 1827.
45. Wolfenbüttel, Niedersächsisches Staatsarchiv, MS 264 N II s. 12 Nr 23, XIIe liasse, 'Couplets chantés à l'occasion d'un dîner offert aux bains de Bade, le 23 août 1827, par une réunion d'Alsaciens à l'honorable M. Benjamin Constant, Député du Département de la Seine', one printed sheet in French and German.
46. Benjamin et Rosalie de Constant, *op. cit.*, p. 300.
47. C. P. Courtney, *A Guide to the Published Works of Benjamin Constant, op. cit.*, pp. 268–72.
48. Benjamin et Rosalie de Constant, *op. cit.*, p. 303.
49. *Ibid.*, pp. 304–7.
50. *Memoirs of the Life of the Right Honourable Sir James Mackintosh*, ed. Robert James Mackintosh, London: Edward Moxon, 1835, 2 vols, vol. II, pp. 270–2. By a remarkable coincidence, Constant's Edinburgh friend Mackintosh was related by marriage to Constant's Swiss friend, the historian Sismondi – and both thereby became distantly related to the young Charles Darwin.
51. Paris, Bibliothèque nationale, Fonds Monamy-Valin [formerly Fonds Jean Mistler], 'Correspondance de Benjamin Constant, carton IV, II, Lettres adressées à Benjamin Constant par diverses personnalités', two letters from Sir James Mackintosh dated 29 May 1828 and 2 July 1829.
52. *Ibid.*
53. C. P. Courtney, *A Guide to the Published Works of Benjamin Constant, op. cit.*, pp. 274–7. Courtney mentions the *Le Temps* articles (p. 96); on these, see Benjamin Constant, *Positions de combat à la veille de juillet 1830. Articles publiés dans le 'Temps' 1829–1830*, texte établi, annoté et commenté par Ephraïm Harpaz, Paris–Geneva: Champion–Slatkine, 1989.
54. *Ibid.*, p. 161.
55. *Ibid.*, p. 142. The text is reproduced in Constant, *Œuvres*, pp. 935–62.
56. Kurt Kloocke, *op. cit*, p. 369, and Constant, *Œuvres*, pp. 1601–2.

57. Benjamin et Rosalie de Constant, *op. cit.*, pp. 309–10.
58. The story of Coste's invitation to return to Paris is told by J.-J. Coulmann in his *Notice sur Benjamin Constant lue à la séance générale de la Société de la morale chrétienne* . . . *Avril 1831*, Paris: Crapelet, 1831, p. 19. On the gift of money see Louis de Loménie's *Galerie des contemporains illustres par un homme de rien*, Paris, 1845, tome VIII, quoted by Elizabeth W. Schermerhorn, *Benjamin Constant. His Private Life and his Contribution to the Cause of Liberal Government in France 1767–1830*, Boston and New York: Houghton Mifflin, 1924, pp. 336–7. The existence of the gift is confirmed by J.-J. Coulmann, *op. cit.*, p. 19.
59. On Constant's brief parliamentary career under the July Monarchy, see the well-researched article by Jean-Pierre Aguet, 'Benjamin Constant parlementaire sous la monarchie de juillet (juillet–décembre 1830)', *ABC*, no. 2 (1982), pp. 3–45.
60. Benjamin et Rosalie de Constant, *op. cit.*, pp. 321–2.
61. Quoted in Kurt Kloocke, *op. cit.*, p. 296.
62. On Constant's fondness for this image, see Georges Poulet, *Benjamin Constant par lui-même*, Paris: Du Seuil (Les Ecrivains de toujours, 78), 1968, pp. 47–8.
63. C. P. Courtney, *A Bibliography of Editions of the Writings of Benjamin Constant to 1833*, *op. cit.*, pp. 132–3, item 58a (4–5).
64. Dorette Berthoud, *La Seconde Madame Benjamin Constant*, Lausanne: Librairie Payot, 1943, p. 239.
65. Dennis Wood, *op. cit.*, p. 8. Beaune was well informed on Constant's thinking, and was sought out possibly by Loève-Veimars and certainly by Sainte-Beuve in 1834, according to Bengt Hasselrot (Benjamin Constant, *Lettres à Bernadotte. Sources et origine de l'"Esprit de conquête et de l'usurpation"*, ed. Bengt Hasselrot, Geneva–Lille: Droz–Giard, 1952, p. lxi). The material in the Niedersächsisches Staatsarchiv, Wolfenbüttel, appears to be the only extant collection of documents concerning Constant and Charlotte by Beaune.
66. J.-J. Coulmann, *op. cit.*, vol. III, p. 219.
67. Coulmann's *Réminiscences* are a rich source of vivid anecdotes about his much admired friend's life – about Constant's love of cats, for example, animals which symbolized freedom and independence for him, and about his unfailing good humour and patience with the increasingly vague and forgetful Charlotte who would even arrive late at her own dinner parties. Coulmann gives one piece of information about Constant that is not, I believe, to be found elsewhere: Constant was not only obsessed with death but also feared being buried alive while in a cataleptic state. Charlotte saw to it that his coffin was made larger than was customary, that five days elapsed between his death and burial, and that his head rested on a pillow (vol. III, p. 231). A death mask was made of Constant by the sculptor Gois. Subsequently lost for many years, the mask was rediscovered by Kurt Kloocke in the anthropological collection of the Musée de l'Homme in Paris.

EPILOGUE

1. Quoted by Edouard Laboulaye writing in the *Revue nationale et étrangère politique, scientifique et littéraire*, Paris, 1861, Tome V, p. 346.
2. *Ibid.*, p. 327.
3. *Ibid.*, p. 332.
4. *Ibid.*, p. 343.

5. Han Verhoeff, *'Adolphe' et Constant: une étude psychocritique*, Paris: Editions Klincksieck, 1976.
6. See above, Chapter 10, note 18.
7. Alfred Fabre-Luce, *Benjamin Constant*, Paris: Librairie Académique Perrin, 1978, p. 327.
8. Constant's hopes were undoubtedly disappointed and he was disillusioned with the July Monarchy by November 1830, as he himself hinted in a speech to the Chamber on 19 November 1830 and as several of his obituarists emphasized. On this subject, see Jean-Pierre Aguet, 'Benjamin Constant sous la monarchie de Juillet (juillet–décembre 1830)', *ABC*, no. 2 (1982), pp. 5–6.
9. C. P. Courtney, *A Bibliography of Editions of the Writings of Benjamin Constant to 1833*, London: Modern Humanities Research Association, 1981, pp. 132–3 and 147–50, items 58a(4–5) and 63a(1–2). Among the Von Marenholtz papers in the Niedersächsisches Staatsarchiv, Wolfenbüttel, there are numerous contracts and documents dating from both before and after Constant's death relating to the printing and sale of his books, proof if any were needed that Charlotte continued to be active in the service of her late husband's literary reputation.
10. A photograph of the bust is to be found in the Bibliothèque nationale exhibition catalogue *Benjamin Constant*, Paris, 1967, plate VIII.
11. Dorette Berthoud, *La Seconde Madame Benjamin Constant*, Lausanne: Librairie Payot, 1943, pp. 240 and 242. The Von Marenholtz papers in the Niedersächsisches Staatsarchiv, Wolfenbüttel, MS 264 N II Nr 23 and 23a, contain the draft of a letter by Charlotte referring to 'le Masque en Platre moulé sur feu mon epoux' ('the plaster cast taken of my late husband'); a letter from Théophile Bra to Charlotte dated 9 October 1833 praising Constant and describing Bra's plans for a bas-relief frieze in memory of him (in the 'Xe liasse'); the letter from 'Fort Royal M^{que}/Le [*hole in letter*]r 1831' (in the 'Xe liasse'); and a letter of condolence dated Toulouse, 30 July 1845, sent to Charlotte's son Wilhelm by Jean-Pierre Pagès, a close friend of both Constant and Charlotte and a liberal deputy after 1830, in which Pagès refers to Wilhelm's being at Charlotte's side to comfort her as she lay dying. For an up-to-date listing of Constant's manuscripts and their whereabouts, see Etienne Hofmann, *Catalogue raisonné de l'œuvre manuscrite de Benjamin Constant*, Geneva: Slatkine (Travaux et recherches de l'Institut Benjamin Constant, No. 1), 1992.
12. On the history of *Adolphe*'s reputation, see Paul Delbouille, *Genèse, structure et destin d''Adolphe'*, Paris: Les Belles Lettres, 1971.
13. To be published by Max Niemeyer Verlag of Tübingen in approximately forty volumes from 1993 onwards.

INDEX